Dangers of Narrative and Fictionality

LITERARY AND CULTURAL STUDIES, THEORY AND THE (NEW) MEDIA

Edited by Monika Fludernik and Sieglinde Lemke

VOLUME 7

PETER LANG

Berlin - Bruxelles - Chennai - Lausanne - New York - Oxford

Samuli Björninen / Pernille Meyer / Maria Mäkelä /
Henrik Zetterberg-Nielsen (eds.)

Dangers of Narrative and Fictionality

A Rhetorical Approach to Storytelling in Contemporary Western Culture

PETER LANG

Berlin - Bruxelles - Chennai - Lausanne - New York - Oxford

Bibliographic Information published by the Deutsche Nationalbibliothek
The Deutsche Nationalbibliothek lists this publication in the Deutsche Nationalbibliografie; detailed bibliographic data is available in the internet at http://dnb.d-nb.de.

Cover Illustration:
fcscafeine/istock.com

ISSN 0935-4093
ISBN 978-3-631-85173-9 (Print)
E-ISBN 978-3-631-89475-0 (E-Book)
E-ISBN 978-3-631-89476-7 (E-Pub)
DOI 10.3726/b21221

info@peterlang.com - www.peterlang.com//

This publication has been peer reviewed.

Acknowledgement

We thank Anna Ramsing Lindhardtsen for her untiring help

Table of Contents

Samuli Björninen, Pernille Meyer, Maria Mäkelä and Henrik Zetterberg-Nielsen

Dangers of Narrative and Fictionality: Introduction

This volume stems from our joint recognition of the pitfalls of *narrative* and *fictionality* in contemporary Western culture. Moreover, it stems from our interest in how narrativity and fictionality, understood as rhetorical strategies, may be problematically entwined.

In the public sphere and in humanist research, narrative has predominantly been seen in a positive light. From a hermeneutic perspective, narrative repertoire is linked to understanding texts and persons, self and others. From a cognitive perspective, narrative is a crucial mental tool for understanding mental processes and experiences. From a rhetorical perspective, storytelling is considered an asset against today's information overflow and an efficient means of persuasion. Moreover, there are historical reasons for equating personal storytelling with authenticity. Stories of personal experience coming from the margins and challenging the dominant narratives sustaining the status quo played a crucial role in Western democracies in the twentieth century, and the narrative turn in political, social, and historical sciences owes much to this storytelling ethos.[1]

Fictionality, similarly – yet typically with more caution – has been described as a source of creativity and – recently – also as an excellent means to persuade.[2] While we do not want to be lied to, we typically enjoy overtly invented stories and use fictionality to create humour and demonstrate wit. As the popularity

1 See Amy Shuman, *Other People's Stories: Entitlement Claims and the Critique of Empathy* (Urbana: University of Illinois Press, 2005); Francesca Polletta, *It Was Like a Fever: Storytelling in Protest and Politics* (Chicago: University of Chicago Press, 2006); Sujatha Fernandes, *Curated Stories: The Uses and Misuses of Storytelling* (New York: Oxford University Press, 2017).

2 See Stefan Iversen, 'Disruptive Communication in Political Campaigning: On the Rhetoric of Metanoic Reflexivity', *Rhetoric Society Quarterly* 52/4 (2022); Stefan Iversen and Henrik Skov Nielsen, 'Invention as Invention in the Rhetoric of Barack Obama', *Storyworlds* 9/1–2 (2017), 121–142; see also Sam Browse, Alison Gibbons and Mari Hatavara, 'Real Fictions: Fictionality, Factuality and Narrative Strategies in Contemporary Storytelling,' *Narrative Inquiry* 29/2 (2019), 245-267.

of fiction genres such as the novel, the feature film, the computer game and the tv-series attests, such stories have historically been an important source of entertainment and enjoyment – and remain so to this day. All of this is true but not the whole picture.

The widely recognized benefits of storytelling and fictional rhetoric, if viewed from a critical perspective, amount to dangers as well. Therefore, even the best of communicative intentions may have unsolicited, contradictory rhetorical effects. The emancipatory ethos of personal narratives has been put in service of political extremism. An invitation to imagine may foster fear. This volume is dedicated to both analysing the complex relations between rhetorical intentions and effects as well as outlining a rhetorical approach to contemporary cultural phenomena at the intersection of narrativity and fictionality.

The dangers of storification and fictionalization are largely not unique to our own age. Their history is long and closely associated with, for example, the development of the novel as a genre, which was widely used for moral guidance and education but also accused of corrupting the minds and wishes of (not least female) readers by giving them unrealistic expectations or triggering romantic desires better not evoked. Yet what makes these dangers today perhaps more pertinent than ever is the uncritical instrumentalization and commodification of narrative and fictionality across virtually all spheres of life, and increasingly loose usage of both terms – narrative and fiction – in public debate. During the twenty-first century, storytelling has become a business model and considered a solution to various social ills.[3] Social media, transforming everyone from individuals to corporations into *storytellers*, are an important factor in this development. The result has been a ruthless instrumentalization of stories of personal, often disruptive experiences that have the maximum potential for going viral on social media. This is a phenomenon recently studied by Maria Mäkelä and her team in the *Dangers of Narrative* and *Instrumental Narratives* research projects.[4] The volume at hand expands the inquiry of the contemporary story economy into the realm of fictionality as a rhetoric.

---

3 E.g., Christian Salmon, *Storytelling: Bewitching the Modern Mind*, David Macey, trans. (London and New York: Verso, 2010).

4 E.g., Maria Mäkelä, Samuli Björninen, Laura Karttunen, Matias Nurminen, Juha Raipola and Tytti Rantanen, 'Dangers of Narrative: A Critical Approach to Narratives of Personal Experience in Contemporary Story Economy', *Narrative* 28/2 (2021), 139–159.

For example, *literary* fiction is increasingly considered on a par with all other types of 'storytelling', with fiction author becoming a subcategory for influencer.[5] At the same time, popular 'true stories' going viral on social media replace referential or journalistic truth with shareable, representative experiences. Corporate storytellers urge organizations to imagine with the help of speculative fiction. Political opponents accuse each other of fabricated and ideologically biased narratives. Commercial discourses around storytelling draw from a scholarly vocabulary and research to argue for the great moral and cognitive benefits gained through narrative imagination. How can the existing theories of fictionality accommodate such fuzzy uses of imaginary construction? The shared theoretical point of reference for the contributions in this volume is the twenty-first-century rhetorical fictionality theory outlined in the work of narratologists Richard Walsh, Henrik Zetterberg-Nielsen, Simona Zetterberg-Nielsen, James Phelan and others. The theory described in more detail below suggests that fictionality is a communicative strategy across genres and media which a sender intentionally employs for some purposes. Yet contemporary storytelling environments foster collective and emergent narrative authority,[6] making it often difficult to attribute communicative intentionality – for example, using an unverified or even falsified story of personal experience on social media to argue for a political position does not qualify as rhetorical use of fictionality.

The current volume does not dispute the benefits of storytelling and invention and imagination in communication, but sheds light on their problematic, and even dangerous, side in times when compelling stories are quickly and uncontrollably usurped, and post-truth politics feeds on narrative invention. Popular discourse on the benefits of storytelling and fiction typically draws on studies in cognitive sciences, narrative psychology and empirical research on reading. Our approach, in contrast, focuses on the rhetoric and ethics of narrative and fictionality as *communicative strategies* with ethical and rhetorical consequences, whether used by fiction authors, social media users or institutions. Next, we will outline recent developments in 'story-critical' narrative theory and rhetorical fictionality theory, in order to contextualize our volume at the nexus of these two paradigms.

---

5 Maria Mäkelä and Hanna Meretoja, 'Critical Approaches to the Storytelling Boom', *Poetics Today* (2022), 191–218.

6 Paul Dawson and Maria Mäkelä, 'The Story Logic of Social Media: Co-Construction and Emergent Narrative Authority', *Style* 54/1 (2020), 21–35.

Story-critical narrative theory

As pointed out by Hanna Meretoja,[7] a 'story-critical' outlook has a long history in philosophy and literature, manifesting itself, for example, in the complete rejection of the narrative form in the French *nouveau roman* in the mid-twentieth century; or the postmodern deconstruction of *grands récits* – grand narratives – as once diagnosed by François Lyotard.[8] Critical approaches to storytelling in social sciences are much more recent and are clearly related to the increased instrumentalization of stories of personal experience by political movements, journalism and corporate storytelling.[9] As Maria Mäkelä and her team have demonstrated, in the contemporary story economy fuelled by social media, a story of disruptive personal experience becomes the most valued currency. A recognizable stock of 'compelling' stories of transformative encounters and personal struggles leading to an epiphany populates the public sphere and can be appropriated by any 'storyteller'. Moreover, personal stories going viral often create disturbing and potentially harmful mismatches in representative and rhetorical scale: individual viral stories of experienced injustice affect political decision-making,[10] while an individual citizen may at any moment become a viral emblem of human goodness or evil, her story appropriated for promoting whatever partisan view or social movement.

Both academic and lay criticism of such instrumentalized stories is made difficult by two narrative features. First, the strategic foregrounding of experientiality frustrates any attempt at fact checking: how can you refute another person's experience? Second, the narrative affordances of social media transform individual experiences into representative exempla through sharing: once shared, an experience becomes collective and thus validated. In this regard, social media experientiality tends toward fictionality that is not intended, but simply results

---

7 Hanna Meretoja, *The Ethics of Storytelling: Narrative Hermeneutics, History, and the Possible* (Oxford: Oxford University Press, 2018); Hanna Meretoja, *The Narrative Turn in Fiction and Theory: The Crisis and Return of Storytelling from Robbe-Grillet to Tournier* (London: Palgrave Macmillan, 2014).

8 François Lyotard, *La Condition postmoderne. Rapport sur le savoir* (Paris: Minuit, 1979).

9 Shuman, *Other People's Stories*; Polletta, *It Was Like a Fever*; Salmon, *Storytelling*; Fernandes, *Curated Stories*.

10 Maria Mäkelä, 'Through the Cracks in the Safety Net: Narratives of Personal Experience Countering the Welfare System in Social Media and Human Interest Journalism', in Klarissa Lueg and Marianne Wolff Lundholt, eds., *Routledge Handbook of Counter-Narratives* (Abingdon: Routledge, 2020), 389–401.

from the foregrounding of general relatability. As such, contemporary viral storytelling seeks legitimacy through moral rather than referential truthfulness, reminiscent of premodern storytelling cultures that recycled canonized exempla and did not differentiate between fact and fiction in the modern, generic sense. The crucial difference between, say, Medieval conversion stories as Christian exempla and personal stories going viral lies in the processes through which they acquire moral narrative authority. Whereas premodern exempla and the doctrines they carried originated in a top-down fashion – from pre-established religious, intellectual or political authority – the contemporary exemplum story gains its authority through the bottom-up mechanism of affective networks of users and algorithms granting personal experiences the status of moral truth.

What kind of 'truths' are we talking about, then? Francesca Polletta and Nathan Redman demonstrate in their recent comprehensive literature review that personal storytelling, while largely considered a driver of social change in contemporary Western societies, rarely alters people's political views, particularly on structural issues such as economic inequality.[11] Social media as narrative environments amplify the conservative story logic of experiential narratives cementing the audience's pre-existing conceptions, values and ideologies, as the push to create easily likable and shareable stories directs the storyteller to conform to familiar masterplots with easily recognizable moral positioning.[12]

While stories of personal, often disruptive experience are largely considered the primary currency in the contemporary story economy, accusations of sticking to and promoting one's ideologically biased 'narrative' loom large within the contemporary public sphere and political debate. As Paul Dawson demonstrates in this volume,[13] the popular uses of the terms 'narrative' and 'story' have a clear tendency to diverge: 'story' is still typically considered something authentic, positive and even emancipatory (quite in the spirit of the twentieth-century Civil Rights movements aiming at 'giving voice' to the oppressed through storytelling), while 'narrative' tends to refer to an ideologically biased position or construction of events. Yet social media polarization feeds on the link between authentic individual stories and biased collective narratives by way of the chain reaction from

11 Francesca Polletta and Nathan Redman, 'When Do Stories Change Our Minds? Narrative Persuasion About Social Problems', *Sociology Compass* 14/4 (2020), e12778.

12 Mäkelä et al., 'Dangers of Narrative'.

13 See also Maria Mäkelä and Samuli Björninen, 'My Story, Your Narrative: Scholarly Terms and Popular Usage', in Paul Dawson and Maria Mäkelä, eds., *Routledge Companion to Narrative Theory* (Abingdon: Routledge, 2022), 11–23.

experientiality to representativeness and normativity. Even an unverified individual experience thus often ends up as a token in polarized story wars, either as a 'true story' supporting a partisan 'narrative', or as a 'fiction' emblematic of the falseness and dishonesty of the opposing camp.

The #metoo solidarity movement constitutes a compelling example of the complex representational, rhetorical, and ethical issues related to viral storytelling. Arguably the viral campaign, prompting users to simply identify with experience of gendered or sexual misconduct or abuse, was hugely influential in most Western societies and made such conduct considerably less socially accepted. What was remarkable was the participants' pronounced abstinence from sharing full-blown experiential narratives. The mere narrative stance-taking constituted a sufficient 'small story'[14] to generate networked affect and solidarity that finally succeeded in concretizing and reflecting a *structure* of oppression. The dark moments of #metoo were invariably experienced due to full-fledged personal stories with potentially falsifiable storyworld particulars and a focus on individual motives and actions; the more experiential detail, the more likely an individual narrative was to end up weaponized in the hands of the social media backlash. Hanna-Riikka Roine analyses in her chapter of this volume a case of #metoo storytelling that takes the questions of the dominance of personal cum collective storytelling in social media, and the resultant problematic relation between relatability and fictionality, to their extreme: the *New Yorker* fictional short story 'Cat Person' by Kristen Roupenian that came to be read as a #metoo exemplary testimony by the affectively networked social media audiences.

The relationship between personal storytelling and 'post-truth' discourse is thus complex and challenges contemporary narrative theory in myriad ways. In public debate, stories supporting one's pre-existing stances are typically considered compelling and illustrative, while those of heretics are deemed strategic, manipulative and 'fictional'. Yet research by narratologists in the two abovementioned research projects, *Dangers of Narrative* and *Instrumental Narratives*, attests that the elements often considered necessary for a compelling story – relatable storyworld particulars, disruptive experience and a clear moral – *as such* are susceptible to rhetorical and epistemic hazards that may actualize in collision with other forms, such as social media platforms promoting certain types of storytelling and audience engagement. Moreover, as proposed by these projects,

14 See, e.g., Alexandra Georgakopoulou, 'Small Stories Research and Social Media: The Role of Narrative Stance-Taking in Circulating A Greek News Story', *Sociolinguistica* 27 (2013), 19–36.

contemporary storytelling cultures should be able to recognize the *limits* of narrative sensemaking and rhetoric; most familiar story formulae, foregrounding the personal and the disruptive, are ill-suited to communicate supra-individual structures and processes, or at least their storification requires particular narrative innovation.[15]

As an antidote to polarized discourses on 'stories' and 'narratives', and somewhat diverging from the philosophical debates between 'narrativist' and 'anti-narrativist' camps,[16] the volume at hand does not focus on ideology or identity as 'narrative', but instead approaches the dangers of narrative and fictionality from a pronouncedly narratological-rhetorical angle, with an emphasis on contemporary narrative environments such as social media. Contemporary narrative theory is well-positioned to promote critical reading that looks beyond good intentions and the ideological lines dividing contemporary audiences.

Rhetorical fictionality theory

A rhetorical approach to fictionality separates the quality of *fictionality* from a one-to-one relationship with *fiction* as a genre. This means that we need to understand and define it independently of any single genre. In 'Distinguishing Fictionality', Henrik Zetterberg-Nielsen and Simona Zetterberg-Nielsen suggest defining fictionality as 'intentionally signaled invention in communication'.[17] Defining a complex concept in only four words will often call for elaboration and clarification; and indeed, there are some provisos to fully reflect the pragmatic approach. First, fictionality is conceived of as the result of an assumption

15 See e.g., Juha Raipola, 'Unnarratable Matter: Emergence, Narrative, and Material Ecocriticism', in Sanna Karkulehto, Aino-Kaisa Koistinen and Essi Varis, eds., *Reconfiguring Human, Nonhuman, and Posthuman in Literature and Culture* (London and New York: Routledge, 2019), 263–279; Samuli Björninen and Merja Polvinen, 'Limits of Narrative: Introduction', *Partial Answers* (2022), 191–206.

16 E.g., Matti Hyvärinen, 'Foreword: Life Meets Narrative', in Brian Schiff, A. Elizabeth McKim and Sylvie Patron, eds., *Life and Narrative: The Risks and Responsibilities of Storying Experience* (Oxford: Oxford University Press, 2017), ix–xxvi; Hanna Meretoja, 'Life and Narrative', in Paul Dawson and Maria Mäkelä, eds., *Routledge Companion to Narrative Theory* (Abingdon: Routledge, 2022), 273–285.

17 Simona Zetterberg Gjerlevsen and Henrik Skov Nielsen, 'Distinguishing Fictionality', in Cindie Aaen Maagaard, Daniel Schäbler and Marianne Wolff Lundholt, eds., *Exploring fictionality: conceptions, test cases, discussions* (Odense: Syddansk Universitetsforlag, 2020), 23.

about the communicative act rather than as an ontology of the represented object.[18] Second, the definition is meant to imply that fictional discourse is communicated as invented regardless of whether or not it coincidentally corresponds to facts in the world. Thus, an assumption about the invented status of a sentence like: 'Once upon a time there was a caterpillar, who…' does not hinge upon whether or not there was or is an actual caterpillar somewhere. Therefore, a more cumbersome version of the same approach is to say that: 'A receiver will assume that a communicative act is fictional when he assumes that the sender has intentionally signaled that she wants it to come across as invented'. What this inevitably implies, however, is that the use of fictionality is always intentional. 'No-one produces fiction by mistake',[19] as Richard Walsh has it. Similarly, it implies that fictionality is signaled or it is not fictionality. Without any signal of any kind – be it contextual, paratextual, based on genre conventions or semantic conventions, or shared socio-cultural horizons; nothing would prompt a receiver to an assumption that fictionality is in play. One consequence is that a concept of communication that does not entail assumptions about intentions is unintelligible from this perspective.

How does fictionality work in the service of misinformation or other nefarious purposes, then? In 'Defining "Fake News"', Edson C. Tandoc, Zheng Wei Lim and Richard Ling examined thirty-four academic articles that use the expression 'fake news'.[20] The authors suggest a typology comprising six types: (1) news satire, (2) news parody, (3) fabrication, (4) manipulation, (5) advertising and (6) propaganda, and distinguish among them partly based on whether there is an 'intention to deceive'.[21] In her 2017 article, 'Fake news. It's complicated', Claire Wardle distinguishes between seven types of fake news, one of which is 'Satire or parody ("no intention to cause harm but has potential to fool")', whereas the remaining six are different examples of intentionally misleading communication.[22]

---

18 Richard Walsh, 'Fictionality as Rhetoric: A Distinctive Research Paradigm', *Style* 53/4 (2019), 399–400.

19 Walsh, 'Fictionality as Rhetoric: A Distinctive Research Paradigm', 402.

20 Edson C. Tandoc, Zheng Wei Lim and Richard Ling, 'Defining "Fake News"', *Digital Journalism* 6/2 (2018), 137–153.

21 Tandoc, Lim and Ling, 'Defining "Fake News"', 148.

22 Claire Wardle, 'Fake news. It's complicated', *First Draft* 16 (2017), 1–11.

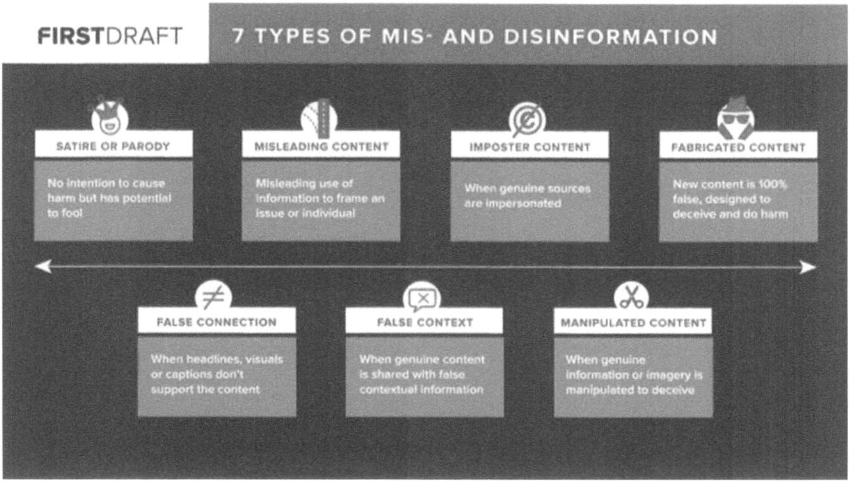

Fake news as satire includes outlets such as theonion.com, *The Daily Show*, *The Colbert Report* and thedailymash. Fake news in the satirical sense uses fictionality as a rhetorical strategy. Both Wardle and Tandoc et al. use assumptions about intention to typologize, which a rhetorical approach endorses. Some important provisos, though, are: (1) The fact that invention is signaled in satire does not justify the conclusion that there is no intention to harm. (2) Fake news as satire is a subtype of fictional discourse, a sine qua non, which is that it intentionally signals invention. Conversely, in fake news understood as deceit and misinformation, such intentional signals will, by definition, be absent, because the utterance is meant to come across as truth. Therefore, it may appear that intention to misinform is hard to imagine in a combination with signaled invention. This is a clear consequence of what Sidney already said: '... the poet, he nothing affirmeth, and therefore never lieth'.[23] The distinction between fictionality and lie is one of the most fundamental communicative and rhetorical distinctions that exists. Notwithstanding, we wish to pursue the consequence a bit further and ask if there are boundaries to its validity, and if even overt fiction can be designed to misinform. Consider the following two imaginary statements; both outrageous and completely untrue. Imagine number one is claimed by a politician in parliament while number two is included in a novel written by the same

23 Sir Philip Sidney, *A Defence of Poesie and Poems*, David Price, ed. (London, Paris and Melbourne: Cassel and Company, [1595] 1891).

imaginary politician. Can we say with certainty that the second can by nature never misinform?

1. 'Muslims committed 9000 out of 9022 rapes in Denmark last year.'
2. 'The kind, intelligent war hero and professor looked up from his research and thought to himself: "Are we not obliged as a country to react to the fact that muslims committed 9000 out of 9022 rapes in Denmark last year?"'

It does not seem justified to say that there is an absolute and categorical distinction between the two statements in a way so that the second can never intend to misinform, let alone cause harm. Many actual cases attest to the fact that also examples of the second kind can be felt to misinform. For example:

> In February, Kosoko Jackson pulled his young adult debut novel, 'A Place for Wolves,' a story set in the 1990s during the Kosovo war that features two gay American teenagers. Jackson decided to cancel the publication after a firestorm erupted on social media over his decision to set the story against the backdrop of genocide, and to make the story's villain an Albanian Muslim.[24]

The last fact is the most crucial one. It feels to many as if actual victims are represented as alleged villains. This volume has no intention to obscure the crucial distinction between fictionality and lie. Rather, it wishes to examine how and why fictionality is used for better and worse to make arguments and intervene in real world discussions. This also helps explain why representation matters, and why audiences routinely discuss and like and dislike novels, tv-series and movies based on perceptions on how they represent immigrants, the relation between genders, experts, mental diseases etc. We have a special focus on the dangers of fictionality and how fictional representations can sometimes circumvent logos-based reasoning and provide strong affective arguments about how to navigate issues of feminism, sex education, ideology, poverty and other important aspects of human existence.

Pragmatic and critical approaches to the relationship between narrative and fictionality

Approaching fictionality as a rhetorical strategy to communicate about the non-actual and overtly invented rather than as a quality belonging only to the genre of fiction, we find that just like narrative, it is very pervasive across discourses and

24 Alexandra Alter, 'She Pulled Her Debut Book When Critics Found It Racist. Now She Plans to Publish', *New York Times* (29 April 2019).

media. This does not mean, however, that we should collapse the two concepts, which has been and is frequently done. Hayden White is perhaps the best-known proponent of the view that Marie-Laure Ryan has dubbed as the pan-fictionality thesis. This view holds that all narrative inevitably amounts to fiction.[25]

Here, we wish to distinguish between narrative and fictionality. In contemporary narrative theory there are three predominant ways to approach narrative. A) Narrative is defined in terms of plot and causality, including approaches ranging from Aristotle via Paul Ricoeur to Peter Brooks and others.[26] B) Narrative is defined qualitatively as a representation that evokes or conveys temporal human experience. Monika Fludernik calls this quality of narrative 'experientiality',[27] and David Herman treats the capacity to convey 'What it is like' as a basic element of narrative.[28] C) Narrative is seen as a rhetorical act of somebody telling something on an occasion and with a purpose. James Phelan is the foremost contemporary theorist working in this tradition.[29] None of the definitions above posit a necessary correlation between narrative and fictionality.

Our working definition of narrative in this volume combines the experiential (B) and the rhetorical (C) views. We define narrative as a representation of what it was like for someone to experience certain events. Furthermore, we understand narrative pragmatically and as socially situated: a particular story is always told in a particular situation for particular purposes. For us, narrative is not *definitionally* about plotting events into a salient whole, which is not to deny that this is often a form or purpose of narrative. However, experientiality and communicative situatedness constitute a more workable definition in that it both delimits the scope of inquiry to experiential representations across different media and encompasses storytelling in new narrative environments, which is often less about recounting events and more about communicating experiences and feelings.

---

25 Marie-Laure Ryan, 'Postmodernism and the Doctrine of Panfictionality', *Narrative* 5/2 (1997), 177.

26 cp. also Karin Kukkonen, 'Plot', in Peter Hühn, Jan Christoph Meister, John Pier and Wolf Schmid, eds., *The Living Handbook of Narratology* (Hamburg: Hamburg University, 2014).

27 Monika Fludernik, *Towards a 'Natural' Narratology* (London and New York: Routledge, 2010).

28 David Herman, *Basic Elements of Narrative* (Hoboken: John Wiley and Sons Ltd, 2009).

29 Phelan's contribution to this volume can be found in Chapter Three, 'Assessing the Genre of Docudrama: The Case of Aaron Sorkin's *The Trial of the Chicago 7*'.

We should not conflate the inevitable constructedness of all narratives with the overt and intentional invention of some narratives. In a pragmatic view, some narratives are fictional and others are not. To describe the full range of communicative phenomena, from stories intended to misinform to fictional narratives to non-fictional narratives that aim to be truthful and informative, we need both the distinction between fiction as a genre and fictionality as rhetoric and the distinction between narrative construction and fictional invention.

The outline of the volume

The volume results from an intense 15-year professional exchange between the narrative scholars at Aarhus and Tampere Universities. In addition, the volume features chapters from some of our closest collaborators in the USA and Australia. The most influential collaborative work has been made on fictional and factual strategies in literature and other media as well as critical approaches to the contemporary story economy. The two research environments are unified in their interest in several research foci: the strategies and devices that travel from literary fiction to other textual contexts, and the application of concepts developed in literary studies to narrativity and fictionality in other communicative contexts. Both research environments operate in the interdisciplinary field of narrative studies and engage in intersectoral and societal collaboration.

There is a loose consensus within this community that literary fiction and literary studies have informed the ways in which narrative and fictionality have been adopted in various media as well as in the interdisciplinary study of narrative. Our work – and this volume – springs from the conviction that a thorough knowledge of literary techniques and traditions provides one with crucial means to tackle narrative and fictionality across spheres of life. However, while much of the existing work springs from literary narratology, many of the chapters pay particular attention to *media affordances* as a decisive factor shaping the rhetoric of storytelling and its relation to fictionality. The volume aims to present the jointly formed theories, methods and analytical approaches in an accessible form, both through theoretical chapters and illuminating case studies. The particularity of the volume lies in its emphasis on the *rhetorical* uses of both narrativity and fictionality – even if the rhetoric is emergent or unsolicited in nature as in many cases of viral storytelling – and the potential ethical and epistemic *dangers* involved. As will become clear to the reader of this volume, not all contributors assign unanimously to the same theoretical frameworks – such as rhetorical fictionality theory – and we hope that the volume will foster new debate and advances in the study of narrative and fictionality in contemporary storytelling environments.

The volume is divided into four parts, and the topics proceed from the public sphere and networked rhetoric to literary texts and transgeneric forms. Part I, 'Narrative, Fictionality and the Public Sphere', opens with Paul Dawson's chapter, 'Bad Press: The Rhetoric of Narrative in Public Discourse'. Dawson focuses on the rhetorical deployment of the term 'narrative' in public discourse. Looking into the contemporary use of the words 'narrative' and 'story' in news media such as *The New York Times*, *Politico*, *The Washington Post* and *The Sydney Morning Herald*, Dawson shows how 'narrative', due to its use in politics and the polarized media sphere, has fallen into disrepute, while 'story' retains positive connotations of experiential truth and empathy. In recent years, 'narrative' has increasingly been associated with lies, misinformation and conspiracy theories. The latter are narrative in nature and, thus, Dawson argues, highlight the dangers of narrative.

The next chapter, 'Dangers of Media Hoaxing', by Louise Brix Jacobsen delves into the dangers of fictionality in media hoaxing. Drawing on a rhetorical approach to fictionality, Jacobsen proposes a new definition for hoaxing, 'deceptive communication designed to be revealed', which places hoaxing between deceit and fictionality. Jacobsen analyses two examples of media hoaxing: The Yes Men's Dow Chemical news hoax and Chris Ume's Tom Cruise deepfake on TikTok, thereby illuminating how and why hoaxes can be dangerous and ethically challenging. Jacobsen ends by suggesting a method for analysing hoaxing through four connected research questions, thus showing how the study of hoaxing can benefit from combining the theoretical framework of fictionality and media affordances.

In Chapter Three, 'Assessing the Genre of Docudrama: The Case of Aaron Sorkin's *The Trial of the Chicago 7*', James Phelan discusses the genre of docudrama; a hybrid genre situated between the documentary film and the historical fiction film. Through his analysis of Aaron Sorkin's film *The Trial of the Chicago 7* (2020), Phelan asks whether Sorkin deceives his audience when combining fact and fiction. Is it potentially dangerous when a director transforms historical events into engaging drama? Or is a director perfectly allowed to make 'a fresh interpretation' of historical events? The chapter demonstrates how a rhetorical approach to fictionality and nonfictionality can help illuminate the appeals and dangers of both Sorkin's film and the genre of docudrama in general.

In Part II, 'Networked Rhetoric', the contributors look closely at the consequences of social media affordances for narrative rhetoric and ethics, as well as for our notion of the fictional. Chapter Four, 'The Message is not the Truth: Uses and Affordances of Narrative Form on Social Media Platforms', by Hanna-Riikka

Roine studies the contemporary variations of the premodern bardic system and the exemplum in digital narrative environments. Following Maria Mäkelä, Roine argues that the relative irrelevance of narrative referentiality and the narrative's detachment from any identifiable author in digital storytelling does not only contribute to the 'post-truth' condition but can also be understood as a 'return' to the premodern storytelling culture. Roine analyses Kristen Roupenian's short story 'Cat Person' (2017) as an example of how complicated content gets reframed as an exemplum-like story with an unambiguous moral lesson.

In Chapter Five, 'Storytelling and Participatory Immersion in the Niilo22 Experience', Jarkko Toikkanen, Mari Hatavara, Maria Laakso and Hanna Rautajoki chart the peculiarities and dangers of YouTube narration such as the lack of rhetorical anchoring that may result in overly normative projections from the audience's part. Drawing on the concepts of immersion and participation, the authors study Finnish Niilo22, a livestream blogger who conveys his idle – and, in narrative terms, 'pointless' – everyday activities to an audience who is eager to read him as a morally alarming example of an unemployed person. Toikkanen, Hatavara, Laakso and Rautajoki demonstrate how the audience engages in participatory storytelling through both narrative immersion and moral judgement.

Part III, 'Repositioning the Novel', contains case studies of novels that complicate the routine dichotomy of fiction and fact and, further, challenge the alignment of fictionality and factuality with the genres of fiction and nonfiction, respectively. Chapter Six, '"It […] cannot do any harm to anyone whatsoever": Fictionality, Invention and Knowledge Creation in Global Nonfictions, Joseph Conrad's Prefaces and *Chance*', by Sarah Copland investigates the potential and dangers of fictionality and invention as forms of knowledge creation in global nonfictions, i.e., works partaking in genres that are conventionally understood as nonfictional such as documentaries, biographies and prefaces. Copland focuses on Joseph Conrad's prefaces and his novel *Chance* (1913). While the prefaces are global nonfiction, *Chance* is a fictional representation of nonfictional conversational storytelling. In both cases, fictionality and invention are central to the creation of knowledge and credibility, respectively, but with very different consequences. The chapter thus brings attention to the dangers of conflating fictionality and invention in nonfictional conversational storytelling, thereby contributing to both rhetorical fictionality theory and Conrad scholarship.

In Chapter Seven, 'Positioning You: Fictionality and Interpellation in Janne Teller's *War: What If It Were Here?*', Pernille Meyer asks what ethical implications narrative interpellation may have when 'forced' on the reader in the nonreciprocal communicative situation of fiction. Meyer's analysis of the use of second-person narration in Janne Teller's fictional essay *War: What If It Were*

Here? (2016) expands into an investigation of political activism through readerly engagement and the ethical pitfalls of reaching outside of the fictional construction with a penetrating second-person address. What kind of dangers of narrative and fictionality are we facing when an author makes the reader play the role of a refugee as part of a political debate, allegedly in order to elicit empathy?

Engaging in the contemporary debate emerging from the popularity of autofiction, Chapter Eight, '"But it hurts like I killed someone": Character Assassinations and Karl Ove Knausgaard's *My Struggle*', by Rikke Andersen Kraglund discusses the ethical implications of using actual family members and friends as 'material' in literary texts. As a case in point, Kraglund focusses on Karl Ove Knausgaard's autobiographical novel in six parts, *My Struggle* (2009–11), which caused strong reactions from people close to the author. Kraglund calls for a heightened sensitivity with regard to other people's narrative identities and story ownership at a time when the instrumentalization of personal narratives is a cultural megatrend.

The final Part IV, 'Broadening the Scope of Rhetorical Fictionality Theory', addresses issues that are not limited to contemporary concerns but rather pose a perennial challenge to theories of fictionality and factuality, namely the rhetorical and epistemic hybridity of factuality and fictionality. In Chapter Nine, 'On being Lectured in and by Fiction: Rhetorical Directness and Indirectness of Fictional Instructiveness', Samuli Björninen complements and challenges the rhetorical fictionality theory by exploring the rhetoric of presenting factual or factual-looking information in fiction. Through his analyses of fictional lectures appearing in three novels – David Foster Wallace's *The Pale King* (2011), Laura Lindstedt's *Oneiron* (2015) and Colson Whitehead's *The Underground Railroad* (2016) – Björninen studies the implications and risks of embedding facts and instructive texts in fictional narrative. The chapter aims to broaden the theoretical view about the ways fictionality and factuality are entangled in the narrative form.

The volume closes with Henrik Zetterberg-Nielsen's chapter, 'Dangers of Fictionality, Human Sexuality and Sexual Fantasies', that continues his work on fictionality theory by exploring the relation between fictionality and human sexuality. Discussing three possible dangers in the context of sexual fantasy – 'assuming that what is rare in reality is also rare as fantasy; that fictionality does not have much real-world impact; and finally, that fantasies always amount to wish fulfilments' – Zetterberg-Nielsen stresses the importance of distinguishing between fantasies of an overtly imagined nature and real wishes and acts, thus moving towards a de-pathologization of common sexual fantasies. Moreover, Zetterberg-Nielsen argues that sexuality is a common purpose of fictionality and demonstrates how a rhetorical approach to fictionality can shed new light on highly debated topics such as coercion fantasies, the importance of consensuality and unhealthy, sexist didactics of some fictional narratives.

Part I: Narrative, Fictionality and the Public Sphere

Paul Dawson

1. Bad Press: The Rhetoric of Narrative in Public Discourse

Abstract: By virtue of its association with empathy, the art of literature, and the empowering nature of personal storytelling, narrative has long **been** considered an essential and positive element of our humanistic sense of self. However, in recent years the invocation of narrative as a strategic element in political campaigning, social activism, corporate branding, and advertising seems to have led to increasingly bad press for the concept. This chapter interrogates the rhetorical deployment of the term 'narrative' in public discourse by examining its appearance in news media reportage of major political events throughout the year 2020 leading up to the US presidential election. By analysing recurring phrases such as 'control the narrative,' 'change the narrative,' and 'false narrative'; the semantic differences between 'a narrative' and 'the narrative'; and the range of lexical substitutes that accompany the word in any given news article, the chapter demonstrates how political culture and media discourse frame the daily news cycle as an ongoing struggle between competing narratives in a digital age marked by epistemological crisis. At the same time that 'narrative' continues to receive bad press by virtue of its association with anything from spin to misinformation, its positive valences have been ceded to 'story', with its connotations of authentic expression and experiential truth.

Keywords: narrative, rhetoric, US politics, journalistic discourse

By virtue of its association with empathy, the art of literature and the empowering nature of personal storytelling, narrative has long been considered an essential and positive element of our humanistic sense of self. However, in recent years the invocation of narrative as a strategic element in political campaigning, social activism, corporate branding and advertising seems to have led to increasingly bad press for the concept. Notes of caution have been sounded by scholars such as Sujatha Fernandes who writes of a 'contemporary boom of instrumental storytelling' that 'presents carefully curated narratives with predetermined storylines as a tool of philanthropy, statecraft, and advocacy',[30] and by journalists such as Mark Leibovich, who laments a 'narrative glut' in political commentary produced by the rise of social media and the campaign success of Barack

30 Sujatha Fernandes, *Curated Stories: The Uses and Misuses of Storytelling* (Oxford: Oxford University Press, 2017), 2.

Obama.[31] This glut has only increased, and the prevalence of the term 'narrative' in media coverage and analysis of the extraordinary events of 2020 is ample evidence of its widespread use beyond scholarship. The particular nature of this use also demonstrates that narrative came to be seen in a negative light throughout the year by virtue of its association with strategic manipulation, spin, lies, misinformation, conspiracy and, ultimately, alternative reality. Its association with empathy, experiential truth, authenticity and the political critique of hegemonic truth, on the other hand, appears to have been ceded to 'story' which retains positive connotations of reclaiming or asserting one's voice in phrases such as share or tell your story.

The aim of this chapter is to examine how the theoretical relationship between narrativity and fictionality is complicated by the performative negotiations of truth being played out in the terminological contortions of narrative that inform contemporary public debate. My argument is that these contortions are symptomatic of a political culture and media environment both pragmatically attuned to and wary of the dangers of narrative, criticizing its strategic misuse and epistemological pitfalls while nonetheless defaulting to narrative analysis. I will interrogate the rhetorical deployment of the term 'narrative' in public discourse by examining its appearance in news media throughout the year 2020, ranging from the reported quotes of public figures to journalistic analysis of current events, particularly in relation to: the impeachment trial of President Donald Trump; the global Covid-19 pandemic; the Black Lives Matter movement; and ongoing partisan politics leading up to the US presidential election. In what follows I will focus mainly on how these events were covered in *The New York Times*, but will also make reference, where salient, to other publications including *Politico*, *The Washington Post* and *The Sydney Morning Herald*.

What even is a narrative?

The first observation to make is that the term narrative itself has become highly protean. If we might conventionally define narrative as the representation of a causally related sequence of events, or simply the telling of a story, its relationship to eventhood often seems tenuous in public discourse, as attested by these two examples:

31 Mark Leibovich, 'When the "Narrative" Becomes the Story', *The New York Times Magazine* (8 December 2015).

> Yes and no. The prevailing narrative is that the polls got the 2016 result catastrophically wrong.[32]

> Each of these escalation points appear designed to bait Mr. Trump into reinforcing the false narrative that there are only two choices when it comes to Iran: war, or a return to the flawed 2015 nuclear deal.[33]

Where is the narrative? In both cases, one could easily substitute the word 'opinion' or 'assessment', or 'argument' or 'viewpoint', with little appreciable semantic difference. Why does the first example not simply say 'The consensus is that …'? In both cases, narrative seems to refer not to the telling of events, but to the interpretation of those events (the inaccuracy of polls; the potential responses to Iran). Furthermore, the term is used in a pejorative sense, referring to the received opinion that needs to be contested. The semantic laxity and protean range of the word makes more sense when we recognize how often it is used as a substitute for other words. For instance, in *The New York Times* Nicholas Fandos and Emily Cochrane write:

> Leading Republicans rallied on Monday around President Trump's refusal to concede the election, declining to challenge the false narrative that it was stolen from him or to recognize President-elect Joseph R. Biden Jr.'s victory even as party divisions burst into public view.[34]

Again, one must wonder where the narrative is (beyond the simple eventfulness contained in the clause 'it was stolen'). Later in the article, the word assertion is used as a substitute: 'Rather than openly rebuke the false assertion that the election was stolen, Mr. McConnell instead said that "this process will reach its resolution"'. This substitution is telling, for if a narrative is also an assertion, the emphasis lies in its rhetorical function and, crucially, in its referential status as a speech act.

The word narrative may have become a recurring cliché in journalistic discourse, a linguistic tic to add variety to the prose, but we can track the implications of its many nominal and adjectival uses and meanings by addressing the synonyms and lexical substitutes that are employed alongside it. As I will

32 Matthew Knott, Can You Trust the US Election Polls?, *The Sydney Morning Herald* (4 August 2020).

33 Richard Goldberg, 'Trump Has an Iran Strategy. This Is It', *The New York Times* (24 January 2020).

34 Nicholas Fandos and Emily Cochrane, 'Republicans Back Trump's Refusal to Concede, Declining to Recognize Biden', *The New York Times* (9 November 2020).

explore further, the list of substitutions can include a trope, an opinion, an idea, a message, an argument, a (partisan) perspective or a fabrication. I will begin by observing a curious grammatical inversion in common usage: the use of the definite article ('the' narrative) to refer to something that in fact has an amorphous agentless generality, while the indefinite article ('a' narrative) is used to refer to something more specifically attached to an agent and a rhetorical design.

'A Narrative' versus 'The Narrative'

While Leibovich argues that political narratives emerge from the consensus opinion of 'a critical mass of narrators', what characterizes *the narrative* as a phrase is its independence of any teller. It more resembles what linguists, anthropologists and cognitive psychologists would call a cultural script: a way of thinking and articulating that frames expectations and guides behaviour, typically encoded in a simple phrase or referring to socially embedded and historically recurring patterns (see Wierzbicka, 1994; McLean and Syed, 2015). While this notion of narrative as cultural script can denote something as broad and deeply rooted in a national psyche as 'the American Dream', its use in the news media appears slightly different. The most conventional use of the definite article is to label a prevailing perspective or consensus opinion in the public sphere about ongoing events. As a result, *the narrative* is more contingent than a typical cultural script; it is an evolving discourse attached to no specific teller, and linked to no particular text, that agents (either individuals, organizations or nations) nonetheless compete to control or change in the daily news cycle. Here is a typical example, in an article by Li Yuan in *The New York Times* entitled 'Coronavirus Weakens China's Powerful Propaganda Machine'. In the context of rising domestic discontent about the Communist Party's mishandling of the coronavirus pandemic, Yuan writes: 'Beijing is doing everything it can to take back the narrative'.[35] What is 'the narrative'? Who owns it? The article does not explain these things. However, it appears to be shorthand for public opinion coherent and substantial enough to be denoted by a definite article. The particular dynamic referred to is Communist Party propaganda being criticized online by citizens, suggesting that *the narrative* is not simply something issued by Beijing so much as it is the site of a discursive struggle between organic lower-level individual agents and the top-down state media.

---

35 Li Yuan, 'Coronavirus Weakens China's Powerful Propaganda Machine', *The New York Times* (26 February 2020).

In journalistic discourse, *the narrative* is often part of a prepositional phrase, such as 'the narrative of ----.', in which the narrative belongs to an idea or to ongoing events. Writing of the attempts of Senator Lindsay Graham to use the United States Senate Committee on the Judiciary to undermine the Mueller report, Catie Edmondson observes:

> The effort mirrors one by Mr. Trump himself to rewrite the narrative of the Russia investigation. Late last week, he publicly vented that neither his administration nor Republicans were adequately investigating unsubstantiated accusations that former President Barack Obama masterminded a plot to spy on his campaign.[36]

Here 'the narrative' is not the story that the Mueller report tells of Russian interference, multiple contacts with the Trump campaign, and attempts to obstruct justice, but the narrative in the public sphere of how and why the investigation came about and how it was received. To 'rewrite' this narrative is to attempt to shift public perception – and thus the narrative is not so much a specific text or a cultural script (that can be encoded in a phrase such as 'the American Dream') as a kind of collectively established perspective on events emerging from the aggregate of public commentary about the Russia investigation.

Cultural scripts are set; they are pre-existing. Hence the phrase 'change the narrative' in social activism. The way *the narrative* is employed in journalistic discourse still implies the same framing function but tends to refer to the flux of recent events. Hence a phrase such as 'control the narrative' in political campaigning refers to manipulating or intervening in the daily news cycle where ongoing events occur and are reported almost instantaneously. This phenomenon of breaking news as a storytelling genre, according to Alexandra Georgakopoulou, is defined by its continuous reporting of recent events, the portability of stories across online and offline environments, and its co-construction through multiple tellers.[37] It also underpins Zizi Papacharissi's concept of 'affective publics' produced by the 'soft structures of storytelling' on Twitter. Papacharissi's focus is the instantaneity of news, where unfolding events are reported as they happen 'through processes that instantly turn events into stories'.[38] According

---

36 Catie Edmonson, 'Graham to Call Mueller to Testify Before Senate Judiciary Committee', *The New York Times* (12 July 2020).

37 Alexandra Georgakopoulou, 'Storytelling on the Go: Breaking News as a Travelling Narrative Genre', in Mari Hatavara, Lars-Christer Hydén and Matti Hyvärinen, eds., *The Travelling Concepts of Narrative* (Amsterdam: John Benjamins, 2013), 201–224.

38 Zizi Papacharissi, *Affective Publics: Sentiment, Technology, and Politics* (New York: Oxford University Press, 2015), 44.

to Papacharissi: 'Personal views and takes on events are woven into developing narratives through the organizational logic of hashtags'.[39] In this diagnosis of breaking news and its perpetual updates, 'developing narratives' emerge from the technological affordances of the networked public sphere, a sphere connected yet fragmented enough to enable multiple publics to form around the instant and continuous reportage of events.

In this context, the phrase *a narrative* becomes a salient counterpoint to *the narrative*. Here is one particularly overt use of the phrase by Republican Senator John Cornyn to dismiss an unpalatable observation put to him by journalists. As reported by Nicholas Fandos and Catie Edmondson:

> Asked whether Mr. Trump had been emboldened since his acquittal, Mr. Cornyn dismissed the idea as a 'narrative,' declining to elaborate as he disappeared into a committee room.[40]

It is certainly a shame that Mr. Cornyn did not elaborate on either the narrative he dismissed or what he meant by narrative. It is interesting to note, though, that what the journalists quote as 'a narrative' they describe as an idea: Trump's post-impeachment emboldenment. To dismiss an idea as a narrative is clearly to use the term in a pejorative sense, but it also stops short of labelling an assertion as lie, leaving open the possibility that it is fanciful speculation. The rhetorical force of Cornyn's statement also betrays his belief that 'a' narrative cannot be 'the' narrative because he ascribes it to a specific group of Trump critics rather than to general consensus. This explains the grammatical inversion to which I referred: *the narrative* refers to no specific artefact and belongs to no teller, but it is a singular dominant script framing unfolding events; *a narrative* is but one of many vying for the status of accepted explanation in the public sphere, and thus could refer to a plurality of possible counter-narratives.

A term sometimes used to clarify this understanding is 'the public narrative.' To identify the different concepts of narrative at play, I will analyse its use in an article that explains how misinformation about the outcome of the US presidential election spread online and led to a number of protest rallies across the country. In 'How Misinformation "Superspreaders" Seed False Election Theories', Sheera Frenkel refers to collaborative research that revealed a small number of right-wing personalities with large social media followings 'helped

---

39 Papacharissi, *Affective Publics*, 70.

40 Nicholas Fandos and Catie Edmondson, 'As a Post-Impeachment Trump Pushes the Limits, Republicans Say Little', *The New York Times* (12 February 2020).

spread the false voter-fraud narrative that led to those rallies.'[41] Likening these figures to coronavirus 'superspreaders', the article quotes a researcher claiming that the apparently organic viral spread of misinformation is in fact cleverly designed: 'These superspreaders show that there is an intentional effort to redefine the public narrative'.[42] This public narrative is presumably a consensus emerging from the mainstream opinion that can nonetheless be altered because it is part of an ongoing news cycle. In describing the method of analysis for tracking such efforts, Frenkel describes how researchers 'compiled a list of 95,546 Facebook posts that included narratives about voter fraud'.[43] These narratives are presumably more specific textual artefacts, micro-narratives contained in the Facebook posts themselves. Finally, in charting the outsized viral influence of such posts, she writes: 'Those 33 posts had created a narrative that would go on to shape what millions of people thought about the legitimacy of the U.S. elections'.[44] Frenkel's analysis of viral misinformation thus involves three different uses of narrative, necessary for charting the path of misinformation through a social media ecology in which influencers game the algorithmic models: (1) narratives contained in individual posts that (2) create *a* narrative about voter fraud that achieves a viral spread in order to (3) redefine *the* public narrative of consensus opinion emerging from the daily news cycle. With this taxonomy in mind, we can proceed to analyse the language that accompanies these different senses of the word narrative.

Narrative as political rhetoric

Journalistic commentary on politics tends to focus on the rhetorical nature of narrative, equating narrative with campaign messaging, and employing verbs such as craft, create and spin to highlight the dubious nature of these strategic acts of communication. For instance, in commentary on the presidential debates, Annie Karni and Maggie Haberman write:

---

41 Sheera Frenkel, 'How Misinformation "Superspreaders" Seed False Election Theories', *The New York Times* (23 November 2020).

42 Frenkel, 'How Misinformation "Superspreaders"'.

43 Frenkel, 'How Misinformation "Superspreaders"'.

44 Frenkel, 'How Misinformation "Superspreaders"'.

> Mr. Trump has been crafting a narrative depicting the former vice president as having a diminished physical and mental stature, in the hope of making voters believe that Mr. Biden is unfit for office.[45]

The phraseology of crafting and depicting has echoes of literary composition but the narrative referred to here is not a textual artefact that tells a story so much as a series of public statements and advertisements that collectively produce a general perception. This is made clear later in the article when narrative is replaced with a synonym: 'It is a message that Mr. Trump's campaign has spent millions of dollars amplifying'.

A little further along the rhetorical spectrum, we see narrative being associated with political spin. Nick Akerman, a prosecutor for the Watergate investigation, writes in 'Did Mueller Ever Stand a Chance Against Trump and Roger Stone?':

> But as a result of those limitations, Mr. Trump, with the assistance of Mr. Barr, spun the narrative to affect the impact on the American public of the Mueller report and, as we have seen with Mr. Stone and Michael Flynn, undermined the criminal convictions obtained by Mr. Mueller's team.[46]

That Trump spun *the* narrative rather than *a* narrative implies an existing narrative that can be manipulated if presented in the right way, although it is not clear whether Akerman is referring to the Mueller report or to the daily news cycle. On other occasions, the verb to 'spin' seems closer to fabrication, such as when Linda Qiu and Michael D. Shear observe that Trump's 'falsehoods are the foundation of his campaign rallies and the connective tissue of the often 90-minute narrative he spins at every stop'.[47]

This use of the word spin is more closely aligned with another verb: to create. In a *Politico* article analysing Trump's attempts to overturn the presidential election, Michael Kruse first observes: 'He's spinning a myth to serve his own interest'.[48] Later in the article, he quotes a Republican strategist as saying 'He's constantly creating a legend, frankly, about himself rather than a truthful narrative'.[49] Both

---

45 Annie Karni and Maggie Haberman, 'By Lowering the Debate Bar for Biden, Has Trump Set a Trap for Himself?', *The New York Times* (27 September 2020).

46 Nick Akerman, 'Did Mueller Ever Stand a Chance Against Trump and Roger Stone?', *The New York Times* (13 July 2020).

47 Linda Qiu and Michael D. Shear, 'Rallies Are the Core of Trump's Campaign, and a Font of Lies and Misinformation', *The New York Times* (26 October 2020).

48 Michael Kruse, 'Trump's Crazy and Confoundingly Successful Conspiracy Theory', *The New York Times* (13 November 2020).

49 Kruse, 'Trump's Crazy and Confoundingly Successful Conspiracy Theory'.

instances invoke older forms of storytelling that historically were unhampered by referentiality and link political spin with the creativity of fiction, managing to give bad press not only to narrative but to creativity.

Other articles refer to Steve Bannon and Rudy Giuliani 'labouring to create a narrative that former Vice President Joe Biden's son Hunter was corrupt' (which makes narrative a lexical accomplice to the word 'allegation'); and to Trump marshalling and pressuring Republican allies in the hope of overturning the election or 'at least creating a narrative to explain his loss'.[50] These quotes demonstrate that attempts to create *a* narrative must be widely accepted in order for it to become *the* narrative. One cannot 'create' *the narrative*: such a script is more organic and emergent. In this instance, the typically positive correlation of creativity with literature becomes a negative correlation with fiction, which is then contrasted with fact. For instance, in 'Trump's Blueprint for Victory', Ryan Lizza writes 'Trump is good at creating narratives that stick even when they defy reality'.[51] And in 'The Intelligence Director Who Is Undermining Trust and Truth', John Sipher asserts, even more overtly, that 'Creating a fictional narrative for political purposes requires corrupting a system that relies on in-depth, contextual and all-source analysis'.[52] Narrative is presented as the opposite of this analysis because, like fiction, it simply invents. In these two examples the verb 'to create' is used to associate narrative first with fabrication, then with fiction, specifically an older, negative meaning of fiction as feigning, rather than the modern understanding of fiction as a mode of nonreferential discourse that is neither truth nor lie. The phrase 'to create a fictional narrative', which would typically refer to the act of composing a work of literature can, in this context, be considered a dangerous and deluded form of political gamesmanship.

Narrative as political commentary

Political commentary throughout 2020 was dominated by speculation over the US presidential campaign, much of it concerned with extrapolating from the results of regular election polling. This commentary took the form of both

---

50 Benjamin Weiser, Michael S. Schmidt and William K. Rashbaum, 'Steve Bannon Loses Lawyer After Suggesting Beheading of Fauci', *The New York Times* (6 November 2020); Peter Baker and Lara Jakes, 'Fighting Election Results, Trump Employs a New Weapon: The Government', *The New York Times* (10 November 2020).

51 Ryan Lizza, 'Trump's Blueprint for Victory', *Politico* (28 August 2020).

52 John Sipher, 'The Intelligence Director Who Is Undermining Trust and Truth', *The New York Times* (20 October 2020).

reporting the prevalence of narrative, and resorting to narrative analysis as it tried to diagnose and psychoanalyse the electorate. Halfway through the year, in 'The Real Reason Biden Is Winning? He's a Man', Peter Beinart writes:

> A narrative has formed around the presidential race: Donald Trump is losing because he's botched the current crisis. Americans are desperate for competence and compassion. He's offered narcissism and division — and he's paying the political price.[53]

This suggests there is a narrative not so much being told as somehow emerging from and enveloping events ('has formed around'). This narrative (which, Beinart seems to suggest, has assumed the status of *the narrative*) is then dismissed as not entirely true. 'For progressives', Beinart writes, 'it's a satisfying story line, in which Americans finally see Mr. Trump for the inept charlatan he truly is. But it's at best half-true'.[54] The real reason (as opposed to a mere competing narrative) we are told, is that Biden leads the race because, unlike his predecessor, Hillary Clinton, he is not facing a culture of misogyny. But why must Beinart set up a narrative that must be contested, rather than refer to an argument that is not entirely convincing or plausible? The significant phrase seems to be 'a satisfying story line', that ultimately a form of emplotment is taking place to account for ongoing events in order to project a future in which there is narrative resolution and moral restoration. In other words, the language of narrative is being employed not only to analyse the campaign rhetoric of politicians, but increasingly to analyse journalistic commentary on politics.

As we know, Biden prevailed, but Trump performed much more creditably than expected and than was predicted by the polls. In 'A Simple Theory of Why Trump Did Well', Jamelle Bouie takes aim at 'professional commentators' seeking to explain these results:

> Two narratives about what happened stand out. First, the idea that left-wing slogans like 'defund the police' cratered the Democratic Party in down ballot fights for the House and Senate, and second, that President Trump's modest gains with Black and Hispanic voters herald the arrival of a working-class, multiracial Republican Party.[55]

What is wrong, for Bouie, is not simply fanciful thinking but flawed logic, establishing a chain of cause and effect where no evidence exists, and believing that

53 Peter Beinart, 'The Real Reason Biden Is Winning? He's a Man', *The New York Times* (7 July 2020).

54 Beinart, 'The Real Reason Biden Is Winning?'.

55 Jamelle Bouie, 'A Simple Theory of Why Trump Did Well', *The New York Times* (18 November 2020).

correlation equals causation. This critique leads him to present an argument in opposition to these narratives which is also an implicit critique of narrative itself. 'At the risk of committing the same sin as other observers and getting ahead of the data', Bouie writes, 'I want to propose an alternative explanation for the election results'. It is instructive that he offers not an alternative 'narrative', but an alternative explanation, by which of course he means 'the real reason'. Explanation appears more reliable than narrative, not least because of its association with science, and throughout the article, Bouie employs phrases such as 'hard evidence' and 'little data to support a direct causal relationship', as if pitting scientific explanation against narrative speculation. And in doing so he has recourse to the same kind of positivist claims that narrative analysis was designed to critique in the social sciences.

Journalistic emplotment and competing narratives

Narrative analysis was also the source of challenges to positivist thinking in historiographic method, most forcefully in the work of Hayden White, and I suggest that White's anatomy of historical discourse can be applied to journalistic commentary. In 'Historicism, History, and Figurative Imagination', White contends:

> A rhetorical analysis of historical discourse would recognize that every history worthy of the name contains not only a certain amount of information and an explanation (or interpretation) of what this information 'means,' but also a more or less overt message about the attitude the reader should assume before *both* the data reported *and* their formal interpretation.[56]

According to White, history takes a narrative form that relies upon emplotment, that is, upon invoking the structural patterns of literary plots to frame events and fashion historical meaning according to broad genres such as Romance, Tragedy, Comedy and Satire. Emplotment also involves the various ideological positions historians can take in relation to their account of events: Anarchism, Conservatism, Liberalism and Radicalism. One can see the same features emerging from a rhetorical analysis of journalistic discourse that relies upon the language of narrative. Or rather, a simultaneous critique of and participation in the ongoing work of emplotment in public discourse. A bit like an addicted smoker, pundits and commentators know narrative is bad for them, but cannot resist continuing to narrativize.

---

56 Hayden White, 'Historicism, History, and Figurative Imagination', *History and Theory* 14/4 (1975), 53.

An example of how journalistic emplotment shapes discussion of the daily news cycle in narrative terms can be found in an article by Peter Baker about Trump's political rhetoric and campaign strategy:

> Mr. Rufo, though, said on Sunday that Mr. Trump was pitting his America First narrative celebrating the nation's heritage against what he called the Black Lives Matter narrative that America was founded on racism. 'The president is framing the election for voters in these terms,' he said. 'Do they want to preserve the American way of life or do they want to burn it down?'[57]

Here, the analysis being cited is that Trump claims ownership of a cultural narrative emerging from historical accounts of America as a successful frontier nation rather than a nation stained by its history of slavery. Which is to say, the article frames the political stakes of Trump's campaign in terms of the genres adopted by historians to emplot America's heritage as a Romance or a Tragedy. In 'The MAGA movement hits the streets — and Trump latches on', Tina Nguyen writes:

> Though the narrative of American cities being overrun with violence has percolated through conservative media, it's picked up in the past few years as anti-Trump, pro-BLM, and anti-police protests have snowballed. Scenes of looting, vandalism and property destruction only bolstered this worldview, and last year, right-wing extremists started clashing with antifa groups in Portland.[58]

In keeping with my observation that we can understand how narrative is being used by attending to the synonyms or substitutes used in surrounding sentences, we can see that Nguyen is using 'the narrative' to mean 'worldview'. This is the other element of emplotment that White refers to: the ideological positions that accompany generic story patterns. The idea of competing narratives being modelled in these articles is not just one of differing partisan perspectives on how current events relate to American national history, but of different world views that dictate what type of narrative can be constructed. In 'Trump, Not so Statuesque', Maureen Dowd argues that while Trump is brandishing 'the same old narrative' that Republicans have employed for decades, his racist appeals are out of touch with 'the national psyche' because: 'The actual narrative gripping America is, at long last, about white men in uniforms targeting black and brown people'.[59]

---

57 Peter Baker, 'More Than Ever, Trump Casts Himself as the Defender of White America', *The New York Times* (6 September 2020).

58 Tina Nguyen, 'The MAGA Movement Hits the Streets - and Trump Latches On', *Politico* (4 September 2020).

59 Maureen Dowd, 'Trump, Not so Statuesque', *The New York Times* (27 June 2020).

If emplotment in journalism operates through a comparison of unfolding events with the structures of literary genres, journalistic commentary is itself attuned to how strategic campaigning seeks to influence this emplotment of the daily news cycle by generating 'storylines'. *Politico's* post-election analysis of the failure of Trump's campaign to discredit Joe Biden is instructive of how narrative analysis echoes literary criticism in the context of actual events. In 'How "Obamagate" and Hunter's "laptop from hell" fizzled', Kyle Cheney and Andrew Desiderio seem to offer an aesthetic critique of the ineffective storytelling produced by a last-minute campaign strategy, as much as a condemnation of its lack of evidence. This operates by a comparative analysis of Trump's 'tangled narratives' with earlier successful ones:

> In 2016, Republicans turned Hillary Clinton's emails into a salient and effective cudgel, bolstered by the daily headlines about the Russian-hacked emails promoted by Wikileaks and lingering questions about the FBI's probe of her private server. Those storylines fed a narrative about Clinton that had been decades in the making.[60]

In this construction, the 'storylines,' or plot developments, are considered part of a larger ongoing 'text' authored by Republican strategists that nonetheless had assumed a status in the public imaginary akin to a cultural narrative. In comparison, Trump's 2020 efforts are considered failed acts of storytelling:

> The narratives were often convoluted even for intense followers of the Russia investigation and Rudy Giuliani's efforts to gather dirt on the Bidens in Ukraine. The storylines appealed almost exclusively to Trump's diehard political base, and were featured on right-wing websites and the Fox News primetime lineup — a large audience indeed, but a narrow sliver of the wider electorate.[61]

This use of literary terms (there is also a reference to unreliable narrators) is less about reducing narrative to fiction, than about recognizing the generic overlaps, but what it does do is suggest that narratives are judged by plausibility and coherence rather than factual accuracy, by verisimilitude rather than verifiability. By association fiction becomes equated with falsehood rather than nonreferentiality, thus receiving bad press by default.

---

60 Kyle Cheney and Andrew Desiderio, 'How "Obamagate" and Hunter's "Laptop from Hell" Fizzled', *Politico* (8 November 2020).

61 Cheney and Desiderio, 'How "Obamagate"'.

Narrative falsehood: Fiction, misinformation and conspiracy

It is evident that partisan politics has become increasingly understood as a battle of competing narratives. The weak version of this battle involves conflicting perspectives on events or interpretations of facts. The stronger version highlights incommensurable ideological differences that are concerned with emplotting different versions of reality. The rhetorical weaponization of what White calls the 'inexpungable relativity in every representation of historical phenomena'[62] has led simply to the rejection of competing views by labelling them narratives. This can be seen in reportage on the Black Lives Matter protests that surged in the wake of George Floyd's death. For instance, in *The New York Times*, Nicholas Kristof writes:

> We see dueling narratives. One is Trump's, and it portrays Portland and other cities with protests against police brutality as teetering on the abyss and requiring his Lincolnesque hand to hold America together. The other is — well, shall we call it reality?'[63]

This opposition seeks to resist any default equivalence between 'dueling narratives', instead arguing that a narrative construction is being pitted against reality. A clear example of the synonymic chain that enables narrative to be linked to a range of terms at odds with reality can be found in Davey Alba's discussion of the viral spread of misinformation after the US presidential election. In this article Alba writes:

> On Monday evening and into Tuesday, a strain of false information that Democratic presidential candidate Joseph R. Biden Jr. had lost Pennsylvania and his president-elect status began to surge.[64]

The phrase 'false information' gets abbreviated later in the article: 'The falsehood was then picked up and posted to YouTube by a verified account, The Next News Network'. From this point, a number of synonyms are introduced to demonstrate the elaborate nature of the 'false claims' that the title refers to:

---

62 Hayden White, 'Historical Emplotment and the Problem of Truth', in Saul Friedlander, ed., *Probing the Limits of Representation: Nazism and the 'final Solution'* (Cambridge, MA: Harvard University Press, 1992), 37.

63 Nicholas Kristof, 'Help Me Find Trump's "Anarchists" in Portland: The President Has His Politically Driven Narrative. And Then There's Reality', *The New York Times* (29 July 2020).

64 Davey Alba, 'False Claims That Biden "Lost" Pennsylvania Surge, and Tech Companies Struggle to Keep Up', *The New York Times* (11 November 2020).

> The false narrative follows other surging falsehoods during election week. From Nov. 3 to Nov. 9, unfounded story lines about widespread voter fraud and ineligible ballots spread across Facebook, Twitter and YouTube as votes were tallied in the swing states of Arizona, Michigan and Georgia. On Election Day, more misinformation about allegations of fraud or election-stealing focused on Pennsylvania than any other state, according to misinformation researchers.[65]

In this synonymic chain, false information becomes false narrative becomes unfounded story lines become misinformation. Information is not necessarily narrative in nature: it could be a list of raw data. To be narrativized, it requires a causal sequence of events, or at least an event, reported through a mediated perspective. Here is where storyline comes in, implying the temporal unfolding of events according to some design, and providing the link to the term misinformation. There is yet another word in this long chain, however, embedded in the quoted remarks of an expert interviewed for the article:

> Melissa Ryan, chief executive of Card Strategies, a consulting firm that researches disinformation, said that she expected misinformation would continue for as long as Mr. Trump's campaign 'continues peddling the fiction that Trump actually won the election'.[66]

The equation of misinformation with fiction may confirm its status as falsehood or lie, but it also highlights the narrative construction at play, the development of a storyline that we would typically associate with the genre of fiction. Ryan is further quoted as saying because the facts are against Trump, 'his campaign only has conspiracies and disinformation to make their argument'.[67] This final association of narrative with conspiracy theories is perhaps the apotheosis of its bad press today (see Dawson, 2022).

With protests against coronavirus lockdowns and claims of election fraud dominating the year, political discourse and national security strategy became increasingly concerned with conspiracy theories being fostered and spread virally online. Given that conspiracy theories seek underlying patterns to explain events and behaviour and link them to intentional agents, one can see the natural fit of narrative analysis for those seeking to investigate the phenomenon. Rather than scholarship on conspiracy theories, though, I am concerned with how the term narrative is deployed in public discourse. Here is one example, from an

65 Alba, 'False Claims'.
66 Alba, 'False Claims'.
67 Alba, 'False Claims'.

article in *The New York Times* by Davey Alba and Ben Decker entitled 'Trump Spread Multiple Conspiracy Theories on Monday. Here Are Their Roots':

> In a wide-ranging interview with the Fox News host Laura Ingraham on Monday night, President Trump spread multiple conspiracy theories about the protests that have erupted across the nation. Many of his unfounded claims can be traced back to narratives that have been swirling online for months.[68]

In this quote, we see a semantic chain from 'conspiracy theories' to 'unfounded claims' to swirling 'narratives'. The core term appears to be the claims that Trump makes, but the semantic chain has the effect of linking conspiracy theories closely to narrative. As well as this sort of commentary that positions both misinformation and narrative as strategic tools for conspiracy theorists, we see commentary on the danger of narrative cognition itself: the faulty narrativization of experience that leads to conspiratorial thinking. In 'Trump Lives in a Hall of Mirrors and He's Got Plenty of Company', Peter Wehner observes:

> This is injurious to Trump supporters because people who believe conspiracy theories can become consumed by them. It is not good for your brain (or your family life) when you see patterns — secret plots by powerful, sinister figures — that don't exist, in order to give meaning to events.[69]

Here is the connection between conspiracy theory and narrative: both are cognitive modes for making sense of experience by drawing connections between events and attributing them to a design. Narrative cognition is not necessarily conspiratorial, of course, but conspiracy theories are fundamentally narrative in nature and thus highlight the dangers of narrative.

Narrative versus story

While narrative and story are often used interchangeably, it is instructive to consider their different rhetorical valences in relation to the foundational narratological distinction between story and discourse, between the events of the fictional world and the manner in which they are reported. Of course, 'story' has long been a key journalistic term, referring to the genre of news itself. But in common parlance, story has become associated with personal empowerment,

---

68 Davey Alba and Ben Decker, 'Trump Spread Multiple Conspiracy Theories on Monday. Here Are Their Roots', *The New York Times* (1 September 2020).

69 Peter Wehner, 'Trump Lives in a Hall of Mirrors and He's Got Plenty of Company', *The New York Times* (2 November 2020).

and with giving individuals a voice. The exhortation to tell one's story has been nowhere more prominent or more positively received than in the global viral phenomenon that emerged around the MeToo hashtag. In an article in *The Guardian*, Bri Lee writes: 'Being able to share our stories is the strength at the heart of #MeToo. It's how patterns emerge, how group courage is fostered and garnered, and how these issues maintain momentum in the public sphere'.[70] A recent book that builds on this momentum is entitled *#MeToo: Stories from the Australian Movement*. In these instances, it simply would not work to substitute narrative for story. Why is this the case?

A story belongs to an individual. It is their personal experience. It is an authentic expression of their self. A narrative is a rhetorical construct that can be used by anyone and detached from any experiencing agent. The validity of a narrative can be contested, but the experiential truth of an individual story cannot. A story need not even be told for it to exist, as this line from Jessica Bennett's 'After #MeToo, the Ripple Effect' in *The New York Times* indicates: 'But recorded or not, nearly every woman seems to have a #MeToo story'.[71] Stories are something we own, that belong to us. Narratives are collective. Stories are private, narratives are public.

I am, of course, describing what has become a cliché in public discourse. An example of the banal instrumentalization of personal storytelling can be found in an article by Herminia Ibarra and Kent Lineback entitled 'What's Your Story?' in the January 2005 issue of *Harvard Business Review*, promoting the importance of individual stories for potential job applicants:

> Let's be clear: In urging the use of effective narrative, we're not opening the door to tall tales. By 'story' we don't mean 'something made up to make a bad situation look good.' Rather, we're talking about accounts that are deeply true and so engaging that listeners feel they have a stake in our success.[72]

Here is an attempt to distinguish story from narrative, even while talking about the importance of narrative. The key claim is that stories are 'deeply true'. Even though they may be harnessed for utilitarian purposes, they are not fabrications, and their truth cannot be contested because they are rooted in the felt experience of the individual.

---

70 Bri Lee, 'Sharing Our Stories Is the Strength at the Heart of #MeToo. We Must Repeal Gag Laws', *The Guardian* (19 November 2018).

71 Jessica Bennett, 'After #MeToo, the Ripple Effect', *The New York Times* (28 June 2018).

72 Herminia Ibarra and Kent Lineback, 'What's Your Story?', *Harvard Business Review* (January 2005), <https://hbr.org/2005/01/whats-your-story>, accessed 17 September 2013.

Clear evidence for the different tonal register of story can be found in Frank Bruni's 'The Undertold, Undersold Story of Kamala Harris'. If political commentary is typically cynical about the strategic manipulations of campaign narratives, Bruni evinces enthusiasm for the political potential of Kamala Harris' personal story:

> She did poorly in the Democratic primary because, yes, her campaign was a mess. But she also did poorly because she never discovered the right, stirring way to tell and sell her story.[73]

Similar to the *Harvard Business Review* advice for job applicants, Bruni is publically advising the vice-presidential candidate not to employ political spin, but to more effectively engage the electorate with the truth of her own personal experience. The 'right' way to tell her story appears to be to focus on biographical detail in order to encourage emotional investment, and to relate her experience to the cultural narrative of the American Dream in order to influence the narrative of the daily news cycle:

> Although Trump would cringe at the following thought and never understand it, Harris reflects this country's ideals and its reality much better than he does. 'Her story's America's story,' Biden said when he and she first appeared together as running mates on Wednesday afternoon. He's right, and I want her to embrace that and flesh it out at every turn.[74]

This may be a partisan exhortation, but it is also a recognition of the authenticity vested in personal storytelling in this cultural moment, as opposed to the scepticism towards broad, collectively generated narratives. It is not just that Harris espouses a certain ideal view of America, but that she is able to embody and express this ideal as her own story, in a way that Trump cannot. 'Storytelling is everything', Bruni notes, before outlining its different types:

> Trump won the presidency with a story about America that appealed to many Americans. It mixed imaginary villains with real ones, lies with truths. But he told it expansively. He told it effectively.[75]

It is notable that Trump has not told *his* story, only *a* story, something closer to spin and to fiction, despite its effectiveness. Trump could not tell his story,

---

73 Frank Bruni, 'The Undertold, Undersold Story of Kamala Harris', *The New York Times* (14 August 2020).

74 Bruni, 'The Undertold'.

75 Bruni, 'The Undertold'.

because his personal experience cannot resonate with voters. Rather he worked on channelling the grievance of some voters, encoded in the phrase 'Make America Great Again'. Personal storytelling is of a different register:

> Obama's rise was rooted in his own story, in the eloquence with which he spoke of Kenya and Kansas and how their commingling inside him was the American dream. I can't count the number of times, on his path to the White House, that he put a lump in my throat.
> Harris's story is the rival of Obama's. She just has to give it a comparably mythic shimmer. I know 'that little girl' was her. But I want to know more *about* her, and I want to hear her voice.[76]

Story is founded in the rhetorical power of the sublime; story is compared favourably to 'mythic shimmer' that transcends its referential status with an appeal to higher truth, as opposed to the association of narrative with untruths in phrases such as spinning a myth or creating a legend; and, in more contemporary terminology, story reveals the personal and is synonymous with the teller's authentic voice, expressing herself, and representing herself both aesthetically and politically. The word 'story' appears eight times in this short article, but the word 'narrative' is never used. There is no synonymic chain, because to write 'her narrative' or 'our narrative' could not carry the same connotations. Story and narrative are not interchangeable either theoretically or politically because their rhetorical deployment carries different assumptions.

Post-truth: Narrative and possible worlds

The idea of competing narratives has a noble origin: to give voice to marginalized identities. If this became the basis for promoting the value of counter-narratives that can contest hegemonic knowledge, it also became the basis for an epistemic collapse. Rightly or wrongly, this has enabled the concept of narrative to become associated with post-truth. As Ralph Keyes wrote, in his 2004 book *The Post-Truth Era*: 'This is the post-truth credo: creative manipulation and invention of facts can take us beyond the realm of mere accuracy into one of narrative truth'.[77] In this context, the conspiracy theory has become the extreme result of a dysfunctional public sphere in the digital post-truth age, and, as I have discussed, the supreme example of bad press for narrative today in which the dynamic of

---

76 Bruni, 'The Undertold'.

77 Ralph Keyes, *The Post-Truth Era: Dishonesty and Deception in Contemporary Life* (New York: St. Martin's Press, 2004), 153.

'competing narratives' has become the default mode of both enacting and analysing political debate. The confluence of these concepts can be found in this comment in *The Washingon Post* by Max Boot:

> First, conspiracy theories spread more efficiently by social media than by previous communications media. The online world is a post-truth space where there are no undisputed facts, only competing narratives, and even the most deranged claims (e.g., QAnon) can aggregate an audience.[78]

As has been noted by many commentators, with the encouragement of conservative politicians, conspiracy theories have reached well beyond the fringes of the online world. The refusal of Donald Trump to concede that he lost the 2020 election led to a flurry of articles in which narrative was construed not just as the presentation of an opposing perspective, or political spin, but as the active construction and maintenance of an alternative reality: one in which Trump actually won. As Ross Douthat writes in '2020 will not be Decisive':

> One factor [in the finality of election results] is the increasingly immersive power of *ideological narratives and virtual realities*. If you can react to an election loss by retreating immediately into a storyscape where the outcome was a cheat, carried about by means of voter fraud or Russian interference, then the decisiveness of any given outcome will inevitably diminish.[79]

The phrase 'immersive power' is instructive, for immersion is considered one of the vital features of our affective engagement with fiction. The ethical value of this immersion is said to reside in its capacity to stimulate our investment in characters and thus develop our empathy. However, if we are immersed in a narrative that is false rather than fictional, or that we believe to be true rather than knowing it is fiction, then it becomes a problem. In 'How Trump Almost Broke the Bounds of Reality', Bruno Maçães offers a critique of Trump's 'narrative tricks' that 'create deeply immersive storylines', promising voters a fantasy world that could not be sustained. 'The main binary in American politics now', Maçães writes, 'may not be between left and right, but between fiction and reality. At some point, fictions must be revealed as no more than fictions — and they must be switched off'.[80] This diagnosis of the problems of American politics

78 Max Boot, 'The Three Reasons Conspiracy Theories Are More Dangerous Than Ever', *The Washington Post* (23 May 2020).

79 Ross Douthat, '2020 will not be Decisive', *The New York Times* (3 November 2020).

80 Bruno Maçães, 'How Trump Almost Broke the Bounds of Reality', *The New York Times* (12 November 2020).

exemplifies the ambiguous use of the word fiction in contemporary public discourse, referring to a fabrication rather than to the genre of fiction, yet meaning more than simply a lie and gesturing instead to a narrativisation of events that can be as immersive as fiction.

The idea of competing narratives creating alternative realities rather than different perspectives relates to a fragmented public sphere in which no consensus exists to be debated, and instead is comprised of almost independent news cycles. For my final example, I refer to an article entitled 'Trump, a Post-truth Man for a Post-truth World' in *The Sydney Morning Herald* by the Australian commentator, Waleed Aly, which provides a textbook diagnosis of the election result in narrative terms. According to Aly, 'American democracy seems to have reached a point that has nothing to do with facts and everything to do with stories'. He positions Trump's 'attitude' towards facts as prime evidence for a post-truth sensibility in which '[a]ll that matters is the narrative and how you feel about it'.[81] What constitutes narrative truth is therefore not so much a rejection of or manipulation of fact, as an indifference to fact, and narrative is important less for its coherent ordering of experience than for its affective power. For Aly, Trump is not a singular phenomenon because both sides of politics are less concerned with productive debate than with choosing 'which narrative suits you', resulting in the replacement of 'a political culture of disagreement with a political culture of contempt'.[82]

The idea here is that competing narratives offer not different perspectives, but in fact different versions of reality. 'We need a better word than polarisation', Aly contends, 'because that just implies serious disagreement. We're beginning to see something much bigger than that: people who inhabit completely different worlds'.[83] Here is where the conflation of narrative and story becomes significant. In Aly's usage the terms are mutually supportive, if not interchangeable, in a way that resonates with the deconstructionist inversion of the story/discourse hierarchy where narrative does not report the events (i.e., 'facts') of the story world, but instead constructs them. The association with critical theory is apparent in this line: 'In a way, Trump is the world's first major post-modern politician: subordinating notions of objective truth to a narrative of anti-elite resistance'.[84]

81 Waleed Aly, 'Trump, a Post-truth Man for a Post-truth World', *The Sydney Morning Herald*, (5 November 2020).
82 Aly, 'Trump, a Post-truth Man'.
83 Aly, 'Trump, a Post-truth Man'.
84 Aly, 'Trump, a Post-truth Man'.

Rather than presenting Trump as the logical outcome of a certain mode of critique, though, I think it would be more accurate to present him as symptomatic of the ethically impoverished ontology of reactionary cultural politics that confronts liberalism with a caricature of its own intellectual positions. Regardless, Aly's point is that the phenomenon we are witnessing is profound in its reach and that the current reliance on narrative as a form of public rhetoric is ultimately anti-democratic. At the same time, his article is evidence of the extent to which narrative analysis has become a default mode of political commentary in the public sphere. By invoking the concept of an alternative reality, he is also arguing that narrative has shifted from modelling possible worlds to constructing fictional worlds. If competing narratives become unyoked from the facts and events of the world to the extent that they cease to be referential, the opposite of narrative is not non-narrative, but reality.

Louise Brix Jacobsen

2. Dangers of Media Hoaxing

Abstract: Hoaxes come in various forms and in various media. In 1998, William Boyd used the Nat Tate biography hoax to mock the glitterati of the New York art world and the media reception processes. Alan Sokal submitted his hoax essay to the journal Social Text in 1996 to demonstrate scientific weak peer review processes and their preference for fashionable scientific buzz words, and The Yes Men continue to practice media hoaxes to expose large corporations' failure to take responsibility for environmental disasters. Recently, the use of deepfake technology has added a new dimension to hoaxing practices and intensified the debate about the ethical concerns of faking. Hoaxes are often related to comic amusement, but they hold a potential for societal critique that can be dangerous and ethically challenging to the hoaxers as well as to the people and institutions being hoaxed. In this chapter, I investigate the dangers of fictionality in media hoaxing. Through a case study of two diverse examples of media hoaxing, The Yes Men's Dow Chemical media hoax on BBC World and the deepfake of Tom Cruise on TikTok, the chapter uncovers how hoaxes possess potential dangers because they are equally dependent on both an initial deceit and the exposure of this deceit. It is a key argument that the latter can be explained as an evoking of fictionality. Thus, the aim of this chapter is to contribute with a new definition of hoaxing (hoaxing = deceit plus fictionality) and an analytical framework designed to analyse hoaxing and its implications. The framework is created through an interlinking of fictionality as a rhetorical strategy with the idea of media affordances which can take into account how a hoax is both fully dependent on and shaped by a given media platform and its affordances.

Keywords: hoaxing, fictionality, deepfake, TikTok, The Yes Men, Tom Cruise

In February 2021, movie star Tom Cruise surprised users as the centrepiece of a series of videos on the social media platform TikTok. In the viral videos, some of which have millions of views, Cruise is playing golf, doing magic tricks and telling anecdotes. These performances were unexpected from an exclusive star like Tom Cruise, and it also quickly turned out to be too good to be true. It was not really him in the videos. It was instead a hoax made with artificial intelligence 'deepfake' technology.[85]

---

85 Deepfake applications are audio-visually manipulated applications based on AI (artificial intelligence). See also the analysis of the Tom Cruise hoax in this chapter.

Hoaxes come in various forms and in various media. In 1998, William Boyd used the Nat Tate biography hoax to mock the glitterati of the New York art world and the media reception processes. Alan Sokal submitted his hoax essay to the journal *Social Text* in 1996 to demonstrate scientific weak peer review processes and their preference for fashionable scientific buzzwords, and The Yes Men continue to practice media hoaxes to expose large corporations' failure to take responsibility for environmental disasters. Recently, the use of deepfake technology has added a new dimension to hoaxing practices and intensified the debate about the ethical concerns of faking.

Hoaxes are often related to comic amusement, but they hold a potential for societal critique that can be dangerous and ethically challenging to the hoaxers as well as to the people and institutions being hoaxed. In this chapter, I investigate the dangers of fictionality in media hoaxing. The investigation uncovers how hoaxes possess potential dangers because they are equally dependent on both an initial deceit and the exposure of this deceit. It is a key argument that the latter can be explained as an evoking of fictionality. Thus, the aim of this chapter is to contribute with a new definition of hoaxing and an analytical framework designed to analyse hoaxing and its implications.

The chapter comprises two main parts. In the first part, I discuss the concept of hoaxing and the range of the term by introducing and comparing various scholarly works on hoaxing and by addressing the concept through the lens of fictionality as a rhetorical strategy. This leads to a new definition of hoaxing (hoaxing = deceit plus fictionality) that will help distinguish the hoax from other kinds of faking. In the second part of the chapter, I introduce and analyse two diverse examples of media hoaxing that address various configurations and degrees of the dangers of hoaxing: The Yes Men's Dow Chemical media hoax on BBC World and the deepfake of Tom Cruise on TikTok. I end by suggesting a framework for hoaxing analysis.

Theoretical and methodological framework

The theoretical framework in this chapter is fictionality as rhetoric. As shown by Nielsen, Phelan and Walsh (2015), Jacobsen (2015), Iversen (2019), Grumsen and Jacobsen (2020) and others, fictionality can be regarded as a communicative strategy operating across media and genres. In this chapter, hoaxing is explored as a distinct rhetorical instrument characterized by a combination of deceit and fictionality (elaborated below). Hoaxes can function within and across a variety of media such as film, literature, social media, newspapers, news TV shows, online news platforms etc. Furthermore, they can copy various forms and genres such as documentaries, biographies, news, campaigns, social media profiles and journal articles. This calls for a theory of hoaxing that can operate independently of genres and media. Yet since hoaxing adapts to and is dependent on the media form it copies, explores and criticizes, the particular affordances of the individual media platform must also be taken into consideration. The ambition of this chapter is thus to contribute to the intersection between fictionality and media studies by methodologically combining the research question central to fictionality in the rhetorical vein: 'When, where, why, and how does someone use fictionality in order to achieve what purpose(s) in relation to what audience(s)?'[86] with the concept of affordances as it is used in media and communication studies.

According to Bucher and Helmond, affordance as a concept is often used to characterize what media technologies (or other material artefacts) allow people to do.[87] Ian Hutchby states that communicative affordances 'are functional and relational aspects which frame, while not determining, agentic action in relation to an object'.[89] In their work on social media affordances, Bucher and Helmond wish to extend extant conceptualizations in order to further consider what users do to the technology in question, and Nagy and Neff address user expectations and designer intentions by introducing the concept of 'imagined affordances'. This allows them to address affective responses: 'Affordances can include the expectations and beliefs of users, whether or not they are "true" or "right." Affordances can and should be defined to include properties of technologies that are "imagined" by users, by their fears, their expectations and their uses, as well as by those of the designers'.[90] A focus on media affordances will situate the interplay between sender, media text and audience, which is essential to the fictionality research question in a specific media ecology.

86 See Henrik Skov Nielsen, James Phelan and Richard Walsh, 'Ten Theses About Fictionality', *Narrative* 23/1 (2015), 61–73, 63.

87 Taina Bucher and Anne Helmond, 'The Affordances of Social Media Platforms', in Jean Burgess, Thomas Poell and Alice Marwick, eds., *The SAGE Handbook of Social Media* (London and New York: Sage Publications Ltd, 2018), online PDF version, 2-19, 3, <http://dx.doi.org/10.4135/9781473984066.n14>, accessed 5 October 2021.

88 For a survey of the term, its origin, development and various meanings see Bucher and Helmond, 'The Affordances of Social Media Platforms' and Peter Nagy and Gina Neff, 'Imagined Affordance: Reconstructing a Keyword for Communication Theory', *Social Media and Society* 1/2 (2015), 1–9.

89 Ian Hutchby, 'Technologies, Texts and Affordances', *Sociology* 35/ 2 (2001), 441–456, 444.

90 Nagy and Neff, 'Imagined Affordance', 4.

The interlinking of fictionality as a rhetorical strategy with the idea of media affordances allows for an analytical framework that can take into account how a hoax is both fully dependent on and shaped by a given media platform and its affordances. How does a hoax work when performed on a TV news show? And what should be considered when it is launched on the social media platform TikTok? Media affordances are important for understanding both The Yes Men's hoaxing practices and the Cruise hoax, but I will unfold the discussion of media affordances more fully in the analysis of the latter. The theoretical conflation of fictionality with affordances helps us understand how the communicative success of a hoax depends on a number of contextual factors, such as different users with different knowledge and expectations. A focus on media affordances also helps us understand the fragile process of orchestrating a hoax, and thereby why hoaxing can go wrong and be ethically problematic or even potentially dangerous. Timing, media skills and a grasp of potential user interplay are crucial.

Hoaxing

The scholarly work on hoaxes contains numerous definitions and discussions about the range of the term. According to James Fredal, hoaxes are a 'public form of deception'[91] which is staged in order to attract attention and create awareness of conditions in society. Hoaxes can target institutions, norms or behaviour, and/ or specific groups or individuals, and while the target risks severe ridiculing, the audience of the hoax is 'the object of entertainment and instruction'.[92] The target may, however, simultaneously be the hoax's audience, making the audience reflect on their own deception seems to be an inherent feature of the hoax.[93] Hoaxes deceive through false statements by imitating a host genre.[94] They are

91 James Fredal, 'The Perennial Pleasures of the Hoax', *Philosophy & Rhetoric* 47/1 (2014), 73–97, 76.

92 Fredal, 'The Perennial Pleasures of the Hoax', 76.

93 Lynda Walsh, *Sins against Science: The Scientific Media Hoaxes of Poe, Twain, and Others* (Albany, NY: State University of New York Press, 2006); Joanna Scott, 'On Hoaxes, Humbugs, and Fictional Portraiture', *a/ b: Auto/ Biography Studies* 31/ 1 (2016); Louise Brix Jacobsen, 'Paratext', in Lasse R. Gammelgaard, Stefan Iversen, Louise Brix Jacobsen, James Phelan, Richard Walsh, Henrik Zetterberg-Gjerlevsen and Simona Zetterberg-Gjerlevsen, eds., *Fictionality and Literature: Core Concepts Revisited* (Columbus: The Ohio State University Press, 2022), 141–160.

94 Fredal, 'The Perennial Pleasures of the Hoax', 76.

parasitic to the host because they inhabit it and are fully dependent on the audience's expectations of the given host.[95]

Brian McHale distinguishes between three types of literary hoaxes: the genuine hoax, the trap hoax and the mock hoax. The genuine hoax is 'perpetrated with no intention of [its] ever being exposed',[96] whereas the trap-hoax and the mock-hoax involve initial deception as well as an intention of exposing the hoax, either to punish and critique (trap-hoax) or for more aesthetic purposes (mock-hoax). The idea of the genuine hoax makes McHale's understanding of the hoax very inclusive. A narrower conception is represented by Alyson Miller's work on fraudulent literature. She distinguishes between hoax and fraud. While fraud is an attempt to remain hidden, a hoax's 'agenda in misleading an audience is usually made explicit, and publicly analysed in the interests of maximising its effect'.[97] This distinction indicates a conception of hoaxing that matches McHale's subcategories (trap-hoax and mock-hoax) but leaves out the broader definition reflected by the idea of the 'genuine hoax'. The crucial point seems to be whether the misleading is 'made explicit'. The same distinction constitutes film scholars Craig Hight and Jane Roscoe's typology of mock-documentaries. If a mock-documentary is categorized as a hoax, it involves an initial deceit meant to be revealed. They argue that hoaxes 'trigger reflexive interpretations among viewers because of the subsequent uncovering of their fictional status'.[98] In this way, the 'uncovering' is part of the designed deception, and the 'subsequent uncovering' triggers the critical reflexive potential of a hoax.

In her work on the scientific media hoax, Walsh describes hoaxing as a rhetorical form or machine functioning through a mechanism of 'illusion and revelation'.[99] The illusion or 'fooling' is usually created by a transparent style, where

---

95 Ian Reilly, *Media Hoaxing. The Yes Men and Utopian Politics* (Lexington Books, 2018), 12.

96 Brian McHale, '"A Poet May Naot Exist": Mock-Hoaxes and the Construction of National Identity', in Robert J. Griffin, ed., *The Faces of Anonymity: Anonymous and Pseudonymous Publication from the Sixteenth to the Twentieth Century* (New York: Palgrave Macmillan, 2003), 233–252, 236.

97 Alyson Miller, 'Stylised Configurations of Trauma: Faking Identity in Holocaust Memoirs', *Arcadia* 49/2 (2014), 229–253, 233.

98 Craig Hight and Jane Roscoe, *Faking It* (Manchester: Manchester University Press, 2011), 72.

99 Lynda Walsh, 'The Scientific Media Hoax: A Rhetoric for Reconciling Linguistics and Literary Criticism', in Patricia Bizzell, ed., *Rhetorical Agendas: Political, Ethical, Spiritual* (Taylor & Francis Group, 2005), 165–175, 171.

the features of the media in question are copied in order to avoid attention to form and authorship. Like Miller, Walsh somewhat distinguishes between hoax and fraud. Fraud usually implies a monetary gain, while hoaxers seek recognition, reflection and potentially even remorse.[100] Hoaxes are indeed intended to be revealed because the revelation displays the 'indirect message'[101] or the critical potential.

As investigated in Jacobsen, some hoaxes are intended to be decoded while reading or watching the media text, while others are meant to dupe the reader throughout the text.[102] Alan Sokal's debated hoax essay in the journal *Social Text* (1996) is an example of the former.[103] Sokal submitted a manuscript that formally resembled a scientific essay with fashionable buzzwords. Once readers encountered the text, however, several invention signals (for example sheer nonsense) were detectable – gradually changing readers' assumptions about the text. The faking was not detected during the peer review process, causing humiliation for the scientific journal, which was displayed as apparently eager to publish anything containing the right buzzwords. The Sokal Hoax shows that we can differentiate between duped readers (in this case the journal editors) and readers in the know (the readers who can decode the essay as a hoax).

I regard media hoaxing as deceptive communication orchestrated to be exposed. In order to clarify this definition further I will elaborate on the two parts of this initial definition: the deception and the exposure. In this next section, I will conflate the rhetorical definition of hoaxing with the idea of fictionality as rhetoric.

If we turn to encyclopedia entries, hoaxes are defined as 'humorous or malicious deception' and hoaxing will then be '[t]o deceive, especially by playing a trick on someone'.[104] In these definitions, deceit is the central characteristic. If we look at definitions of deceit, it becomes clear why the concept of deceit is essential – but not sufficient – for understanding the nature of the hoax. Cambridge defines deceit as '(an act of) keeping the truth hidden, especially to get an advantage'.[105] Merriam-Webster defines deceit as 'the act of causing someone to accept

---

100 Walsh, *Sins against Science:* 24.

101 Walsh, *Sins against Science*, 25.

102 Jacobsen, 'Paratext'.

103 See Allan Sokal, 'Transgressing the Boundaries: Towards a Transformative Hermeneutics of Quantum Gravity', *Social Text* 46/47 (1996), 217–252.

104 Lexico, 'hoax', <https://www.lexico.com/definition/hoax?locale=en>, accessed 1 October 2021.

105 Cambridge Dictionary, 'deceit', <https://dictionary.cambridge.org/us/dictionary/english/deceit>, accessed 1 October 2021.

as true or valid what is false or invalid'.[106] The definition of deceit sheds light on the first crucial part of hoaxing: Receivers of hoaxes are ideally deceived to 'accept as true or valid what is false or invalid'. This aligns with McHale's definition of the genuine hoax, but is insufficient in describing how the majority of hoaxes actually work, and how we can detect them as hoaxes. Fredal places the hoax between the prank and the con to combine the diverse feelings of amusement and embarrassment with the importance of deception and exposure.[107] I find this description enlightening, yet we still need to further explore which mechanisms are at work rhetorically in orchestrating the revelation of the deception. For Fredal it is essential that hoaxes 'employ rhetorics of truth (or plausibility), but they also use rhetorics of falsehood (or implausibility), and successful hoaxes balance these two strategies in order to create a productive tension between belief and doubt'.[108] In the following, I will argue that what distinguishes hoaxes from deception and lies, and what lifts them above a discussion of true or false, is the evoking of fictionality.

Fictionality and hoaxing

My conception of fictionality is rooted in Richard Walsh's theory of fictionality as described in *The Rhetoric of Fictionality* (2007) and further developed in 'Fictionality as Rhetoric' (2019). Walsh characterizes fictionality as a 'distinctive rhetorical resource, functioning directly as part of the pragmatics of serious communication'.[109] He describes fictionality 'as a quality of fiction as communication, not a quality of its referent or object of representation'.[110] Thus, fictionality is tied to the communicative intent and how the author invites readers to interpret and reflect on the fictional text. According to Walsh, fictionality can be invoked by paratexts that help the receiver decode a message as fictional.[111] Communication is culturally embedded, and the cultural context is crucial for its interpretation. This is of particular interest when it comes to hoaxing as a

---

106 Merriam-Webster, 'deceit', <https://www.merriam-webster.com/dictionary/deception>, accessed 1 October 2021.

107 Fredal, 'The Perennial Pleasures of the Hoax', 78.

108 Fredal, 'The Perennial Pleasures of the Hoax', 80.

109 Richard Walsh, *The Rhetoric of Fictionality: Narrative Theory and the Idea of Fiction* (Columbus: Ohio State University Press, 2007), 1.

110 Richard Walsh, 'Fictionality as Rhetoric: A Distinctive Research Paradigm', *Style* 53/4 (2019), 397–425, 398.

111 Walsh, *The Rhetoric of Fictionality*, 45.

rhetorical mechanism. The fictionality of a hoax cannot (at least not initially) be signalled text-internally, and hoaxes very often depend on epitexts as the sole source for signalling and determining its fictionality.[112]

In recent research on fictionality, the notion of invention has been highly debated. According to Nielsen, Phelan and Walsh, 'the intentional use of invented stories and scenarios'[113] is considered one form of fictionality, but in Gjerlevsen and Nielsen's definition of fictionality as 'intentionally signalled, communicated invention',[114] invention is a defining feature. For Walsh, fictionality entails 'independence from directly informative kinds of relevance'.[115] Invention is not crucial or necessary in his understanding of fictionality, but once independent of informative kinds of relevance, 'there is every reason to take advantage of the creative opportunities afforded by invention'.[116]

I adhere to the conception that 'when a sender invokes fictionality, the receiver is invited to conceive of the communicated or parts of the communicated as invented'.[117] At the same time, however, I also find it crucial to put forward Walsh's notion on the importance of the paratext, because the signalling – which is also at the core of Gjerlevsen and Nielsen's definition – may be completely absent in a first encounter with fictionalized communication. Gjerlevsen and Nielsen state that a 'paratext is not the only criterion for determining the status of fictionality'.[118] I agree that fictionality can be and is often signalled text-internally, yet, this might not be the case and sometimes a distant paratext might be the only signal available. It is important that a theory of fictionality is able to encompass communication which is 'set up ("signaled") in one way but later revealed ("re-signaled") in a different light.'[119]

Invention is also at the core of hoaxes. The hoaxer invents in order to show us that we have just trusted something we should not have trusted. Gjerlevsen and Nielsen state: 'Like the true statement, fictionality is not aimed at deceiving

112 Cf. Louise Brix Jacobsen, 'Paratext'.

113 Nielsen, Phelan and Walsh, 'Ten Theses About Fictionality', 62.

114 Simona Zetterberg Gjerlevsen and Henrik Skov Nielsen, 'Distinguishing Fictionality', in Cindie Aaen Maagaard, Daniel Schäbler and Marianne Wolff Lundholt, eds., *Exploring Fictionality: Conceptions, Test Cases, Discussions* (Southern Denmark University Press, 2020), 19–41, 23.

115 Walsh, 'Fictionality as Rhetoric', 399.

116 Walsh, 'Fictionality as Rhetoric', 415.

117 Jacobsen, 'Paratext', 142.

118 Gjerlevsen and Nielsen, 'Distinguishing Fictionality, 29.

119 Jacobsen, 'Paratext', 143.

anyone'.[120] This is actually not quite the case with hoaxes. The aim is indeed to deceive, but unlike fraud or genuine deception, deceiving an audience is not the end goal. It is part of the overall design of the hoax and the first step in the decoding process. At the same time, fictionality can be regarded as the tool that can help us distinguish hoaxes from genuine deceptive communication. If fictionality is not signalled at some point – either as part of the message (for example through a surprising ending) or in epitexts after the release of the initial message, it is not possible to recognize a hoax as a hoax. If a hoax is not exposed, it does not exist in our world as a hoax. Instead, it exists as unintended deceit functioning as true communication, because its full purpose was never detected. Therefore, it is crucial for the hoaxer to orchestrate a hoax carefully. Fictionality cannot be signalled too early, because the initial deception must be allowed to work, but failing to signal also ruins the communicative potential of the hoax. Thus, in decoding a hoax, we are indeed encouraged to conceive of the message as invented, but it occurs retrospectively and changes our initial conception.

This observation pinpoints the fragility of the hoax: 'Some might decode signals of invention, and some might not be able to perform such a decoding'.[121] As the much-debated *Marbot Eine Biographie* [Marbot A Biography] (Wolfgang Hildesheimer, 1981) has shown, some readers would decode it as a real biography despite the author making epitextual proclamations prior to the release. In the German newspaper *Die Zeit*, Hildesheimer introduced the book as a 'gefälschte... Biographie' [faked biography].[122] As shown by Mikkonen (2006), even some readers of the English translation either did not see or were not convinced by the blurb labelling it as fiction. This could be explained by 'the author's reputation as a Mozart biographer, the subtitle "biography," and other paratexts, such as Marbot's "image" on the cover, the text's formal mimesis, and its historical referentiality'.[123] Thus, sometimes audience expectations can overrule signals of invention and we can only guess whether the author of *Marbot* wanted the rather subtle fake-revealing paratexts to ensure the reader of the biography's falseness. Regardless of intentions, Hildesheimer is playing with genre codes and

---

120 Gjerlevsen and Nielsen, 'Distinguishing Fictionality' 24.

121 Jacobsen, 'Paratext', 150.

122 Cf. Julia, L. Abramson, 'Translation as Metaphor in Hildesheimer's Marbot Eine Biographie', *Paroles gelées*, 14/2 (1996), 103–114.

123 Kai Mikkonen, 'Can Fiction Become Fact? The Fiction-to-Fact Transition in Recent Theories of Fiction', *Style*, 40/4 (2006), 291–312, 299.

audience expectations.[124] The Marbot case is an interesting liminal example because the initial signals of faking in principle disqualify it as a hoax. However, it did have a hoaxing effect on readers who were either not exposed to these signals or simply persuaded by other contextual matters.

Understanding the hoax as planned deception intended to be revealed (for a variety of purposes, depending on the type of hoax) places it between deceit and fictionality – or rather as a concept depending and drawing on both. This can be illustrated through a simple model. [Figure 1]

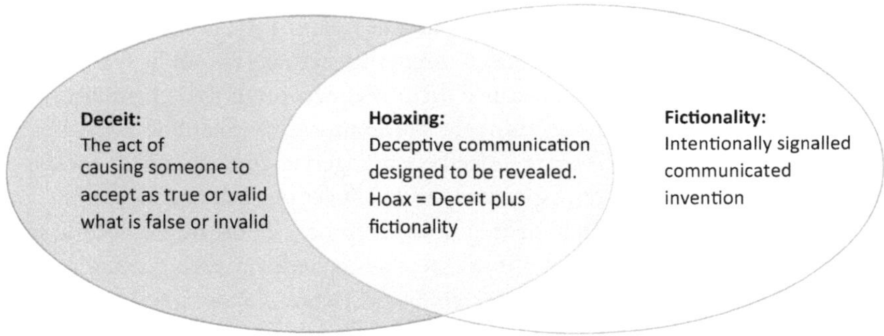

Figure 1: Hoaxing: Deceit plus fictionality

The model illustrates how hoaxing always entails deception and fictionality. Hoaxes exist and operate in the intersection between deceit and fictionality, and without one or the other, a hoax fails. Without the initial deception, the illusion cannot be created, and without fictionality, which requires a signalling of invention, the critical potential created by the exposure will be absent. The audience may guess and be suspicious, but if not exposed, the hoaxing will exist as either true statements or persisting ambiguous communication.

Hoaxes can be categorized according to a range of different qualities such as their host media (biography hoax, social media hoax, radio hoax), topic (scientific hoax, environmental hoax, news hoax), effect and ambition (the activist

124 For a further discussion of the Marbot case see also Dorrit Cohn, *The Distinction of Fiction*. (Baltimore: Johns Hopkins UP, 1999), Jean-Marie Schaeffer. *Why Fiction?* [1999] Lincoln: Nebraska University Press, 2010, Francoise Lavocat, 'Pseudofactual Narratives and Signposts of Factuality', in Monika Fludernik and Marie-Laure Ryan, eds., *Narrative Factuality: A Handbook* (Berlin, Boston: De Gruyter, 2020), 577–592.

hoax, the political hoax), and target (ideology-hoax, villain-hoax, company-hoax). These types of categorizations can be useful in understanding the function and potential of various hoaxes. However, hoaxes usually have several qualities: an activist hoax targeting big companies may take the form of a news hoax spreading on social media. Thus, for purposes here of identifying a new common definition and analytical method, I will focus on perspectives that work across these categorizations.

Inspired by Brian McHale's distinction between the trap-hoax and the mock-hoax, I find it useful to distinguish between hoaxes primarily conducted 'for the fun of it' or as aesthetic experiments, and hoaxes designed to conduct societal critique or cause humiliation in order to expose illegal and/or unethical business. Yet I will work with a somewhat different conception, because trapping and mocking, rather than being distinctive features of some hoaxes, seem to be defining characteristics of hoaxing altogether. Trap-hoaxes also tend to be mocking in their nature because leading the hoaxed into the trap requires mocking in the sense of imitation. When supplemented with the definition of mock 'to treat with contempt or ridicule',[125] this is often very descriptive of the more coarse humiliating hoaxes. In addition, despite a harsh critique, trap hoaxes can function as satire and be mockingly funny. At the same time, mock-hoaxes can contain a trap effect, because the audience is deceived for a longer or shorter timespan. All hoaxes trap (deceive the dupes to believe something which is not) and mock (imitate and sometimes ridicule), but some hoaxes are harsher and potentially more dangerous than others.

Rather than working with two or more distinct types of hoaxes, I will focus on the degree of danger and the ethical concerns of hoaxing. All hoaxes are to some extent linked to humour and danger. As Ian Reilly states, 'Hoaxes often channel both serious and comic motivations'.[126] They can produce everything from a harmless giggle to the punishing laughter of ridicule. In a similar way, all hoaxes – because of their initial deceit – are potentially dangerous. In pursuit of higher purposes, hoaxes can be damaging to (1) the hoaxer, (2) the target of the hoax and (3) potential victims. Especially in the more activist coarse hoaxes, hoaxers risk their reputation, surveillance by their targets and lawsuits filed against them. The targets risk public ridicule and sometimes even shaming which can be devastating to their reputations. Politicians can lose votes and

125 Merriam-Webster, 'mock', <https://www.merriam-webster.com/dictionary/mock>, accessed 1 October 2021.

126 Reilly, *Media Hoaxing*, 12.

companies can be financially weakened. As previously mentioned, the audience is also the target of a hoax, but there is a difference between the broader audience and the person, group or company named as villains. The named villain will typically be the main target of humiliation and shaming, while the rest of the audience will reflect on their own deception. If hoaxes go wrong, however, or if the audience finds that the hoax cannot be considered performed for a higher cause, the audience may feel deceived and humiliated. This creates a potential retrospective danger to the hoaxer.

In the following case studies, I will explore two examples of hoaxing which are dangerous for different reasons: the hoaxing practices of The Yes Men, with specific attention to The Dow Chemical news hoax on BBC World, and the Tom Cruise deepfake on TikTok, created by Chris Ume.

The Yes Men

The Yes Men are an activist group famous for using hoaxing strategies to expose dehumanizing behaviour and lack of environmental concern. Their primary targets are usually specific governments and big corporations, but their critique is also directed at the surrounding culture that accepts the unethical behaviour. They have made fake editions of *The New York Times*, *The New York Post* and recently *The Washington Post* claiming that Donald Trump would resign from his presidency.[127] They also use another hoaxing recipe involving the fabrication of fake websites (for example for George Bush and the World Trade Organization) that secure them invitations to conferences, press gatherings and even TV interviews broadcasted globally. The Yes Men impersonate spokespersons from major companies such as Dow Chemicals and Shell, and influential organizations like the WTO. They call this performative practice 'identity corrections', in the sense that they perform according to how they think representatives of these companies should behave.[128] This usually entails apologizing on behalf of targets for their wrongdoings and promising to pay compensation, donate and change their course of action. This is done through a hoaxing strategy in order to vivify an alternative reality (through the illusion) and to make the world reflect and take a stand (by exposing the illusion).

---

127 See theyesmen.org. (The Yes Men's official site), <http://theyesmen.org/>, accessed 20 June 2021.

128 Andy Bichelbaum, Michael Bonanno and Kurt Engfehr (dir.), *The Yes Men Fix the World* (2009).

One of the most illustrative examples of The Yes Men's hoaxes is the Dow Chemical hoax from 2004, when a Dow representative called Jude Finesterra appeared on BBC World. Dow owns Union Carbide, which is responsible for the Bhopal disaster in India in 1984. In the interview, Jude Finesterra apologizes on behalf of Dow, promising compensation for the victims of the disaster.[129] The Dow representative was in fact Jaques Servin also known by the pseudonym Andy Bichlbaum from The Yes Men, who successfully secured an invitation to the BBC to give an interview because it was the twentieth anniversary of the disaster. Dow Chemicals, the BBC and BBC viewers were all hoaxed. The BBC was duped because it allowed the interview in the first place. The fact that the BBC interviewed a fictive character on global television threatened its credibility and cast doubt upon its gatekeeping competences. It had to explain the mistake and retract the interview, and it had to apologize to Dow for putting it in a compromising position. Dow was ultimately humiliated when it had to deny the enormous act of goodwill The Yes Men had suggested on their behalf. The Yes Men led it into a trap, where Dow itself provided the final critique by refusing to do good and thereby exposing what powerful organizations actually can get away with.

Amber Day categorizes the activist practice of The Yes Men as 'identity nabbing', referring to their 'exaggerated caricatures of their opponents'.[130] She describes identity nabbing as part of the artistic activist practice of 'culture jamming': 'the practice of using forms of mass culture against itself through tactics like parody and irony'.[131] When it comes to The Yes Men, this strategy is applied in order to affect public discourse. They use a 'shaming strategy',[132] and when their opponents try to act against it, they only make things worse. The Yes Men's hoax did influence the direction of the public discourse and was damaging for Dow: not only did it contribute to an increasingly poor reputation, but share prices also dropped.

The Yes Men use the combination of deception and the signalling of fictionality to perform a three-layered critique. The deception leading to the creation

129 See Louise Brix Jacobsen, 'Fictional Characters in a Real World: Unruly Fictional Encounters in *Borat*, *The Ambassador*, and the Yes Men's Media Hoaxes', *European Journal of English Studies* 23/2 (2019), 206–223.

130 Amber Day, *Satire and Dissent* (Bloomington, IN, USA: Indiana University Press, 2011), 146f.

131 Day, *Satire and Dissent*, 148.

132 Day, *Satire and Dissent*, 154.

of the illusion of the apology is damaging to Dow – but not until Dow breaks the illusion. This is when Dow is ridiculed for its dehumanizing practices, for which Dow refuses to apologize and compensate. Yet this also creates a subsequent critique of gatekeeping processes and a potential lack of critical scepticism towards sources. Finally, the hoax reaches its full potential the moment people realize that the hoax was believed and accepted as true. The exposure is an invitation for the news consumer to reflect both on politically and ethically troubling issues and on reception processes and the truth value of media messages.

The Dow Chemical hoax can be categorized as a media hoax functioning as satirical fake news.[133] It parasitizes a TV news show, utilizing the affordances of this media platform to practice satirical ridicule. The BBC broadcasts worldwide and The Yes Men take advantage of its reputation as a reliable news source. The audience's expectations are also incorporated in the hoaxing strategy: when we turn on the TV to watch BBC World, we expect well-researched news living up to journalistic demands, so when The Yes Men are invited to participate in an interview of this calibre, the public is easily deceived.

Making the world aware of big corporations' exploitation of third-world countries is usually considered a heroic endeavour. It seems sympathetic and admirable to risk lawsuits and reputation in order to secure justice. Yet there is a downside to this type of hoaxing that reinforces the hoax's position as dangerous. The hoaxing strategy can be considered unethical when it comes to the deception of the BBC and the unsuspecting TV host, whose career is on the line. It is also highly problematic to dupe the people in India into believing that finally, after all these years of suffering, they would be financially compensated. The hoax is dangerous to the hoaxer and the hoaxed due to its high degree of ridiculing, but the potential harm to innocent people creates another kind of awareness: Does the end always justify the means?[134]

@deeptomcruise: Deepfake technology and initial scepticism

The Tom Cruise deepfakes were posted on the account @deeptomcruise in February 2021 on the social media platform TikTok. They consist of a number of short videos showing the celebrity performing magic tricks, practicing his golf

---

133 See Reilly, *Media Hoaxing*; Jacobsen, 'Fictional Characters in a Real World'.

134 For an analysis of the ethical implications of encounters between fictive characters and (unsuspecting) real people in The Yes Men's media hoaxes, see Jacobsen, 'Fictional Characters in a Real World'.

swing and telling an anecdote about a meeting with Mikhail Gorbachev [figure 2]. Since the exposure of the use of deepfake, the account has remained active and continues to post new videos. Currently, the account has 1.5 million followers and 4.4 million likes. The first video has more than fourteen million views.

Figure 2: The deepfaked Tom Cruise. Image: @deeptomcruise/TikTok

In the videos, Cruise is not shown in any particularly compromising situations, although he does act rather goofy and worked up. He constantly laughs (his characteristic loud laugh) and he seems rather self-centred. Several media have focused on the problematic aspect of the videos. CNN states: 'A series of deepfake videos of Tom Cruise is confusing millions of TikTok users. See the convincing videos and learn how this technology could be used to spread misinformation'.[135] In order to understand how this deepfake-hoax works, a focus on the social media affordances of TikTok and the technology of deepfaking is crucial.

135 CNN.com, 'No, Tom Cruise isn't on TikTok. It's a Deepfake', CNN (2021), <https://edition.cnn.com/videos/business/2021/03/02/tom-cruise-tiktok-deepfake-orig.cnn-business/video/playlists/business-originals-counterprogramming/>, accessed 20 June 2021.

TikTok is already one of the most popular applications in the world and is the fastest growing.[136] TikTok is a video-sharing platform developed in 2019 by the Chinese company ByteDance. Videos on TikTok 'incorporate music samples, filters, quick cuts, stickers and other creative add-ons that allow users to make the most of the short length'.[137] Users can apply a user handle (@deeptomcruise) and a display name that appears on the profile, and make use of hashtags to enable trending on the app.[138] Furthermore, algorithms are used to recommend videos, since TikTok is a 'personalised video feed based on what you watch, like, and share.'[139]

Bucher and Helmond stress how the interaction between user, producer and technology is crucial to the understanding of social media affordances: 'By clicking and liking end-users fuel the algorithms, which in their turn generate the information flows fed back to end-users.'[140] Orchestrating a hoax on TikTok requires taking this interaction and particularly the importance of the user and the spreadability into account. In order to convince an audience, the hoax must contain suitable content matching the TikTok vein and the user's expectations, and in order to reach a wider audience, the content must be remarkable enough to spread.

According to Karine Nahon and Jeff Hemsley, the nature of virality is influenced by a complex blurring of top-down and bottom-up forces, combined with the structure of networks.[141] Content can go viral if powerful actors, institutions or networks promote it (top-down), but it can also spread through algorithms when media platforms are designed to show and circulate content already

---

136 Gabriel Weimann and Natalie Masri, 'Research Note: Spreading Hate on TikTok', *Studies in Conflict & Terrorism* (2020), 1–14, 1. See also Yunwen Wang, 'Humor and Camera View on Mobile Short-Form Video Apps Influence User Experience and Technology-Adoption Intent, an Example of *TikTok* (*DouYin*)', *Computers in Human Behavior* 110/9 (2020), 1: 'By April 2019, *TikTok* has gained 200% market-share in a two-year growth period (Lee and Nass, 2005): The app had 1.17 million ratings on the iPhone app store, 9.67 million ratings on Google Play (2019 April), and over 9.67 million downloads'.

137 Weimann and Masri, 'Research Note', 4.

138 Weimann and Masri, 'Research Note', 9.

139 'TikTok – Make Your Day, App Store', <https://apps.apple.com/us/app/id835599320>, accessed 20 June 2021.

140 Bucher and Helmond, 'The Affordances of Social Media Platforms', 14.

141 Karine Nahon and Jeff Hemsley, *Going Viral* (Cambridge and Malden: Polity Press, 2013), 41f.

trending (network structure). Content can also go viral through bottom-up processes based on user reactions. According to Nahon and Hemsley, a message has viral potential if it is surprising or new, easily related to, contextually important (e.g., newsworthy), and if it creates emotional or humorous impact. On TikTok content primarily goes viral due to the network structure and bottom-up processes. Users share what they find remarkable, surprising, funny etc., and based on their viewing practices, related content will appear in their feeds.

The Tom Cruise deepfakes are remarkable because they show a famous actor performing in rather trivial situations seemingly without any clear purpose. In fact, Cruise appearing on TikTok is in itself surprising and funny. At the same time, it seems easy to relate to, precisely because he appears in situations created for fun like many other TikTok users do. When the audience begins to wonder if this really is Tom Cruise, the conversational qualities of social media take over. On the one hand, Cruise posting rather contentless videos on TikTok seems unlikely. On the other hand, receivers might remember his much-debated performance on the Oprah Winfrey Show in 2005 where he is overtly worked up, constantly laughing and jumping on the couch.[142] Or the Scientology promotion video leaked in 2008, in which he laughs hysterically and is difficult to understand.[143] These performances could make the realness of the videos more plausible. Rumours spread, and gossiping about the status of the videos spread them even further. Even after the exposure of the use of deepfake, the conversation continues, and the technology is debated in the commentary section.

When working with social media platforms, it must be stressed 'how a platform's infrastructure extends its affordances beyond its own environment and how they may be integrated in other platforms and services, as well as how these activities afford back to the platform and its multiple users.'[144] This is also what Jose van Dijck labels the 'ecosystem of connective media'.[145] When something is affected at one end of the system, it has consequences for the ecosystem as a whole. Trending on a social media platform can be very difficult since everyone is there as competitors. However, if successful, the outreach can be enormous.

142 Kate Nibbs, 'The Couch Jump That Rocked Hollywood', *The Ringer* (1 August 2018), <https://www.theringer.com/tv/2018/8/1/17631658/tom-cruise-oprah-couch-jump>, accessed 30 August 2021.

143 'The Tom Cruise Scientology Video' (2008), posted on *Aleteuk*, <https://www.youtube.com/watch?v=UFBZ_uAbxS0>, accessed 30 August 2021.

144 Bucher and Helmond, 'The Affordances of Social Media Platforms', 14.

145 Jose van Dijck, *The Culture of Connectivity* (Oxford: Oxford University Press, 2013), 4.

The attention to the Cruise hoax spread beyond TikTok to Twitter, Reddit etc., and it was discussed as news material on several media platforms as well. This was, however, predominantly because of the skilled use of deepfake that made it almost impossible to distinguish real from fake. The inability to distinguish real from fake is what makes deepfaking potentially dangerous.

Oppenheim and Yadlin-Segal describe deepfakes as 'a set of AI algorithms used to synthesize multiple audiovisual products into one manipulated media item (usually videos), for example through face-swap (Floridi, 2018).'[146] The videos are created through deep learning algorithms resulting in what Mika Westerlund characterizes as 'hyper-realistic videos digitally manipulated to depict people saying and doing things that never actually happened'.[147] The deepfake phenomenon was first seen on Reddit in December 2017, and has been the centre of critical attention ever since. Initially, it was primarily associated with pornographic content, but recently the technology has been applied for a range of purposes. According to Westerlund, it can be a helpful tool in film editing (voice and face reconstruction), branding (trying clothes online) or in social or medical fields to allow transgender people to see themselves as their preferred gender or people with Alzheimers to recognize a younger face.[148] However, deepfake is a new technology, and as Yadlin-Segal and Oppenheim have shown through their studies of the framing of deepfake in mainstream news media, deepfake is generally considered a threat that 'carries the potential to harm vulnerable groups, to undermine indicators of a shared reality, and to jeopardize the ability to distinguish between real and fake.'[149] Historically there has always been a scepticism towards new media: the telephone, radio, TV, the internet. There have been optimistic as well as dystopian predictions whenever new technology was introduced.[150] We are in the midst of the development of deepfake technology and we do not yet know whether it will persist as a threat to society. The insecurity surrounding the technology sparks predictions and anxiety.

Westerlund demonstrates how most deepfakes on social media platforms are quite harmless and made for fun or artistic purposes.[151] Several deepfakes exist

---

146 Yael Oppenheim and Aya Yadlin-Segal, 'Whose Dystopia Is It Anyway? Deepfakes and Social Media Regulation', *Convergence: The International Journal of Research into New Media Technologies* 27/1 (2021), 36–51, 41.

147 Mika Westerlund, 'The Emergence of Deepfake Technology: A Review', *Technology Innovation Management Review* 9/11 (2019), 39–52, 40.

148 Westerlund, 'The Emergence of Deepfake Technology', 41.

149 Oppenheim and Yadlin-Segal, 'Whose Dystopia Is It Anyway', 41.

150 See also Oppenheim and Yadlin-Segal.

151 Westerlund, 'The Emergence of Deepfake Technology', 43.

where the mashing up of images is so poorly executed that the technology itself is in the foreground. In these cases, the deepfaking is signalled, and it is rather unlikely anyone would believe that we actually see Donald Trump as a little girl or Steve Buscemi with Jennifer Lawrence's body. These instances are created to make people laugh and they are only dangerous in the sense that they can be humiliating for the celebrities involved. Yet if the technology is used to create revenge porn, it is dangerous no matter how amateurish it appears. Deepfake is, however, most likely to deceive, and therefore generally more dangerous, when used seamlessly. As soon as the technology is rendered invisible or very hard to detect, a range of other possibilities occur. Westerlund offers two examples of deepfake as serious political manipulation:

> In Central Africa in 2018, a deepfake of Gabon's long-unseen president Ali Bongo, who was believed in poor health or dead, was cited as the trigger for an unsuccessful coup by the Gabonese military. And in Malaysia, a viral clip deepfake of a man's confession to having sex with a local cabinet minister caused political controversy.[152]

In these examples, deepfake technology is applied as genuine deception and not as hoaxing. All types of fakes of real people often spread quickly and go viral, but fakes like these can be a dangerous tool in the creation of disinformation.[153]

It is when the technology is used skilfully and seamlessly, and applied in order to be exposed, that it can be exploited as part of a hoaxing strategy. This is the case of the Tom Cruise deepfake, where deepfake is used to create a hoax through the strategy of illusion and exposure. This is executed via exceptional deepfaking skills and the help of a talented impersonator [figure 3]. Deepfake can theoretically be used to create hoaxes on the whole range of the scale. At this point in media history, however, the technology itself sparks debates about the dangers of faking, and deep fake-hoaxes seem to be biased towards highlighting the dangers. This initial scepticism is also at the heart of @deeptomcruise, and the deepfake creator Chris Ume utilizes it to highlight the potential dangers and possibilities of the new technology.

---

152 Westerlund, 'The Emergence of Deepfake Technology', 44.
153 Westerlund, 'The Emergence of Deepfake Technology', 46.

Figure 3: 'Tom Cruise impersonator Miles Fisher (left) and the deepfake Tom Cruise created by Chris Ume (right).' Image: Chris Ume

Ume uses the short format characteristic of TikTok posts, and the videos easily blend in visually with other TikTok material. At first, there appear to be no signs of faking. It really looks like Tom Cruise performing trivial and frivolous activities. Retrospectively, one can come to the conclusion that fictionality is actually partially signalled internally through the user handle @deeptomcruise. However, this signal is integrated in the recognizable TikTok graphics, and without the knowledge of the use of deepfake technology, the word 'deep' could also refer to something else. It is striking that Cruise says: 'This is all real' while gesticulating towards his face, but since he says this after doing a magic coin trick there is no immediate reason to believe that he is addressing anything else. The attention to the realness of his face can be interpreted as an intertextual reference to the *Mission Impossible* spy movies, in which Cruise stars as the agent Ethan Hunt, who changes faces through the use of super-realistic latex facemasks as an important part of the plot. This use of intertextuality can function as an in-joke regardless of the audience's assumptions, but with the knowledge of the use of deepfake, it adds another dimension to the face-swap theme. The signalling of fictionality instead occurs primarily paratextual, when the illusion is exposed.

Ume has chosen a rapidly developing platform that reaches billions of people worldwide. By choosing TikTok, Ume can not only benefit from the viral potential to reach a huge audience, but the platform is also extremely well suited to address the use of artificial intelligence, since many popular and seemingly harmless apps and filters used on TikTok are based on face recognition. The videos direct attention to how TikTok could work in the future. What if deepfake ends up being yet another filter one can apply by pushing a button? In his statements to the press, Ume himself attempts to balance his explanation of the purpose of the account:

> I don't intend to use it in any way where I would upset people – I just want to show them what's possible in a few years (…) I just strongly think that there should be laws to help with the responsible use of AI and deepfakes.[154]

Awareness and appeal to responsibility are at the core here: 'What now takes an inventive impersonator, a beefy computer, and a skilled practitioner days of work could be done by a simple Snapchat filter by 2025'.[155] In another statement, he points to the benefits of the technology and says that people should not worry. New technology such as Photoshop has been created before without undermining our conception of true and fake.[156] These statements seem to blur the intention of @deeptomcruise, or at least point to a double intention. In another statement, the less serious aspects are emphasized: '"I created awareness. I showed my skills. We made people smile."'.[157] Chris Ume is a visual effects specialist, and according to Vincent, the flashing of media technology skills is an attempt to fulfil a lifelong dream of working with Peter Jackson. TikTok provides a platform where awareness and skills can spread simultaneously with great haste. In order to make people reflect on the possibilities of the technology, Ume uses the hoax as a rhetorical instrument. The initial deception encourages reflection on the possibilities and potential pitfalls of the deepfake technology. The reflexive potential is created when we begin to realize that this might not be the real Tom Cruise. Again, the exposure of the hoax is crucial to getting the message across to an audience. Yet the deception is also necessary in order to demonstrate his skills. It is characteristic of the hoax that it can function as a tool to draw attention to the hoaxer: 'After getting over our embarrassment when a spectacle is revealed as a hoax, we might enjoy a wry, humbling admiration for the trickster's

---

154 Alex Hern, '"I Don't Want to Upset People": Tom Cruise Deepfake Creator Speaks Out', *The Guardian* (5 March 2021), <https://www.theguardian.com/technology/2021/mar/05/how-started-tom-cruise-deepfake-tiktok-videos>, accessed 20 June 2021.

155 Hern, '"I Don't Want to Upset People"'.

156 James Vincent, 'Cruise Deepfake Creator Says Public Shouldn't Be Worried about "One-Click Fakes"', *The Verge* (5 March 2021), <https://www.theverge.com/2021/3/5/22314980/tom-cruise-deepfake-tiktok-videos-ai-impersonator-chris-ume-miles-fisher>, accessed 20 June 2021.

157 Vincent, 'Cruise Deepfake Creator Says Public Shouldn't Be Worried about "One-Click Fakes"'.

ingenuity.'[158] If Ume can deceive millions of users, he could also work convincingly with the technology in other contexts, such as moviemaking.

Ume utilizes the specific affordances of TikTok by performing in alignment with other TikTok content and users' expectations of TikTok content and the technology of deepfake. Ume applies fictionality as a rhetorical strategy in the form of hoaxing in order to create awareness, entertain and demonstrate the possibilities of technology. @deepTomCruise is not dangerous in the same way as the Dow Chemical hoax. It does not reveal dehumanizing behaviour, and Tom Cruise is not the target in the same way as Dow. Tom Cruise instead functions primarily as a tool for creating awareness. Celebrities generate attention, and once the audience is hooked, Ume can show off his skills and make viewers reflect on the possibilities and potential dangers of deepfaking. Yet the Cruise deepfake still raises a number of ethical concerns. Is it okay to use celebrities to create awareness without their consent? The real Tom Cruise created a TikTok account, but he has not posted anything or reacted to the deepfake. Many of the concerns the hoax generated were not about Tom Cruise as an individual, but about the technology itself. Could anyone with pictures available online be the victim of deepfake? This aligns with one of the concerns Westerlund raises. If it becomes impossible to distinguish real from fake, people will be deceived, but the greatest concern deepfake raises is the possibility of people regarding everything as deception.[159] The Tom Cruise hoax can create admiration for Ume, but it can also cast doubt upon his motives. Does he really want to create awareness of the technology for the greater good of society, or is it simply a career stunt? Although @deeptomcruise is not damaging to its content target in the same way as the Dow hoax, it nonetheless demonstrates and highlights the dangers of deepfake, which have been debated across a range of media, not because of the ridiculing of a particular individual, but because of the concerns this specific ridiculing creates for society as a whole.

Findings: A method for analysing hoaxes

In this chapter, I have investigated the dangers of media hoaxing. In order to understand how hoaxes work and are potentially dangerous, I have established a new theoretical understanding and definition. I define hoaxes as deceptive communication designed to be revealed. The definition can also be formulated with

158 Scott, 'On Hoaxes, Humbugs, and Fictional Portraiture', 27–32, 29.
159 Westerlund, 'The Emergence of Deepfake Technology', 43.

the equation: Hoax = deceit + fictionality. In order to explore the full potential as well as the dangers and ethical implications of hoaxing, I have combined fictionality theory with the media and communication-based notion of media affordances. This enables an interlinking of essential research questions of fictionality as rhetoric with the importance of media possibilities and expectations. A hoax parasitizes its host text and cannot be understood without attention to the specific characteristics of this host. The case studies of The Yes Men and Ume's Cruise deepfake showed the importance of the combination of rhetorical interest (who wants to move whom with what) with the role of media affordances. News shows on broadcast TV can reach a global audience by duping a respected news distributer and its target audience. The Yes Men utilize the audience's expectations of news on BBC World, and they are dependent on the news format for the hoax to fulfil its potential. Likewise, Chris Ume can benefit from the logic of the social media network when conducting his @deeptomcruise hoax on TikTok. The contagion of viral phenomena underlines the dangers of spreading fake material, and using a social media platform known for its filters makes the illusion all the more effective when it is exposed: this could be real, right here, very soon. At the same time, Ume can play with the initial fear associated with deepfake technology in order to point to necessary precautions for the future. Furthermore, the media technology enables Ume to show off his skills and situate his qualifications in a viral message that exposes him as a potent trendsetter in a rapidly developing SoMe culture.

The case studies and the large amount of various existing media hoaxes show that the dangers of media hoaxing are not in the media as such, but in the use of it when they are used to deceive. Books, film, TV and social media can all be hosts to the parasitic practice of hoaxing, and since hoaxing implies an initial deceit, it also contains a potential danger. This makes the hoax a risky form of communication.

The case studies also show that hoaxes can be dangerous and ethically problematic in various ways. The degree of danger depends not only on the degree of harshness and ridiculing, but also on the target of the hoax, and who ends up being affected by it. In the case of The Yes Men, the hoax was very dangerous for its main target, Dow, but also quite damaging to the host media. In the case of @deeptomcruise, the hoax mocks, but not in order to present Tom Cruise as a villain. Instead, he is used as a tool for the purpose of raising technology awareness, eliciting a good laugh and demonstrating technological skills.

Based on the theoretical framework of fictionality and media affordances and the new definition of hoaxing, I suggest an analytical method for analysing hoaxing and its implications. The overall analytical question can be aligned with

Nielsen, Phelan and Walsh's: 'When, where, why, and how does someone use fictionality in order to achieve what purpose(s) in relation to what audience(s)?'.[160] The important attention to media affordances can to some extent be encompassed by the 'where' question. Yet since hoaxing depends on its host media and a fragile reception process that must account for several media ecological perspectives, I have found it necessary to apply a more fine-grained method directly addressing the affordance approach. To understand the complicated rhetorical machine of the hoax, it is important to ask:

> When, where, why, and how does someone use fictionality [in hoaxing] in order to achieve what purpose(s) in relation to what audience(s)?
> How does the hoax address which target? Is it dangerous or ethically questionable, and to whom?
> How are the affordances of the host media accounted for in the design of the hoax?
> How does the hoax fulfil its communicative potential in the media ecology it is inscribed in?

These supplementing research questions are potentially beneficial for fictionality as rhetoric in general, but in the case of the hoax, they are unavoidable. Hoaxing for a greater good can be dangerous and comes at a price. Paying attention to the rhetorical machine of the hoax and the media environment it parasitizes and influences give us a better understanding of this peculiar communicative phenomenon that keeps duping both enemies and allies.

160 Nielsen, Phelan and Walsh, 'Ten Theses About Fictionality', 63.

James Phelan

3. Assessing the Genre of Docudrama: The Case of Aaron Sorkin's *The Trial of the Chicago 7*

Abstract: This chapter uses a rhetorical approach to fictionality and nonfictionality to consider the dangers of narrative and fictionality inherent in the film genre of docudrama. The dangers are inherent because the genre is devoted to the representation and interpretation of nonfictional events via re-enactments of them, even as it licenses non-signaled uses of fictionality to heighten the dramatic quality of the re-enactments. I use Aaron Sorkin's 2020 film, *The Trial of the Chicago 7*, as a test case because assessments of it vary from scornfully negative to admiringly positive depending on whether the critic focuses on Sorkin's gifts as a dramatic storyteller (positive) or on the adequacy of his representations of the historical record (negative). I come down on the side of the negative assessments because Sorkin's non-signaled uses of fictionality for salient elements of his narrative distort the historical record in ways that undermine his ultimately optimistic interpretation of the trial. In that way, I find that Sorkin's narrative is both ethically and aesthetically deficient. At the same time, I refrain from an indictment of the genre itself, arguing instead that a rhetorical approach can help us (a) recognize that the non-signaled quality of the genre's inventions indicate that audiences need to be aware of its dangers; (b) that some inventions can add to the efficacy of a docudrama's interpretations; and (c) that we therefore should judge not the genre itself but individual narratives located under its umbrella.

Keywords: Aaron Sorkin, *The Trial of the Chicago 7*, docudrama, history, salience, ethics, aesthetics

> 'Aaron Sorkin's movie … crosses historical lines to incite a fairy tale'.[161]
>
> – Tod Gitlin

> 'You don't just want to dramatize a Wikipedia page. … It's no longer going to be a photograph; it's going to be a painting'.[162]
>
> – Aaron Sorkin (in Wood)

---

161 Todd Gitlin, 'Retrying the Chicago 7', *The American Prospect* (30 October 2020), <https://prospect.org/culture/retrying-the-chicago-seven/>, accessed 17 September 2021.

162 Aaron Sorkin in Jennifer Wood, 'The Unwavering Optimism of Aaron Sorkin', *GQ* (16 October 2020), <https://www.gq.com/story/the-unwavering-optimism-of-aaron-sorkin>, accessed 17 September 2021.

As I write in the spring of 2021, the American film industry has just concluded its annual awards season, and the results suggest that Aaron Sorkin's *The Trial of the Chicago 7* (hereafter *The Chicago 7*) is one of 2020's best films. This docudrama, which Sorkin wrote and directed, re-enacts the U.S. government's lengthy prosecution (September 1969 to February 1970) of seven U.S. citizens for their roles in the violent protests during the 1968 Democratic Convention in Chicago. Sorkin's film was nominated for six Academy Awards, including Best Picture and Best Original Screenplay. The American Film Institute named *The Chicago 7* one of the Ten Best Films of 2020, and the Golden Globe Awards bestowed their trophy for Best Screenplay upon Sorkin.[163] Yet, as my first epigraph shows, Todd Gitlin, one of the most important historians of the American 1960s, has excoriated the film with a line that adapts one of the charges brought against the Chicago 7: crossing state lines to incite a riot. For Gitlin, the film's many departures from what really happened during the Convention and during the trial are, well, hanging offenses. And other critics such as Charlotte Rosen and Joshua Furst join Gitlin in offering withering assessments of the ethics of the telling in the film, that is, the moral values underlying Sorkin's treatment of the material and his relation to his audience.[164] In Sorkin's case, the key ethical question is whether his playing fast and loose with the historical record dishonours the protestors and deceives his audience.[165] If so, then this award-winning film would become a powerful exhibit in a case about the dangers of fictionality. The second epigraph represents Sorkin's concise, metaphorical defense against such

---

163 For a full list of awards ad nominations that the film has received in the 2021 awards season, see <https://en.wikipedia.org/wiki/List_of_awards_and_nominations_received_by_The_Trial_of_the_Chicago_7>, accessed 20 September 2021.

164 Charlotte Rosen, 'Aaron Sorkin's Inane, Liberal History Lesson', *The Nation* (3 November 2020), <https://www.thenation.com/article/culture/aaron-sorkins-inane-history-lesson/>, accessed 17 September 2021;Joshua Furst, 'Aaron Sorkin's Moralizing Liberal Fantasy Betrays the Real Chicago 7', *Forward* (20 October 2020), <https://forward.com/culture/456814/aaron-sorkins-moralizing-liberal-fantasy-betrays-the-real-chicago-7/>, accessed 17 September 2021.

165 For more on the ethics of the telling, see James Phelan, *Living to Tell about It: A Rhetoric and Ethics of Character Narration* (Ithaca: Cornell University Press, 2005); James Phelan, *Experiencing Fiction: Judgments, Progressions, and the Rhetorical Interpretation of Narrative* (Columbus: Ohio State University Press, 2007); James Phelan, 'Narrative Ethics', in Peter Huhn et al., eds., *Living Handbook of Narratology*, <https://www.lhn.uni-hamburg.de/node/108.html>, accessed 20 September 2021.

charges: I was not going for a strict reproduction of the historical record but rather for a fresh interpretation of it.

Although Sorkin doesn't explicitly invoke the genre of docudrama, his defense fits with its contours and conventions. Docudrama, as its name suggests, is a hybrid genre, one that occupies the space between documentary film and historical fiction film. Reasoning back, in the standard method of rhetorical narratology, from the practices and purposes of a range of films concerned with historical events, we can distinguish among docudrama, documentary film and historical fiction film in the following ways. All three genres are devoted to the interpretation of history, but they ground their interpretations in different approaches to storytelling. Documentary film such as David French's reconstruction of the Act Up movement's efforts to end the AIDS epidemic in the United States, *How to Survive a Plague*, bases its interpretations in its synthesis of multiple elements of the historical record, including commentary on that record at the time of the telling. The fundamental claim of the documentary is 'this is the way it was'. Historical fiction film (sometimes called docufiction) such as Steven Spielberg's *Saving Private Ryan* roots its interpretations of history in plausible inventions of characters and their actions within historically accurate contexts. It uses those inventions to shed new light on those contexts typically by thematizing particular aspects of them, as Spielberg does with the effects of war on the soldiers who wage it. Docudrama such as Ron Howard's *Apollo 13* and *The Chicago 7* grounds its interpretations in re-enactments of historical events. Unlike documentary, it has a license to depart from the historical record in advancing its interpretations, but unlike historical fiction film, it does not invent major characters.

Sorkin's defense, then, is an implicit appeal to judge his film according to its appropriate genre. Docudrama does not share documentary's claim that 'this is the way it was' but exercises a license to depart from strict adherence to the historical record in order to advance its interpretations of the way it was. Nevertheless, by remaining more tethered to the historical record than the historical fiction film, docudrama does claim, 'this take on what happened, enabled in part by its uses of fictionality, deserves a hearing in debates about the way it was'.

Understanding the genre of docudrama as occupying the space between documentary and historical fiction suggests that the gap between the negative assessments (by Gitlin, Furst, Rosen and other like-minded critics) and the positive ones (by the nominators and voters in the 2021 awards season and many reviewers) stems from the first group focusing on 'docu' piece of the hybrid and the second group privileging the 'drama' piece (even as this group values the film's engagement with real events). These differences also point to possible tensions between the two halves of the genre, especially when the drama piece, as it does in Sorkin's film, relies heavily on departures from the historical record.

In this chapter, I propose to use a rhetorical approach to fictionality and nonfictionality to investigate those tensions in the genre and to adjudicate the differing judgments of Sorkin's film. I shall contend that those assessments arise not only from the different positionalities of the judges (of course the sociologist-historian and the politically-oriented critics would privilege the documentary side and the members of the film industry the drama side) but also from Sorkin's particular synthesis of the two sides. More specifically, I shall argue that, while Sorkin stays within the generic borders of docudrama, his handling of its hybridity does indeed make it an exhibit in the case for the dangers of fictionality. In my view, Sorkin's film is ethically deficient, and the ways it is deficient stem from his uses of affordances of the genre itself, though I stop short of concluding that the genre is itself ethically deficient. Ultimately, I find that *The Chicago 7* is more successful as drama with an internal emotional logic than as a contribution to debates about the significance of the trial itself for our understanding of the late 1960s in U.S. history. In making this case, I shall rely in part on the concept of *salience* by which I mean the degree of importance given to particular scenes or ideas in a teller's efforts to achieve their purposes in relation to their particular audiences.[166] This concept allows us to recognize that (a) not all adherences to and departures from the historical record have the same consequences for an assessment of docudrama in general and *The Chicago 7* in particular and (b) that the assessment of invented scenes with high salience depends on whether the inventions ultimately illuminate the historical record or distort it.

I begin my case with a fuller account of *The Chicago 7*, attending both to what makes it compelling and to how it follows and departs from the historical record. I shall then explain my rhetorical approach and use it to assess the film and the genre by analysing the salience and the relationship between illumination and distortion in four instances of fictionality in Sorkin's film.

166 For more on this concept, see James Phelan, 'Local Nonfictionality within Generic Fiction: Huntington's Disease in McEwan's *Saturday* and Genova's *Inside the O'Briens*', in *The Edinburgh Companion to Contemporary Narrative Theories*, Zara Dinnen and Robyn Warhol, eds., (Edinburgh: Edinburgh University Press, 2018), 362–374.

The Trial of the Chicago 7

Sorkin's film is yet another demonstration of his impressive storytelling skills. His famous ability to write dialogue that both explores sophisticated ideas and moves the narrative action along is once again on display, as is his ability to construct a narrative arc that connects multiple threads and provides a powerful, affective experience.[167] If one applies only the criterion of 'creating compelling drama', the film deserves its multiple nominations and awards.

Sorkin generates the forward motion of the film by introducing and complicating two main conflicts, that between the U.S. government and the Chicago protestors and that within the protestors themselves. The U.S. government is represented by Richard Nixon's Attorney General John Mitchell (John Doman), the two prosecutors he instructs to bring in a conviction, Richard Schultz (Joseph Gordon-Levitt) and Thomas Foran (J. C. MacKenzie), and the presiding judge at the trial, Julius Hoffman (Frank Langella). The government initially charges eight men, Tom Hayden (Eddie Redmayne), Rennie Davis (Alex Sharp), Jerry Rubin (Jeremy Strong), David Dellinger (John Carroll Lynch), Abbie Hoffman (Sacha Baron Cohen) – no relation to the judge – Lee Weiner (Noah Robbins), John Froines (Danny Flaherty) and Bobby Seale (Yayah Abdul-Mateen II). These eight come from different factions of the American left in the 1960s, all opposed to the Viet Nam War. Hayden, Davis and Dellinger from MOBE (National Mobilization Committee to End the War in Vietnam and closely allied with the Students for a Democratic Society), Hoffman and Rubin from the Yippies (the Youth International Party), and Seale from the Black Panther Party. Froines and Weiner were volunteer protestors rather than leaders, and they were included in the government's case, Sorkin suggests, so that the government could look more measured in its response when it acquitted two of the defendants.

Sorkin clearly sides with the protestors in this conflict, and he shows them losing the battle of the trial but winning the war of ethical and political values rooted in a commitment to the better part of the U.S. democratic system. Sorkin

167 Sorkin gained notoriety for his use of these skills in his screenplays for the television series *Sports Night* and *The West Wing* and for the films *The Social Network* and *Molly's Game*, which he wrote and directed. Alison Willmore titles her positive review 'Aaron Sorkin's Annoying Tics Are Actually Good in *The Trial of the Chicago 7*', *Vulture* (25 September 2020), <https://www.newsbreak.com/news/2069977337585/aaron-sorkins-annoying-tics-are-actually-good-in-the-trial-of-the-chicago-7>, accessed 17 September 2021.

contrasts the mostly noble motives of the protestors with Judge Hoffman's clear bias against the defendants.

Judge Hoffman's handling of Bobby Seale eventually leads to his case being declared a mistrial (more on Seale's important role in the film below). The titular seven protestors are defended by William Kunstler (Mark Rylance) and Leonard Weinglass (Ben Shankman). The internal conflicts among the protestors are primarily between Tom Hayden, whom Sorkin represents as conventionally respectable, and Abbie Hoffman, whom Sorkin represents initially as more interested in disrupting the proceedings than in mounting a defense. Hayden finds him cavalier and self-indulgent, to say the least. At one point, Sorkin has Hayden deliver the following set-piece to Hoffman:

> My problem is, for the next 50 years, when people think of progressive politics, they're gonna think of you. They're gonna think of you and your idiot followers passing out daisies to soldiers and trying to levitate the Pentagon. They're not going to think of equality or justice. They're not going to think of education or poverty or progress. They're gonna think of a bunch of stoned, lost, disrespectful, foulmouthed, lawless losers, and so we'll lose elections.[168]

Sorkin resolves the Hayden-Hoffman conflict by having Hayden acknowledge, after a mock cross-examination by Kunstler, that Hoffman would be a better witness for the defense and by Hoffman showing that he has read everything that Hayden has written. Sorkin then clinches the resolution by having Hoffman offer serious and politically astute testimony that further aligns the audience with the protestors. The resolutions to the two sets of conflicts converge in the final scene.

Given a chance by Judge Hoffman to speak before the sentencing, Hayden reads aloud the names of the American soldiers that have died in Viet Nam since the trial began. As the judge futilely bangs his gavel on his bench, all the defendants, the spectators (except a few who run for the exits), and even prosecutor Schultz stand up to honor the deceased, and, by extension, the anti-war position that led to the protests in the first place. Hayden's reading is accompanied by a triumphant musical score and by scrolling text recounting what happens to all the major figures in the years after the trial. This recounting includes the facts that Hayden, Abbie Hoffman, Rubin, Davis and Dellinger were sentenced to five years for inciting the riots, that their convictions were overturned on appeal, and that in a biannual survey 78% of Chicago trial lawyers gave Judge Julius Hoffman

168 Aaron Sorkin (dir.), *Trial of the Chicago 7: The Screenplay* (New York: Simon and Schuster, 2020), 156.

a rating of 'Unqualified'. The recounting also notes that Seale was acquitted of an outstanding charge against him in Connecticut of having killed a police officer.

In going from the photographs of the historical record to the painting of his docudrama, Sorkin constructs the narrative so that any spectator coming to the film with an open mind about the protests and the trial will be likely to leave convinced about the righteousness of the protests and protestors, about the government's violation of their rights throughout the trial, and about their ultimate triumph. More generally, Sorkin constructs the narrative so that viewers cognizant of President Donald J. Trump's weaponizing of the U.S. government against those whom he regarded as his enemies will recognize parallels to the trial. Such viewers will also find in the triumphant ending reasons to hope. Many of Sorkin's uses of fictionality, including those involving its conclusion, are motivated by this purpose of giving his audience hope. In my view, however, Sorkin's handling of docudrama's license to deploy fictionality ultimately works against his purpose and demonstrates the potential dangers of the genre.

The Chicago 7 and the historical record

Following the contours of the genre, Sorkin's orchestration of the narrative relies upon both references to the historical record and invention. Samantha Putterman on *Poynter* and Matthew Dessem on *Slate* compare key aspects of Sorkin's representation against the historical record, and they come to the same conclusions about where Sorkin accurately follows that record and where he deviates from it.[169] Combining their findings with the reviews by Gitlin, Rosen and Furst and giving special weight to their overlaps yields the following results about the most striking features of Sorkin's representation (these lists would be much longer if one went scene by scene).[170]

---

169 Samantha Putterman, 'What Aaron Sorkin's *The Trial of the Chicago 7* Gets Right and Wrong', *Poynter* (20 April 2021), <https://www.poynter.org/fact-checking/2021/what-aaron-sorkins-the-trial-of-the-chicago-7-gets-right-and-wrong/>, accessed 25 September 2021; Matthew Dessem, 'What's Fact and What's Fiction in *The Trial of the Chicago 7*', *Slate* (15 October 2020), <https://slate.com/culture/2020/10/trial-chicago-seven-aaron-sorkin-accuracy-netflix.html>, accessed 17 September 2021.

170 For more extensive histories, see Bruce A. Ragsdale, *The Trial of the Chicago Seven: The True Story behind the Headlines* (e-artnow, 2021); John Schultz, *The Conspiracy Trial of the Chicago Seven* (Chicago: University of Chicago Press, 2020 [1993]); and Jon Weiner, ed., *Conspiracy in the Streets: The Extraordinary Trial of the Chicago Eight* (New York: The New Press, 2006). Ragsdale's book includes the transcript of the trial.

Historically accurate representations

The film is replete with historically accurate representations and, indeed, is deeply invested in them, as its use of newsreel footage indicates. Here I'll highlight the accuracy of two especially striking representations.

1. Judge Julius Hoffman's behavior was as egregiously out-of-line as Sorkin represents it to be. Putterman notes that when in 1972 the U.S. Court of Appeals for Seventh Circuit overturned the sentences of Davis, Dellinger, Hayden, Hoffman and Rubin, they concluded that 'the demeanor of the judge and the prosecutors would require reversal, if other errors did not'.[171]
2. Bobby Seale's lawyer, Charles Garry, was unable to represent him because Garry had to undergo gall bladder surgery. Garry had made a motion for a continuance, but Hoffman denied it. This situation led to multiple conflicts between Hoffman and Seale and between Hoffman and Kunstler.

Partially accurate representations

1. In the film, Abbie Hoffman and Jerry Rubin early in the trial show up in the courtroom in judges' robes. When they remove the robes in response to Judge Hoffman's order, they reveal that they have police uniforms on underneath. The historical record shows that Hoffman and Rubin did wear judges' robes, but they did so toward the end of the trial and that only Hoffman had a police uniform on underneath.
2. In the film, Sorkin represents Fred Hampton, the Vice-Chairman of the Black Panther Party, as giving advice to Bobby Seale during the trial, until he is killed in his apartment by the Chicago police. After the killing, Seale launches an attack on Judge Hoffman that the Judge uses as the pretext for an order that Seale should be bound in chains and gagged. The historical record shows that Seale was bound and gagged on 29 October 1969, and that Hampton was killed on 4 December 1969. Seale had to endure four days of such treatment, while the film focuses on only one.

Distortions/Inventions

1. In the film, a female undercover FBI agent, Daphne O'Connor, approaches Jerry Rubin in a bar, befriends him and through him gains access to the plans

---

171 Putterman, '*What Aaron Sorkin's The Trial of the Chicago 7 Gets Right and Wrong*'.

of the protestors. The historical record shows that the protestors were infiltrated by three male undercover FBI agents, one of whom (Robert Pierson) paid special attention to Rubin. In the film, Prosecutor Richard Schultz is sympathetic to the defense, pointing out to John Mitchell that the conspiracy charge is bogus, calling Judge Hoffman to task for binding and gagging Bobby Seale and standing with the defendants during the last scene. The historical record does not contain any evidence of these behaviors.

2. In the film, Kunstler and Hayden visit Seale in jail to give him the news that Fred Hampton, Seale's fellow member of the Black Panther Party, has been killed. Seale tells them he already knows, and pointedly addresses Hayden about the difference between his kind of protest and the plight of Black men in America. He ends by saying that he also knows that Hampton was executed by the Chicago police. This conversation never happened.
3. Sorkin uses Abbie Hoffman to reveal that Tom Hayden misspoke in his speech to the crowd in Grant Park, before one of the violent confrontations with police, when he said, 'If blood is gonna flow, let it flow all over the city'. Hoffman contends, and Hayden agrees, that Hayden meant to say, 'If our blood', thus changing his intent from inciting the crowd to violence to exhorting them to accept being on the receiving end of it. The historical record does not support this interpretation of Hayden's speech or this account of Hoffman's reading of it.
4. In line with this distortion, Sorkin generally misrepresents Hayden's character throughout and Abbie Hoffman's in the film's latter half. Sorkin shows Hayden as more focused on acting within the system by keeping the actions of the protestors peaceful and law-abiding and on winning elections than the historical Hayden was in 1968. The historical figure was, as Gitlin puts it, 'vastly, and fascinatingly, more complicated'.[172] Based on his personal knowledge of Hayden and his own research, Gitlin reports that Hayden went into the Chicago anti-war protests hoping to provoke Mayor Richard Daley and the police into an overreaction that would demonstrate to the world that the unjust violence of the war could only be defended by more unjust violence at home. The historical Hayden would not have delivered that set piece about progressive politics and elections to Abbie Hoffman. As for Hoffman, Sorkin does capture what the historical record shows about both his irreverent humour and his interest in disrupting the trial. But he would not have been the

172 Gitlin, 'Retrying the Chicago 7'.

one to float the hypothesis about Hayden's intending to say, 'if our blood is gonna flow', and he did not defend the ideals of democracy on the witness stand in the way that Sorkin shows him doing.

5. The stirring final scene never happened. The closest event in the historical record occurs earlier in the trial. On 15 October 1969, a national day of protest against the Viet Nam War, David Dellinger began to read aloud the names of both Americans and Vietnamese who lost their lives in the war, but Judge Hoffman soon shut him down.

This fuller consideration of *The Chicago 7* leads me to formulate some more specific questions about the interactions of fictionality, nonfictionality and the ethics of the telling. Is there a point at which Sorkin's distortions and inventions undercut his interpretations of what happened at the Convention and the trial? Is there a point at which Sorkin's transformation of the historical photograph into his own painting crosses an ethical line and becomes a narrative act that misleads or even deceives its audience? Alternatively, given that docudrama licenses the combination of history and invention, are the two previous questions misguided or even downright hostile to the genre itself, a refusal to acknowledge Sorkin's artistry, the affective power of his film, and his invitation to find relevance between the era of the trial and the era of Trump? Do those questions arise only because those who ask them fail to heed the warning baked into the genre: 'many objects in this narrative that appear historical are invented'? Let's consider how a rhetorical approach to fictionality and nonfictionality can help answer these questions.

A rhetorical approach to fictionality and nonfictionality

This approach is indebted to Richard Walsh's *The Rhetoric of Fictionality* (2007) and to further developments of his ideas by Walsh and others, including 'Ten Theses about Fictionality' (2015) by Walsh, Henrik Skov Nielsen and me, and the essay collection *Fictionality in Literature: Core Concepts Revisited* (2022). The key principles are as follows:

1. Nonfictionality is intentional communication that makes direct reference to actual states of affairs in order to report on, interpret, evaluate or otherwise engage with those states. Fictionality is intentional communication that relies on invention, projection or other means of directing an audience to consider nonactual states or sets of events in order to indirectly report, interpret, evaluate or otherwise engage with actual states of affairs.

2. Fictionality and nonfictionality are not binary categories rooted in different ontological commitments (nonfictionality to the actual world and fictionality to an imagined world) but rather are two distinct ways of communicating about the actual world. In other words, they use different means – one direct, the other indirect – toward the same ends of intervening in the actual world.[173] Literary criticism's longstanding practice of offering thematic readings of fictional narratives is just one example of the widespread acceptance of this idea.
3. Although fictionality and nonfictionality are two broad categories of communicative discourse, they are not the only ones. Some communicative discourses such as autofictions and some unstable ironies deliberately blur the lines between them. Other communications such as hoaxes initially present as one mode but ultimately (want to) become exposed as instances of the other. As noted above, docudrama is a hybrid mode. See #6 for commentary on lying.
4. This conception of fictionality situates generic fictions such as the novel, the short story and the fiction film as subsets of the larger mode. Fictionality is all but ubiquitous in discourse: it's a staple of political speeches, advertising, legal and philosophical arguments, and it appears in countless other contexts.
5. The pervasiveness of fictionality calls attention to the frequent cross-border traffic between its rhetoric and that of nonfictionality. Global nonfictions often contain instances of local fictionality, and global fictions contain instances of local nonfictionality. Docudrama is unusual because it does not signal its border crossings or presuppose that its audience will recognize them.
6. Fictionality and nonfictionality are analytically distinct from truth and falsehood. Nonfictional statements can be erroneous, but the discovery of their errors does not transform them into instances of fictionality because, by definition, they refer to actual states of affairs. Thus, we can distinguish between accurate and erroneous nonfictionality. Similarly, lying is not a subset of

173 Walsh's work connects this principle to an approach to communication that privileges relevance over truth. Speakers and listeners seek to maximize the relevance of any discourse to its communicative context. Nonfictionality strives for direct relevance and fictionality for indirect relevance. For a fuller discussion, see the introductions to Richard Walsh, *The Rhetoric of Fictionality* (Columbus: Ohio State University Press, 2007) and Lasse Gammelgaard, Stefan Iversen, Louise Brix Jacobsen, Henrik Zetterberg Nielsen, Simona Zetterberg Nielsen, James Phelan and Richard Walsh, eds., *Fictionality in Literature: Core Concepts Revisited* (Columbus: Ohio State University Press, 2022).

fictionality but rather a deceptive use of nonfictionality. The liar claims to be making a direct intervention in actual states of affairs, but they know something that they don't want their audience to know: the claim has no basis in the actual. Lying, thus, is ethically deficient nonfictionality.

7. In line with #6, ascriptions of fictionality and nonfictionality arise not from the degree of correspondence between what the rhetor expresses and the actual world but rather from the rhetor's intended claims about that correspondence. Since the genre of docudrama licenses invention, Sorkin and other makers of docudrama do not claim that their films faithfully correspond to the historical record, and, thus, their inventions are not lies. But that acknowledgment clarifies rather than settles the issue of how to assess the genre.

This rhetorical approach also helps separate two concepts that sometimes get conflated in discussions of fictionality: construction and invention. That conflation often leads to the conclusion that the distinction between nonfictionality and fictionality cannot hold because everything is fiction.[174] The argument works like this: people, the things that they do and that happen to them, and countless objects and other phenomena in the world are real, but any effort to capture those entities must be mediated – by language and/or other signifying systems. That mediation inevitably introduces a gap between the real and its representation, and, what's more, every specific deployment of a mediating system will select and emphasize some aspects of the real while overlooking or downplaying others, thereby further magnifying the gap. The trouble with the concept of nonfictionality is that it ignores or denies that gap. Consequently, nonfictionality is as constructed as fictionality is, though its construction is less out in the open. Far better to acknowledge that similarity by joining in with the narrator of *The French Lieutenant's Woman* when he declares that 'fiction is woven into all'.[175]

From a rhetorical perspective, the weaknesses of this argument are that (1) it erases the distinction between construction and invention; and (2) it ignores the way tellers and listeners use and respond to discourse and representation. Rhetoricians fully endorse the position that both fictionality and nonfictionality involve mediation and construction. In any rhetorical act, a rhetor shapes some raw material – whether events and people in the world, events and people in the

---

174 For a rich discussion of what she calls the doctrine of panfictionality, see Marie-Laurie Ryan, 'Postmodernism and the Doctrine of Panfictionality', *Narrative* 5/2 (1997), 165–187.

175 John Fowles, *The French Lieutenant's Woman* (Boston: Little, Brown, 1969), 104.

imagination, or combinations of the real and imagined – in some ways rather than others in order to achieve some purposes in relation to some audience. There's construction all the way down. Yet, the shaping of real-world materials and the shaping of invented materials are different activities with different constraints and opportunities, and we can better explain how we use and respond to our discourses by separating construction and invention. The same claim in a newspaper, a novel or a lie will have a significantly different meaning for its audience (in the case of a lie, the difference emerges when the deception gets exposed). Far better to acknowledge the inescapability of construction and to simultaneously recognize that constructing to directly intervene in the actual world is qualitatively different from constructing to indirectly intervene, and that both of these acts are different from constructing to deceive one's audience about something that happened in the world.

In this rhetorical view, then, such features of docudrama as the use of actors to stand in for historical people and the substitution of movie sets for historical places are overt signs of construction but not necessarily signs of invention. Given the nature of the genre, if the actors behave in ways that reflect the historical record and if the sets reasonably represent the historical places, then the tellers are using construction in the service of nonfictionality. And if the actors behave in ways that depart from the historical record, then the tellers are using construction in the service of fictionality. Both uses of the construction have specific functions in relation to the tellers' purposes of offering persuasive new interpretations of history.

Q&A about *The Chicago 7*

With these principles in mind, I now turn to some Q&A about the genre and the potential dangers of Sorkin's specific uses of fictionality.

Q. Does Sorkin's purpose of reinterpreting history, while seamlessly crossing between fictionality and nonfictionality, inevitably lead to a deficient ethics of the telling?

A. No, not inevitably, as a return to documentary film and historical fiction film indicates. In these genres, interpreting and reinterpreting history are standard operating procedures. In each case, the teller shapes materials in the service of their purpose of conveying an interpretation or reinterpretation of historical events to a particular audience. What's sauce for these generic geese is sauce for the docudrama gander. In other words, different means, similar ends. This position, in turn, means that Sorkin's interpretation *has the potential* to be a viable entry into the contest of narratives about the demonstrations in 1968 and the trial in 1969. The politically oriented reviewers who assess the film negatively are, in effect, saying that, because it deploys fictionality, it is not a worthy participant in that contest. I'm interested in whether and how Sorkin's specific uses of fictionality enable or prevent it from realizing its potential.

Q. Do the departures from the historical record inevitability weaken Sorkin's interpretation?

A. Not by themselves. The rhetorical approach to fictionality notes that its departures from actual states of affairs can serve the valuable function of indirectly intervening in the way that those states are interpreted or evaluated. Consequently, assessing the film is not simply a matter of giving some points for historical accuracy and deducting others for departures from the historical record and seeing whether the total number of points is a positive or a negative number. Furthermore, such a tally assumes that all departures are created equal, and, as I'll discuss below when I take up the concept of salience, that's a flawed assumption.

The answers to these first two questions support the idea that the genre of docudrama gives Sorkin a fair amount of leeway for his inventions. But now let's move to some more pointed questions.

Q. Is Sorkin's film dangerous because, more than fifty years after the events of the Convention and the trial, many audience members will not know much, if anything about them, and will therefore get their history from the film?

A. Yes, but. First, note that saying 'yes' entails saying that the genre is potentially dangerous even if Sorkin's film stays within its rather elastic boundaries. Second, from a rhetorical perspective, an outcome in which many viewers end up with a false understanding of the historical record is a problem that no amount of theoretical foo-foo dust can erase. Third, this danger is part and parcel of Sorkin's taking advantage of the genre's license to seamlessly move back and forth between referentiality and invention. If the movement were signaled, the danger would be greatly reduced, but such signaling would disrupt the drama.

Now I come to the 'but'. To some extent, the adage that 'the abuse of a thing is no argument against it' applies here. Viewers who take the film as history are treating it as if its ultimate goals are the same as those of documentary and thus misapprehending Sorkin's claims for it. Such viewers do, indeed, fail to heed the genre's implicit warning (in its license to combine fictionality and nonfictionality) that 'many objects in this narrative that appear historical are invented'.

Q. Is there a point at which Sorkin's inventions and distortions undercut his interpretations of what happened at the Convention and the trial? And how do we determine that point?

A. Yes to the first question. The second requires a more extended answer. We make such determinations by examining the interaction between salience and the rhetorical and ethical efficacy of the indirect approach to the actual in any given scene. Let me start with salience. It is a concept aligned with but different from Peter J. Rabinowitz's analysis of Rules of Notice.[176] As the term 'Rules' indicates, Rabinowitz seeks to identify conventions that operate across narratives that help readers recognize that some textual phenomena (e.g. beginnings and endings) carry more weight than others (e.g. sentences marking a transition from one temporal moment to another). Salience is not a rule but a concept that applies in different ways to different narratives. It refers to the relative importance of a narrative element's function in the teller's rhetorical action, or to put it another way, salience is determined by how crucial the element is for the teller's achievement of their purpose in relation to their audience.

Rules of Notice can help readers recognize and enhance the salience of a narrative's element as, for example, happens with Sorkin's ending. Other markers include space given to an element, rhetorical flourishes or other ways of heightening the presentation. But like most other interpretive claims, those about salience are hypotheses that can be tested against others' views on the teller's shaping of a narrative.

As for efficacy, the key issue is whether the indirection of the fictionality illuminates the actual states of affairs as reflected in the historical record or dangerously distorts them. Let's look at some specific examples.

Assessing *The Trial of the Chicago 7*: Salience and efficacy in four instances of fictionality

Instance 1: Sorkin's invention of Daphne O'Connor to be the undercover agent attached to Jerry Rubin during the Democratic Convention. This invention shows that the government did regard the protestors as a serious threat. The invention also functions to portray Rubin as naïve and easily duped, a lightweight radical who is in over his head. Sorkin shows Rubin falling for O'Connor after she tells him a silly joke ('Jerry, do you know why the French only eat one egg for breakfast? .... Because in France one egg is an oeuf'). This portrayal, in turn, supports Sorkin's ultimate privileging of the allegedly more respectable Hayden

176 Peter J. Rabinowitz, *Before Reading: Narrative Conventions and the Politics of Interpretation* (Columbus: Ohio State University Press, [1987] 1998), 47–75.

and MOBE over Rubin, Abbie Hoffman (in the first two-thirds of the film) and the Yippies.

Again, the two key questions are: (1) does the invention indirectly capture something essential about the FBI, Rubin and their roles in the demonstrations and the trial?; and (2) how salient is it for Sorkin's achievement of his overall purpose? The answer to the first question is that the invention works better for illuminating the FBI than for illuminating Rubin. Inventing O'Connor and dramatizing her interactions with Rubin captures something important about the lengths to which the FBI went in their surveillance of the protestors. With Rubin, however, the invention results not in illumination but in ethically dubious distortion. The historical record indicates that Rubin, like Abbie Hoffman, was a disrupter but he was neither lightweight nor naïve. Both were serious and aware political actors, whose antics were motivated by a belief in the power of disruption. The responses they received to those antics indicated that they had good warrants for their beliefs.[177] By departing from the historical record about Rubin, Sorkin misrepresents him and weakens rather than strengthens his interpretation of the way it was.

Turning to salience, I find that the inventions are not particularly significant for Sorkin's achievement of his larger purposes. He already makes the case about the FBI surveillance by briefly and accurately showing two other undercover agents among the protestors. Although Sorkin's characterization of Rubin functions as another means to give greater importance to his version of Hayden's position in the debates among the protestors, Sorkin's position would be clear without this characterization. All in all, despite the appealing drama of the O'Connor-Rubin relationship, Sorkin's case for his interpretation of the protests and the trial would, on the whole, have been more effective without it.

Instance 2: The scene in which Kunstler and Hayden visit Seale in jail to tell him the news that Fred Hampton was killed. Seale and Kunstler sit at a table across from each other and Kunstler delivers the news, while Hayden stands several feet to the side. After Seale tells Kunstler that he already knows, the following exchange occurs:

177 See Wiener, *Conspiracy in the Streets: The Extraordinary Trial of the Chicago Eight*, and Schultz, *The Conspiracy Trial of the Chicago Seven*, on Rubin. See also Rubin's *Do It: Scenarios of the Revolution* (New York: Simon and Schuster, 1970).

Seale (to Hayden): The seven of you, you've all got the same father, right? (Pause)
I'm talking to you. You've all got the same father, right? Cut your hair, don't be a fag, respect authority, respect America, respect me. Your life, it's a fuck you to your father, right? A little.
Hayden: (beat) Maybe.
Seale: Maybe. And you can see how that's different from a rope on a tree.
Hayden: Yeah.
Seale: Yeah. He was shot in the wrist first. You can't hold a gun if you've been shot in the wrist. You can't pull a trigger. The second shot was in the head. Fred was executed. (pause)
Anything else?
Kunstler: No.[178]

By contrast with Sorkin's invention of Daphne O'Connor, this invention is both efficacious and salient. It indirectly and effectively captures some important truths about U.S. history in the late 1960s, and it has ripple effects on Sorkin's larger interpretation of the historical record. Sorkin uses Seale's account of Fred Hampton's killing to illuminate what actually happened. Cook County State's Attorney Edward Hanrahan, whom Hampton had recently criticized, organized the raid on Hampton's apartment in Hyde Park, and the heavily armed police force shot him multiple times, despite his offering no resistance. What's more, they covered up their execution. As for Sorkin's use of Seale to characterize Hayden and the other white defendants, it runs the risk of being too simplistic, but Sorkin uses it to make valid larger points about the difference race makes in the U.S. Seale's speech highlights both the relative freedom of each racial group to act up and act out and then the huge differences in the consequences for each of falling into disfavor with the government. It's one thing to be put on trial and quite another to be lynched.

Sorkin gives the scene substantial salience because it connects with the film's previous treatment of Seale's position in the trial – separate and unequal, singled out for more abuse by Judge Hoffman and ultimately bound and gagged. Sorkin adds to the salience by having Seale himself articulate the larger truths: they have more force coming from him than they would coming from Kunstler, Hayden, Abbie Hoffman or any other character. Most importantly, all the scenes involving Seale function as a counterweight to the triumphant ending: Sorkin's affirmation of the American system does not include the system's treatment of African Americans.

178 Sorkin, *Trial of the Chicago 7*, 123.

Instance 3. Sorkin's invention of Hayden's speech to Abbie Hoffman about the essence of progressive politics and the importance of elections. Here I'll start with the substantial salience of the speech. It is a crucial part of Sorkin's efforts to achieve his purpose of advancing his optimistic view of the past and the present. Sorkin constructs the speech as a turning point in the conflict between Hayden and Abbie Hoffman: shortly after it, Hoffman reveals that he has read everything Hayden wrote and delivers his astute testimony. In that sense, the set piece becomes one of the thematic takeaways of the film: Hayden viewed progressive politics as rooted not in disruptions of the system but in commitments to education, justice and winning elections.

As for ethical efficacy, Gitlin persuasively argues that, whatever Hayden came to believe later, when he entered politics and served as a representative from California for multiple years, the speech misrepresents the historical figure. Gitlin cites evidence that Hayden was far more interested in disruption and open to violence during the Convention. But even more than that, Gitlin persuasively contends that the last thing on Hayden's mind – and on the minds of the others – was the likely practical consequences of their behavior during the Convention: they were actually paving the way for the election of Richard Nixon.

Given the salience and the distortion of Sorkin's invention, it ultimately works to undercut his larger purposes. Presented as capturing something key to our understanding of Hayden, it actually functions only as an expression of Sorkin's own beliefs. To put it another way, the speech becomes an instance of mask narration[179] in which Sorkin uses his construction of the respectable Hayden to express his own views in 2020 about the importance of elections in a film released during the days of early voting in the 2020 election. In these ways, Sorkin's invention leads him to lose touch with the history his film seeks to engage with.

Instance 4. The final scene. As the ethical, political and affective climax of the film, it has the greatest salience of any scene. When Judge Hoffman invites Hayden to speak, the judge comments that Hayden is different from the others because he has behaved respectfully, and the judge indicates that, if Hayden briefly expresses remorse, he will take that into account in his sentencing. This lead-in allows Sorkin to construct Hayden's reading of the names as simultaneously an unselfish act of civil disobedience, a(nother) protest against the war and a means of honoring those Americans who lost their lives in the war. Each dimension of Hayden's reading reinforces the others. In addition, the reading demonstrates the strength of the new solidarity between Hayden and Abbie

179 Phelan, *Living to Tell about It*, 201.

Hoffman, whom Sorkin shows fully supporting Hayden's unexpected action. That solidarity then extends to all the defendants and to the spectators in the courtroom who stand at attention. While prosecutor Schultz's standing does not display the same kind of solidarity, it does acknowledge the ethical and political value of Hayden's act. Sorkin reinforces the triumphant quality of the scene not only with the rousing score but also by showing Judge Hoffman futilely banging his gavel on the bench and by the information about what happens to the key players in the coming years. In short, Sorkin packs everything into this climactic scene but confetti and balloons.

Sorkin's implicit claim is that this invention indirectly captures something about the historical record: the good guys' commitment to superior values, reflected both in the protests and in their present solidarity, allowed them to triumph over John Mitchell, Julius Hoffman and the U.S. government. Furthermore, because the good guys ultimately won in the era of Richard Nixon and John Mitchell, we can be confident that they will win again in the current era. Our systems, despite bad actors such as Mitchell, Judge Hoffman, Donald Trump and Bill Barr, are sound.

It's a stirring conclusion, but it evokes in me the response of 'Isn't it pretty to think so?'. A look at the historical record suggests that it's not just difficult but also dangerous to accept Sorkin's interpretation. First, Sorkin's playing fast and loose with the historical record means that Hayden does not read names of Vietnamese killed in the war. It's as if only American lives matter to Hayden and the other defendants, to Sorkin and to the authorial audience. Second, it's striking that the film, unlike most trial dramas, does not represent the reading of the verdict or the scene of sentencing. Dramatizing them would obviously work against the triumph Sorkin goes for, but, more importantly, their presence in the historical record works against the confidence underlying his interpretation. It's not just that five of the defendants were found guilty and sentenced to five years in prison but it's also that the overwhelming evidence in the historical record is that the Chicago police were the ones who incited the violence. And there were no charges against the police. In short, the historical record contains too much recalcitrant evidence for Sorkin's interpretation of it to be persuasive.

These findings, then, suggest that Sorkin uses his brilliant storytelling skills to create a highly engaging drama but a seriously compromised docudrama. Whatever one thinks of Sorkin's own politics, his effort to impose them on *The Chicago 7* leads him into unmarked fictionality that too often fails to indirectly capture truth and too often distorts history. In short, it's dangerous to believe that this appealing drama offers a sustainable new interpretation of the way it was. This conclusion in turn means that both the ethics and aesthetics of the film, despite its appealing drama, are seriously flawed.

Assessing the docudrama

In conclusion, I want to underline two points I've made about the genre in connection with Sorkin's film and then articulate a third one that has been implicit in the discussion so far.

1. *Caveat videntium*: audiences should recognize that the genre's authorization of seamless crossing from fictionality to nonfictionality means that many narratives within its boundaries may use the license less to illuminate history than to advance implausible and even dangerous interpretations of it.
2. Audiences can effectively follow that caveat by considering (a) whether the docudrama's inventions capture larger truths about the historical record and (b) how salient the uses are for the tellers' achievement of their purposes.
3. Since the genre is based on the principle of 're-enact in order to (re)interpret,' it allows for a considerable range in the quantity of fictionality any particular narrative within it can employ. In other words, the genre's elastic boundaries allow both for the frequent uses of fictionality that we find in Sorkin's film and for rare, or even no, uses of it. Choices about quantity will depend on the nature of the material and the degree to which a re-enactment that stays close to the historical record will fit the tellers' (re)interpretations of it. For example, Ron Howard in *Apollo 13* uses much less fictionality than Sorkin does. Howard's material has a great deal of inherent drama, as suggested by its most famous line, 'Houston, we have a problem.' Since the explosion of an oxygen tank in the Apollo spacecraft actually threatened the lives of the three astronauts on board, accurately re-enacting what happens in the spacecraft, in Houston's mission control, and in the interactions between them provides ample drama to make the narrative arresting. Just as important, staying with a predominantly accurate re-enactment serves Howard's purposes of interpreting the events as evidence of American grit, ingenuity and heroism.

Again, though, a rhetorical assessment of the ethics of the telling in relation to the film's uses of fictionality would proceed in the same way: attend to how the fictionality indirectly illuminates the historical record and to how salient it is. For example, the famous line is, in fact, not strictly accurate, since the record shows that the astronauts said 'Houston, we've had a problem'[180]. The alteration is obviously salient – the line functions as an abstract of the film's main action – and it is ethically sound since the shift to the present tense better captures the ongoing challenge the astronauts and ground control face.

More generally, then, a rhetorical approach to fictionality and nonfictionality helps us to understand both the appeal and the dangers of docudrama, even as it turns away from any overall indictment or endorsement of the genre. The approach instead turns us toward an examination and assessment of how individual docudramatists make particular uses of both fictionality and nonfictionality in their efforts to achieve their purposes in relation to their audiences.

180 Elizabeth Howell and Kimberly Hickok, 'Apollo 13: The moon-mission that dodged disaster', *Space.com* (31 March 2020), <https://www.space.com/17250-apollo-13-facts.html>, accessed 20 September 2021.

Part II: Networked Rhetoric

Hanna-Riikka Roine

4. The Message Is Not the Truth: Uses and Affordances of Narrative Form on Social Media Platforms

Abstract: Understanding narrative from an instrumental perspective has increasingly enabled researchers to study the ways in which it is used as well as the contexts where such uses take place. This chapter continues the work of focusing on potential dangers that emerge from the narrative form itself, widening the scope from the affordances of the narrative form to those of social media platforms as contexts where uses of narrative increasingly take place today. First, the chapter aims to build an affordance concept that closes the gap between the constraints and possibilities of narrative form and its uses in specific environments, which in this case are social media platforms as digital architectures. It is argued that this way narrative theorists can better understand 'the point' of using narrative in divergent ways on the platforms as well as the ongoing erosion between the categories of fact and fiction. Furthermore, the chapter suggests that on social media platforms, narrative must be approached both as a form of content and a form of agency. By building on previous theories of narratives in digital media, the chapter draws out the interplay between these two forms and examines how fictionality of narratives in social media is based on the affordances as dynamics and conditions enabled by platforms as much as in the published and shared content itself. The discussion is illustrated with the example of Kristen Roupenian's 'Cat Person', a short story published on *The New Yorker* website in 2017.

Keywords: social media platforms, fictionality, affordance, narrative form, content, agency, Kristen Roupenian

Understanding narrative from an instrumental perspective has increasingly enabled researchers to study the ways in which it is used as well as the contexts where such uses take place. Perhaps the most widely known theorizations of narrative as an instrument fall under the rhetorical tradition, where narrative is seen as told by someone to someone else *for some purpose(s)*, canonized in criticism by Wayne C. Booth and James Phelan.[181] After the so-called 'narrative turn' in

181 Wayne Booth, *The Rhetoric of Fiction* (Chicago: University of Chicago Press, 1983); James Phelan, *Experiencing Fiction. Judgments, Progression and the Rhetorical Theory of Narrative* (Columbus: Ohio State University Press, 2007).

social sciences and humanities, the idea of narrative as not only indispensable but also inherently beneficial for us has been widely spread, thus sharing Paul Ricoeur's statement that only 'a life *narrated*' can be 'a life *examined*' and hence worth living.[182] Such an outlook has given rise to more critical approaches to uses of narrative, most recently by the *Dangers of Narrative* project, seeking to 'bring into focus those dangers of narrative that stem from the affordances of the narrative form itself'.[183] This chapter continues the work of drawing out such potential dangers by widening the scope from the affordances of the narrative form to those of social media platforms as contexts where uses of narrative increasingly take place today.

As an object of use, narrative can naturally be understood as a form that carries certain affordances with it. Among the most influential studies of the affordances of literary forms is Caroline Levine's *Forms* (2015), which outlines forms as transhistorical, portable and abstract ways of making order, travelling across time and space while taking their particular affordances along.[184] Affordance, in turn, is defined by Levine as 'a term used to describe potential uses or actions latent in material or design'.[185] With this definition, *Forms* accepts without criticism the designer-centred understanding of affordance put forward by cognitive scientist Donald Norman in his book *The Psychology of Everyday Things* (1988), thus associating literary forms with materials and designs.

Levine's move in connecting broadly all sorts of abstract forms from free indirect speech to racism with the concept of affordance is intriguing and yields interesting analyses, but her approach entails two inherent problems that narrative theorists should consider before adopting her usage of the term. Firstly, Levine's analysis often evokes the affordance perspective to describe phenomena that concern *a feature* of a specific form:[186] she suggests, for instance, that 'glass

182 Paul Ricoeur, *A Ricoeur Reader: Reflection and Imagination*, Mario J. Valdés ed., (New York and London: Harvester Wheatsheaf, 1991), 435, emphases in original; see also Hanna Meretoja, *The Ethics of Storytelling: Narrative Hermeneutics, History and the Possible* (Oxford: Oxford University Press, 2018), 2.

183 Maria Mäkelä et al., 'Dangers of Narrative: A Critical Approach to Narratives of Personal Experience in Contemporary Story Economy', *Narrative* 28/2 (2021), 139–159.

184 Caroline Levine, *Forms: Whole, Rhythm, Hierarchy, Network* (Princeton, NJ: Princeton University Press, 2015), 4, 10–11.

185 Levine, *Forms*, 6.

186 Cf., Sandra K. Evans et al., 'Explicating Affordances: A Conceptual Framework for Understanding Affordances in Communication Research', *Journal of Computer-Mediated Communication* 22/1 (2017), 35–52.

affords transparency' while narratives 'afford the connection of events over time'.[187] Secondly, Levine's use of the concept lacks relationality, which results in a problematic gap between an abstract form and its uses by an actual or potential, situated agent. In a footnote, she further explains this through her interest 'in the ways that affordance allows us to think about both constraint and capability – that is, what actions or thoughts are made possible by the fact of a form'.[188] Thus, although Levine argues that the 'meaning and values' of a pattern or shape may change as they travel and that 'specific contexts … matter',[189] both forms and their affordances (or 'constraints and capabilities', as she calls them) come across as predetermined and inscribed.

In this chapter, I start by building an understanding of affordance that is both functional and relational for narrative theory, as I see that this greatly benefits our understanding of the contemporary uses of narrative, especially on social media platforms that are, basically, programmable digital architectures designed to organize interactions between different users, driven by algorithms and fuelled by data.[190] Instead of following Norman's definition of affordance as 'the perceived and actual properties of the thing, primarily those fundamental properties that determine just how the thing could possibly be used',[191] I turn to ecological psychologist James J. Gibson's original idea of the affordance as cutting 'across the dichotomy of subjective-objective' and pointing 'both ways, to the environment and the observer'.[192] For Gibson – as well as for the more contemporary researchers in the fields of communication and human-computer interaction studies attempting to 'rethink' the concept after Norman's reign – affordance emerges in constellations of objects and environment.[193] Here, my

187 Levine, *Forms,* 6.

188 Levine, *Forms,* 152.

189 Levine, *Forms,* 7.

190 Dijck, José van, Thomas Poell, and Martijn de Waal, *The Platform Society: Public Values in a Connective World* (New York: Oxford University Press, 2018), 4.

191 Donald Norman, *The Psychology of Everyday Things* (New York: Basic Books, 1988), 9.

192 James J. Gibson, *The Ecological Approach to Visual Perception* (London: Routledge, 1979), 129.

193 See Ashley Scarlett and Martin Zeilinger, 'Rethinking Affordance', *Media Theory* 3/ 1 (2019), 1–48; Taina Bucher and Anne Helmond, 'The Affordances of Social Media Platforms', in Jean Burgess, Thomas Poell and Alice Marwick, eds., *The SAGE Handbook of Social Media* (London and New York: Sage Publications Ltd, 2018), online PDF-version, 2-19, <http://dx.doi.org/10.4135/9781473984066.n14>, accessed 5 October 2021.

aim is to create an affordance concept that closes the gap between the constraints and possibilities of narrative form and its uses in specific environments, which in this case are social media platforms as digital architectures. This way narrative theorists can, in my view, better understand 'the point' of using narrative in divergent ways on the platforms as well as the ongoing erosion between the categories of fact and fiction.

Furthermore, my argument is not only that we must understand affordance as situated *between* the object and the user, but also that on social media platforms, narrative must be approached both as *a form of content* and *a form of agency*. As digital architectures, social media platforms are multi-layered, or, as Ashley Scarlett and Martin Zeilinger argue, made up both as material and social spaces of 'different-yet-intersecting layers'.[194] While narrative theory has mostly focused on the layer that is immediately available to human perception and on features of content that scales in visibility or 'goes viral' in social media, I argue that we must pay similar attention to the forms of agency which are inherent to these platforms as digital architectures. These forms configure (both enable and constraint, but not simply dictate)[195] our engagements on the platforms. Interestingly, narrative theorists analysing digital media have already identified narrative from these two perspectives, although not explicitly in these terms: Maria Mäkelä's *viral exemplum*[196] insightfully opens up the forms of content, while Janet Murray's *bardic system*[197] delves into the different forms of agency. By building on these two approaches, I draw out their interplay and examine how fictionality of narratives in social media is based on the affordances as dynamics and conditions enabled by platforms as much as in the published and shared content itself. Finally, I illustrate this with the example of a fictional story published on *The New Yorker*

194 Scarlett and Zeilinger, 'Rethinking Affordance', 18.

195 danah boyd, 'Social Networking Sites as Networked Publics: Affordances, Dynamics, and Implications', in Zizi Papacharissi, ed., *Networked Self: Identity, Community, and Culture on Social Network Sites* (London: Routledge, 2011), 39–58.

196 Maria Mäkelä, 'Disagreeing with Fictionality? A Response to Richard Walsh in the Age of Post-Truth Politics and Careless Speech', *Style* 53/4 (2019), 457–463; Maria Mäkelä, 'Lessons from the Dangers of Narrative Project: Toward a Story-Critical Narratology', *Tekstualia* 1/4 (2018), 175–186.

197 Janet Murray, *Hamlet on the Holodeck: The Future of Narrative in Cyberspace* (New York: Free Press, 1997).

website, Kristen Roupenian's 'Cat Person' (2017),[198] which was reframed into an exemplum-like content through certain forms of agency.

Towards a relational understanding of affordance in narrative theory

First, I set out to outline an approach to narrative affordances that sees them as relational. This allows us to analyse both the affordances of narrative form as well as the ways in which the environment shapes users' perception of narrative as an instrument. Various affordances for narrative have, of course, been proposed by several approaches. In post-classical narrative theory, *experientiality* is probably the most often mentioned through Monika Fludernik's redefinition of narrativity as 'mediated experientiality' as opposed to structuralist definitions.[199] The more classically minded definitions, opposed by Fludernik and echoed by Levine in her description of narratives affording 'the connection of events over time',[200] would then emphasize *temporality* or *causality*. In the popular discourse, *universality* is often raised to the fore, such as in Jonah Sachs's discussion of 'great stories' as universal in his storytelling manual *Winning the Story Wars*, bringing up the unifying function of stories through evoking shared human emotions, myths, cultural reference points and values, for instance.[201]

The above descriptions of what narrative is for illustrate why Levine's conceptualization of literary forms as fixed 'ways of making order' with 'particular affordances'[202] is quickly troubled by the fact that instead of objects existing in our environment as things of nature (such as stones or tree branches) or even as designed (such as chairs or doorknobs), abstract forms such as narrative are actualized through the very practices they enable and shape. Furthermore, affordance can be seen to mark a relation between an object and user in the case of much more concrete objects of use: in Gibson's decidedly environmental approach, an object's affordances may be grounded within its material form but are ultimately realized through processes of identification and purposeful

---

198 Kristen Roupenian, 'Cat Person', *The New Yorker* (4 December 2017), <https://www.newyorker.com/magazine/2017/12/11/cat-person>, accessed 28 June 2021.

199 Monika Fludernik, *Towards a 'Natural' Narratology*, (London: Routledge, 1996), 12–13, 28–30.

200 Levine, *Forms*, 6.

201 Jonah Sachs, *Winning the Story Wars. How Those Who Tell – and Live – the Best Stories Will Rule the Future* (Boston, MA: Harvard Business Review Press, 2012).

202 Levine, *Forms*, 4.

implementation through an agent. Thus, an affordance is inherently 'relative to' and 'unique for' the agent in question as well as tied to socialisation and learning of humans, since environment's affordances may exist independently from a potential agent's ability to recognize them.[203]

While Gibson's original approach to affordance was geared to open up our understanding of the relational ontology of objects and environments, technologically oriented accounts of affordance have been developed within numerous fields.[204] The concept of communicative affordance promoted by, for instance, sociologist Ian Hutchby attempts to find a 'third way' between technological determinism and social constructivism. Hutchby's definition of affordances as 'possibilities for action that emerge from … given technological forms'[205] emphasizes how affordances are both *functional and relational*: functional 'in the sense that they are enabling, as well as constraining', and relational in terms of drawing 'attention to the way that the affordances of an object may be different from one species than for other'.[206] In this, the concept of communicative affordance moves away from Norman's applied perspective of seeing affordances as features that can be designed and subsist independently from environments and technologies. Furthermore, it recognizes that while the material and structural constitution of media technologies 'request, demand, allow, encourage, discourage, and refuse'[207] particular kinds of use, they are also comprised of 'a set of practices that cannot be defined *a priori*, and [that] are not predetermined outside of their situated everyday actions and habits of usage'.[208]

---

203 Scarlett and Zeilinger, 'Rethinking Affordance', 10.

204 These include particularly the fields of interaction design, software development, information science and information architecture, interface design and user experience design. For more about affordance concept in Communication and Media Studies, see e.g., Tarleton Gillespie, 'The Politics of "Platforms"', *New Media & Society* 12/3 (2010), 347–64; and Lev Manovich, *The Language of New Media* (Cambridge, Ma: The MIT Press, 2001).

205 Ian Hutchby, *Conversation and Technology: From the Telephone to the Internet* (Cambridge: Polity Press, 2001), 30.

206 Ian Hutchby and Simone Barnett, 'Aspects of the Sequential Organization of Mobile Phone Conversation', *Discourse Studies* 7/2 (2015), 151.

207 Jenny L. Davis and James B. Chouinard, 'Theorizing Affordances: From Request to Refuse', *Bulletin of Science, Technology & Society* 36/4 (2017), 241.

208 Elisabetta Costa, 'Affordances-in-practices: An Ethnographic Critique of Social Media Logic and Context Collapse', *New Media & Society* 20/10 (2018), 3642; emphasis in original.

When adopting an instrumental approach to narrative, we see that the users' perception of narrative as a form guides their understanding of what actions are available to them. The actions and thoughts made possible through narrative point both ways – both to the instrument and its users instead of being located within a historically and socially fixed form carrying its similarly fixed affordances from one environment to another. From this angle, the 'story-critical' approach adopted by the *Dangers of Narrative* project, used to 'elaborate on the risks of storytelling perceived by non-narratological audiences'[209] through the analysis of crowdsourced corpus in media and the social sphere, can be seen as an attempt to affect users' perception of narrative. This would not only make users more conscious of the actions available to them but also change the subsequent uses.

So, users' perception of what narrative is for shapes their understanding of its affordances, but we must also acknowledge the environment where the uses take place. As such environments, social media platforms are not value-free constructs but digital architectures that come with specific forms and values inscribed in them[210] as well as with their own affordances for agents.[211] Technology scholar danah boyd has discussed the platforms or social networking sites as networked publics: they are publics that are simultaneously 'the space constructed through networked technologies' and 'the imagined collective that emerges as a result of the intersection of people, technology and practice'.[212] The affordances of these publics, according to boyd, follow from the properties of bits building these architectures instead of atoms, including persistence, replicability, scalability and searchability.[213] I will return to these affordances in detail a bit later on in this chapter – for now it is important to keep in mind that these

---

209 Mäkelä et al., 'Dangers of Narrative', 155.

210 Van Dijck, Poell, and de Waal, *The Platform Society*, 3.

211 Here, I focus on the affordances of social media platforms for human agents, especially end-users, while the nonhuman agents are addressed in e.g., Hanna-Riikka Roine and Laura Piippo, 'Authorship vs. Assemblage in Computational Media', in Susanna Lindberg and Hanna-Riikka Roine, eds., *The Ethos of Digital Environments: Technology, Literary Theory and Philosophy* (London and New York: Routledge, 2021) and other human agents such as developers and advertisers are analysed in e.g., Bucher and Helmond, 'The Affordances of Social Media Platforms'.

212 boyd, 'Social Networking Sites', 39.

213 boyd, 'Social Networking Sites', 46; see also Jeffrey W. Treem and Paul Leonardi, 'Social Media Use in Organizations: Exploring the Affordances of Visibility, Editability, Persistence, and Association', *Communication Yearbook* 36 (2012), 143–189.

affordances do not, as boyd argues, 'dictate participants' behaviour' but rather 'configure the environment in a way that shapes participants' engagement'.[214] Furthermore, as Scarlett and Zeilinger note, boyd's turn to bits as the definitive grounds of digital affordances identifies how each layer of materiality in the digital initiates a different sense of where and how these affordances arise and operate.[215]

The digital can be usefully illustrated to operate on three entangled layers: content, software and hardware.[216] Of these three, only content can be directly perceived by human end-users, because it is designed as such. Others include various imperceptible dimensions of computation, such as blackboxes and microtemporal operations, all of which have their own affordances that unfold and come into existence through the processual operations of computation despite being 'hidden' from human users.[217] Although quite a few aspects of the digital operate out of users' view, these hidden affordances still affect what users can and cannot do on social media platforms. Scarlett and Zeilinger even argue that imperceptibility, or invisibility, might be conceived of as an affordance in and of itself in the digital: this usefully points towards the ways in which users 'imagine', construct and project the affordances of computational technologies.[218] The concept of imagined affordances, suggested by Peter Nagy and Gina Neff, illustrates this further: they argue that what users believe and expect technologies to be able to do shapes 'how they approach them and what actions they think are suggested'.[219]

While narratives on social media platforms have been mostly discussed on the layer that is immediately available to us – as users' updates, blog posts, tweets, and so forth – it would be dangerous to see narratives simply as limited to the layer of content. To illustrate this, as well as the ways in which narrative affordances are both functional and relational, I differentiate between two categories of forms, operating on different layers of the digital. In brief, the affordances of social media platforms as constructed through networked technologies and

---

214 boyd, 'Social Networking Sites', 39.

215 Scarlett and Zeilinger, 'Rethinking Affordance', 18.

216 See e.g., Sy Taffel, *Digital Media Ecologies. Entanglements of Content, Code, and Hardware* (New York and London: Bloomsbury Academic, 2019).

217 On hidden affordances see William Gaver, 'Technology Affordances', *Proceedings of CHI'91* (1991), 79–84.

218 Scarlett and Zeilinger, 'Rethinking Affordance', 21.

219 Peter Nagy and Gina Neff, 'Imagined Affordance: Reconstructing a Keyword for Communication Theory', *Social Media + Society* July-December (2015), 4.

as imagined collectives configure them as environments in a way that shapes users' engagement: from the perspective of narrative practices, they are forms of agency. The ways in which users' engagement is shaped, then, inevitably shape their perception and usage of the 'abstract ways of making order', or forms of content. Next, I look at how these two categories of forms can be approached and evoke the affordance perspective that does not simply reflect features of a form or an outcome of an affordance in narrative theory.

Forms of content and forms of agency

As a starting point, forms of agency configure (both enable and constrain) the engagement of human users and correspondingly shape their perception of the abstract and symbolic objects they use on social media platforms. Forms of agency are thus closely intertwined with those of content, a phenomenon that can be seen in the way in which the *Dangers of Narrative* project attempts to pursue both of them all at once in the discussion of 'the viral exemplum', the prominent narrative prototype in the social media corpus they collected. The concept is defined as both an exemplar of a compelling story 'optimized for social media visibility, which, in large part because of its viral success on social media, becomes unduly representative'[220] and 'the chain reaction, typically fueled by social media shares, from narrative experientiality to representativeness and normativity'.[221] In my view, however, making the distinction between forms of content and agency is crucial when attending to the specificities of particular kinds of use to understand the ways in which forms and their affordances overlap and collide.[222] In what follows, I use the viral exemplum together with the concept of bardic system to draw out some of these overlaps and collisions.

As a form of content, the exemplum originates in the pre-modern tradition: structurally, it is a maxim-like, concise expression of a moral rule or principle. Larry Scanlon, researcher of medieval literature, describes the integral outcome of the usage of exemplum as 'a narrative enactment of cultural authority',[223] persuading 'by conveying a sense of communal identity with its

220 Mäkelä et al., 'Dangers of Narrative', 147; see also Mäkelä, 'Disagreeing'; Mäkelä, 'Lessons'.

221 Mäkelä et al., 'Dangers of Narrative', 154.

222 Cf., Levine, *Forms*, 7.

223 Larry Scanlon, *Narrative, Authority, and Power: The Medieval Exemplum and the Chaucerian Tradition* (Cambridge: Cambridge University Press, 1994), 34.

moral lesson'.[224] Today, the exemplum has emerged in social media to serve the same purpose, asking everyone in its audience to be convinced by its *sententia* or maxim because it expects them to put themselves in the position of the protagonist's personal experience. Thus, it asks to emulate the protagonist's righteous affective responses or to avoid their moral failure.[225] The key affordance of such a form that enables the enactment of cultural authority or conveys a sense of communal identity is, of course, universality. Compared with the medieval version of exemplum, however, neither those in charge for the narrative enactment of cultural authority nor the protagonists in the contemporary version are necessarily dependent on the support of institutions such as the church. Instead, today's exemplum relies on creating a sense of sharedness through a personal experience as representative of a larger phenomenon. It is paradoxical, though, that the universality of the exemplum's moral on contemporary social media platforms depends on its 'personality, alleged authenticity and particularity' as a guarantee of its worth.[226]

A similar change has occurred in the role of media as regards upholding the cultural consensus. In *Reading Television*, one of the seminal books of television studies originally published in 1978, John Fiske and John Hartley interestingly connect the central cultural role of television with the return of an old form. They coin the idea of 'television as our own culture's bard', performing a 'bardic function', a social ritual of sorts, for the culture at large and all the individuals who live in it.[227] They argue that television does this, for example, in articulating the main lines of the established cultural consensus about the nature of reality and convincing the audience that their status and identity as individuals are guaranteed by the culture as a whole.[228] However, as Djoymi Baker aptly notes in her book on the effects of transmedia merchandising and marketing on the viewers' experience of the *Star Trek* franchise, Fiske and Hartley underplay the significance of formula both to the bard and the television.[229] In Murray's

224 Scanlon, *Narrative, Authority, and Power*, 35.

225 Mäkelä, 'Lessons' 184; Scanlon, *Narrative, Authority, and Power*, 35.

226 Maria Mäkelä, 'Viral Storytelling as Contemporary Narrative Didacticism: Deriving Universal Truths from Arbitrary Narratives of Personal Experience', in Susanna Lindberg and Hanna-Riikka Roine, eds., *The Ethos of Digital Environments: Technology, Literary Theory and Philosophy* (London and New York: Routledge, 2021), 50.

227 John Fiske and John Hartley, *Reading Television* (London: Routledge, 2004), 64.

228 Fiske and Hartley, *Reading Television*, 66–67.

229 Djoymi Baker, *To Boldly Go: Marketing the Myth of Star Trek* (London and New York: I.B. Tauris, 2018).

visionary work, *Hamlet on the Holodeck*, formula takes centre stage in the discussion of bardic system as a model for storytelling in digital architectures. Murray's model shows bardic storytelling as a system of interplay between formula and innovation: authorship, for instance, is seen as the innovation and arrangement of expressive patterns that constitute 'a multiform story'.[230]

Murray's approach emphasizes that what the bardic system conserves 'is not a single particular performance but the underlying patterns from which the bards can create multiple varied performances'.[231] In other words, while specific details of a story narrated may change with each telling and are thus in flux, the formulae are preserved. As I have argued elsewhere, authorship in contemporary digital media does not lie within the design of a particular plot or other such patterns of meaning, but within the designed processes and structures that allow and invite us as users to construct such patterns in real time as we manage the data.[232] Baker describes Murray's vision as all users becoming bards, 'constructing stories with the morphemes laid out by a programming bard'.[233] In its contemporary manifestation, the bardic system conserves a host of formulae to navigate through and make sense of a vast amount of data. We are not only performing patterns of meaning such as the plot as members of the audience but can also create our own versions of the processes and structures we come across.

Compared with the idea of television as the culture's bard – a single authoritative source sending messages to the many in the audience – the affordances of the contemporary bardic system make possible actions related to the distribution of authorial power within large communities. An outcome that occurs simultaneously with such distribution is the blurring of the distinction between the source and the alteration, challenging, for instance, the traditional ways of analysing the narrative-ethical effects of storytelling as linked with the question of the ownership of a story being shared. As in code-driven – or bit-based, to use boyd's terminology – media users' interpretative work is placed in a reciprocal relationship with their ability to manage, define and manipulate representations, the digital bardic system allows everyone to (re)use the formulae conserved by it. In other words, the key affordance of such a system that enables the aforementioned distribution of authorial power is replicability.

230 Murray, *Hamlet*, 188–194.

231 Murray, *Hamlet*, 194.

232 Hanna-Riikka Roine, 'Computational Media and the Core Concepts of Narrative Theory', *Narrative* 27/3 (2019), 322.

233 Baker, *To Boldly Go*, n.pag.

Therefore, as a model for storytelling in digital architectures, the bardic system configures our actions in a manner that enables and constrains our understanding of what narrative is for, resulting in the rise of forms of content like the exemplum. Actions such as cutting, pasting, sharing and liking on social media platforms are concrete manifestations of such configurations shaping our perception of content. It is important, however, to maintain the balance between the affordances of forms of agency and forms of content: for instance, as ethnographer Elisabetta Costa has argued, the concept of affordance has been often used to emphasize the power of the architecture and to minimize the agency of users.[234] According to her, the affordance concept fails to inscribe the possibilities not actualized by media users as the properties that shape, constrain or generate practices cannot be known outside the actual, situated uses.[235] This is also why I am slightly wary of the term viral and the connotations it carries. Mäkelä's treatment of virality, for instance, does indeed not inscribe the possibilities not actualized – what about the content that does not scale in visibility, i.e., go viral? – although it is, of course, relevant to ask why certain kind of content *does* scale in visibility. As boyd argues, the internet does not guarantee an audience: scalability in networked publics 'is about the *possibility* of tremendous visibility'.[236]

However, if that which is not actualized is completely ignored, the different dimensions to which scalability is subject – socio-political divisions, such as 'filter bubbles', and manipulations by multiple actors such as algorithms, bots, and trolls as well as advertisers[237] – remain imperceptible. Furthermore, as Henry Jenkins, Sam Ford and Joshua Green suggest in their book coining the concept of spreadable media, 'the viral metaphor does little to describe situations in which people actively assess a media text, deciding who to share it with and how to pass it along'.[238] We are not simply 'infected' by an idea or a narrative in a way that we would be by a virus, without our own choice in the matter. In addition to users' intentions, we must keep in mind that human perception of content is enabled and constrained by the affordances as dynamics and conditions

234 Costa, 'Affordances-in-practices', 3438.
235 Costa, 'Affordances-in-practices', 3651.
236 boyd, 'Social Networking Sites', 47; emphasis in original.
237 boyd, 'Social Networking Sites', 54; see also Bucher and Helmond, 'The Affordances of Social Media Platforms' on the expanded notion of the user.
238 Henry Jenkins, Sam Ford and Joshua Green, *Spreadable Media: Creating Value and Meaning in a Networked Culture* (New York: New York University Press, 2013), 20.

enabled by platforms. We thus need to engage with ethical readings that not only acknowledge the affordances of narrative form and possible dangers inherent in them, but also the ones connected with the nature of social media platforms as digital architectures.

The irrelevance of the 'original'

Social media platforms are often seen to favour content that is structurally, rhetorically, and ideologically unambiguous, such as redemption or conversion narratives.[239] This may not, however, inherently be a matter of the affordances of these narratives as content, but also of the affordances as dynamics and conditions enabled by platforms. Here, I focus on affordances that, following boyd,[240] can be argued to emerge out of the properties of bits: persistence, replicability, scalability and searchability. I already briefly discussed scalability, the possibility for content to scale in enormous visibility, while here I look at affordances of persistence and replicability in more detail.[241] While the exemplum, in its current manifestation, retains its affordance of universality and thus makes the narrative enactment of cultural authority possible, the ways in which it intersects with the affordances of social media platforms as digital architectures – which, for their part, make actions such as reframing and remaking readily available – brings up an important shift in the communicative relevance of 'the original'. Although the narrative-rhetorical dynamics of sharing and liking are accounted for in the concept of the viral exemplum, for instance, the affordances of social media platforms are currently not sufficiently fleshed out.

By communicative relevance of the original, I simply mean the evaluation of the source of the updated or shared content in social media, such as asking whether the source is trustworthy or authentic. The evaluations often bring up the process of fact-checking as a kind of cure for fake news and other manifestations of 'post-truthfulness':[242] the logic is, in brief, that if we can prove that a viral story or similar spreadable content is not based on facts, we can show it to be irrelevant. However, there are two particular affordances of social media

239 Mäkelä, 'Lessons', 184.

240 boyd, 'Social Networking Sites', 46.

241 For its part, searchability simply points toward the fact that content in networked publics can be accessed through search, thus radically reworking the ways in which information is retrieved; see boyd, 'Social Networking Sites', 46, 48.

242 See Mäkelä, 'Disagreeing', 459.

platforms as digital architectures – persistence and replicability – that complicate the notions of authenticity.

Persistence, in brief, means that as online expressions are, by default, recorded and archived, what remains may lose its essence when consumed outside of the context in which it was created.[243] Persistence is also one contributor to collapse of contexts, the lack of spatial, social and temporal boundaries in digital environments which makes it difficult to maintain distinct social contexts.[244] When a media text or other such content is shared, for instance, its original point can be lost or ignored at the expense of what the person sharing it has in mind. As Jenkins, Ford and Green argue, '[a]s people listen, read, or view shared content they think not only – often, not even primarily – about what the producers might have meant but about what the person who shared it was trying to communicate'.[245] This also means that the author of a particular text does not control the ways in which it is reused and reframed.

Replicability, for its part, is based on the fact that content made out of bits can be duplicated: there is no way to differentiate the original bit from its duplicate. Content can be remade in ways that make it hard to tell which is the source and which is the alteration.[246] As a result, communicative acts and information are not located in a particular space and time and, because of the nature of bits, it is easy to alter content, making it more challenging to assess its origins and legitimacy.[247] This has also been studied in terms of media surfaces perceptible to human users and the layer of software 'beneath' these surfaces: while in physical media adding new properties means modifying its physical substance, in digital media new properties can always be easily added or even new types of media invented simply by changing existing or writing new software. For users who only interact with media content through application software (such as Adobe Photoshop), the properties of digital media are defined by the particular software as opposed to being contained in the layer of content.[248]

Furthermore, even if we got to the 'original' source, discerning what is true is not a matter of a straightforward fact-checking operation. Algorithms and other

243 boyd, 'Social Networking Sites', 46.
244 boyd, 'Social Networking Sites', 49.
245 Jenkins, Ford and Green, *Spreadable Media*, 13.
246 boyd, 'Social Networking Sites', 47.
247 boyd, 'Social Networking Sites', 53–54.
248 Lev Manovich, *Software Takes Control: Extending the Language of New Media* (New York and London: Bloomsbury, 2013), 91–92, 152.

computational agents are even less interested in such operations, as most of them are merely intent on – and responsible for – increasing human engagement on various platforms. In the case of viral exemplum discussed by Mäkelä, for instance, the informative content of the exemplary narratives is downplayed, and it is their afterlife on social media platforms that determines their 'truthfulness', appearing as '*a material manifestation* of the alleged universality of narrative truth'.[249] Fact-checking 'the universal' represented through a singular event or experience by means of an exemplary story is, of course, an impossible task. As such, this brings to mind cultural historian Mary Poovey's useful comparison between 'modern facts', originating in the institutions of early mercantile capitalism in the seventeenth century, and 'ancient facts' which, according to Aristotle, depend upon the recognition of 'the universal', or 'that which is always or that which is for the most part'.[250]

Over the centuries, such debates over truth have been frequent in countless discussions concerning the ways in which fiction can be relevant to us despite concerning non-existent people and events. Starting from Aristotle's 'universal' or higher truths,[251] fiction has, for instance, been seen as a prop in the game of make-believe,[252] and, more recently, enjoyable because it abstracts and simulates social experience,[253] cultivates sympathy by means of 'narrative imagination'[254] or as intentionally signalled, communicated invention.[255] What unites all these ideas of relevance is the roundabout way of approaching it: it seems as if the particulars (following Aristotle) would not be as relevant as the universals, the game, the abstraction, the imagination or the signalling. In other words, as

249 Mäkelä, 'Disagreeing', 460; emphasis in original.

250 Mary Poovey, *A History of the Modern Fact: Problems of Knowledge in the Sciences of Wealth and Society* (Chicago: University of Chicago Press, 1998), 8.

251 Aristotle, *Poetics*, Malcolm Heath, trans. (London: Penguin Books, 1997).

252 Kendall Walton, *Mimesis as Make-Believe: On the Foundations of the Representational Arts* (Cambridge, Ma: Harvard University Press, 1990).

253 Raymond A. Mar and Keith Oatley, 'The Function of Fiction is the Abstraction and Simulation of Social Experience', *Perspectives on Psychological Science* 3 (2008), 173–192.

254 Martha Nussbaum, *Not for Profit. Why Democracy Needs the Humanities* (Princeton: Princeton University Press, 2010).

255 Simona Zetterberg Gjerlevsen and Henrik Skov Nielsen, 'Distinguishing Fictionality', in Cindie Aaen Maagaard, Daniel Schäbler, and Marianne Wolff Lundholt, eds., *Exploring Fictionality: Conceptions, Test Cases, Discussions* (Odense: Syddansk Universitetsforlag, 2020), 19–40.

particulars such as characters or events cannot be evaluated as factual or authentic, the point of the story must lie elsewhere.

This (admittedly very short) discussion of the relevance of fiction illustrates the messiness of distinguishing between fact and fiction as a matter of reference – in brief, the idea that to be meaningful, fiction must have fictional referents instead of real ones.[256] The question of reference is similarly tricky in the case of social media platforms, as the affordances such as persistence and replicability feed into forms that favour the universal, duplicable and formulaic over the particular and unique. As a form of agency, bardic system enables us to see forms of content as replicable, as something that can be cut, pasted and reassembled with ease, as Murray has suggested.[257] The motor of universality is thus partly based on the recognizable formulae being conserved and re-used to fashion content. Particulars can always be changed. As a result, the authorial power is distributed and, simultaneously, distinguishing the source from the alteration becomes not only impossible but also irrelevant.

Against this backdrop, narrative theorist Richard Walsh's definition of fictionality as 'a contextual assumption prompting us to understand an utterance's communicative relevance as indirectly, rather than directly, informative'[258] can be useful. He continues to note that a striking consequence of this definition is 'that it does not assume that the utterance is false, only that the issue of literal truth does not arise, because it is not the point'.[259] In the case of an exemplary story, for instance, the point of the story is the moral example it provides, and therefore it is not evaluated referentially but against the shared sense of communal identity and values[260] – in other words, that which we know to exist, if not always, then 'for the most part'. When we combine Walsh's rhetorical approach to fictionality with the social media platforms dominated by actions such as reframing and

---

256 Richard Walsh, 'Fictionality as Rhetoric: A Distinctive Research Paradigm', *Style* 53/4 (2019), 401. See e.g., possible worlds semantics, where fictional worlds function as the referential grounds for the sentences of fictions, e.g., in Lubomír Doležel, *Heterocosmica: Fiction and Possible Worlds* (Baltimore: Johns Hopkins University Press, 1998), and ontological approaches to fictional worlds as worlds both constructed and referred to by fictions e.g., in Marie-Laure Ryan, *Possible Worlds, Artificial Intelligence, and Narrative Theory* (Bloomington: Indiana University Press, 1991).

257 Janet Murray, *Inventing the Medium: Principles of Interaction Design as a Cultural Practice* (Cambridge, Ma: The MIT Press, 2011), 57.

258 Walsh, 'Fictionality as Rhetoric 414.

259 Walsh, 'Fictionality as Rhetoric 414.

260 Cf., Mäkelä, 'Disagreeing', 460.

remaking, made possible by the affordances of these platforms, we see that the contextual assumption crucial for the users to understand the relevance of content is not prompted by the 'original' message, but rather the actions related to its use.

As a result, actions such as reframing and remaking override what the content 'is supposed to' mean. Thus, published or shared content in social media does not simply entail 'post-truthfulness' in the sense that the distinction between fact and fiction would be eroding – what is eroding is the relevance of an authentic source while the distinction between the original and alteration is simultaneously being blurred. On the one hand, this has further contributed to the blurring of conventions between doing things with facts and doing things with fiction – to paraphrase J.L. Austin's influential book *How to Do Things with Words*.[261] On the other hand, however, the affordances of social media platforms have made us more aware of the existence of various cultural and social formulae, such as more conventional frameworks and models for storytelling.[262] In the contemporary bardic system, both formulae and more particular elements such as characters are increasingly conceptualized as content, ownership of which is not attributed to any one person. In the last section of this chapter, I illustrate this with an example of a more complicated content reframed into an exemplum-like story with an unambiguous moral.

Changing the contextual assumption: Readings of 'Cat Person'

At the end of 2017, Kristen Roupenian's fictional short story 'Cat Person', published on the website of *The New Yorker*, dominated social media feeds in a way that pieces of fiction rarely do. Most of the story focuses on a miserable sexual encounter from the perspective of Margot, a twenty-year-old college sophomore who realizes too late that she would rather not have sex at all with Robert, a man fifteen years senior to her. In their social media shares, quite a few readers associated 'Cat Person' with a personal essay and viewed it as weighing in on a timely issue, most obviously the #MeToo movement. Despite the fact that it is told in

261 Cf., Samuli Björninen, 'The Rhetoric of Factuality in Narrative: Appeals to Authority in Claas Relotius's Feature Journalism', *Narrative Inquiry* 29/2 (2019), 352–370.

262 For an illustrative example of such awareness, see e.g., Ebony Elizabeth Thomas, *The Dark Fantastic: Race and the Imagination from Harry Potter to Hunger Games* (New York: New York University Press, 2019).

third person, there is a certain resemblance in the confessional, feminine narrative voice of the story to the 'It happened to me' -style first-person narratives. Consider, for instance, the moment when, after several weeks of texting with Robert and building a certain image of him in her mind, Margot goes to a movie with him and finally gets a kiss from him:

> He kissed her then, on the lips, for real; he came for her in a kind of lunging motion and practically poured his tongue down her throat. It was a terrible kiss, shockingly bad; Margot has trouble believing that a grown man could possibly be so bad at kissing. It seemed awful, yet somehow it also gave her that tender feeling toward him again, the sense that even though he was older than her, she knew something he didn't.[263]

The excerpt aims for an evocation of Margot's experience both in terms of bodily and emotional responses: it describes in detail what Robert's kiss feels like, but also Margot's tender feelings. However, as the story is filled with overshadowing of this sort, it hardly comes as a surprise for the reader that when Margot and Robert have sex later on the date night, it is an even more terrible experience for Margot than their initial kiss. After recoiling at the sight of Robert's 'belly thick and soft and covered with hair' Margot decides to 'bludgeon her resistance into submission', as she is afraid that 'insisting that they stop now, after everything she'd done to push this forward, would make her seem spoiled and capricious'.[264] Then, over the next day or so, she realizes missing something, and that it was 'not the real Robert but the Robert she'd imagined on the other end of all those text messages'.[265] Despite this realization, Margot finds it hard to tell Robert that she does not want to pursue a relationship with him, and finally her roommate sends a rather rude break-up text to Robert who answers politely. The story ends with a poisonous note, though: a month later Robert sees Margot at the bar with her friends, and then texts Margot, asking what he did wrong and then moving to questions such as 'When u laughed when I asked if you were a virgin was it because youd [sic] fucked so many guys' and finally ending with 'Whore'.[266]

While the topic and content of 'Cat Person' make it possible to connect it with the #MeToo movement, it is neither an unambiguous nor an instructive story. Robert is not simply presented as 'a bad guy' despite his behaviour towards the end, Margot is shown to happily get on with her life, and there are no clear moral guidelines given. As Laura Miller aptly summarizes the story in *Slate*, 'Cat Person'

---

263 Roupenian, 'Cat Person'.
264 Roupenian, 'Cat Person'.
265 Roupenian, 'Cat Person'.
266 Roupenian, 'Cat Person'.

is about a relationship that is 'no relationship at all, but two imaginary constructs colliding with each other until they fall apart'.[267] However, many social media shares of the story framed it with a clear message of warning against the failure of its protagonist and thus to be read as an exemplum-like moral lesson. In a more confusing twist, a smaller but still significant portion of the readers did not only associate the story with a personal essay but outright mistook it as 'a piping hot thinkpiece' and framed it as such when sharing it – despite the fact that it was explicitly categorized under 'Fiction' in *The New Yorker* site, which is, as its own section, a well-known venue for publishing fiction.

'Cat Person' shows how framings enable people sharing content to use it in divergent but specific ways. In the case of this story, it was typically reframed as a representative example of contemporary dating culture. The moral ambiguity of the story was completely ignored as its 'point' was turned into an example of 'how men (or women) are'. Thus, by evoking the universal we (presumably) know to exist 'for the most part', it enabled the enactment of, if not cultural, at least communal identity. In other words, readers' perception of what narratives such as 'Cat Person' are for shaped their understanding of its affordances when shared on social media. Reframings of this sort guided the people coming across the story through shares to overlook the artifice of the text and, consequently, many of them failed to recognize it as fictional. This obviously had a great impact on the ways in which the communicative relevance – or the 'point' of the short story was understood: whether it was seen as a fictional story about, for instance, a failure of relationship depicted through a collision of imaginary constructs, or as a direct account of the horrors of dating culture, authorized by the first-hand experience of such culture. What was being shared was not only a link or even an affective reaction to Roupenian's story but also instructions for reading: an invitation to adopt a specific position, to use a story in a specific way, to see it as an instrument with a specific purpose – that of narrative enactment of a moral lesson, of exemplum.

This further shows why forms of content and forms of agency cannot be lumped together under a single concept, as 'Cat Person' was not a story optimized for social media visibility in the sense of prototypical narratives of personal experience being instrumentalized in the service of political campaigning

---

267 Laura Miller, 'The *New Yorker*'s "Cat Person" Story Is Great. Too Bad the Internet Turned It Into a Piping Hot Thinkpiece', *Slate* (11 December 2017), <https://slate.com/culture/2017/12/too-bad-twitter-turned-the-new-yorker-s-cat-person-story-into-a-piping-hot-thinkpiece.html>, accessed 28 June 2021.

discussed by the *Dangers of Narrative* project.[268] Instead, 'Cat Person' was given a certain form of content with associated affordances through a form of agency. Compared with other phenomena ignorant of the culturally upheld boundary between fact and fiction, this was not a communicative act aimed at creating confusion and mistrust. So-called 'fake news', for instance, contribute to a political climate where our speech acts may be doing something, but cannot be called to account for their repercussions.[269] In the case of Roupenian's story, perceiving universality as its main affordance enabled people sharing it to appeal to it as a source about, for instance, what it is like for women to experience unpleasant sexual encounters in their everyday life. In the process, Roupenian's story acquired a status usually reserved for facts in political or social debates: to inform opinions.[270] Samuli Björninen follows up on this idea in his article on the rhetoric of *factuality*, arguing that factual rhetoric is distinctive as it involves an appeal to something that has the authority to inform an opinion.[271] According to him, factuality is thus not so much a case of appealing to facts in the sense of modern fact discussed by Poovey, but rather about authority.[272]

The ways in which 'Cat Person' was appealed to as an authority on experience that is universal at least from a perspective of a certain community demonstrate the quality of social media platforms as environments where the author of a text, image or other content cannot control its afterlife consisting of reframings and re-uses. They further bring out the nature of the viral metaphor as unfitting in these situations, as the framings show the active assessment of people sharing content instead of being 'infected'.[273] In other words, it seems that the one who sets the tone of the contextual assumption also controls the ways in which the meaning and significance of the so-called 'main text' are approached. I have previously made a similar point with Laura Piippo in our discussion of the paratextuality of the digital interfaces which affect the material users write and publish on them – in effect, *the context of reading* defines the paratext: 'The logic affects, for instance, elements of an online discussion, where the intentions of a singular commentator are not necessarily the ones that matter but the ways in which their

268 Mäkelä et al., 'Dangers of Narrative', 147.

269 See Ari-Elmeri Hyvönen, 'Careless Speech: Conceptualizing Post-Truth Politics', *New Perspectives* 26/3 (2018), 1–25.

270 Hyvönen, 'Careless Speech', 7.

271 Björninen, 'The Rhetoric of Factuality in Narrative', 359.

272 For more on the different types of authority, see Björninen, 'The Rhetoric of Factuality in Narrative', 360–361.

273 See Jenkins, Ford and Green, *Spreadable Media*, 20.

comments may come to contextualize the whole discussion – and may be recontextualized again by either human or nonhuman actors'.[274] Analysis of the interplay between the reading context and paratext also highlights problems in the concept of authorship, as the authorial power is distributed and the distinction between the original and alteration is irrelevant.

In the environment dominated by actions such as reframing and re-using, made possible by the affordances of platforms, the conventions for doing things with facts and for doing things with fiction are particularly liable to blurring. Furthermore, narrative reframing and re-using illustrate the fact that the point of stories and other content published and shared on social media platforms rarely concern literal truth that could be fact-checked. It would hardly make sense to call all such content *fictional*, though. I have already suggested that crucial for understanding 'points' of this sort is prompted by the active role of people sharing, not only the 'original' message of the content. On contemporary social media platforms, the acts of communication are typically aimed at creating as well as strengthening communities, and in this process, not only is universality seen as the most important affordance of narrative as a form but also is sharing an act of (re)fashioning content through forms of agency. These operations – as well as their potential dangers – need to be recognized if we want to investigate the point of publishing and sharing stories.

Conclusions

The main driver behind this chapter was the need to delve deeper into the ways in which narratives are used as instruments on social media platforms as digital architectures and draw out the dangers of focusing on these uses predominantly in the layer of content. While narratives may not be, as singular performances, able to change our minds, for instance, the ways in which they are used for purposes of enacting cultural or communal authority speak for their effectiveness as instruments. What this chapter has argued, however, is that the ways in which these instruments are used must be recognized as equally important. Furthermore, the affordances as dynamics and conditions enabled by social media platforms as digital architectures need to be analysed side by side with the affordances of forms, as they shape users' perception of what instruments such as narrative are for. The uses enabled by the affordances as dynamics and conditions include, for instance, strategies involved in sharing and reframing content, and

274 Roine and Piippo, 'Authorship vs. Assemblage', 70.

the irrelevance of the 'original' compared with the refashioning of the material according to a formula that is recognizable to the wider community. In this sense, human experiences are transformed into data as the 'fourth fictional commodity' not only in the sense of making profit – as Shoshana Zuboff has argued of surveillance capitalism[275] – but also as a guarantee of (performed) authority instead of authority being (solely) supported by social or cultural institutions.

In her important critique of curated stories, Sujatha Fernandes recognizes the significance of the ways in which formulae are used in her call for 'new kinds of organisings' that would open the spaces for different kinds of tropes, subjectivities, storylines and narratives – or 'we will be constrained to stories that conform to what is acceptable in the narrow vision of the mainstream'.[276] In my view, this already happens within numerous digital communities, which support and bolster new 'organisings' as well as reworkings of the older ones: a logic that is visible in the ways in which 'Cat Person' was repurposed and reframed and that also showed that a formula need not to be clearly present in the 'original'. We still need, however, a better understanding of the ways in which these organisings and constraints function in relation to the individual agency of people participating in the communities: the disconnections between the experiences and formulae discussed by Fernandes as well as the ways in which the affordances of two forms I have discussed here – those of content and those of agency – intertwine. In other words, we need to learn to read both content and their uses in specific environments even better to assess both the dangers and possibilities inherent in this entanglement, and my approach to the affordances of narrative as functional and relational is designed to help with that.

275 Shoshana Zuboff, *The Age of Surveillance Capitalism: The Fight for a Human Future at the New Frontier of Power* (London: Profile Books, 2019), 71.

276 Sujatha Fernandes, *Curated Stories: The Uses and Misuses of Storytelling* (Oxford: Oxford University Press, 2017), 170.

Jarkko Toikkanen, Mari Hatavara, Maria Laakso and Hanna Rautajoki

5. Storytelling and Participatory Immersion in the Niilo22 Experience

Abstract: The social media personality Niilo22, real name Mikael Kosola, is a keen user of several platforms and most famous as a highly active YouTuber since 2008. Over the years, he has gained popularity with his video clips that show him engaged in everyday activities. In the eyes of the social media crowd, he can transition from being just his own individual to representing a broader societal trend of voluntary unemployment and living off welfare. Following the antics of a single person, on a social media platform with specific technological features, risks affecting the crowd so that the interaction becomes both generative and representative of collectively judging individuals such as Niilo22. Our aim is to survey the dangers of creating such inequalities in today's digitalized society. Fictionalizing narrative modes may turn real-world people into stereotypes in the YouTube storyworld through the medium-specific qualities of online storytelling that constitute a special kind of activity and potentially escalate the controversy on societal issues such as unemployment. We observe Niilo22 as a new kind of experience in the social media that distinctly draws on the medium-specific qualities and technological features of the YouTube environment for storytelling purposes. The phenomenon involves users who assume different roles and positions in an ongoing and dynamic process of online storytelling, and we analyse scenes of this interaction as participatory immersion in the Niilo22 experience.

Keywords: online storytelling, participatory immersion, medium specificity, Niilo22 experience

The social media personality Niilo22, real name Mikael Kosola, is a keen user of several platforms and most famous as a highly active YouTuber since 2008. Over the years, he has gained popularity with his video clips that show him engaged in everyday activities, chatting on sundry issues in Finnish, and interacting with his followers – the number of which now ranks at around 104,000 when his main channel and live channel are combined (November 2022). In the analysis that follows, we observe some of the striking qualities in this particular case of social media interaction. In his video clips, Niilo22 can often appear as a somewhat simple character who may have trouble articulating himself and finding the right words to explain whatever issue seems topical on the day – he has been diagnosed with dyslexia[277] – and he can also give the impression of somebody who does not want to go to work but only spends his time at home, or around the neighbourhood, every day. In the eyes of the social media crowd, he can transition from being just his own individual to representing a broader societal trend of voluntary unemployment and living off welfare. Following the antics of a single person, on a social media platform with specific technological features, risks affecting the crowd so that the interaction becomes both generative and representative of collectively judging individuals such as Niilo22. Our aim is to survey the dangers of creating such inequalities in today's digitalized society. Fictionalizing narrative modes may turn real-world people into stereotypes in the YouTube storyworld through the medium-specific qualities of online storytelling that constitute a special kind of activity and potentially escalate the controversy on societal issues such as unemployment.

In this chapter, we analyse the whole of this interaction as the *Niilo22 experience* – a phenomenon that takes place online, involving users that assume different roles and positions in an ongoing and dynamic process. First of all, we study the Niilo22 experience from the perspective of storytelling, what kind of a story Niilo22 is telling and how, or if any impression of a story is only there to provide a medium of expression for the many voices participating in the narrative. Using narrative modes characteristic of fiction, Niilo22 embeds and attributes vicarious minds in his storytelling, obscuring the levels of story and storytelling in an engaging way.[278] Secondly, we study the Niilo22 experience as a technologically mediated, audio-visual phenomenon with tools from literary and media studies, as well as sociology.[279] The key concepts applied are immersion and participation. Immersion has been defined in several ways across the disciplines from the mental simulation of textual worlds to technological advancements in producing creative immersive experiences in, for instance, journalism and virtual reality cinema.[280] In our analysis, we contrast a traditional view of

277 Satu Vasantola, 'Lukihäiriöinen nuori jäi ilman apua ja sitten ilman töitä – nyt Niilo22 on aikamies ja Youtube-tähti, joka lukee ylpeänä videoillaan, vaikka väärin menisi', *Helsingin Sanomat* (15 April 2017).

278 See Mari Hatavara and Jarmila Mildorf, 'Fictionality, Narrative Modes, and Vicarious Storytelling', *Style* 51/3 (2017a), 391–408.

279 Hanna Rautajoki, Jarkko Toikkanen and Pirkko Raudaskoski, 'Embodied Ekphrasis of Experience: Bodily Rhetoric in Mediating Affect in Interaction', *Semiotica* 235 (2020), 91–111.

280 See Marie-Laure Ryan, *Narrative as Virtual Reality II: Revisiting Immersion and Interactivity* (Baltimore: Johns Hopkins University Press, 2015); Niels Christian Nilsson,

immersion as a passive activity[281] with a contemporary view of immersion as active participation.[282] As we are using them, immersion and participation are not interchangeable terms with one another – instead, immersion in the Niilo22 experience is produced through active participation in the storytelling that occurs as the social media users assume different roles and positions in the process. In other words, participation is one of the ways that brings about an immersive experience, actuated in the form of discursive variation in the voices maintaining the ongoing narrative.

In becoming immersed in the Niilo22 experience, the social media users firstly interact in the dimension of communicating with the individual known as Niilo22 and the other participants, and secondly, in transitioning to the dimension of collective values that Niilo22 with his stories may represent and risk being judged for. We hypothesise that Niilo22's video clips provide compelling evidence of this kind of 'participatory immersion' being sustained through storytelling on YouTube. At times, as the exchanges between Niilo22 and his followers turn heated, the immersion in the Niilo22 experience may explicitly come across as affectively charged whereas, at other times, the interaction can appear as more disinterested or distanced in terms of emotional involvement. This latter attitude could be called the ironic attitude – a less obvious manner of participating in the storytelling to produce the immersive Niilo22 experience we are going to focus on in the analysis.

Rolf Nordahl and Stefania Serafin, 'Immersion Revisited: A Review of Existing Definitions of Immersion and Their Relation to Difference Theories of Presence', *Human Technology* 12/2 (2016), 108–134; Gary M. Hardee and Ryan P. McMahan, 'FIJI: A Framework for the Immersion-Journalism Intersection', *Front. ICT* 4:21 (2017), doi: 10.3389/fict.2017.00021; Jayesh S. Pillai and Manvi Verma, 'Grammar of VR Storytelling: Narrative Immersion and Experiential Fidelity in VR Cinema', *VRCAI '19: The 17th International Conference on Virtual-Reality Continuum and its Applications in Industry*, Article 34 (2019), 1–6.

281 See Norman Holland, *Literature and the Brain* (Cambridge, MA: PsyArt Foundation, 2009).

282 See Susan Turner, Huang Chih-Wei, Luke Burrows and Phil Turner, 'Make-Believing Virtual Realities', in Phil Turner and J. Tuomas Harviainen, eds., *Digital Make-Believe* (Cham: Springer, 2016).

Social media and YouTube as technological platforms

As claimed by Mäkelä et al. (2021) among others, social media have changed contemporary storytelling. Mäkelä and her colleagues argue that the urge today 'to tell and share experiential stories results in collisions between the narrative form and other forms, such as those of social media'.[283] However, there are differences, as van Dijck has stated.[284] Whereas social networking sites including Facebook and Twitter are based on establishing and maintaining interpersonal contact between individuals, platforms like YouTube rely on user-generated content and allow for the sharing of media content. Bronwen Thomas adds that YouTube actually hosts a range of networking and 'social' aspects,[285] whereas van Dijck classifies it in his second category as a content-sharing platform. In our analysis on the potential of storytelling to enable immersion in social media, it is important to bear in mind that YouTube is at the same time a platform to publish content and a site for sharing experiences and connecting with others. The sharing and telling functions coincide both in the video streaming situation and as video clips posted on the YouTube channels are further commented on and shared.

Due to the specific technological features of YouTube, the popularity of the social media platform is not only based on shared audio-visual material easily accessible through different devices. YouTube is indeed an interactive medium where users actively participate. They can create their own profiles, like and dislike video clips, and build a network of their own or participate in others by subscribing to their channels. As Ruth Page has noted, YouTube's commercial and formal development has been remarkable since 2005 when the site was founded with the slogan 'Broadcast yourself'.[286] The new platform that allowed anyone to share their personal everyday experiences in video format was treated as a promising example of a new participatory culture in social media. However, as early as in 2006, YouTube was sold to Google, and it became possible for members to benefit commercially from their video clips by adding advertisements to them.

---

283 Maria Mäkelä, Samuli Björninen, Laura Karttunen, Matias Nurminen, Juha Raipola and Tytti Rantanen, 'Dangers of Narrative: A Critical Approach to Narratives of Personal Experience in Contemporary Story Economy', *Narrative* 29/2 (2021), 142.

284 Jose van Dijck, *The Culture of Connectivity: A Critical History of Social Media* (Oxford: Oxford University Press, 2013).

285 Bronwen Thomas, *Literature and Social Media* (London: Routledge, 2020), 17–18.

286 Ruth Page, *Narratives Online: Shared Stories in Social Media* (New York: Cambridge University Press, 2018), 160–161.

Page summarizes: 'The interactivity that YouTube templates offer to audiences, which can add their evaluations of and comments on the content, is by no means a democratic gesture, but rather the means which advertisers and Google can generate revenue'.[287] Despite the commercial aspect, YouTube is a lively platform for popular culture, democratic in the sense that anyone can load content and gather followers – Niilo22 included. Niilo22 may actually make a living out of telling and sharing a story of his unemployed life.

Storytelling online

Telling stories as part of social media communication has changed what is prototypical to narrative, especially in what comes to the basic expectation of narrating taking place only after the narrated events. The duality between the time of the told and the time of the telling is crucial to narrative analysis, and also fundamental to how David Herman identifies four elements of a prototypical narrative: a) a narrative representation is situated, that is, it occurs in a specific occasion for telling, b) the representation is about particularized events in a structured time-course, c) the represented events introduce a disruption in the represented world, and d) the representation conveys how it feels for a human-like agent to live through the represented events.[288] The distinction between the situated telling and the events represented in this telling implies a temporal distance between the two, which enables forming a structured time course of the past, identifying a disruption and conveying the experience of living through. However, in online sharing on a media platform such as YouTube, this is not the case because the narrative representation partially concurs with the taking place of the events, living along them through transitions and disruptions.

Alexandra Georgakopoulou has demonstrated how the practices of creating and sharing stories out of the lived moment in online media indeed depart from the idea of teller-led lengthy communication of particularized story content in the past.[289] In its place, Georgakopoulou identifies the prominent features of online story sharing to be the taking of a narrative stance and story-linking, and she argues that storying the moment would in classic narrative terms rather be

---

287 Page, *Narratives Online*, 162.

288 David Herman, *Basic Elements of Narrative* (Oxford and Malden, MA: Wiley Blackwell, 2009), 14.

289 Alexandra Georgakopoulou, 'Sharing the Moment as Small Stories: The Interplay between Practices and Affordances in the Social Media Curation of Lives', *Narrative Inquiry* 27/2 (2017), 313.

showing than telling the moment. Filming one's life as it is happening emphasizes the narrator-experiencer as opposed to a narrator relating the happenings from a temporal or evaluative distance. Stories come into existence at the moment of sharing and develop relationally.[290]

We argue that even though the times of the telling and that of the told partially collapse in online storytelling, it is important to keep in mind that the distinction between story – what is told – and discourse – the act and representation of the telling – is not only temporal in nature but also involves agency. This duality between content and representation stands even when tellers and characters in interactional storytelling are situated both in the story, or the happenings depicted, and in the discourse depicting them.[291] Literary narratology has developed methods to identify linguistically the discursive movement between agentive voices on the story and storytelling levels. These methods apply both in the case of portraying vicarious experience and in the case of portraying the former or ongoing experiences of a self.[292]

We believe that in order to fully capture the elements of telling and showing, narrating and sharing in the online storytelling of Niilo22, narrative analysis needs to bring together the linguistically nuanced narratological analysis of voices and positioning theory with insights into identity work and social norms in interaction.[293] Positioning theory distinguishes positions on three levels: (1) positions taken and given in the story, (2) positioning in the interaction and (3) positioning related to identities and social norms.[294] Positioning analysis applies

290 Georgakopoulou, 'Sharing the Moment as Small Stories', 330.

291 cf. Seymour Chatman, *Story and Discourse: Narrative Structure in Fiction and Film* (Ithaca and London: Cornell University Press, 1980), 81–88; Gérard Genette, *Narrative Discourse* (Oxford: Cornell University Press, [1972] 1980), 27; H. Porter Abbott, 'Story, Plot, and Narration', in David Herman, ed., *The Cambridge Companion to Narrative* (2007), 39–40.

292 Dorrit Cohn, *Transparent Minds: Narrative Modes for Presenting Consciousness in Fiction* (Princeton: Princeton University Press, 1978), 14–17, 145–158.

293 Hanna Rautajoki and Matti Hyvärinen, 'Aspects of Voice in the Use of Narrative Positioning in Polyphonic Storytelling: Ventriloqual Moves within a Biographical Interview', *Journal of Interdisciplinary Voice Studies* 6/1 (2021), 55–73.

294 Michael Bamberg, 'Positioning Between Structure and Performance', *Journal of Narrative and Life History* 7/1–4 (1997), 337; Michael Bamberg, 'Positioning with Davie Hogan: Stories, Tellings, and Identities', in Colette Daiute and Cynthia Lightfoot, eds., *Narrative Analysis. Studying the Development of Individuals in Society* (Thousand Oaks: Sage, 2004), 136–137; Arnulf Depperman, 'Positioning', in Anna de Fina and

to the teller positioning both others and themselves in the projected story (level 1) from the position of telling (level 2).[295] Together with the discourse narratological methods to identify voices that express agency on those levels of positioning,[296] our analysis can trace the moulding and modifying agencies in the online storytelling that is part of the Niilo22 experience.

An important narrative feature often overlooked in the analysis of social media narratives is the ability to portray and position several minds within one's storytelling. As a narrator-experiencer, a YouTuber is showing and telling ongoing happenings, but they also have the ability to use several voices and attribute several minds in their story with the use of such narrative techniques as blending two voices (free indirect discourse), internal focalization and the use of mental verbs on other persons.[297] Attributing other minds and using the voices of others has traditionally been considered as confined to fictional narratives, but recent scholarship has demonstrated that cross-fictional narrative modes used to portray other minds are also used in nonfictional narrative environments,[298] such as political journalism[299] and online political discussions[300]. Whereas the rhetorical approach to fictionality, with its understanding of fictionality as signalled invention, concentrates on the invented nature of the story content and the intention of an author,[301] cross-fictionality zooms into narrative modes of

---

Alexandra Georgakopoulou, eds., *The Handbook of Narrative Analysis* (Oxford: Wiley Blackwell, 2015), 377–380.

295 Depperman, 'Positioning', 377–380.

296 See Cohn, *Transparent Minds* Alan Palmer, 'Thought and Consciousness Representation (Literature)', in David Herman, Manfred Jahn and Marie-Laure Ryan, eds., *Routledge Encyclopedia of Narrative Theory* (London and New York: Routledge, 2005), 602–606.

297 See David Herman, 'Introduction', in David Herman, ed., *The Emergence of Mind. Representations of Consciousness in Narrative Discourse in English* (Lincoln: The University of Nebraska Press, 2011).

298 Hatavara and Mildorf, 'Fictionality 391–408.

299 Sam Browse and Mari Hatavara, 'I Can Tell the Difference between Fiction and Reality. Cross-fictionality and Mind-style in Political Rhetoric', *Narrative Inquiry* 29/2 (2019), 245–267.

300 Samuli Björninen, Mari Hatavara and Maria Mäkelä, 'Narrative as Social Action: A Narratological Approach to Story, Discourse and Positioning in Political Storytelling', *International Journal of Social Research Methodology* 23/4 (2020), 437–449.

301 Henrik Skov Nielsen, James Phelan and Richard Walsh, 'Ten Theses about Fictionality', *Narrative* 23/1 (2015), 61–73.

mind representation characteristic of fiction.[302] Those modes, when used outside of fiction, introduce a degree of fictionality in storytelling, where the contextual frame is nonfictional, but vicarious experience and the minds of others are presented as if from within. This blurs the origins of voices and the instances of agency highlighting the need for a nuanced interpretation of narrative modes and their functions.[303] Particularly in social media storytelling with its emphasis on the simultaneous sharing and relational development of stories, the search for authorial intention seems unnecessary compared to the analysis of voices and positionings in a narrative.

The cross-fictionality approach enables us to analytically identify the layering of voices in Niilo22's video clips as he at the same time shows himself living his everyday life, accounts for other events and people that come to his mind during the streaming of the clips and engages in communication with his followers. Our analysis maintains the difference between showing the happenings unfolding and telling about the ongoing, past and projected events. Together, the cross-fictional attention to embedded voices and positioning analysis invested in how the levels of story and interaction address social norms help us to identify different voices in our examples and locate their relation to agency and expectations in producing the immersive Niilo22 experience.

Immersion and irony

Norman Holland has viewed immersion as a passive activity that requires aesthetic distance because becoming too closely involved in the presentation transforms the experience into something that requires action instead of contemplation.[304] When the users are made to take an active part, such as deciding on courses of action, they are denied the chance to reflect on the imaginary environment and fully become immersed in its detail and construction. Obviously, Holland's traditional view of immersion is at odds with the Niilo22 experience in social media. As an alternative, game theorists have recently proposed that active participation in the presentation is indeed a prerequisite for immersion.[305] If the player cannot engage with the game environment by way of playing – that

302 Mari Hatavara and Jarmila Mildorf, 'Hybrid Fictionality and Vicarious Narrative Experience', *Narrative* 25/1 (2017b), 66–69; Hatavara and Mildorf, 'Fictionality', 404.

303 Hatavara and Mildorf, 'Hybrid', 79–80.

304 Holland, *Literature and the Brain.*

305 See Turner, Chih-Wei, Burrows and Turner, 'Make-Believing Virtual Realities'.

is, by making moves and choices, as well as filling in plot holes and atmospheric detail – the experientially immersive qualities vanish, and it may be questioned whether the presentation is a game at all.

In our analysis, we will not delve into game studies any further but will argue that the social media user, similar to the video game player, becomes engaged in producing the immersive Niilo22 experience by way of active participation in the storytelling. The Niilo22 experience consists of the protagonist and his followers affectively interacting with one another, producing content for new clips, and while the process may not be about immersion in Holland's passive sense, it is very much immersive in the active sense, as demonstrated in our analysis. In making their discursive moves, the interaction between the participants in the Niilo22 experience transitions from merely involving the single YouTuber to broadly impacting collective judgment on individuals such as Niilo22 in today's society.

The question of normativity – or what one should be like and do – becomes much more important in terms of this collective judgment. While Niilo22's individual coffee-making habits might not be intensely commented on, what he represents in the broader sense can have the opposite effect. When considering normativity in the comments and responses Niilo22 receives, it is important to notice that followers and commentators tend to play around with normative and moral stances. Online communities like YouTube allow their users to stay anonymous and therefore adopt identities they do not represent in real life. YouTube users can create avatars to join the imagined community in any role they wish. These specific technological features of social media platforms make the morality of certain social media communities diffused and divided. Moral responsibility of one's actions depends on the idea of unity of a moral agent. In social media, personal identities are not necessarily coherent, and users may not consider their actions as moral actions. Studies on online anonymity have proven that anonymity in communication often causes users to engage in more uninhibited behaviour like violence and aggression.[306]

Consequently, the affective logics of online communities can actually encourage mean, provocative and antisocial behavior. Especially so-called trolling is common among anonymous online collectives such as Niilo22's followers. Trolling is a rhetorical strategy by which the 'troll' tries to affect unsuspecting participants and engage them in a conflict. Claire Hardaker has defined trolling

306 Lisa S. Nelson, *Social media and Morality. Losing Our Self Control* (New York: Cambridge University Press, 2018), 14–15.

as online antagonism undertaken for amusement's sake.[307] Elsewhere, Hardaker has claimed the rhetorical range of trolling strategies to include digression, '(hypo)criticism', antipathy, endangering, shocking and aggression.[308] In effect, trolls pretend to be serious in adopting a provocative point of view that might be contrary to real life.

The possibility of trolling and adopting different normative or moral stances is part of the Niilo22 experience, and most participants may be aware of this. Their participation does not necessarily result in sincere willingness to immerse themselves in Niilo22's personal world, as they might remain at a certain emotional distance that could be called ironic but still take part in the Niilo22 experience in a less obvious manner. Ironic distance can signal an attitude where users position themselves as recipients rather than participants. This ironic distance may be explicitly marked by the phrase 'get the popcorn' or similar memes, meaning that the person wants to identify as an onlooker sitting back in their chair, enjoying the heated conflicts or emotions expressed by others.

Trolling can also include ironic distance, or indifference, towards the actual topic at hand. However, the ironic attitude does not necessarily dissolve the Niilo22 experience because, in their indifference, followers still actively participate to immerse themselves in a world that includes both Niilo22's video clips and the world or community that operates around them. They can try to affect the plot of the clips by making rude or provocative comments, and in doing so they become active agents in the Niilo22 experience, notwithstanding their real-life intentions or opinions.

The Niilo22 'appreciation community' in the Ylilauta platform (at Ylilauta.org) is an interesting example of a thoroughly ironic community. It is not a traditional fan base, but rather a venue where Niilo22's fans both love and hate their hero. The participants create avatars with Niilo22's pictures and become Niilos themselves, even if they did not really want to be Niilo22 themselves but saw him as a mock or anti-hero. In a sense, Ylilauta may constitute a Bakhtinian counter-cultural space[309] where institutional orders are temporarily overturned

---

307 Claire Hardaker, 'I refuse to respond to this obvious troll. An overview of responses to (perceived) trollin', *Corpora* 10/2 (2015), 202.

308 Claire Hardaker, '"Uh.....not to be nitpicky,,,,,but...the past tense of drag is dragged, not drug.": An overview of trolling strategies', *Journal of Language Aggression and Conflict* 1/1 (2013), 80.

309 Mikhail Bakhtin, *Rabelais and his world*, Helene Iswolsky, trans. (Bloomington: Indiana University Press, [1965] 1984).

and mixed up with one another. Indeed, Ruth Page has recognized points of resonance between the Bakhtinian carnival and unruly social media spaces such as YouTube.[310] Perhaps Niilo22 is king of the carnival, a king of fools that allows his followers to feel emotions and ironic superiority at the same time. What is more, while carnivals with their upside-down worlds have been known to emancipate and challenge existing orders and authorities, carnivalistic practices can also operate as a spare valve for the power holders which eventually reinforces the existing boundaries – similar to how Durkheim described criminality to be the necessary flip side of social norms.[311] Who holds the upper hand in the constellations of Niilo22 remains unresolved.

Linda Hutcheon has stated that irony often has a cutting edge, and it is carnivalesque in the sense that it denies all certainties and creates ambiguity.[312] However, as Hutcheon recalls, it can also mock, attack, ridicule, embarrass and humiliate. Although Niilo22 is constantly ridiculed in the comments that he receives in his clips, it is hard to objectify him as a victim. While he may be uneducated, unemployed and lives an uneventful life, sharing his everyday life and thoughts that might not be especially clever or rhetorically brilliant, he has thousands of followers that help him benefit financially. The YouTuber can be interpreted as a jester figure who by his command of a technological platform and understanding of the social media environment becomes the mock hero whose humdrum life is turned into an immersive spectacle.

Telling and following as participatory immersion

In this section, we reframe our discussion on participatory immersion sociologically for a further research perspective. As regards communication, Niilo22 is a social media personality at the point of convergence for different communicative settings. He presents himself as a humoristic caricature figure with repetitive slogans and gestures who speaks a lot but says quite little. There are recurring repetitive loops of utterances in the talk, bearing zero information. The topics seem spontaneous and unstructured and, instead of having a message to deliver or a retrospective story to tell, the words uttered appear as an occasioned stream of mind outspoken to the viewer as the situation evolves from one moment to the

310 Page, *Narratives Online*, 179.

311 Emil Durkheim, *Suicide: A Study in Sociology* (London: Routledge and K. Paul, 1952).

312 Linda Hutcheon, *Irony's Edge. The Theory and Politics of Irony* (London and New York: Routledge, 1994).

next. For Niilo22, the reporting activity itself, having the YouTube channel open regularly, seems to be the primary goal of getting into contact with his audience. The primacy of the phatic function and the weak tellability of the accounts in the video clips does not, however, diminish the usability or the 'followability' of the channel, as is evident from the number of subscribers and commentary in the clips. The video material is regular and recurrent, which makes it easy to follow and view as habitual. Who, as a matter of fact, are involved in this communicative exchange? What kinds of recipients is Niilo22 talking to and who is responding back to him? How is the content of Niilo22 used and repurposed in the commentaries?

The communicative setting in the Niilo22 experience is intriguing because the time of the story and the time of the telling are partly intertwined, feeding into the ways his stories are evaluated in the commentaries. Niilo22 is storying the ongoing time of his unemployed everyday life through his video recordings. This material, the story told, includes the events unfolding on the screen (immediate time) and the verbalized descriptions of events Niilo22 is telling about his life (past time). All elements in the story about and by Niilo22 are embedded in the broader societal context that is thematized in the video, identifying him as an unemployed person. He is thus the protagonist of the story, the teller of the narrative and the carrier of a social category that affects the interpretations made about his story. This entanglement of different positions makes it challenging to inspect the communicative situation from the perspective of stable participation framework in storytelling.[313] The rough division into the teller and the recipients does not function in Niilo22's setting, even if the wording and ideas were differentiated from the utterances[314] or if the fine details of versatile recipient addresses were analysed.[315] The production format of Niilo22 video clips is infused in several ways, making it particularly appealing in terms of participatory immersion. To grasp this aspect of the Niilo22 experience, it is crucial to recognize the complexity reaching beyond the story being transmitted from one origin to its destination. Our tools to unravel this dynamic of participation come from narrative positioning analysis.[316]

313 Cf. Charles Goodwin, 'Notes on Story Structure and the Organization of Participation', in J. Maxwell Atkinson and John Heritage, eds., *Structures of Social Action: Studies in Conversation Analysis* (London: Cambridge University Press, 1984), 225–246.

314 Erving Goffman, *Forms of talk* (Philadelphia: University of Pennsylvania Press, 1981).

315 Goodwin, 'Notes'.

316 Bamberg, 'Positioning between Structure and Performance', 335–342.

As explained above from the narratological perspective, the three levels of participative positionings instantiated in the Niilo22 experience portray shifting movement across the levels of the story, the interaction and the broader societal categories in the way participant roles and identifications are produced. Adding to the communicative complexity, Niilo22 is often verbalizing in the video clips the feedback received from the users of the channel. Interactionally, perceiving the ongoing time that unfolds in the clips as a story locates the commentaries on them in the position of story evaluation.[317] Paradoxically, Niilo22's explicit references to the feedback make the recipients with their evaluations characters in the story whom Niilo22 is at times addressing directly in his talking to the camera. This two-way exchange unfolds in the channel often starts from an apparently coincidental remark by Niilo22, provoking feedback, which then ends up back in the clips as he comments on the commentaries and provides justification for his prior words.

The most prominent interpretive resource in the feedback seems to be the broader societal context of the ongoing time and talk content of the video clips, especially Niilo22's societal identification as an unemployed person. There is variation in the way he refers to the societal context and thematizes it in the clips, and the outlooks persist in the comments. In the negatively critical reading, Niilo22 is accused of acting improperly as a citizen of the welfare state, while others may positively celebrate him as a hilarious and unique caricature embodying unemployment in the landscape of social media. As a result, the category of an unemployed person does not mean that Niilo22's role would be fixed and settled. Quite the contrary, as a social media celebrity Niilo22 exhibits carnivalistic qualities that challenge given ideas about a long-term unemployed person – exposing him to negative attention and provocative comments. Commentators may also team up with one another and nurture ties that bind followers together through references to Niilo22's catchphrases and imitating his use of words. The rich variety in the feedback gives evidence that engaging in the Niilo22 experience takes many different forms and the video channel can be deployed for multiple purposes. The charm of taking part in the channel is rooted in the strong affective and attitudinal reactions the video material arouses, particularly in the opportunity to take action, take a stance and bounce the messages back into the storytelling via feedback channels to create the immersive Niilo22 experience.

---

317 William Labov and Joshua Waletzky, 'Narrative analysis: Oral versions of personal experience', *Journal of Narrative and Life History* 7/1 (1997), 3–38.

Key scenes: 'Weather' and 'Sleep'

We analyse the audio-visual content and verbal commentaries in two video clips originally produced in Finnish: 'Mikä Ilma Ja Kotiin Menossa'['What Weather And Going Home'] from now on shortened to 'Weather',[318] and 'Ei oikee kiinosta mennä vielä nukkuu' ['Don't feel like going to sleep'] from now on shortened to 'Sleep'.[319] In 'Weather', clocking in at 23 min and shot in real time, Niilo22 is first seen at the grocery store, playing slots and buying a soda, before walking back home while it is windy and snowing. The weather aside, the topical point of his discourse concerns the Finnish presidential election. In 'Sleep', at 9 min and shot in non-real-time, Niilo22 is sitting in his kitchen, talking to the camera late in the evening with his topics ranging from television shows to his recent business with the Social Security office and his amazement in learning that liver casserole is actually a meat product. We apply narratological analysis and sociological positioning theory to study how active participation in the social media environment with specific technological features produces the immersive Niilo22 experience. The interaction may come across as either explicitly affectively charged or less obviously so because of an ironic attitude on the part of Niilo22's followers, moving from just involving the social media personality to risking collective judgment on individuals like him.

Firstly, as regards the individual, one might think the often hostile responses Niilo22 is subjected to create affective interaction in which his followers hold the upper hand, but analysing the clips in terms media technological agency can tell a different story. While the audience's narrativization of the YouTuber's story may miss its ground in the storyteller's personal world, and be shaped by their own normative expectations, it can be argued the persistent him–them setup produces the Niilo22 experience. This setup does neither primarily concern who Niilo22 (or Mikael Kosola) is or what he thinks, nor is it about the true thoughts and feelings of the followers – first and foremost, the Niilo22 experience is about negotiating understandings of the roles assumed by the protagonist and his antagonists to generate mutual immersion. Each party has their own part to play in the layering. Indeed, it is Niilo22 who runs the YouTube show by controlling

318 Niilo22, 'Mikä Ilma Ja Kotiin Menossa' ['What Weather And Going Home'], *YouTube* (24 January 2018), <https://www.youtube.com/watch?v=H6qKb7eg47c>, accessed 27 April 2021.

319 Niilo22, 'Ei oikeen kiinosta vielä mennä nukkuu' ['Don't feel like going to sleep'], *YouTube* (8 October 2018), <https://www.youtube.com/watch?v=YApgeoA9rIM>, accessed 27 April 2021.

the technological platform at his disposal, as becomes evident in the key scenes, while users bear their participatory weight through responsive commenting. The various media involved – including the technological platform and storytelling as a medium of expression – operate in specific ways to devise the structure of the interactional situation within which a myriad of discursive roles and positions is possible.

Secondly, the individual dimension turns into something collective through the content on display and under discussion in the video clips. Whereas Niilo22's everyday activities from making coffee to commenting on the weather and enthusing about video games can be uncontroversial and relatable in a way that rarely bothers his followers, any talk that edges towards ideas and opinions on the life of the unemployed freeloader is liable to spark response on a level in which Niilo22 only serves as a cautionary example of a broader malaise. The question is how does this shift from the followers reacting to Niilo22's individual tomfoolery to the collective judgment of societal spite appear in the interaction that takes place? How is participatory immersion in the Niilo22 experience sustained, or potentially disrupted, in the storytelling that moves between the dimensions, and where can the line between them be drawn? In analysing the key scenes, an important aspect will be to observe the themes that most forcefully provoke response while they also demand identification with the him–them setup. The rules and roles of the Niilo22 experience are recognized and sustained but, at the same time, storytelling as discussion on societal themes has the potential to disrupt the familiar dynamic as followers dispute, through imitative commenting and use of catchphrases, if their own positions are all that different from Niilo22.

In the key scenes, as regards the individual, Niilo22's level of control is evident in different ways in his real-time and non-real-time clips. In 'Weather', shot in real time using the now discontinued Periscope application, there is a moment when he receives a comment whose content he will not share with the audience at all but instead deletes it immediately with the spoken remarks 'should I ban it' and 'delete it away'. Similar instances occur elsewhere in the video, highlighting Niilo22's constant level of individual control. Towards the end of the clip, there is a telling lapse from this routine when he speaks aloud the comment 'Ski to work' he sees on his mobile screen and responds to it off the side of his mouth with 'you too, let's see you ski there too'. It is only after this point that he deletes the comment, having first made it public to his collective followers, demonstrating the kind of care he must take when curating the technological platform in real time. Of course, while Niilo22 can moderate the comments section after the recording in real time has ended, the behaviour of the 'shot-Niilo' shown in the clip in contrast to the 'shooting-Niilo' who may do anything he likes with the material during or after the shooting session is striking in the scene. The real-time curating requires attention but, in contrast to non-real-time commenting whose content the 'shot-Niilo' may not be instantly able to moderate, the 'shooting-Niilo' can potentially control his materials. In real time, Niilo22 doubles in the role of an object and subject of the storytelling, actively resorting to ways of balancing between the individual and collective dimensions of the ongoing experience.

In non-real-time clips such as 'Sleep', Niilo22 is not concerned with comments he might be receiving while talking on the spot, and instead, he focuses on addressing the theme of the clip. In disregarding the chat that might be happening at the same time on the social media platform, Niilo22 surrenders some of his technological level of control. His performance thus appears, in terms of the authenticity of the individual dimension, more vulnerable and exposed to hostile commenting. In the process, however, the Niilo22 experience may be reinforced as the followers are led to believe they are taking the upper hand and letting him have it. At the start of 'Sleep', Niilo22 enthuses over a *Walking Dead* episode in which a man who has been hurting other people gets himself hanged in the end by a 'hanging lady'. Without much spoiler alert, Niilo22 describes the show as excellent and seems to find satisfaction in the justice meted out to the villain, with a sense of moral superiority.

However, Niilo22's appreciation as an individual fan of the television show is soon reversed. After praising the episode, he goes on to elaborate on what has been happening between him and the Social Security office – he has not been receiving his welfare in time. In promising to make some people hurt for this oversight, a mirroring structure is created between the *mise en abyme* of the TV show and a personal grievance. Whereas Niilo22 seems to remain unaware of the analogy, his followers recognize it and turn the tables on him, accusing him collectively of violations against society. In due process, the storytelling in 'Sleep' consists of a layering of narrative positionings that includes both the voices used by Niilo22 and the *Walking Dead* references made by him.

Niilo22's interpretation of the show's ending with the hanging lady getting to hang the villain is that the lesson demonstrates how provocative behaviour with falsely high self-esteem leads to downfall: 'that story really taught you that this is what happens when you start to talk big'. As he then concentrates on making coffee, talking about his own life and what he plans to do the following day, he says he has to use his own money to call the Social Security office and continues that he will be forced to use swear words to make the people in the Social Security office understand. Then Niilo22 tells the viewers the unidentified officials must understand and make the payments, and he insists emphatically, looking straight at the camera, that the payments are late. A bit later he expresses a violent urge against the person who has reported him to the Social Security officials – apparently because he has been gaining income from YouTube activities while still collecting welfare. In this story, Niilo22 positions himself in the story level (1) as a victim of both the Social Security office who do not understand and the person who had reported his activities to them. In the projected future story (level 1), he corrects the wrongdoings by making the Social Security office see things his way while fantasizing about physical violence against the person who reported on him. All this is carried out in the interaction (level 2) with emphasized eye contact with the camera and some fatherly shaking of a fist as if to admonish a child, inviting the assumed viewers to see his point of view too and provoke a reaction.

The non-real-time viewers' comments in 'Sleep' reveal a gap in the interpretation (level 2) of the stories (level 1) Niilo22 has offered. Whereas the story in the fictional TV series (level 1) is presented (on level 2) as having ended and exposing a clear lesson (level 3), the story Niilo22 is uncovering about his own situation with the Social Security office unfolds in a reversed order, starting with Niilo22's current frustration and need (on level 2) to convince the officials of his view of his situation and if needed, even to use force in achieving this (level 1). The story events that have led to the current situation are mostly only implied, and the YouTube audience participates in constructing the sequence. At an early stage, a commentator nicknamed Rempseä heinämies ['Rowdy hick'] brings out the similarities between the stories (level 1) of Niilo22 and *Walking Dead*: 'When are you right there going to stop talking big to the viewers, Social Security office and whole society? Did you happen to get what's coming to you, therebirdinthesnow?'. This comment engages in interaction with Niilo22 (on level 2) with the ironic repetition of the same words he had used about the story in the TV show (level 1): Niilo22's phrase 'talk big' uses Niilo22's voice in his comments on the TV series to instead comment on what Niilo22 claims he will do the next day. What is more, the partly nonsensical 'therebirdinthesnow' ['sillälintulumen' in the original Finnish] imitates the way Niilo22 talks in general. In this way, the commentator in the interaction (level 2) draws a parallel between what Niilo22 had interpreted as talking big and then getting the deserved punishment with what he had just revealed about his own situation (level 1) without the same normative conclusion (level 3). The comment makes evident the similarities between Niilo22's behaviour and his interpretation of the TV show, suggesting that the lesson to be drawn on positioning level 3 based on social norms should be the same for Niilo22 as it is in his interpretation of the TV show: he is talking big and should receive his punishment.

A follower named Eero engages in the forming of the story too: 'Wonder how it is. Is it enough for the Social Security office if you say that "building houses is only my hobby, not my job! I get some money but not enough. So you owe me my unemployment and housing payment." Seems to work for this Niilo…'. Using the voice of a hypothetical construction worker – Niilo22 is not one – Eero creates a parallel between what Niilo22 is allegedly trying to tell the Social Security office: that his online activities are only a hobby, and he is qualified to receive unemployment benefits in spite of his activities in YouTube that bring him income. By partially imitating what Niilo22 claims about the Social Security office, in the hypothetical voice of an individual, Eero enlivens the backstory (level 1) to question Niilo22's reasons and sincerity in the interaction (level 2), as well as his interpretation of his situation as regards the collective dimension of social norms and regulations (level 3).

In 'Sleep', there are followers whose participatory immersion in the Niilo22 experience both sustains and disrupts the familiar him–them setup, as they imitate Niilo22's catchphrases in the non-real-time comments section and some of them also identify with Niilo22 visually by an image of his as their profile picture. On the one hand, as regards affectively interacting with the individual, such use of avatars signals sustained immersion in the Niilo22 experience as the followers identify with the storytelling for a sense of shared appreciation also when the usual roles begin to mix and merge with one another. On the other hand, as the interaction transitions to the collective level, Niilo22 appears to remain unaware of the analogy between himself and the scene with the hanging lady of the TV show in his response to the incident with the Social Security office. Mutual immersion in the Niilo22 experience is 'spoiled' to the degree of the followers being more aware of the ongoings than the protagonist.

In the real-time clip 'Weather', the transitioning between the individual and collective happens in a more controlled and conscious way, with Niilo22 curating the technological platform in real time, as indicated above. After leaving the grocery store, Niilo22 is walking home in the snow when he reads out a question from the comments section asking if he has voted. He replies no and repeats twice that he does not tend to vote. The video changes subject for a couple of minutes, after which there is a short pause during which he probably reads a question from a viewer, and he returns to the topic. Niilo22 explains why he does not vote by saying that nobody is really in line with his thinking and all representatives have been turncoats. Commenting on politics further, Niilo22 uses several voices to attribute the actions of others and build up to his own argument and conclusion. He talks about the previous presidential election in 2012 and candidate Sauli Niinistö who went on to win the election:

> And Sauli was so shameless in what he said that they have, if he gets to be president, that he has this workgroup who'll look after unemployed benefits so that the unemployed can get work, and that was total bullshit.
>
> There's been no workgroup, in the media or anywhere else, that there was a group like that, that was looking after the unemployed, it doesn't exist. And I was pissed off how he just said that, just does it like that, says it out aloud with emotion. Does it with emotion and gets you convinced, convinces people that he's a good guy with a good agenda, and bullshit he had nothing, just jerks people around, that's how I see it. I remember it clearly when he said it. (Our translation).[320]

Niilo22 starts with attributing Niinistö as a deliberately unscrupulous person, taking the position of an omniscient narrator who is able to directly name the intention (shameless with the intention to deceive) of another person. In Cohn's model of consciousness representation,[321] this would be psychonarration, in which the narrator relates a character's stance not consciously known to the character themselves.[322] In Niilo22's case, the portrayed intention of Niinistö to boldly and knowingly be deceptive would most likely be disclaimed by Niinistö, had he a chance to comment. This attribution of an intention, positioning Niinistö on the story level (1) as a crooked politician, is followed at the end of the same line by Niilo22's positioning on the level of interaction (2), telling the audience that Niilo22 finds the promise given to be 'bullshit'. The positioning on the story level of Niinistö as crooked and on the discourse level of Niilo22 realizing the deception reinforces Niilo22's knowledge and authority in real time.

This positioning of Niilo22 as an authoritative teller is reinforced by forging the alleged words by Niinistö himself in the middle of the line after the 'he said', in the form of free indirect discourse, mixing the voices of Niilo22 with the words attributed to Niinistö.[323] In this free indirect discourse, Niilo22 produces a semblance of what he claims Niinistö said, and only the personal nouns are changed from the 'I' of Niinistö to the 'him' of Niilo22, with accompanying changes in verb forms ('if he gets to be president, that he has this workgroup' implies *if *I get* to be president, that *I have* this workgroup*). Using this form, Niilo22 can forcefully argue, almost straight from the horse's mouth, what Niinistö promised to do if elected president: to have a committee to look after the unemployed and see that they get work. By giving this approximation of Niinistö's promise at the

---

320 Niilo22, 'Mikä Ilma Ja Kotiin Menossa' ['What Weather And Going Home'].

321 Cohn, *Transparent Minds*.

322 Alan Palmer, 'Thought and Consciousness Representation (Literature)'.

323 cf. Hatavara and Mildorf, 'Fictionality, 391–408.

time it was made in the storyworld (level 1 positioning) and evaluating it at the online storytelling moment (level 2) Niilo22 emphasizes both the unscrupulousness of Niinistö in the story and his own ability to see through the deception and uncover it in the storytelling interaction.

Niilo22 then moves between the voices and subject positions of Niinistö, the people and himself. The group is described as Niinistö had described it on the story level, portrayed as looking after the unemployed, but Niilo22 knows that such a group was never founded. Using first the perfect and then the present tense at the beginning of the second paragraph, Niilo22 brings together the telling and the told by stating the group has not been there and then draws a conclusion at the time of the telling that no such group exists. With high emotion, Niilo22 tells how upset and annoyed he is because Niinistö had made such an empty promise. What makes him particularly annoyed is that he saw Niinistö doing it 'with emotion' which had resulted in people believing in him. What the people were led to believe is again expressed in their voice – Niinistö's 'a good guy with a good agenda.' This exhibits two minds portrayed on the story level (1), that of Niinistö and that of the people who believed him. This belief of the people is starkly contrasted with Niilo22 in his own voice telling at the time of the interaction (level 2) that Niinistö had no such group formed and was only conning people with his promise. Within these couple of sentences, Niilo22 moves between immersing in his former self in the past (level 1) as part of the group of people who believed Niinistö because of his false emotion and his storytelling self in the present (level 2) reflecting on the experience of having been deceived. Niilo22 restores his identity (level 3 on positioning) by drawing the lesson (on level 2) to never be involved in politics again, not at least in the form of voting. In this short period of communicating, Niilo22 uses several conflicting voices, including a known politician and the people as a collective to introduce several positions and draw a lesson to be learned.

The final effect in the dialogue is created between Niilo22, Niinistö and the people who believed in Niinistö. Niilo22 gives strong epistemic support to his claim at the moment of telling (level 2) stating how he remembers Niinistö's speech that included the promise very well – 'I remember it clearly when he said it' – bringing together the moment of telling, when the remembering happens (level 2), and the moment of the told where Niinistö had made the promise (level 1). After this reassurance, Niilo22 emphasizes the importance of the moment and his apparent resentment by spitting on the ground. After this Niilo22 proceeds to the more general lesson of his story and concludes that what he has told is just an example of how turncoats like Niinistö tend to act and how everybody in Finland deceives everyone else regularly. In this way, Niilo22 has exposed a prevailing social practice and positioned himself morally on a higher ground (level 3). From the viewer's point of view, it is noteworthy that a contradiction in content can be detected. Even though Niilo22 says he has not been following politics, a little later he says he has not seen the group Sauli Niinistö promised to establish anywhere, or he would have noticed that such a group existed, making a stand for himself. In 'Weather', the real-time environment of the video clip makes the role of the followers small in comparison to 'Sleep', but the layering of narrative voices and positionings in Niilo22's commenting on the presidential election transitions from presenting an individual annoyance to expressing a collective political grievance, generating participatory immersion in the Niilo22 experience.

Conclusion

We have observed Niilo22 as a new kind of experience in social media that distinctly draws on the medium-specific qualities and technological features of the YouTube environment for storytelling purposes. The phenomenon involves users who assume different roles and positions in an ongoing and dynamic process of online storytelling, and we have analysed scenes of this interaction as participatory immersion in the Niilo22 experience. We have studied the difference in the level of control in curating real-time and non-real-time clips on YouTube, the impact of the layering of narrative voices and positionings in generating immersion, and how social media users participate and interact in the telling and following of the Niilo22 experience including the audio-visual content of the video clips and their verbal commentaries. We have demonstrated how transitions between the individual and collective are vital to the immersive appeal of the Niilo22 experience.

Niilo22 is not only a fascinating social media text and a narratively complex storyworld to explore, since it involves an actual human being living his everyday life embedded in real societal frameworks. The multifaceted embeddedness of layers and transitions between them should thus be treated with a degree of caution and negotiation on the dangers of narrativity. As Bakhtinian carnivalism can be hilarious and entertaining, getting swept away by participatory immersion in the Niilo22 experience is a potential risk whose gravity we have studied with both sociological and narratological tools.

Firstly, from the sociological perspective, the field of textual representation (characters on the level of the story) and the field of situated exchange (individuals on the level of interaction) are accompanied by the field of social co-existence (cultural orders and categories on the level of the broader societal framework).

The danger is that the laughter may stop from being harmless fun here and now, with Niilo22's followers reacting to his individual tomfoolery. As the interaction shifts towards the collective judgment of societal spite, the laughter risks being indelibly rooted in social hierarchies, cultural stereotypes and inequalities related to unemployment in today's society. The risk becomes especially hefty on the individual scale when the one laughed at may not be aware of it – as in the Walking Dead analogy ('Sleep') that we have analysed. At other times, when the king of the carnival is in control, as in banning his users and deleting their comments in real time ('Weather'), the state of danger can be lifted, even if the potential for equal interaction is diminished as Niilo22 assumes the position of the authoritative teller. Our case study displays how YouTube as a technological platform and storytelling as a medium of expression operate in specific ways to devise the structure of the interactional situation within which a myriad of discursive roles and positions is possible, and which may influence different views on societal issues such as unemployment.

Secondly, in the narratological perspective, the danger is evoked by using fictionalizing narrative modes that may turn real-world people into stereotypes in the online storyworld. In these modes, vicarious experience and the minds of others are attributed in the storytelling action. Participants in the ongoing interaction may also often seem more occupied by playing with and ironically mimicking what the YouTuber is showing and telling rather than exhibiting an affectively charged stance towards the issues addressed. In such a communicative setting of spontaneous response, Niilo22 as the primary teller and storysharer uses vicarious voices and stories instrumentally for his argument only, turning real people into characters in his stories. Subsequently, as the levels of story and interaction are flattened together, the level of commenting and sharing comes to dominate the dimension of the individual, and the comments produce a vicarious alternative to Niilo22's experience imitating his voice and style. The danger, then, is that provocation matters more than collectively dealing with societal issues. In this kind of participatory immersion, the telling of the story and having a laugh with or at Niilo22 forgoes the complexity of the multi-layered and societally sensitive communicative setting, whereas, in another kind of less antagonistic immersion, the Niilo22 experience can promote and reward participation in online storytelling in the social media environment.

Part III: Repositioning the Novel

Sarah Copland

6. 'It […] cannot do any harm to anyone whatsoever': Fictionality, Invention and Knowledge Creation in Global Nonfictions, Joseph Conrad's Prefaces and *Chance*

Abstract: *Chance* explores the intersection of two of novelist Joseph Conrad's life-long fascinations: fictional representations of nonfictional conversational storytelling and the relationship between truth, credibility and invention. The latter is also apparent throughout Conrad's prefaces, in which he works through long-held anxieties about the truthfulness and credibility of his representations and about critics' concerns on these fronts. To reconcile the relationship between invention and truth or credibility, he describes a process of constructing, via invention, fundamentally truthful and credible stories about real-world events and figures. In *Chance*, Conrad depicts a character narrator, Marlow, doing the same thing. There are, however, two salient differences between Marlow's and Conrad's undertakings: one is their distance from the events and figures they are telling about and telling to (Conrad very distant from them vs. Marlow literally living amidst them), and the other is the genre claims they make for their narratives (Conrad's literary fictions vs. Marlow's conversational nonfictions). Conrad depicts Marlow using invention (through fictionality and otherwise) to supplement the limitations of his knowledge about other people, their motivations and their relationships, so that he can narrate a credible and compelling nonfictional conversational tale for his narratee. But because Marlow lives amidst and communicates with the subjects of his tale and presents his communications as nonfictional, the knowledge he creates through invention is consequential for his own and others' involvement in the unfolding action. Failure to signal must have beens and hypotheticals as invention contributes to significant outcomes for the people with whom Marlow communicates in the told. Conrad thus qualifies his portrait of the affordances of invention for knowledge creation in global nonfictions with a cautionary note related to narrating situations like Marlow's: telling nonfictional conversational stories about and to our acquaintances.

Keywords: fictionality, invention, knowledge creation, truth, credibility, signaling, nonfictional conversational storytelling

Fictionality theory has been remarkably generative in the past decade or so, its decoupling of fictionality from generic fiction constituting a watershed moment in rhetorical theory and narrative theory.[324] Specifically, reconceiving fictionality as 'a rhetorical resource available within communicative contexts of all sorts' means that the distinction between fictionality and factuality can be 'detached from, and [cut] across, any generic distinction between fiction and non-fiction'.[325] Consequently, generic classifications cease to be ontological distinctions and instead serve as indicators of 'which of these two modes is rhetorically dominant in the global communicative act'.[326] Among other interventions, the shift from an ontological to a rhetorical- or communication-based conception of fictionality enabled scholars to account for the presence and role of fictional discourse in global nonfictions and for the presence and role of nonfictional discourse in global fictions.[327]

In this chapter, working with fictionality as 'intentionally signalled, communicated invention',[328] I focus on the relationship between fictionality and invention. In doing so, I explore the potential and affordances of fictionality and the limitations and dangers of shifts among fictionality, ambiguously signalled communicated invention, and unsignalled communicated invention as forms of knowledge creation in global nonfictions. While fictionality can, of course, take many forms, I am interested in standard examples, such as what-if projections, thought experiments, hypotheses, hypotheticals, counterfactuals, speculations

---

324 See Richard Walsh, *The Rhetoric of Fictionality* (Columbus: Ohio State University Press, 2007) for the first formulation of fictionality theory; Henrik Skov Nielsen, James Phelan and Richard Walsh, 'Ten Theses about Fictionality', *Narrative* 23/1 (2015), 61–73 for its elaboration and refinement; and Cindie Aaen Maagaard, Daniel Schäbler and Marianne Wolff Lundholt, eds., *Exploring Fictionality: Conceptions, Test Cases, Discussions* (Odense: University Press of Southern Denmark, 2020) for a representative sample of leading theorists' recent work.

325 Richard Walsh, 'Exploring Fictionality: Afterword', in *Exploring Fictionality: Conceptions, Test Cases, Discussions*, 213–238, 214.

326 Walsh, 'Exploring Fictionality', 214.

327 For the latter, since nonfictional discourse in global fictions has received less attention in fictionality studies, see James Phelan, 'Local Nonfictionality within Generic Fiction: Huntington's Disease in McEwan's *Saturday* and Genova's *Inside the O'Briens*', in Zara Dinnen and Robyn Warhol, eds., *The Edinburgh Companion to Contemporary Narrative Theories* (Edinburgh: Edinburgh University Press, 2018), 362–374.

328 Simona Zetterberg Gjerlevsen and Henrik Skov Nielsen, 'Distinguishing Fictionality', in Cindie Aaen Maagaard, Daniel Schäbler and Marianne Wolff Lundholt, eds., *Exploring Fictionality: Conceptions, Test Cases, Discussions* (Odense: University Press of Southern Denmark, 2020), 19–40, 23.

and other deviations from the actual within a globally nonfictional discourse.[329] While it would be fruitful to examine such examples of fictionality, and their potential for knowledge creation, in straightforwardly nonfictional discourses like legal testimony, medical narratives, memoirs or biographies, I turn, paradoxically, back to literary fiction and its paratexts: specifically to modernist writer Joseph Conrad's novel *Chance*[330] and his prefaces to the collected edition of his works.[331] In the prefaces, which offer globally nonfictional accounts of the genesis, composition and reception of his works, Conrad uses fictionality to create knowledge and theorizes invention as central to creating verisimilitude in fictional storytelling that is at times based on nonfictional events and people. *Chance*, like *Heart of Darkness*, *Lord Jim* and 'Youth', offers a fictional representation of nonfictional conversational storytelling. These texts depict an unnamed frame narrator recounting an oral tale that he heard from character narrator Charles Marlow, with most of the frame narrator's narration given over to direct quotation of Marlow's telling; the tale is nonfictional from the point of view of Marlow and the unnamed frame narrator because the incidents recounted really happened to Marlow and his acquaintances. In *Chance*, Marlow uses fictionality, ambiguously signalled communicated invention, and unsignalled communicated invention to create knowledge (specifically knowledge about human psychology, relationships and their attendant affective and ethical entanglements), making invention central to his storytelling about ostensibly nonfictional events and people. As I will demonstrate, Conrad's and Marlow's uses of invention in their ostensibly nonfictional storytelling have very different consequences based on three variables: the extent to which their fictionality shifts into ambiguously signalled or unsignalled communicated invention; their distances from the events they are referring to and figures they are communicating with; and the genre claims they make for their stories.

Working with Conrad's prefaces and *Chance* to explore the relationship between fictionality and invention, and the potential and dangers of invention as a form of knowledge creation in global nonfictions, I also contribute to two long-standing debates in Conrad scholarship: one on Conrad's anxieties about the credibility and plausibility of his representations, and the other on the

329 Nielsen, Phelan and Walsh, 'Ten Theses about Fictionality', 62, 64.

330 Joseph Conrad, *Chance* (Oxford: Oxford University Press, 2002). Published in serial form starting in 1912 and in book form in 1913 (UK) and 1914 (US).

331 Joseph Conrad, *Conrad's Prefaces to His Works* (London: J. M. Dent & Sons, 1937). Published 1917–1920.

relationship between Conrad and Marlow. I tackle the former in the next section, and the latter towards the end of the chapter, where I take a rhetorical narrative theory-informed approach to character narration in *Chance*, drawing in particular on James Phelan's ideas about character narration as an art of indirection,[332] in order to distinguish Conrad's communication with his audience from Marlow's communication with his narratee. This distinction is essential to recognizing Conrad's use of Marlow's fictionality-rich narration to explore the limitations and dangers of shifts between fictionality and other forms of communicated invention in globally nonfictional conversational storytelling. In turn, distinguishing Conrad's communication from Marlow's communication enables us to ascertain the degree of what Phelan's rhetorical approach calls the interpretive, affective and ethical alignment between author and character narrator, in this case, Conrad and Marlow, vis-à-vis the storyworld's action and character-character relationships.

Fictionality as knowledge creation and invention, truth and credibility in Conrad's prefaces

Paratexts such as prefaces have played a central role in fictionality theory's development. By bringing together Conrad's prefaces and fiction, I supplement fictionality theory's current focus on paratexts' employment of fictionality to signal the accompanying texts' global status.[333] First, I analyse examples of intentionally signalled, communicated invention in the prefaces, demonstrating how Conrad

332 See James Phelan, *Living to Tell about It: A Rhetoric and Ethics of Character Narration* (Columbus: Ohio State University Press, 2005).

333 Walsh regards paratexts as the sole determinants of a text's rhetorical dominant (in part because he opposes the idea of text-internal signals); though they embrace the possibility of text-internal signals, Gjerlevsen and Nielsen also regard the paratext as an important potential site for signaling fictionality. Louise Brix Jacobsen's taxonomy of text-paratext relations accommodates not only paratexts featuring local fictionality within a rhetorically dominant factuality (or vice versa) and paratexts in which some elements of the paratextual communication are fictive (or non-fictive) but others are not – which Genette's foundational, binary fictive/non-fictive model cannot accommodate – but also blurry cases that concurrently invoke fictive and non-fictive rhetorics to prevent readers from determining a dominant rhetoric. Such paratexts often accompany texts that are themselves undecidable. See Louise Brix Jacobsen, 'Paratext', in Lasse Gammelgaard, Stefan Iversen, Louise Brix Jacobsen, James Phelan, Richard Walsh, Henrik Zetterberg-Nielsen and Simona Zetterberg-Nielsen, eds., *Fictionality and Literature: Core Concepts Revisited* (Columbus: Ohio State University Press, 2022).

uses them to create and communicate knowledge in a globally nonfictional discourse. Then, I situate these uses of fictionality in Conrad's broader theorization of invention, focusing on his investment in truth and his claims about invention as the means by which he makes the truth credible, even in fiction based on real people and events.

Although chapter seven of Walsh's seminal work *The Rhetoric of Fictionality* (2007) deals with both fictionality and prefaces and examines authors' conceits – often taken from their prefaces – about the discursive and representational authorities that underwrite their narrative creativity, in order to theorize an account of creativity rooted not in mimesis, verisimilitude or correspondence but in 'narrative rightness', Walsh never treats these conceits as examples of fictionality. I, on the other hand, do regard them as examples of fictionality, congruent with both leading definitions of fictionality, Walsh's own ('utterances functioning independent of directly informative relevance') and Gjerlevsen's and Nielsen's ('intentionally signaled, communicated invention'). To take one of the examples Walsh cites, there is, of course, no directly informative relevance to Walter Scott's description, in his prefaces to the Waverley novels, of a demon who 'seats himself on the feather of [his] pen when [he] begin[s] to write, and leads it astray from the purpose'.[334] Surely this is an utterance 'functioning independent of directly informative relevance' and an 'intentionally signaled, communicated invention': Scott uses fictionality to articulate the way the writing process derails his original intentions and takes him into unforeseen creative territory. (Even here I find myself using, for the rhetorical purpose of making my argument, the metaphors of redirected creative intentions as train derailment and literary subject matter as geographical terrain.)[335]

My attention to Conrad's use of fictionality as a rhetorical strategy in his prefaces, however, extends far beyond the conceits writers routinely use to describe their inspiration and composition practices in prefaces, media interviews and other paratexts.[336] In addition to such figures, Conrad uses fictionality to refer to

334 Walsh, *The Rhetoric of Fictionality*, 135.

335 I am struck by the omission of Conrad's prefaces from Walsh's case studies, but, as I demonstrate, Conrad's account of creativity *is* – unlike Walsh's other case studies – based on mimesis or verisimilitude *and* makes frequent use of fictionality.

336 Such figures are pervasive in Conrad's prefaces, especially seafaring metaphors for writing. While many figures have a nautical basis, others take on the themes of the non-seafaring works to which they refer, such as the metaphor for the chemical reaction of creative ingredients for *The Secret Agent*, a novel about a plot to blow up the Greenwich Observatory (Conrad, *Conrad's Prefaces to His Works*, 108).

the sources of his characters and the tales in general, and, as I will demonstrate, these examples of fictionality are key elements in his broader theorization of invention's relationship to truth and credibility.

Discussions of sources are common in retrospective prefaces for a collected edition of an author's works, and they are especially apparent in Conrad's prefaces because his critics (then and now) are preoccupied by the question of his sources, especially the idea that his personal experiences and familial and cultural backgrounds might account for his works' subjects and themes.[337] Knowing the expectations of the genre and his critics' preoccupation, Conrad responds directly in his prefaces, sometimes via factual discourse, refuting critics' assumptions or responding to their commentary, but often via the rhetorical resource of fictionality. He refers to some characters as though he interacted with them in the real world or as though they crossed an invisible boundary between the real world and the world of fiction. Lord Jim 'pass[es] by' '[o]ne sunny morning in the commonplace surroundings of an eastern roadstead',[338] and the man who inspired *Victory*'s Axel Hurst drifts out of Conrad's life and into the tale.[339] Conrad refers to his fictional characters' lives beyond the timeframe depicted in his works, reporting on what the characters from *Nostromo*, for example, are doing now.[340] For the sources of his tales in general, Conrad typically includes publicly available texts and private correspondence or conversation, along with real-world people he met or read about, but such discussions often also employ fictionality: he includes fictional character Don José Avellanos's book *History of Fifty Years of Misrule* as one of his sources for *Nostromo*.[341]

It is, of course, only possible to ascertain the communicative purpose (and informative relevance) of these statements in relation to Conrad's sources and creative process if we regard them as examples of fictionality. No scholar would, for example, upon reading that Avellanos's book was a source for *Nostromo*, undertake an archival search for it. Likewise, no scholar would, upon reading that

337 Conrad responded in his prefaces to critics' preoccupation with tracing the sources of his work in his personal history, but this preoccupation continues even in subsequent scholarship. For the most salient example from Conrad's lifetime, see H. L. Mencken, 'Joseph Conrad', in *A Book of Prefaces* (Garden City: Garden City Publishing Company, 1917), 11–64. For a more recent and comprehensive approach, see Thomas C. Moser, 'Conrad, Ford, and the Sources of *Chance*', *Conradiana* 7/3 (1976), 207–224.

338 Conrad, *Conrad's Prefaces to His Works*, 67.

339 Conrad, *Conrad's Prefaces to His Works*, 163.

340 Conrad, *Conrad's Prefaces to His Works*, 89–93.

341 Conrad, *Conrad's Prefaces to His Works*, 88.

Conrad escaped his first love (upon whom *Nostromo*'s Antonia was modelled) by making a trip to the fictional Sulaco,[342] search archival records for proof of Conrad's travel there. As a rhetorical resource, then, fictionality allows Conrad to adhere to the conventions of the genre and respond to his critics, disclosing information about his sources, while also communicating the limits of his knowledge on this front and gently satirizing the expectation that he know and share everything about his creative process.[343]

Notably, Conrad's use of invention-based fictionality to create knowledge, and to signal the limits of his knowledge, is part of his broader theorization of invention's centrality to truthful, credible representation in fiction based on real people and events. As I have demonstrated, Conrad's defense of the truthfulness of his representations most often centres on sharing – directly or through fictionality – the sources or inspirations for his works' characters and/or incidents, but he typically turns his defense of the factuality or actuality of his representations into a defense of their credibility: that his characters and plots possess the appearance or impression of truth.[344] Perhaps paradoxically, considering his

---

342 Conrad, *Conrad's Prefaces to His Works*, 92.

343 I concur with Vivienne Rundle's assessment that '[b]y blurring the distinctions between real and historical characters (and between biographical and implied author), Conrad undermines the boundaries separating fiction from fact, story from history' (Vivienne Rundle, 'Defining Frames: The Prefaces of Henry James and Joseph Conrad', *Henry James Review* 16/1 (1995), 66–92, 80), but I depart from her ontological conception of the distinction between fact and fiction. See also Anita Starosta's similarly ontological conception, that '[t]he Notes are not of the "real" world but belong, rather, to the fictions' (Anita Starosta, 'Conrad's "Author's Notes": Between Text and Reader', *Yearbook of Conrad Studies* 3 (2007), 31–40, 33).

344 He is clearly concerned about criticism of the credibility of his representations. He mentions, for example, some critics' response to *Lord Jim*'s 'narrative form', which they said was 'not […] very credible' because 'no man could have been expected to talk all that time, and other men to listen so long' (Conrad, *Conrad's Prefaces to His Works*, 65). He refers gratefully to critics who have found his representations believable, such as the critic who praised Vladimir in *The Secret Agent* for being '"not only possible in detail but quite right in essentials"', the French critics who maintained that he captured 'the spirit of the whole epoch' in 'The Duel', and the Russian critics who praised his 'clearness of […] vision and the correctness of […] [his] judgment' in his representation of Russian affairs in *Under Western Eyes* (Conrad, *Conrad's Prefaces to His Works*, 110, 119, 123). As early as 1917, Mencken noted Conrad's efforts to create credibility: 'he is wholly convincing: that the men and women he sets into his scene show ineluctably vivid and persuasive personality; that the theories he brings forward to account for their acts are intelligible; that the effects of those acts, upon actors and

insistence on the truth of his tales and his equation of truth with credibility, Conrad makes it clear that *invention* is what enables him to make truth credible. He admits that he changed the fates of characters based on real-world people (such as Lena in *Victory*, modeled on a girl in a French café),[345] applied the fate of one ship to another,[346] 'fastened onto [...] [one character] many words heard on other men's lips' (such as Axel Heyst in *Victory*),[347] and in general represented 'experience pushed a little [...] beyond the actual facts of the case for the perfectly legitimate [...] purpose of bringing it home to the minds and bosoms of the readers'.[348] He also describes the changes he made to the historical incident upon which *The Secret Agent* is based to make it more credible. He does not regard these inventions and changes to source material as lies or dishonesty, a charge he is quite concerned about, as he insists that the 'essentials' of his fiction are 'true' (that he is opposed to the 'sustained invention of a really telling lie',[349] that it 'bored [...] [him] too much to make believe',[350] and that make believe would be 'dishonest'[351]).

Conrad thus theorizes invention as the primary means by which he achieves his central goal as a fiction writer: making the truth credible. At the same time, the rhetorical strategy of fictionality that Conrad deploys in his prefaces – in order to communicate the limitations of his knowledge of his sources and the impossibility of full disclosure, which the genre and his critics expect of him – has, at its core, invention: intentionally signalled, communicated *invention*. Invention, then, is at the heart of the fictional stories Conrad tells, even though they are based on real-world people and events, and at the heart of the nonfictional but fictionality-rich stories he tells *about* the stories he tells, his accounts of his works' inspiration, composition and reception. I thus read Conrad's nonfictional prefaces as grappling theoretically, through the employment of a rhetoric

---

immediate spectators alike, are such as might be reasonably expected to issue; that the final impression is one of searching and indubitable veracity' (Mencken, *A Book of Prefaces*, 46). See Edward Garnett, 'Introductory Essay', in *Conrad's Prefaces to His Works* (London: J. M. Dent & Sons, 1937), 1–34 for a similar assessment of Conrad's life-like representations.

345 Conrad, *Conrad's Prefaces to His Works*, 168–170.
346 Conrad, *Conrad's Prefaces to His Works*, 117.
347 Conrad, *Conrad's Prefaces to His Works*, 164.
348 Conrad, *Conrad's Prefaces to His Works*, 73.
349 Conrad, *Conrad's Prefaces to His Works*, 59.
350 Conrad, *Conrad's Prefaces to His Works*, 110.
351 Conrad, *Conrad's Prefaces to His Works*, 181.

of fictionality, with the concept at the core of fictionality: invention. In *Chance*, Conrad offers us a fictional representation of another nonfictional genre, nonfictional conversational storytelling, in which the narrator uses fictionality (intentionally signalled, communicated invention) to create knowledge, and invention to make the truth credible – but with very different outcomes from those apparent in Conrad's prefaces, based on three variables: Marlow's shifts between fictionality and other forms of communicated invention; the genre claims Marlow makes for his tale (non-fiction) in relation to those Conrad makes for his novels (fiction); and the distance Marlow has from the events he is recounting and the people he is addressing (very little) in relation to Conrad's distance (much greater).

Contextualizing fictionality and invention in *Chance*'s representation of nonfictional conversational storytelling

In *Chance*, Marlow uses fictionality for knowledge creation, just as Conrad does in the prefaces, and invention for credibility, just as Conrad theorizes in the prefaces, but the outcomes differ, based on the three aforementioned variables. In the next section, I analyse Marlow's fictionality and invention, which he uses to make the characters and events of his nonfictional (from the point of view of Marlow, his narratee and the other characters) oral tale's insights into human psychology, relationships and their attendant affective and ethical entanglements more true, more credible and more clear.[352] In this section, I contextualize my analysis of fictionality and invention in *Chance* in the novel's complex narrative structure and its narrators' and narratees' self-conscious reflections on the tellings, particularly focusing on sources and credibility, seeing as these preoccupations are also apparent in Conrad's prefaces, where fictionality and invention are similarly used to create knowledge and credibility, respectively.

Chance's narrative structure entails an unnamed frame narrator reporting a tale he heard from two sources, his friend Marlow and their new acquaintance Charles Powell. The last twelve of the novel's thirteen chapters consist almost entirely of Marlow's monologue, quoted by the unnamed narrator who serves

---

352 John Attridge notes the novel's 'explicit preoccupation with probability and motivation' and its 'systematic and obtrusive verisimilitude', which he regards as a form of ethos, 'an appeal to the reader's trust' (John Attridge, '"The Yellow-Dog Thing": Joseph Conrad, Verisimilitude, and Professionalism', *ELH* 77 (2010), 267–296, 269, 270, 271), but I supplement this account by foregrounding the role fictionality plays in Marlow's and Conrad's generations of ethos and storytelling capacities.

as Marlow's narratee and who periodically interrupts Marlow. Marlow knows the story of destitute and desperate young Flora de Barral, her imprisoned (and later released) criminal-financier father, her eventual husband naval Captain Roderick Anthony, her friends the Fynes (through whom she meets Anthony) and young Powell (second officer on Anthony's ship after Anthony's marriage to Flora) from conversations with the Fynes and Flora during his temporary residency near the Fynes' home and from his blossoming friendship with Powell, which permits him to reconnect with Flora later in life. Marlow's twelve-chapter monologue itself consists of extended quoted dialogue, reproducing what the other characters told him, seeing as he was not present for most of the events he relates. Likewise, the novel's first chapter is made up mostly of Powell's monologue, which includes extended quoted dialogue and is quoted by the unnamed narrator.

I introduce the narrative structure in such detail because Marlow draws considerable attention to, and attempts to justify, his extended verbatim reports of dialogue and other people's narration, along with other matters pertaining to his construction of the tale and its chronology, as well as his sources. For Conrad and for us, the novel's global rhetoric is fictionality, but for Marlow and his anonymous narratee (the frame narrator), and for the frame narrator and his anonymous narratee, the tellings are global nonfictions: factual accounts of events that really happened to people they know or know of. Extended verbatim report of dialogue is a signpost of fictionality for Conrad and his authorial audience, one that we have naturalized or conventionalized.[353] But for Marlow and his narratee, reporting a tale that is, to them, nonfictional, extended verbatim report of dialogue requires explanation in order to be credible. Consequently, they repeatedly draw attention to it and justify it. Marlow, for example, anticipates and defuses concern about how a much older Powell could remember events and conversations in such detail: 'This would account for his remembering so much of it

353 Nielsen adds extended verbatim report of dialogue to a range of other features of first-person narration that constitute 'transgressions of the limits to what a narrative-I would be able to narrate': 'a quantity of details [...] that [...] would be impossible for any real person to remember', along with 'a very long series of monologues, dialogues, descriptions, and recollections of previous thoughts that part ways with the model of traditional autobiography, which first-person narrative is often assumed to have as its ideal'. See Henrik Skov Nielsen, 'The Impersonal Voice in First-Person Narrative Fiction', *Narrative* 12/2 (2004), 133–150, 135–136. These features are signposts of fictionality that we have naturalized or conventionalized to such an extent that we scarcely register them when we encounter them in fiction.

with considerable vividness'. Where the recollections might strain credibility to a breaking point, Marlow makes concessions: after his long report of what Fyne said he and Captain Anthony discussed in London, Marlow concedes, 'That was the general sense of his remarks, not his exact words'. Likewise, after recounting the conversation that transpired between Flora and her father upon his release from prison, Marlow acknowledges, 'Something like that. Not the very words perhaps but such was the general sense of her overwhelming argument—the argument of refuge'.[354]

Through Marlow (and to some extent through the narratee), Conrad draws attention to extended verbatim report of dialogue as a signpost of fictionality, in effect de-naturalizing it and making Marlow's construction of his tale at times even more central to the reader's attention than the characters and events in the tale itself. Conrad scholar Martin Ray takes Marlow's remark to his narratee, '[t]he means don't concern you except in so far as they belong to the story', as gospel, concluding that Marlow is not as involved in the creation of the tale as he was in Conrad's earlier Marlow novels,[355] but Marlow in fact spends considerable time detailing 'the means', so clearly the means do belong to the story to a significant extent.[356] Marlow's remark, in fact, occurs just as he yet again interrupts his telling to justify the credibility of his means – in this case his source for information about Flora's married life on board the ship with Captain Anthony and her father – to his narratee, before once again minimizing these reflections on the means: 'I have now seen our Powell many times under the most favourable conditions—and besides I came upon a most unexpected source of information .... But never mind that'.[357] Marlow also reflects on his construction of the tale to shore up its credibility, interrupting 'the current of his narrative' to explain that he is incorporating what he learned subsequently to create a more comprehensible chronology.[358] He forecloses any possible concern about the apparent discrepancy between the relatively short time he conversed with Flora in London

354 Conrad, *Chance*, 211, 186, 270.

355 See Martin Ray, 'Introduction', in Joseph Conrad, *Chance* (Oxford: Oxford University Press, 2002), xi–xii, xix.

356 Paul Wake, on the other hand, finds Marlow's claim disingenuous and scholars' agreement with Marlow evaluative, either criticizing or praising the elaborate structure of the telling. See Paul Wake, *Conrad's Marlow: Narrative and Death in Youth, Heart of Darkness, Lord Jim and Chance* (Manchester: Manchester University Press, 2007), 104–105.

357 Conrad, *Chance*, 242.

358 Conrad, *Chance*, 84.

and the extensive information he obtained from and shared with her, pointing out that the account seems long only because he has interposed his own comments throughout.[359]

Far more common than these meta-commentaries on the extended verbatim recounting of dialogue or the means of the telling in general are Marlow's efforts – which mirror Conrad's in the prefaces – to prove the truth of his tale by disclosing his sources. As I will demonstrate in the following section, Marlow uses fictionality – and ambiguously signalled and unsignalled communicated invention – extensively in service of this preoccupation with truth and sources. Marlow and his narratee share this preoccupation, which plays a significant role in their assessments of the truth and credibility of the tellings. When Marlow reports that Fyne passed on the news that Flora 'bolted with […] [his] wife's brother, Captain Anthony', Marlow adds that he asked Fyne '[i]s it a suspicion or does she actually say that …?' seeing as '[t]hey didn't [actually] go together'.[360] The narratee is likewise concerned with Marlow's sources, asking him at one point, 'How do you know all this?' to which Marlow replies, 'You shall see by and by'.[361] The narratee also presses Marlow for a fuller explanation of whether the naïve Powell could possibly be the source of insights Marlow is sharing about events only Powell witnessed, or whether Marlow himself developed the insights on the basis of what Powell told him.[362] When Marlow acts as narratee for Powell's narration, he follows the same line of questioning, asking him whether he talked to Flora a lot when she and her father were on board, as the information he is sharing is quite comprehensive.[363]

In *Chance*, Marlow thus draws considerable attention to, and attempts to justify, his extended verbatim reports of dialogue and other people's narration, along with other matters pertaining to his construction of the nonfictional tale and its chronology, as well as his sources. Within this context of self-conscious narration and preoccupation with credibility and sources, Marlow uses fictionality for knowledge creation and invention for credibility, just as Conrad does in his prefaces, but with very different outcomes.

359 Conrad, *Chance*, 173.
360 Conrad, *Chance*, 51–52.
361 Conrad, *Chance*, 198.
362 Conrad, *Chance*, 212.
363 Conrad, *Chance*, 134.

Knowledge creation and the dangers of shifts between fictionality and ambiguously signalled or unsignalled communicated invention in nonfictional conversational storytelling

In this section, I examine Marlow's use of invention[364] to create knowledge of the psychology and relationships of the tale's key figures, moving from cases of intentionally signalled, communicated invention (fictionality) through cases of ambiguously signalled and unsignalled communicated invention. As I move through these cases, I consider the (deleterious) consequences of these shifts between fictionality and other forms of invention for Marlow's communications in the told, as character narrators who narrate as the action is unfolding are uniquely positioned: their tellings can impact their communications and actions not only in the telling, but also in the told.

Most often, Marlow's use of invention takes the form of fictionality, that is, intentionally signalled, communicated hypotheticals, speculations, what ifs, must have beens and imagined scenarios: for example, a counterfactual to offer insight into the Shipping Master's motives, which Marlow believes malicious rather than altruistic;[365] an imagined scenario of the Fynes' first meeting, replete with phrases like 'most likely', 'probably' and 'I imagine';[366] speculation about what Fyne is saying to Captain Anthony in the London hotel, replete with questions, 'Was he [...]?', 'Had he [...]?', 'Or was he perhaps [...]?', 'How was it [...]?'[367] – and similar speculations about what Anthony's arrival at the Fynes' cottage must have been like for Flora[368] and about why Anthony waited for Flora's father to come on board before meeting him.[369]

When Marlow uses fictionality as a rhetorical strategy to generate knowledge about other people's psychology and relationships, he sometimes presses his narratee for assent to the plausibility of the invention. For example, he speculates

364 While Conrad scholars have not used fictionality theory to explain Marlow's rhetorical strategies, Ray does point out that 'Marlow's task [...] is [...] to assemble facts, to reach and convey a reflective and philosophic understanding of Flora, based on *his imaginative interpretation* of the often indirect knowledge which he receives about her' (Ray, 'Introduction', xii, italics added).

365 Conrad, *Chance*, 22.

366 Conrad, *Chance*, 31–32.

367 Conrad, *Chance*, 154–155.

368 Conrad, *Chance*, 155.

369 Conrad, *Chance*, 260.

about the conversation between Flora's governess and her co-conspirator: 'And we may conjecture what we like. I have no difficulty in imagining that the woman—of forty, and the chief of the enterprise—must have raged at large. And perhaps the other did not rage enough'.[370] Marlow is keen to obtain his narratee's assent to the credibility of his conjectures: he asks, 'Don't you see it—eh …' and the narratee reports, 'I was struck by the absolute verisimilitude of this suggestion. But we were always tilting at each other. I saw an opening and pushed my uncandid thrust. "You have a ghastly imagination"'.[371] Following speculations about what Captain Anthony thought about how his sister treated him, signalled by phrases like '[i]t is possible', 'it may be', 'perhaps' and 'must have', Marlow asks his narratee, 'Don't you think that I have hit on the psychology of the situation?'[372]

At times, though, Marlow undertakes the same operation (speculations, hypotheticals, must have beens, etc.) with the same motive (to generate knowledge of human psychology and relationships) without clearly signalling that what he is intentionally communicating is invented. In other words, he reports things he could not possibly know, yet they are not clearly flagged as invention or accompanied by commentary or justification. Such inventions are at times relatively brief and inconsequential: for example, what Flora's scheming governess and the butler said to each other as de Barral's fate was sealed, or what the governess and her co-conspirator said to each other when the latter returned with a cashed cheque, appropriating whatever remained of de Barral's fortune. On the one hand, we might say that these inventions are relatively close to other flagged inventions, so perhaps the signalling could be taken to encompass large swaths of the reporting. Problematically, however, Marlow references his sources and the 'facts' in between periodic explicit signals of his invention, so it is at times impossible to tell where his signalling begins or ends and thus which material his narratee is supposed to take as intentionally signalled, communicated invention. At best, the signalling is ambiguous.

At other times, however, such inventions cannot even be described as ambiguously signalled. These inventions are extended and much more consequential as they pertain to the motivations and behaviours of major players in the narrative at critical moments in their lives: what Captain Anthony thought – conveyed by Marlow in extensive free indirect style – after Fyne met with him to persuade him against marrying Flora,[373] what Anthony thought in the ten days leading up

370 Conrad, *Chance*, 80.
371 Conrad, *Chance*, 80.
372 Conrad, *Chance*, 120–121.
373 Conrad, *Chance*, 247.

to his marriage to Flora[374] and during his perambulations after their visit to the registry office,[375] and what Anthony felt and assumed about Flora, in the midst of their strife on board, including his contemplation of suicide.[376] It is difficult to imagine even the most attentive narratee regarding these reports about other people's psychology and relationships as invention because so much of the telling features explicit discussion of sources, overt signalling of invention and requests for assent to the plausibility of the invention. Indeed, as I have already demonstrated, Conrad depicts the narratee asking Marlow whether he is sharing what Powell told him or developing the insights himself, so the narratee's failure to ask anything at these junctures surely indicates his reading of Marlow's unsignalled inventions as facts.

The chief danger of shifts among fictionality, ambiguously signalled communicated invention and unsignalled communicated invention lies in the combination of the genre claim Marlow makes for his tale (nonfiction) and his proximity to the figures in it (acquaintances in whose lives he continues to play a role). As a character narrator, Marlow uses fictionality not only in his telling, but also in his communications in the told, in the action itself, where the deleterious consequences of his shifts among fictionality, ambiguously signalled communicated invention and unsignalled communicated invention are most apparent. He offers inventions – some of which take the form of fictionality (intentionally communicated, signalled must have beens, speculations and hypotheticals) – about Flora's and Anthony's psychological motivations and interpersonal relationships to his acquaintances in the action itself, so that they, like Marlow and the narratee, can navigate the ethical tangles they are involved in. But some of these communicated inventions in the told are not signalled, just like some of the communicated inventions in the telling. The most notable instance of such unsignalled invention in the told has a significant impact on the unfolding action, highlighting the dangers of shifts between fictionality and other forms of invention in global nonfiction and further calling into question the critical commonplace that *Chance* is the Marlow novel in whose action Marlow is least involved.[377]

374 Conrad, *Chance*, 252–253.

375 Conrad, *Chance*, 257–258.

376 Conrad, *Chance*, 293–294.

377 Ray, for example, claims that Marlow's 'role in *Chance* is much more passive than on his earlier appearances; he tells us little of his own life and he intervenes in the affairs of Flora much less than he did with Lord Jim' (Ray, 'Introduction', xi-xii). Even Wake, who considers the intersection of narration (telling) and story (told) in *Chance*, does

Conrad's communication to his audience thus includes this representation of Marlow's lack of signalling of his use of invention and its outcome, in the told. This representation constitutes a critical qualification of the celebratory portrait Marlow offers invention in his reflections. Invention, Marlow believes, helps him get to the truth of the matter – but, as Conrad shows us, the truth of the matter is obfuscated, and matters are in fact made worse, when Marlow occasionally shifts from fictionality to other forms of invention in his knowledge-creation endeavour. When Marlow learns from the Fynes that Flora is missing and has had an immensely difficult life, he realizes that when he encountered her earlier on the precipice of a quarry, she was likely not being reckless, as he had assumed at the time, but was attempting suicide. He therefore mentions the quarry as a place the Fynes should search for Flora. After a night of searching, the Fynes learn via a letter from Flora that she has fled with her new acquaintance, Captain Anthony, Mrs Fyne's brother. Marlow formulates a range of hypotheses about Flora's past, present and future actions and motivations, some of which he shares with the Fynes as intentionally signalled, communicated hypotheses (fictionality) but others he presents without signalling them as invention, even though they are as invented as his straightforward uses of fictionality are: that he saved her from a suicide attempt, for example. When Fyne seeks Marlow's advice about Mrs Fyne's request that he go to London to intercede with Anthony, which Fyne does not want to do, Marlow recourses to his own hypotheses to convince Fyne to capitulate. Some of these hypotheses are not signalled as inventions: unlike Marlow's ambiguously signalled or unsignalled communicated inventions in the telling (like his free indirect style-rich account of Anthony's thoughts) these inventions could not be identified as inventions even by the most attentive narratees. Having convinced Fyne to go to London, Marlow offers to accompany him and tells him, 'you are doing what's right since it pleases a lady [Mrs Fyne] and cannot do any harm to anybody whatsoever'.[378]

In fact, the harm done by Fyne's intercession in London is significant. While awaiting Fyne outside Anthony's hotel, Marlow encounters Flora, who forces him to admit that he 'put that notion [of checking the quarry in case she had made another suicide attempt there] into their heads':[379] 'I told them that you were making up your mind and I came along just then. I told them that you were

not consider the impact of Marlow's communications in the told on his own and other people's actions.

378 Conrad, *Chance*, 144.

379 Conrad, *Chance*, 151.

saved by me. My shout checked you'.[380] Flora reports that she had abandoned her suicide attempt before Marlow appeared on the scene because she feared that the Fynes' dog might leap after her and come to harm. Even as Flora tells Marlow this, adding that by the following day she had abandoned her ideas about suicide because she 'remembered what [she] should never have forgotten',[381] Marlow does not understand that she is referring to her father, who has no one else in the world to turn to, and instead continues to act – and encourage others to act – on the basis of a must have been or hypothetical about the reason she abandoned her suicide attempt. She must have remembered 'a vague notion that suicide is a legal crime; words of old moralists and preachers which remain in the air and help to form all the authorized moral conventions'.[382]

The damage has been done: Marlow's unsignalled communicated invention that he saved Flora's life is one of the factors that leads to Fyne's intercession in London, an intercession Marlow believes 'cannot do any harm to anybody whatsoever'.[383] Instead, based on what Fyne tells him, and based on his own insecurities, Anthony is once and for all convinced that Flora does not love him and is instead repulsed by him; as Anthony retreats into himself, he only further alienates Flora, who believes, based on the treatment she faced at the hands of her governess, that no one could possibly love her. The more one retreats, the more the other retreats, in a vicious cycle that culminates in complete estrangement.

When Marlow cannot explain how and why Flora and Anthony became so estranged, he admits to his narratee: 'I must confess at once that it was Flora de Barral whom I suspected. In this world as at present organized women are the suspected half of the population. There are good reasons for that'.[384] This phrasing signals the invention (speculation), but Marlow is yet again wrong, and at the earlier, far more critical juncture in the story, the one that exacerbated the initial tension between Flora and Anthony, Marlow offered no such signals of invention. Indeed, he fails to see, even now, that he played a significant role in their estrangement: their latent insecurities about being unworthy of love achieve full-blown manifestation thanks to Fyne's interference, which Marlow encouraged on the basis of his unsignalled must have beens and hypotheticals. Furthermore, Flora's preoccupation with her father's happiness and her responsibility for him,

380 Conrad, *Chance*, 151.
381 Conrad, *Chance*, 154.
382 Conrad, *Chance*, 161.
383 Conrad, *Chance*, 144.
384 Conrad, *Chance*, 243.

which she had tried to signal to Marlow as the thing she should never have forgotten, is something Marlow overlooked entirely and thus failed to counsel her about. He is so preoccupied with his own must have beens and hypotheticals that he ignores the entirely predictable outcome that the fiercely proud de Barral would try to drive a wedge between his daughter and the man whose charity he resents, only exacerbating their estrangement and eventually resulting in de Barral's (failed) attempt to murder Anthony (after which de Barral commits suicide). Marlow fails to reflect on his shifts between fictionality and other uses of invention, all stemming from the same operation (speculation, hypotheticals, must have beens, etc.) with the same motives (to generate knowledge of human behaviour, motivations and relationships), and to appreciate the impact of his rhetorical strategies on his own actions and the actions of his interlocutors. His failures are, of course, not solely responsible for the outcomes Flora, Anthony and de Barral face, but there is no denying their contributions or Conrad's decision to depict them.

Conclusion: What Conrad's fictional story teaches us about nonfictional conversational storytelling

Chance explores the intersection of two of Conrad's life-long fascinations: fictional representations of nonfictional conversational storytelling and the relationship between truth, credibility and invention. The latter is also apparent throughout the prefaces, where Conrad works through long-held anxieties about the truthfulness and credibility of his representations and about critics' concerns on these fronts. He tries to reconcile the relationship between invention and truth or credibility, describing a process of taking events and figures from his life or history and constructing, via invention, fundamentally truthful and credible stories about them. In *Chance*, Conrad depicts a character narrator doing much the same thing. There are, however, two salient differences between Marlow's and Conrad's undertakings: one difference is their distance from the events and figures they are telling about and telling to (Conrad very distant from them vs. Marlow literally living amidst them), and the other is the genre claims they make for their stories (Conrad's literary fictions vs. Marlow's conversational nonfictions).

Conrad depicts Marlow using invention (through fictionality and otherwise) to supplement the limitations of his knowledge about other people, their motivations, and their relationships, so that he can narrate a credible and compelling nonfictional conversational tale for his narratee. But because Marlow lives amidst and communicates with the subjects of his tale and presents his communications as nonfictional, the knowledge he creates through invention is consequential for his own and others' involvement in the unfolding action. Failure to signal must have beens and hypotheticals *as invention* contributes to significant outcomes for the people with whom Marlow communicates in the told. The limitations on what people know of each other's hearts and minds are clearly at the centre of this novel, as are the ways in which they supplement these limitations with invention to create knowledge - and the ways in which they do and do not signal to each other what they are doing, with significant outcomes. Conrad thus qualifies his portrait of the affordances of invention for knowledge creation in global nonfictions with a cautionary note related to narrating situations like Marlow's: telling nonfictional conversational stories about and to our acquaintances.

Analysing *Chance* through the lens of fictionality theory thus illuminates Marlow's communicated inventions in his telling and in the told, signalled, ambiguously signalled and unsignalled — and illuminates the consequences of these inventions in the told. This new reading of the novel puts Marlow far more at the centre of the action than Conrad scholars have believed him to be and regards Marlow's encouragement of Powell to pursue a relationship with Flora in their early middle age as not the first but the second time he has intervened in Flora's romantic life. This new reading of *Chance* also contributes to key debates in Conrad scholarship about the degree of interpretive, affective and ethical alignment between Conrad and Marlow: Conrad depicts Marlow's use of invention as an inevitable part of nonfictional conversational storytelling, but inevitable does not mean unproblematic or harmless, and authorial attention to the harm signals at least some misalignment between author and character narrator.[385]

Ray points out that the unnamed frame narrator of *Chance*, who acts as Marlow's narratee, was depicted in the original serialized version of *Chance* as a novelist 'preoccupied with the literary mediation of the experiences which Marlow conveys to him'. Ray speculates that Conrad removed from the book version all references to the frame narrator as a novelist because 'this was an excessive and unfruitful complication'.[386] Without hazarding a guess as to the reason for Conrad's revision, I can certainly comment on the effect: the absence of any information about the unnamed narrator's medium, occasion and purpose for

---

385 In *Conrad's Marlow: Narrative and Death in Youth, Heart of Darkness, Lord Jim and Chance*, Wake argues that Marlow's misogynistic statements, along with critical and questioning interruptions by his narratee, also indicate that Marlow is not simply a mouthpiece for Conrad.

386 Ray, 'Introduction', xv.

narration keeps the reader's focus on Marlow's conversational storytelling. This focus entails attention to the two salient differences between Marlow's communication and Conrad's – living amidst or entirely apart from the people they are telling about and telling to, and constructing a nonfictional conversational tale or a literary fiction – and to the impact of these differences on Conrad's portrait of invention's potential for knowledge creation.

Conrad's often-quoted declaration from his memoir *A Personal Record* is relevant here: 'And what is a novel if not a conviction of our fellow men's existence, strong enough to take upon itself a form of imagined life clearer than reality and whose accumulated verisimilitude of selected episodes puts to shame the pride of documentary history?'.[387] My pairing of *Chance* and the prefaces prompts a further question: where does nonfictional conversational storytelling fit? Verisimilitude is as important in nonfictional conversational storytelling as it is in the novel, but ethical responsibility to those we tell about and tell to is as important, perhaps even more important, than it is in documentary history, where there is likely greater spatiotemporal separation between teller, told and addressee. Conrad's fictional representations of the affordances and dangers of invention as a form of knowledge creation in nonfictional conversational storytelling illuminate his fascination with and anxieties about this question. Nonfictional conversational storytelling about our lives and our acquaintances' lives can be beneficial for our self-understanding, wellbeing and social literacy, and fictionality and invention can play important roles in creating knowledge in order to tell stories that achieve these aims. But, as Conrad showed us nearly a century before the rise of fictionality theory, that's not the whole story.

387 Joseph Conrad, *A Personal Record* (Cambridge: Cambridge University Press, 2008), 27–28.

Pernille Meyer

7. Positioning You: Fictionality and Interpellation in Janne Teller's *War: What If It Were Here?*[388]

Abstract: In Janne Teller's illustrated, passport-shaped book *War: What If It Were Here?* (2016), first published as a fictional essay in Denmark in 2002, the refugee crisis is turned upside down. A war has broken out in Europe, and the fourteen-year-old 'you' protagonist is forced to flee from Great Britain to Egypt with his family. Employing fictionality, Teller raises awareness about the current refugee crisis and asks the reader: What would you do? Where would you go? In reality, however, there is, as critical voices have pointed out, no dialogue; the reader is told what she is experiencing, thinking and feeling. Positioning the reader as a refugee, the book is designed to evoke empathy in the reader and, consequently, motivate political action. This chapter explores the ethical implications of ascribing a particular identity to the reader through the use of second-person narration. What responsibilities does the author have in relation to the reader when participating in the public debate? And what are the potential dangers of an interpellative use of second-person narration?

Keywords: second-person narrative, fictionality, interpellation, reader involvement, Janne Teller, humanitarian discourse, refugee narrative

> You shudder every time the missiles whirl off miles away, every time you see a glimmer of light on the horizon, not knowing if this time the missile is headed for you. You shudder every time the explosions sound. How many of your friends were struck this time?[389]

In Janne Teller's illustrated, passport-shaped book *War: What If It Were Here?* (2016), the refugee crisis is turned upside down. A war has broken out in Europe, and the fourteen-year-old 'you' protagonist is forced to flee from Great Britain to Egypt with his family. After two years in a refugee camp, the 'you' protagonist and his family are granted temporary asylum and obliged to move to Aswan in southern Egypt. But everything is different in the new country – the language, the customs, the way to behave – and no matter what the 'you' protagonist does, he is looked at as third tier. Another three years later, when the war is finally over,

388 Parts of this chapter have been presented at ISSN's 2021 Narrative Conference.

389 Janne Teller, *War: What If It Were Here?* (London: Simon and Schuster UK, 2016), 8.

Great Britain has become part of a dictatorship under Danish overrule, and the 'you' protagonist gets permanent residency in Egypt along with the rest of his family. Sadly, the 'you' protagonist still 'feel[s] a stranger',[390] and all he can think about 'is when [to] go home'.[391]

War was originally published as a fictional essay in Denmark in 2002 as a response to the Danish immigration policy.[392] At the time, the centre-right parties had just won a majority together with the extreme right, which, as Teller describes in an interview about the book, resulted in a radical shift in attitude: 'there were very strict policies introduced against asylum-seekers and immigrants [...] [, a]nd the rhetoric against foreigners, particularly against Muslims, became horrible, with politicians claiming that Islam is not a religion but a terrorist organisation'.[393] Since the outbreak of the Syrian refugee crisis in 2011, the book has gained renewed interest, both in Denmark and abroad. It has now been published in around twenty countries, with text and illustrations adapted to the countries in question to make the narrative as relatable to the reader as possible.[394]

The attempt to involve the reader through such adaptations is radically reinforced by the perhaps most striking feature of the book: its consistent use of second-person narration, which immediately pulls the reader into the narrative and positions her as a refugee. Employing fictionality, Teller raises awareness about actual political issues and asks the reader: What would *you* do? Where would *you* go? In reality, however, there is, as critical voices have pointed out, no dialogue; the reader is told what she is experiencing, thinking and feeling.

In this chapter, I explore the potential dangers of ascribing a particular identity to the reader through the use of second-person narration, thereby illuminating one of the many interesting aspects of the subject of this volume: the dangers of narrative and fictionality. I begin by elaborating on Teller's use of fictionality and, most importantly, what she achieves by it. Engaging with positions within rhetorical fictionality theory, I argue that second-person narration can function as

---

390 Teller, *War*, 51.

391 Teller, *War*, 51.

392 In 2004, the fictional essay was turned into a passport-shaped book with illustrations by Helle Vibeke Jensen and published by Dansklærerforeningen as educational material for Danish primary schools.

393 Orsolya Ruff, '"I never write to provoke": interview with Janne Teller', *Hungarian Literature Online* (6 May 2012), <https://hlo.hu/interview/interview_with_janne_teller.html>, accessed 27 April 2021.

394 Ruff, '"I never write to provoke"'.

a local, textual sign of fictionality, which in this case transforms the reader into the protagonist. I, then, focus more specifically on second-person narration as a narrative technique with an immanent ability to involve, define and position and, thus, suggest to describe Teller's use of second-person narration in *War* as interpellative. Turning to the mixed reception of *War* in Denmark, I end by discussing whether Teller is manipulating the reader when employing fictionality, including the interpellative use of second-person narration, to address actual political issues.

What if?

As mentioned above, Teller wrote a *fictional* essay to engage in the *actual* political debate. This interaction between imagination and reality can be understood through a rhetorical approach to fictionality.[396] In *The Rhetoric of Fictionality* (2007), Richard Walsh distinguishes between 'fiction as a generic category'[397] and 'fictionality as a rhetorical resource'.[398] According to Walsh, fictionality is a rhetorical resource that can be used to achieve something in different communicative contexts. Thus, fictionality does not only occur in generic fiction such as classic novels and short stories, but in all forms of communication:

> fictionality should [not] be equated simply with 'fiction,' as a category or genre of narrative: it is a communicative strategy, and as such it is apparent on some scale within many nonfictional narratives, in forms ranging from an ironic aside, through various forms of conjecture or imaginative supplementation, to full-blown counterfactual narrative examples.[399]

From a fictionality perspective, then, the interesting question is not *if* something is generic fiction or not, but *what* someone achieves by employing fictionality in a specific communicative context.

---

395 To avoid too many translations, this chapter focusses on the English edition of the book from 2016.

396 See e.g., Richard Walsh, *The Rhetoric of Fictionality* (Columbus: Ohio State University Press, 2007); Henrik Skov Nielsen, James Phelan and Richard Walsh, 'Ten Theses about Fictionality', *Narrative* 23/1 (2015), 61–73; Simona Zetterberg Gjerlevsen and Henrik Skov Nielsen, 'Distinguishing Fictionality', in Cindie Aaen Maagaard, Daniel Schäbler and Marianne Wolff Lundholt, eds., *Exploring Fictionality: Conceptions, Test Cases, Discussions* (Odense: Syddansk Universitetsforlag, 2020), 19–40.

397 Walsh, *The Rhetoric of Fictionality*, 38.

398 Walsh, *The Rhetoric of Fictionality*, 38.

399 Walsh, *The Rhetoric of Fictionality*, 7.

In the afterword, Teller explains her motivation for writing *War*: 'The discussion about refugees in Denmark [...] seemed to forget that two of our most hailed European philosophical, humanitarian and even Christian, values are: that all human beings are created equal, and to do unto others as you would wish them to do onto you'.[400] These views are confirmed in many interviews where Teller accuses the attitude towards immigrants and refugees in Denmark of being 'hateful'[401] (my translation) and 'rancorous'[402] (my translation).

Although debating real-life political issues, the book does not come across as a traditional contribution to the debate. Instead, as Teller writes in the afterword, it is 'an invitation to the imagination';[403] 'an invitation into life as a refugee'.[404] The fictional status of the book is underlined by several paratextual markers. Among these are the subtitle on the front cover of the book, 'What if it were here?', and the text on the back cover of the book, 'Imagine if war broke out', which explicitly inform the reader that what she is about to read differs from reality. Furthermore, the book is shaped like a passport; the document any refugee hopes to get. The reader is, obviously, well aware that she is not holding an actual passport in her hands, but the passport shape helps situate her in the world of a refugee: arriving in a new country, desperately trying to obtain the necessary papers. Opening the book, coloured illustrations appear on the pages next to and in combination with the text. These, too, help bring the narrative to life in the reader's imagination. Interestingly, however, the 'you' protagonist and his family are never portrayed up close. Instead, both people and places are shown from a distance: a world map with groups of refugees on different continents, small figures wandering in a desert-like landscape, postage stamps with pictures of a minaret and a tent. Thus, the illustrations play a dual role: on the one hand, they create a quite specific universe, and on the other hand, the many small, faceless figures make it easy for the reader to imagine herself as one of them.[405]

---

400 Teller, *War*, 55.

401 Jes Stein Pedersen and Hanne Budtz-Jørgensen, 'Hvis der var krig i Norden', *Bogfolk* (13 May 2016), <https://podtail.com/da/podcast/politiken-bogfolk/uge-19-hvis-der-var-krig-i-norden/>, accessed 27 April 2021.

402 Nordic co-operation, 'Om det vore krig i Norden', *YouTube* (3 October 2012), <https://www.youtube.com/watch?v=LLJFSfKJxVw>, accessed 27 April 2021.

403 Teller, *War*, 55.

404 Teller, *War*, 56.

405 A further investigation of the interplay between text and illustrations is beyond the scope of this chapter.

According to Henrik Skov Nielsen, James Phelan and Walsh, '[f]ictive discourse invites the reader or listener to imagine something – to ask, often tendentiously, "What if?"'.[406] In line with this, *War* can be seen as an open invitation for the reader to ask herself: What if war broke out in my country? What if I were forced to flee? What if I were not accepted because of the colour of my skin? This is reflected by the question in the subtitle and by the opening lines of the book where a string of questions invites the reader into a disturbing thought experiment:

> What if Great Britain were at war? Where would you go? If the bombs had torn most of London, most of Britain, to ruins? If the house that you and your family live in had holes in the walls, all the windows broken, the roof rent off?[408]

The attempt to engage the reader through such questions is closely tied to the use of second-person narration, which inevitably points towards the reader. While Walsh is hesitant to point out textual signs of fictionality, Simona Zetterberg Gjerlevsen and Nielsen argue that 'it is possible to look for, and find, textual signs that point to the fictional status of an utterance independent of contextual knowledge and paratextual markers'.[409] Following Gjerlevsen and Nielsen, I would say that the use of second-person narration becomes such a textual sign of fictionality as part of the 'What if'-scenario established by other paratextual and textual markers. This does not mean that second-person narratives are necessarily fictional, but that second-person narration is a narrative technique that can signal local fictionality in both global fiction and non-

406 Nielsen, Phelan and Walsh, 'Ten Theses about Fictionality', 64.

407 For a philosophical approach to fiction and its 'as if' character, see Hans Vaihinger, *A Philosophy of 'As if': A System of the Theoretical, Practical and Religious Fictions of Mankind* (London: Routledge and Kegan Paul, 1924).

408 Teller, *War*, 7.

409 Gjerlevsen and Nielsen, 'Distinguishing Fictionality', 45.

410 Gjerlevsen's and Nielsen's concept of signs of fictionality should not be conflated with Dorrit Cohn's (Dorrit Cohn, 'Signposts of Fictionality: A Narratological Perspective', *Poetics Today* 11/4 (1990), 775–804), which, according to Gjerlevsen and Nielsen who define fictionality as 'intentionally signaled, communicated invention' (Gjerlevsen and Nielsen, 'Distinguishing Fictionality', 25), concerns fiction and not fictionality: 'We suggest operating with a concept of signs of fictionality different from one of signs of fiction. Whereas signs of fiction have served to identify a genre as such, the idea of signs of fictionality is that these can also be found outside fiction, and that they are therefore not necessarily indicative of any generic relations' (Gjerlevsen and Nielsen, 'Distinguishing Fictionality', 26–27).

fiction.[411] In *War*, the reader is aware that she is not the 'you' protagonist – she is not a fourteen-year-old boy living in a war-torn London with her father, mother, older brother and little sister – and yet, the slippage from the first general 'you' appearing in the question 'Where would you go?' to the specific 'you' protagonist emerging later on the same page pulls the reader into the narrative and transforms her into the protagonist.

Positioning the reader as a refugee, *War* is designed to evoke empathy in the reader and, consequently, motivate political action. Employing fictionality in humanitarian discourse has, as Stefan Iversen argues, become more and more prevalent in recent years. Citing Luc Boltanski, Iversen draws attention to one of the key problems regarding the relationship between sufferers in the southern parts of the globe and spectators in the northern parts of the globe: 'How can we give form to the representation of suffering at a distance, so that it can establish a political connection?'.[412] The relationship between sufferers in the southern parts of the globe and spectators in the northern parts of the globe is, Iversen explains with reference to Boltanski, 'primarily characterized by power hierarchies and distance'.[413] We are terrified when something tragic happens in our own neighbourhood, country or even part of the world, but as the geographical and cultural distance grow, so does the emotional. Thus, the challenge for everyone who wants to motivate political action is to minimize the emotional distance.

As a case in point, Iversen focuses on the 'Most Shocking Second a Day' campaign from 2014 by the British NGO Save the Children, which was launched as a response to the Syrian refugee crisis. The resemblance to *War* is striking: in the video, a war breaks out, and a young girl is forced to flee from London with her family. Turning the refugee crisis upside down, both the 'Most Shocking Second a Day' campaign and *War* move the suffering from the Middle East to the Western world, thereby succeeding in minimizing the emotional distance

---

411 Nielsen, Phelan and Walsh explain the difference between global and local fictionality in the following way: 'Global fictions can contain passages of nonfictionality, and global nonfictions can contain passages of fictionality. Thus, nonfictionality can be subordinate to fictive purposes, and fictionality can be subordinate to nonfictive purposes' (Nielsen, Phelan and Walsh, 'Ten Theses about Fictionality', 67). Paul Auster's autobiographical works *Winter Journal* (2012) and *Report from the Interior* (2013) are examples of the use of second-person narration in global non-fiction.

412 Boltanski, cited in Stefan Iversen, '"Just because it isn't happening here, doesn't mean it isn't happening": Narrative, Fictionality and Reflexivity in Humanitarian Rhetoric', *European Journal of English Studies* 23/2 (2019), 190–205, 194.

413 Iversen, '"Just because it isn't happening here, doesn't mean it isn't happening"', 194.

through the act of fictionalization. In *War*, however, the reader is not 'just' a spectator invited to imagine what it would be like to be a refugee. Because of the use of second-person narration, in a sense, the reader *becomes* the refugee.

Before moving to the potential dangers of this 'transformative' kind of reader involvement, I will focus more specifically on the characteristics of second-person narration; a narrative technique that has occupied an increasingly larger place on the literary landscape since the beginning of the twentieth century, although not receiving considerable attention among narratologists until the 1990s.[414]

Second-person narration and reader involvement

The presence of the second-person pronoun 'you' in literature, or any form of communication, is by no means unusual in itself, and thus, one of the most debated issues in this regard has, as Monika Fludernik writes, been how to find 'the golden proportion between "real" second-person texts and other fiction using the second-person pronoun in interesting and potentially significant ways'.[415] Today, most narratologists agree that second-person narrative is best described as narrative in which the protagonist is designated by the second-person pronoun 'you'.[416][417]

---

414 Brian Richardson, 'At First You Feel a Bit Lost. The Varieties of Second Person Narration', in *Unnatural Voices: Extreme Narration in Modern and Contemporary Fiction* (Columbus: Ohio State University Press, 2006), 17–36, 17–18.

415 Monika Fludernik, 'Introduction: Second-person Narrative and Related Issues', *Style* 28/3 (1994), 281–311, 284.

416 See e.g., Gerald Prince, *A Dictionary of Narratology* (Lincoln: University of Nebraska Press, 1987); Monika Fludernik, 'Second Person Fiction: Narrative *You* As Addressee And/Or Protagonist', *Arbeiten aus Anglistik und Amerikanistik* 18/2 (1993), 217–247; Irene Kacandes, 'Narrative Apostrophe: Reading, Rhetoric, Resistance in Michel Butor's *La Modification* and Julio Cortazar's "Graffiti"', *Style* 28/3 (1994), 329–349; Matt DelConte, 'Why *You* Can't Speak: Second-Person Narration, Voice, and a New Model for Understanding Narrative', *Style* 37/2 (2003), 204–219; Richardson, 'At First You Feel a Bit Lost'; David Herman, Manfred Jahn and Marie-Laure Ryan, 'Second-Person Narration', in *Routledge Encyclopedia of Narrative Theory* (London: Routledge, 2010), <https://www.proquest.com/docview/2137959874?accountid=14468>, accessed 27 April 2021.

417 Throughout the years, many definitions have been proposed. One of them is Helmut Bonheim's: 'You-narration proper takes place when the "you" is used over such large stretches of text that the narrative effect is essentially altered' (Helmut Bonheim, 'Narration in the Second Person', *Recherches Anglaises et Américaines* 16 (1983), 69–80,

[418] Accordingly, Fludernik defines second-person narrative as 'fiction that employs a pronoun of address in reference to a fictional protagonist',[419] while Brian Richardson defines it as 'any narration other than an apostrophe that designates its protagonist by a second-person pronoun'.[420]

Consistently referring to the protagonist with the second-person pronoun 'you', *War* is a classic example of a second-person narrative:

> Your mother has bronchitis and yet another bout of pneumonia is on its way. Your older brother has lost three fingers on his left hand in an episode with a mine. He supports the Militia against the wishes of your parents. Your little sister has been wounded by grenade splinters and lies in a hospital with no equipment. Your grandparents died when a bomb struck their nursing home. You yourself are still well and sound, but scared.[421]

The passage above appears on the very first page, right after the initial string of questions that pulls the reader into the narrative, and marks the shift from a general 'you' to a more specific 'you' protagonist. In the passage, as well as the rest of the book, it does not seem as if the 'you' protagonist is being addressed. [h]e obviously knows it all – that his mother is ill, that his brother has joined the militia, that his little sister is wounded, that his grandparents have been killed, that he is scared – and it is, in Helmut Bonheim's words, very difficult 'to find a believable motive for supplying him with information which would be familiar to him'.[422]

This oddity, I would argue, is exactly what differentiates the use of the second-person pronoun 'you' in second-person narrative from its use in everyday communication. In everyday communication, the first-person pronoun refers to the speaker, the second-person pronoun refers to the one spoken to, and the third-person pronoun refers to the one spoken about, but in second-person narrative,

---

73–74). The definition has been criticized for being too broad, not explicating what is meant by expressions such as 'large stretches of text' and 'narrative effect' (see Jarmila Mildorf, 'Studying Writing in Second Person: A Response to Joshua Parker', *Connotations* 23/1 (2013/2014), 63–78; Pernille Meyer Christensen, 'Hvorfor fortælle dig noget, du allerede ved? Om dufortællinger i dansk litteratur', *Passage* 35/3 (2020), 1–13).

418 For a discussion of this consensus, see Pernille Meyer, 'Exploring the Boundaries of Second-Person Narrative: The Use of "You" in Maria Gerhardt's *Transfer Window*', *The Problems of Literary Genres* 65/4 (2023), 19–33, in which I attempt to develop and challenge the conception of what is considered a second-person narrative proper.

419 Fludernik, 'Second Person Fiction', 217.

420 Richardson, 'At First You Feel a Bit Lost', 19.

421 Teller, *War*, 7–8.

422 Bonheim, 'Narration in the Second Person', 77.

the 'you' protagonist is not addressed by the second-person pronoun 'you'. Or in short, according to Nielsen: 'The protagonist is referred to and designated, but not addressed by the second-person pronoun'.[423] In fact, Nielsen continues, there is nothing except the very use of the second-person pronoun 'you' that suggests that the 'you' protagonist is being addressed: '[h]e [the "you" protagonist] is just as oblivious to being the centre of a narrative as are the protagonists in third person narratives'.[424]

While the 'you' protagonist is not addressed, one of the most distinct features of second-person narration is its ability to involve, and sometimes even address, the actual reader. As Brian McHale notes, the second-person pronoun 'you' is a 'shifter' in Roman Jakobson's sense; 'an "empty" linguistic sign whose reference changes with every change of speaker in a discourse situation: every reader is potentially *you*, the addressee of the novelistic discourse'.[425] This has led several narratologists to state that the reader is likely to feel addressed whenever the second-person pronoun 'you' in a second-person narrative could refer to her as well as the 'you' protagonist.[426] According to Phelan, the unfamiliar, and often surprising, feeling of being addressed will, however, diminish as the reader gains more and more information about the 'you' protagonist:

> the fuller the characterization of the 'you,' the more aware actual readers will be of their differences from that 'you,' and thus, the more fully they will move into the observer role, and less likely this role will overlap with the addressee position. In other words, the greater the characterization of 'you,' the more like a standard protagonist the 'you' becomes, and, consequently, the more actual readers can employ their standard strategies for reading narrative.[427]

This evidently holds true for second-person narratives such as Michel Butor's *La Modification* [*A Change of Heart*] (1957), Italo Calvino's *Se una notte d'inverno un viaggiatore* [*If on a Winter's Night a Traveler*] (1979) or Phelan's own example, Lorrie Moore's *Self-Help* (1985), but in *War*, something significantly

---

423 Henrik Skov Nielsen, 'Fictional Voices? Strange Voices? Unnatural Voices?', in Per Krogh Hansen, Stefan Iversen, Henrik Skov Nielsen and Rolf Reitan, eds., *Strange Voices in Narrative Fiction* (Berlin: De Gruyter, 2011), 55–81, 66.

424 Nielsen, 'Fictional Voices? Strange Voices? Unnatural Voices?', 66.

425 Brian McHale, *Postmodernist Fiction* (New York and London: Methuen, 1987), 223.

426 Irene Kacandes, 'Are You in the Text? The "Literary Performative" in Postmodernist Fiction', *Text and Performance Quarterly* 13 (1993), 139–153; Richardson, 'At First You Feel a Bit Lost'; Mildorf, 'Studying Writing in Second Person'.

427 James Phelan, '"Self-Help" for Narratee and Narrative Audience: How "I" – and "You"? – Read "How"', *Style* 28/3 (1994), 350–365, 351.

different seems to be the case. Even though the characterization of the 'you' protagonist already on the first page becomes quite specific, the reader – or at least this reader – keeps feeling addressed throughout the book. The reason, I believe, can be found in the initial interrogative mode and its invitation to imagine. Because the reader is well aware that she is joining a thought experiment that, in order to work, requires her to take on the role of the 'you' protagonist, the role of a refugee, the address function is sustained. However, the address function is not completely stable, and in some passages, it is clearly intensified. This typically happens in the descriptions of a more emotional character, such as '[y]ou are nothing'[428] and 'you feel a stranger'.[429] At some point in our lives, we have all felt scared, alone or different, and in the descriptions of such widely recognizable emotions, the distance between the textual 'you' and the actual reader decreases. This seems to be a central part of Teller's rhetorical strategy to engage the reader; when the reader is identifying herself with the 'you' protagonist in passages such as the ones cited above, she is probably more likely to do so in other passages as well – because the identification is already established.

In 'Reconsidering Second-Person Narration and Involvement' (2016), Jarmila Mildorf distinguishes between two different types of reader involvement: aesthetic-reflexive involvement and affective-emotional involvement. While the first one 'denotes a more intellectual response to, and pleasure taken from, the (often postmodern) playfulness of *you*-narration', the latter 'is close to what is otherwise labelled as "empathy"'.[430] Since Teller is by no means engaging in any playful postmodern experiment,[431] it is the second type I am interested in here. The link between second-person narrative and empathy has previously been established. For instance, Bonheim suggests the term 'conative solicitude', by which he, as Fludernik writes in her introduction to the 1994 special issue of *Style* about second-person narrative, manages to pinpoint one of the emotional effects of using second-person narration: 'namely, its decidedly involving quality,

---

428 Teller, *War*, 36.

429 Teller, *War*, 49.

430 Jarmila Mildorf, 'Reconsidering Second-Person Narration and Involvement', *Language and Literature* 25/2 (2016), 145–158, 148.

431 Calvino's *Se una notte d'inverno un viaggiatore* is, with its intriguing beginning, the perhaps best-known example of this kind of postmodern playfulness: 'You are about to begin reading Italo Calvino's new novel, *If on a Winter's Night a Traveler*. Relax. Concentrate. Dispel every other thought. Let the world around you fade' (Italo Calvino, *If on a Winter's Night a Traveler*, William Weaver, trans. (London: Picador, [1979] 1982), 3).

which provokes much greater initial empathy with second-person protagonists than with first- or third-person characters'.[432] According to Mildorf, however, one has to consider the linguistic environment of the 'you' protagonist as much as the use of second-person narration: 'emotional involvement may be attributed to other factors alongside the second-person pronoun – for example, internal perspectives and granularity of description'.[433]

In *War*, the 'What if?'-scenario consisting of war, fear and despair is in itself capable of creating strong emotional responses in the reader. Combined with the use of second-person narration, these emotional responses become even stronger, and it is this combination – of second-person narration and the fictionalized event of a war breaking out in Europe – that makes the book and its call for political action so powerful. Moreover, the coexistence of the present tense and second-person narration makes it, at least on a linguistic level, impossible for the reader to refuse the statements put forth by the undefinable voice of the narrator. The reader is given a particular identity, that of a refugee, along with a certain set of values, and in the end, she is supposed to reach only one conclusion: we, the Western countries, should, without hesitation, welcome more refugees.

As we will see in the final part of this chapter, not all readers agree with this conclusion. Yet, Teller's use of second-person narration, and the emotional reader involvement created by it, seem to leave almost no room for disagreement. In what follows, I will suggest describing the specific use of second-person narration in *War* as interpellative.

Second-person narration as interpellation

In 'Ideology and Ideological State Apparatuses (Notes towards an Investigation)' (1969), Louis Althusser introduces his notion of interpellation to express how ideology transforms individuals into subjects:[434]

> ideology 'acts' or 'functions' in such a way that it 'recruits' subjects among the individuals (it recruits them all), or 'transforms' the individuals into subjects (it transforms them all) by that very precise operation which I have called *interpellation* or hailing, and

432 Fludernik, 'Introduction', 286.

433 Mildorf, 'Reconsidering Second-Person Narration and Involvement', 155.

434 Althusser is, as the essay title implies, rooted in a Marxist tradition, but his thoughts on interpellation have gained widespread interest in various areas of academia, such as economy, political science and literature (Vincent B. Leitch, *The Norton Anthology of Theory and Criticism. Second Edition* (New York and London: W. W. Norton & Company, 2010), 1332–1334).

> which can be imagined along the lines of the most commonplace everyday police (or other) hailing: 'Hey, you there!'.[435]

Responding to the police officer's 'Hey, you there!', the person on the street acknowledges the authority of ideology and is thereby subjected to it. In the ordinary use of the term, Althusser writes, 'subject' can in fact mean (1) 'a free subjectivity, a centre of initiatives, author of and responsible for its actions'[436] and (2) 'a subjected being, who submits to a higher authority, and is therefore stripped of all freedom except that of freely accepting his submission'.[437] Taking the second meaning of the term into account, the similarity between interpellation and second-person narration is easily seen: the 'you' protagonist can neither hear nor respond to the narrator's voice and is in that sense stripped of all freedom. In other words, the 'you' protagonist is subjected to the will of the narrative voice and, in the end, the author.

In his review of Butor's *La Modification*, Roland Barthes explicitly describes second-person narration as interpellation. According to Barthes, the vocative in Butor's novel must be understood quite literally: 'it is the creator's address to the creature, named, constituted, *created* in all his acts by a judge and progenitor'.[438] 'This interpellation', Barthes continues, 'is crucial, for it institutes the hero's consciousness: it is by dint of finding himself under surveillance, described by another consciousness'.[439]

Although the review is written before Althusser introduces his notion of interpellation, it is interesting how both Althusser and Barthes use the term in relation to the ultimate authority, namely God. Barthes' language 'rings with biblical overtones, specifically with God's creation of the world through speech acts in the book of Genesis',[440] as Irene Kacandes points out, and Althusser emphasizes how 'the interpellation of individuals as subjects presupposes the "existence" of a unique and central Other Subject':[441] 'God thus defines himself as the Subject par

---

435 Louis Althusser, 'Ideology and Ideological State Apparatuses (Notes towards an Investigation)', in Ben Brewster, trans., *Lenin and Philosophy and Other Essays* (New York: Monthly Review Press, [1969] 1971), 127–183, 174.

436 Althusser, 'Ideology and Ideological State Apparatuses', 182.

437 Althusser, 'Ideology and Ideological State Apparatuses', 182.

438 Roland Barthes, 'There Is No Robbe-Grillet School', in Richard Howard, trans., *Critical Essays* (Evanston: Northwestern University Press, [1958] 1972), 91–95, 93.

439 Barthes, 'There Is No Robbe-Grillet School', 93.

440 Kacandes, 'Narrative Apostrophe: Reading, Rhetoric, Resistance in Michel Butor's *La Modification* and Julio Cortazar's "Graffiti"', 334.

441 Althusser, 'Ideology and Ideological State Apparatuses', 178.

excellence, he who is through himself and for himself ("I am that I am")'.[442] Also, in this connection, it is worth noting that even before any actual studies of the narrative technique have been conducted, Barthes manages to give a very precise account of what is at stake in second-person narration; the 'you' protagonist's consciousness is described by another consciousness – the supreme consciousness of the author – and he seems, as Rolf Reitan expresses it, to be 'created by the [...] reference'.[443]

In recent years, Daniel Newman has brought renewed attention to the relation between second-person narration and interpellation. In 'Your Body is Our Black Box: Narrating Nations in Second-Person Fiction by Edna O'Brien and Jennifer Egan' (2018), Newman argues that second-person narration in its interpellative mode is ideally suited for a specific kind of stories in which the characters are 'coerced',[444] 'shamed'[445] and 'disciplined'[446] by society: 'Against the illusion of autonomy and self-determination, you-narration exposes the characters' vulnerability and submission to societal forces that appear to be inescapable'.[447] While Newman's analysis primarily centres on the interpellative use of second-person narration in relation to the 'you' protagonist rather than the reader, I am here concerned with both.

Throughout *War*, the 'you' protagonist is subjected to the will of others. In Great Britain, the newly established dictatorship is controlling his every move, and in Egypt, his wish of getting permanent residency lies in the hands of the Egyptian authorities who do not want to receive more refugees.

> You have brought your diary. It shall remind you that there was a time before the war: a time when Britons were a mixed people allowed to hold different opinions about everything. A time when you went to Swedish techno parties on Fridays, rode your German roller blades on Saturdays, and ended the weekend with chicken masala at the local Indian food joint [...]. It's so endlessly far away that it is like it never was. Even if it was like this only three years ago.[448]

---

442 Althusser, 'Ideology and Ideological State Apparatuses', 179.

443 Rolf Reitan, 'Theorizing Second-Person Narratives: A Backwater Project?', in Per Krogh Hansen, Stefan Iversen, Henrik Skov Nielsen and Rolf Reitan, eds., *Strange Voices in Narrative Fiction* (Berlin: De Gruyter, 2011), 147–174, 147.

444 Daniel Newman, 'Your Body is Our Black Box', *Frontiers of Narrative Studies* 4/1 (2018), 42–65, 46.

445 Newman, 'Your Body is Our Black Box', 46.

446 Newman, 'Your Body is Our Black Box', 46.

447 Newman, 'Your Body is Our Black Box', 60.

448 Teller, *War*, 22.

The 'you' protagonist has brought his diary to keep his fading memories of the pre-war time alive. He repeatedly has to remind himself that it has not always been like this. Only three years ago, he was in charge of his own life in a multicultural society; he would go to Swedish techno parties, ride German roller blades, eat Indian food. And, most importantly, he was free to have his own opinion. All this is gone now, and instead the 'you' protagonist and his family are faced with one choice: submit to the new rules or flee. The problem, however, is that freedom is not gained in Egypt, even though the Middle East is a peaceful area. At first, the 'you' protagonist experiences a sense of relief living in the Egyptian tent camp: 'Hunger no longer gnaws at your guts, there are no missiles or bombs to fear, there is no Britification Police ransacking your home day and night'.[449] There is nothing to fear anymore, and the 'you' protagonist does not see any reason why his family should not be officially recognized as true refugees – 'Of course you're *true* refugees. What else would you be?'.[450] But the application process is delayed, and soon, the sense of relief is replaced by a growing fear of not ever getting permanent residency. When it finally happens several years later, the 'you' protagonist is not happy. He has kids who speak Arabic and know the Koran better than the Bible, he has a job in the family bakery, he has friends among the locals, but he does not feel at home, which is cemented in the final lines of the book: 'Yet, you feel a stranger. Yet, all you can think about is when you can go home. Home where?'.[451] On the last page, in the bottom right-hand corner, there is a small illustration of a group of refugees and the inscription 'Homeland' in both English and Arabic next to a large question mark. The 'you' protagonist never manages to regain his self-determination, and thus, he continues to feel helpless and vulnerable. This is emphasized by the interpellative use of second-person narration. The 'you' protagonist is subjected to the voice of the narrator as he is subjected to the demands of society: he is unable to answer back, and the opportunity to have a fulfilling life is in the hands of others rather than himself – no matter if he lives in Great Britain or Egypt.

Turning to the reader, it becomes clear that she is just as defenceless as the 'you' protagonist, though in a different way. Stepping into the role of the 'you' protagonist, the reader is, more or less directly, told what to think, which is that every refugee, no matter the circumstances, deserves to be welcomed by the countries in peaceful areas. An important part of the attempt to influence the

449 Teller, *War*, 26.
450 Teller, *War*, 26.
451 Teller, *War*, 51.

reader's opinions in this way is to confront her with her own stereotypes and prejudices regarding refugees through the eyes of the Egyptians who are faced with the challenge of receiving and integrating the many refugees from Great Britain:

> No country wants to receive more of those decadent people from Great Britain. Free thinkers who are good for nothing but the corruption of the lives of the right-minded. They are unsuited for work. They don't speak Arabic, and they aren't used to carrying their load. Refugees from Britain are unable to do anything except sit in an office and turn over documents. Who needs that?[452]

And later:

> Egypt doesn't want any more refugees from Northern Europe. [...] Britons are indecent heathens that corrupt any society who takes them in. The British count themselves superior to everybody, they have no discipline and are unruly and give rise to unrest everywhere, particularly the women, no matter how much you teach them about their host country's ways and habits.[453]

Note that the second-person pronoun 'you' in the last passage does not refer to the 'you' protagonist, but to the Egyptian public who is not interested in receiving more 'indecent' and 'unruly' 'heathens' from the northern part of the globe. In relation to the reader, passages such as the two cited above function as a mirror, reflecting how refugees from the Middle East, especially Muslims, are viewed, and sometimes even spoken about, by many people in the Western world – 'Muslims do not fit in', 'Muslims are not willing to adapt', 'Muslims are not willing to become Danish/British/German, etc.'. The stereotypes and prejudices that the 'you' protagonist is confronted with are by no means unusual. What is unusual is that it is now the other way around. It is not the refugee from the Middle East who is not welcome; it is *you*, the white reader from the North, nobody is willing to help. Therefore, the reader is forced to rethink her own position and ask herself how she would like to be treated if she was the one fleeing from war. By this manoeuvre along with the interpellative use of second-person narration, the reader becomes subjected to the will or values of the author – no matter if she shares them or not. This is, at least, what critical voices of the book have argued and problematized.

Below, I will turn my attention towards the reception of *War* in Denmark and discuss whether it is fair to claim that Teller is abusing her power as an author

452 Teller, *War*, 14–15.

453 Teller, *War*, 41.

when employing fictionality, including the interpellative use of second-person narration, to address actual political issues.

Potential dangers of an interpellative use of second-person narration

In Denmark, the reception of *War* has been very mixed. On the one hand, Teller has been praised for her ability to engage the reader and raise awareness about immigration policy,[454] and on the other hand, she has been accused of manipulating the reader by giving a simplistic and unnuanced account of a highly complicated issue.[455] On both sides, however, Teller's use of second-person narration is foregrounded as a powerful rhetorical tool by which she achieves a unique kind of reader involvement. Below, I will focus on two critical responses to *War* from 2015 and 2017, when the book received renewed interest in Denmark because of the Syrian refugee crisis.

In 'I Was Shocked When I Read a School Book and Discovered How Much Political Slant It Had'[456] (2015), Danish right-wing politician Peter Kofod warns teachers against using *War* as educational material in Danish primary schools. Naturally, he writes, every 11–16-year-old schoolchild who reads the book will be appalled by 'the inhuman refugee policy of Denmark',[457] but the book does by no means give an adequate account; it is 'black/white, primitive and highly unnuanced in its portrayal of the refugee policy'.[458] It is of utmost importance, Kofod continues, that teachers inform about the enormous problems regarding refugees, such as '[h]uman traffickers, asylum shopping, unfounded asylum seekers [and] massive crime'.[459] Kofod ends by encouraging parents to be aware of their children's educational material to avoid what he describes as 'homogenization and propaganda in school'.[460]

---

454 See Jens Raahauge, 'Hvis der var krig i Norden', *Folkeskolen* (14 May 2016); Nikoline Linnemann Prehn, 'Vi glemmer, at flygtninge er individer, der lige så godt kunne være dig eller mig', *Jyllands-Posten* (24 February 2019).

455 See Peter Kofod, 'Jeg fik noget af et chok, da jeg læste en skolebog og opdagede, hvor meget politisk slagside den havde', *Den korte avis* (4 June 2015); Anne-Marie Vestergaard, 'Når litteratur bliver til debatindlæg', *Berlingske Tidende* (13 July 2017).

456 All translations are my own.

457 Kofod, 'Jeg fik noget af et chok'.

458 Kofod, 'Jeg fik noget af et chok'.

459 Kofod, 'Jeg fik noget af et chok'.

460 Kofod, 'Jeg fik noget af et chok'.

A similar position is found in 'When Literature Becomes a Contribution to the Debate'[461] (2017), where MA in comparative literature Anne-Marie Vestergaard concedes that only a reader stripped of all empathy will not be moved by the use of 'second-person narration [...] in this very realistic war and refugee story':[462] 'Using our fantasy and ability to imagine, in a way we experience the horrifying things being told, which naturally provokes a strong emotional reaction.'[463] But, in line with Kofod, Vestergaard argues that the reader involvement is problematic because of the lack of nuances in the book. According to Vestergaard, good literature is characterized by its 'ambiguity, oppositions and paradoxes';[464] qualities that *War*, in Vestergaard's opinion, does not possess. Teller might be striving for true communication with the reader, but in reality, she comes across as 'an author who forces her own opinions on the reader. There is no dialogue, since the reader is driven into a corner from the beginning.'[465] Vestergaard concludes with the following statement:

> I'm almost tempted to say that she [Teller] becomes an evil author when she manipulates the reader and frames herself as the good author with a cause. Which is such a pity because she should take a step back and be confident that the reader is able to think for herself.[466]

In the afterword, Teller comments on the critical responses to *War* and stresses that she does not understand why it is a problem to be political:

> I hear it [*War*] accused of being political. First of all, I've never understood why being political in a political world could be wrong. But secondly, and more importantly, isn't there something awry, something terribly, ominously awry, when the sheer act of trying to envision, to understand and empathize with the situation of *the other* becomes politized? Aren't we then already beyond the brink of our own humanity?[467]

As a former UN conflict advisor and activist, Teller is used to being outspoken about her political views, and since she debuted as an author, she has shared her thoughts on the relation between literature and politics on several occasions. 'Fiction is a contribution to the debate, it's just a more thorough and, hopefully, long-term contribution', she states in an interview about *War* and continues: 'It's

461 All translations are my own.
462 Vestergaard, 'Når litteratur bliver til debatindlæg'.
463 Vestergaard, 'Når litteratur bliver til debatindlæg'.
464 Vestergaard, 'Når litteratur bliver til debatindlæg'.
465 Vestergaard, 'Når litteratur bliver til debatindlæg'.
466 Vestergaard, 'Når litteratur bliver til debatindlæg'.
467 Teller, *War*, 58–59.

a bit sad that we in Denmark don't have this connection between the everyday debate and the immersion of fiction where it, at its best, really adds something to our understanding of our existence and reality'[468] (my translation).

Kofod and Vestergaard, however, are not the only ones to problematize the interpellative use of second-person narration. In 'Notes on Second-Person Narration. Tolstoj's First Sevastopol Story' (2006), Eric De Hard, too, expresses a concern regarding the lack of nuances in many second-person narratives:

> [i]t [second-person narration] seems to leave too little flexibility for the reader to bring nuances to his identification, to distance himself in some respects, and to identify himself in others. Its obtrusive didacticism ('un recit a la deuxieme personne [...] est toujours un recit didactique' ('a narrative in the second person [...] is always a didactic narrative') (Butor 1964a: 66)) and, one may add, its restriction to a single point of view, seem to impose too many limitations, even though it has resulted in a few eminent works of literature.[469]

Compared to first- and third-person narration, second-person narration is capable of ascribing a very specific set of values to the reader who, as the 'you' protagonist, is unable to answer back and refuse the statements put forth. Yet, the interpellative mode is, as Walsh points out in his discussion of the concept of narrative voice, not restricted to second-person narration: '[n]arration always involves perspectival choices, which necessarily carry with them some set of presuppositions, ranging from the physical (spatio-temporal), through the epistemological, to the ideological'.[470] In fact, one could argue that more conventional narrative techniques can be interpellative in a much more subtle way than second-person narration. This, however, does not change the fact that critical voices such as Kofod and Vestergaard have been extremely provoked by Teller's use of second-person narration; even though readers might easily discern Teller's reason(s) for using second-person narration, they are still, on a linguistic level, forced to identify with the 'you' protagonist.

This manoeuvre becomes particularly interesting when second-person narration is used in a work with an explicit political aim. Back in 2001, Teller was

468 Lotte Folke Kaarsholm, 'I krig med de historiske løgne', *Information* (26 August 2004).

469 Eric De Hard, 'Notes on Second-Person Narration. Tolstoj's First Sevastopol Story', *Amsterdam Journal for Cultural Narratology* (2006), <https://cf.hum.uva.nl/narratology/a06_haard.html>, accessed 27 April 2021.

470 Richard Walsh, 'Person, Level, Voice: A Rhetorical Reconsideration', in Jan Alber and Monika Fludernik, eds., *Postclassical Narratology* (Columbus: Ohio State University Press, 2010), 35–57, 53.

encouraged to write an essay about immigration policy, and in order to do so, she chose to employ fictionality to get her message across in the most forceful way. The book is, as Kofod and Vestergaard argue, not an objective account, but Teller's personal contribution to a very complicated debate. The question that remains, however, is whether Teller is obliged to create a narrative that is open to interpretation. In my opinion, she is not, but the reader has to be aware that second-person narration contains an immanent ability to transform the reader into the protagonist and give her a specific point of view and set of values regardless of what she actually thinks or believes. Because of this 'transformative' quality, there is a similarity between second-person narration and Althusser's notion of interpellation; it is a narrative technique that allows the author to tell the reader directly what to experience, think and feel. Thus, second-person narration often requires a lot of the reader, who continuously has to struggle and reflect upon the positioning power of *you*.

Rikke Andersen Kraglund

8. 'But it hurts like I killed someone': Character Assassinations and Karl Ove Knausgaard's *My Struggle*

Abstract: In this chapter, I suggest that character assassination in literary fiction has the following characteristics. First, character assassination is found in works that refer to real people who would be recognizable either in public or in their private lives. Second, the living and deceased individuals in question would most likely not want to see their character portrayed in this way, so they may regard the portrayal as an invasion of privacy. These works will often include private conversations, letters, biographical information about the lives of others, private pictures and life stories. Third, the portrayal of these characters will be negative and often linked to something shameful and to parental confrontations, divorces and stories of infidelity, incest, bullying, abuse and failure; but one also finds character assassinations of politicians, large groups and systems. Fourth, the ethical dilemmas of writing and publishing personal stories about one's family and friends will often be incorporated into the works themselves and may be used to perform an ethical attitude and legitimize one's narrative. The character assassination motif is often associated with meta-reflections such as: How will the surroundings react? How will the media react? Is it okay to reveal family secrets? Should those involved read the work before it is published? Can the version and voice of those affected be included? Fifth, character assassinations often take place on multiple platforms. Literary works elicit a response in the media, in interviews with the author, in reviews and in research, which may reinforce the first character assassination, but which may also arouse new character assassinations and attacks from those who felt offended by the first attack.

Keywords: character assassination, Karl Ove Knausgaard, My Struggle, autobiographical novels, autofiction, fictionality

Imagine reading a novel that follows your life story and describes your worst defeats and biggest personal problems, featuring a character whose name, place of residence and background is identical to your own. This may sound like a nightmare; and yet it is not an uncommon scenario in contemporary literature, which is full of real-life events and personal narratives that are given away to the public. In recent years, an increasing number of individuals have recognized themselves in a literary work and have called for limits to the freedom of authors to appropriate stories from their personal acquaintances. These cases display the tension between freedom of expression and individual rights.[471]

In this chapter, I reflect on the ethical dilemmas arising when novelists damage the images of family members and friends, leaving their targets with little opportunity to clear their names. I have chosen to study the Norwegian author Karl Ove Knausgaard's autobiographical novel in six parts, *My Struggle* (*Min Kamp* in Norwegian), because the text itself goes into the ethical issues arising when authors draw on private lives in their fiction, leading to discussions about the writer's social role and responsibility and conceptions of the literary craft. Knausgaard reflects on the ethical issues he encounters, and the last volume derives its dramatic drive and progress from the interplay of accusation and self-defence.

My Struggle, which was published between 2009 and 2011, details Knausgaard's life, thoughts and experiences in a personal and introspective manner and refers to real persons and events. These portraits of several named individuals and family members led to a heated debate about the relationship between artistic freedom and defamation, violation of privacy, responsibility, guilt and shame, generating negotiations regarding collective norms and values in connection with testimonies presented in autobiographical novels. This chapter contains a brief analysis of two feature articles written by family members in response to the publication of these novels, to shed light on the ethical problem that arose in this connection. This is followed by a study of the accusations made in the novels themselves, focusing on the character assassinations of Knausgaard's uncle and Knausgaard's wife Linda in volume six, and on how the accusations changed as the narrative progressed in response to the reactions of the outside world.

The many autobiographical novels of our time connect to the discussions about the dangers of narrative and fictionality in this volume because they implicate and harm real people if they are regarded as being directly informative. The authors may exploit the communicative resource of fictionality, but the dangers inherent in these kinds of works thus characterize the referential character of the

471 For a more comprehensive overview of court cases connected to literature, see Ralf Grüttemeier, ed., *Literary Trials. Exceptio Artis and Theories of Literature in Court* (New York, London, Oxford, New Delhi, Sydney: Bloomsbury, 2016) and particularly Gisèle Sapiro, 'The Legal Responsibility of the Writer Between Objectivity and Subjectivity: The French Case (Nineteenth to Twenty-First Century)', in Ralf Grüttemeier, ed., *Literary Trials. Exceptio Artis and Theories of Literature in Court* (New York, London, Oxford, New Delhi, Sydney: Bloomsbury, 2016), 21-47'.

novels. The revelations presented in such novels feel like a betrayal of trust to the people depicted in them.

In closing, the chapter claims that there is a need to consider the differences between character assassination inside and outside the novel because *My Struggle* is far more ambiguous, allowing for contradictory interpretations which are not examined in the media coverage.[472]

Character assassinations in contemporary culture and literature

In the last volume of *My Struggle*, the author's wife, Linda, tells her family that she's afraid that Knausgaard is 'performing a character assassination on her' in his forthcoming novels.[473] The term 'character assassination' is otherwise typically used in a political, rhetorical and psychological context but it is also a notable tendency in contemporary culture and communication. 'Character assassination' has been described as 'a practice in which a deliberate and sustained effort is made to damage the reputation or credibility of an individual',[474] and it refers to both the process (the attack itself) and the result (the destruction of a reputation or a negative portrayal of another person). This can be done through a variety of means, including spreading false or malicious rumours, publishing damaging information or accusations, or using other forms of propaganda or manipulation. Character assassination is often used as a political tactic to discredit an opponent or rival and can be particularly effective when the individual being targeted has a high profile or is in a position of power or influence. Politicians and celebrities are common targets for character assassination, but character assassinations are experienced daily by anyone involved in debates in the media, and it can also be used in personal disputes or other situations where an individual seeks to harm the reputation of another. The increasingly competitive

---

472 This chapter incorporates excerpts from my article on Knausgaard's persuasive attack in: Rikke Andersen Kraglund, 'Karaktermord, angreb og selvanklager omkring Karl Ove Knausgårds *Min kamp*', *Rhetorica Scandinavica* 25 (2021),106–122; Rikke Andersen Kraglund, 'Karaktermord i 10'ernes danske skønlitteratur', *Passage* 36 (2021), 7–27.

473 Karl Ove Knausgaard, *My Struggle. VI*, Don Bartlett, trans. (New York: Archipelago Books, [2009–11] 2012–18), 963.

474 Serhei A. Samoilenko, Eric Shiraev, Jennifer Keohane and Martijn Icks, 'Character Assassination', in Alena Ledeneva, ed., *The Global Encyclopaedia of Informality. Volume II* (London: UCL Press, 2018), 441.

discourse in politics has led to an increase in character assassinations, but they are not a new phenomenon. They can be found in a great variety of times and places but have some universal aspects that remain remarkably constant across ages and cultures. In *Routledge Handbook of Character Assassination and Reputation Management* (2020), the editors refer to 'the use of stigma, stereotypes and taboos, the implicit or explicit appeals to morality, the mixing of truth and falsehood, and direct insults'.[475]

When character assassination is committed in a political context, the intention of the attack is often easy to see. Character assassination has been described as a multi-pronged process that takes place in relation to five components: 'the Attacker, the Target, the Medium or Media, the Audience, and the Context'.[476] *The Attacker* makes a deliberate attack on someone else's reputation and history in an attempt to create a public reaction of anger, affect and judgement that will undermine the target's social status, and here it will be particularly interesting to take a closer look at the motivation for the attack and the chosen strategies. *The Target* will often be a prominent and famous person who risks having both his public reputation and his social capital destroyed. *The Medium or Media* can be printed or digital, consisting of text, images or videos, with different effects being achieved with different media. Character assassination will also be addressed and passed on to *The Audience* that the attacker is trying to convince and influence. The Audience can choose to believe or reject the accusations, and they have the power to decide whether the character assassination in question should have an effect. The last factor is *The Context* in which character assassination takes place. Social norms and cultural and historical traditions influence the ways in which an attack is understood, and are also negotiated along the way.

Scholars have only rarely thought about character assassination in autobiographical novels, maybe because in fiction the attacker, target, medium, audience and context are more ambiguous and complicated than they are in a political context. Fiction is written for a greater good and with a higher purpose than the desire to accuse someone of something, and fictional characters are generally either invented or unknown to the general public. But fiction may still feel like an attack on someone's character, especially in novels that include the life stories of real individuals. However, it is not easy to identify the attacker

475 Martijn Icks, Sergei A. Samoilenko, Jennifer Keohane and Eric Shiraev, 'Introduction', in *Routledge Handbook of Character Assassination and Reputation Management* (New York: Routledge, 2020), 2.

476 Icks et al., 'Introduction', 16.

in fiction (is a fictional character carrying out the attack, or is the narrator or author the attacker?). The author may express a different attitude than his character – even though they share the same name. The target may have changed, as the person exposed to an attack is not necessarily based on only one individual but may have been created from several different persons and have partially fictive traits. The audience or readers may of course also differ in terms of how an attack seems to them, depending on how close they are to the author and the person being attacked. It is easier for literary scholars and critics to defend artistic freedom than it is for people who see their own lives on display – or the lives of their families. The context of the work's character assassinations may also change, particularly in relation to where and when the work is published. The attack may seem very diverse, depending for instance on whether it is experienced and interpreted owing to the depth and ambiguity created in fiction or experienced via author interviews, feature articles for the newspapers or blog posts in the epitext.

I suggest that character assassination in literature has the following characteristics. First, character assassination is found in works that refer to real people who would be recognizable either in public or in their private lives. Second, the living and deceased individuals in question would most likely not want to see their character portrayed in this way and these works will often include private conversations, letters, biographical information about the lives of others, private pictures and life stories. Third, the portrayal of these characters will be negative and often linked to something shameful and to parental confrontations, divorces and stories of infidelity, incest, bullying, abuse and failure; but one also finds character assassinations of politicians, large groups and systems. Fourth, the ethical dilemmas of writing and publishing personal stories about one's family and friends will often be incorporated into the works themselves and may be used to perform an ethical attitude and legitimize one's narrative. The character assassination motif is often associated with meta-reflections such as: How will the surroundings react? How will the media react? Is it okay to reveal family secrets? Should those involved read the work before it is published? Can the version and voice of those affected be included? Fifth, character assassinations often take place on multiple platforms. Literary works elicit a response in the media, in interviews with the author, in reviews and in research, which may reinforce the first character assassination, but which may also arouse new character assassinations and attacks from those who felt offended by the first attack.

In *The Rhetoric of fictionality* (2007) and in the article 'Fictionality as Rhetoric. A Distinctive Research Paradigm' (2019), Richard Walsh presents a rhetorical view of fictionality in which fictionality is understood as a quality and resource of fiction, as communication that is closely connected to the readers' inferential process. When we assume that 'a rhetoric of fictionality is in play', then we do not look for the utterance's directly informative relevance but privilege 'the inferential retrieval of less immediate implicatures'.[477] So fictionality changes the way in which we as readers seek to understand the relevance of the communication in question; it reorients our communicative attention because it does not inform the utterance in itself but rather 'the narrative mode in which it participates'.[478] The fiction's aboutness and its communication is something that is worked through in the interpretative encounter with a fictional narrative in process; and therefore a character assassination in fiction must be studied not only locally in a statement or in a scene, but also in the interpretation of the larger context of the narrative.

Offended by *My Struggle*

In 2011, the sixth and final volume of Knausgaard's *My Struggle* was released. By then, the work had become one of the most controversial novels in Scandinavia today, due to the author's ambition to write about his own life without being limited by the interests of his immediate family. On the very day of publication, a feature article was published by Knausgaard's uncle, containing an accusation and an appeal to the readers to use their critical sense and empathy: 'Put yourself in the place of his relatives and imagine how YOU would react. Does it violate what you can legally allow? Are there any ethical concerns?' (my translation).[479] This was not the first time that the family had reacted. Even on the release of the first volume, fourteen family members wrote a feature article in the Norwegian newspaper *Klassekampen* complaining that the project violated their honour:

> This is confessional literature and nonfiction we are talking about. Judas Literature. It is a book full of insinuations, untruths, erroneous descriptions of persons, absolute exposure that clearly violates Norwegian law in this area (my translation).[480]

The family members pointed out that the novel contravened Norwegian law, which caused the same newspaper to consult a solicitor, who recommended

---

477 Richard Walsh, 'Fictionality as Rhetoric: A Distinctive Research Paradigm', *Style* 53/4 (2019), 411.

478 Walsh, 'Fictionality as Rhetoric', 417.

479 Bjørge Knausgaard, 'Hilsen fra onkel Gunnar', *Fædrelandsvennen* (16 November 2011).

480 Knausgaard (14 affected family members), 'Klassekampen, Schiøtz og Knausgaard', *Klassekampen* (3 October 2009).

that the family members should not pursue any legal action. Section 390 of the Norwegian Penal Code states otherwise: 'Any person who by frightening or annoying behaviour or other inconsiderate conduct violates another person's right to be left in peace, or is accessory thereto, shall be liable to fines or imprisonment for a term not exceeding six months'.[481] Despite this statement in the Norwegian Penal Code, the solicitor was unable to provide a single example of a novel which had led to a sentence in the Norwegian courts recently. In Norway, it seems to be virtually impossible to respond to a novel's unwanted representations as violations of one's privacy, and very few cases end up in court.

The family regarded *My Struggle* as a character assassination, and it is true that the novel has some of the defining characteristics of character assassination in literature. It includes private life stories, conversations and biographical information about the lives of others, and Knausgaard's father's family did not want to see their characters involved. The family found the portrayal of the father and grandmother in volume one problematic because of the shameful implication that they had a drinking problem and that the family had neglected the grandmother. In *My Struggle* volume six, the ethical dilemmas of writing and publishing personal stories about the family are incorporated and used to perform an ethical attitude and legitimize the narrative. The book elicited a response from the family in the media and led to new character assassinations, counterattacks and moral judgements.

In the following, I want to present an analysis of the feature articles written by family members, because in responding in this way the family were not only committing new character assassinations on the author and the novels but also negotiating what is socially acceptable in literature and discussing freedom of expression in contradiction with respect of privacy. In this counterattack, Knausgaard's father's family is *the attacker*, *the media* is the Norwegian newspapers *Klassekampen* and *Fædrelandsvennen*, and *the target* is Knausgaard, *My Struggle* and the publisher. The family's attack is an attempt to present a public reaction of anger, affect and judgement by increasing the audience's perceptions of the offensiveness of the act of writing *My Struggle*. I will take a closer look at the family's attacks and show how the attacks are also used as a defence against the character assassinations in the novels (as a form of image repair).

The two feature articles show the public judicial negotiations about the boundaries of what is allowed in literature and what is not. The family uses arguments

---

481 Legislationline, 'Criminal Code of the Kingdom of Norway (English version)', § 390 a, <https://www.legislationline.org/documents/id/8909>, accessed 23 December 2021.

from judicial dealings with literature in courtrooms and they attack both the writing and the publication of *My Struggle*. According to the family, the book is full of 'untruths' and exposes a number of people because the book's cast of characters is still 'identifiable'. The publisher has been 'tricked by the author', as *My Struggle* is not 'a novel', but contains a dangerous mixture 'of reality, fantasy and untruths', which makes it 'impossible for a reader or reviewer to distinguish' and extremely difficult for 'affected living or dead persons to defend themselves'. The discussions about truth and falsehood are a characteristic trait of character assassinations, and several of the accusations against *My Struggle* are directed at the genre tag and the way the author and publisher define it:

> In terms of genre, this is not a novel. Publishing editor Geir Berdahl said in August: 'The novel is based on autobiographical material.' The author July 31: 'This is an autobiographical novel. All names and events are authentic. '[...]. Author September 18: 'The book is based on reality but is not reality.' The author September 25: 'I do not remember much from childhood. What I have experienced must be recreated based on the visual. That is what fictionalisation is all about.' Here it is clear that neither the author nor the publisher knows what they have published. The author turns 180 degrees, from 'authentic' to 'fictionalisation'. The publisher has cold feet but insists on calling it a novel (my translation).[482]

The affected family members see these statements as examples of the publisher and author not knowing what they were publishing and starting to fear the consequences of the book. In the literary tradition of autofiction and autobiographical novels, however, these are not contradictory statements. As long ago as the 1970s, the author and literary theorist Serge Doubrovsky proposed the genre of autofiction to reflect the ambiguity of the autobiographical novel and talked about the 'fiction of strictly real events'.[483] Certain dangers and problems arise in this situation because there is a difference between the definition of genre within and outside the literary institution, which increases miscommunication and different perceptions of artistic freedom. The affected family members want a clear distinction to be drawn between fiction and nonfiction, while publishers, authors and literary scholars are interested in its grey areas and equivocality. A central feature of literary trials from the second haft of the nineteenth century onwards is according to Ralf Grüttemeier 'the judicial acceptance of a certain kind of autonomy for literature'.[484] A text may be judged differently if it is classified as a

482 Knausgaard (14 affected family members), 'Klassekampen, Schiøtz og Knausgaard'.
483 Hywel Dix, ed., *Autofiction in English. Palgrave Studies in Life Writing* (Cham: Palgrave Macmillan, 2018), 2.
484 Grüttemeier, 'Literary Trials as Mirrors', 8.

literary text, but the family do not think that fiction can be invoked in defence of the writer since he at the same time claims the veracity of the narrative.

In the two feature articles written by family members, it is very clear that not only Karl Ove Knausgaard, but also the editor and the publisher are held responsible for the publication and its consequences. They are described as 'cynical', and according to Knausgaard's uncle, they knew what they were doing and benefited from it. Sincerity and good faith are extenuating circumstances in defence for a writer and the same is personal conviction as described by Giséle Sapriro in 'The Legal Responsibility of the Writer Between Objectivity and Subjectivity':

> Personal conviction can be an extenuating circumstance in so far as it is linked both to freedom of thought and freedom of philosophical discussion, or to the particular rules of literature (its autonomy) [...]. Being free to develop and publish his own system of thought, the author who acts out of personal conviction and the writer bound by the constraints of his art are deemed to have acted in good faith, not necessarily intending to do harm, and not having realized the consequences of his acts.[485]

The uncle tries to prove that the act of publication has less pure ends. According to him, the novels were only motivated by two things: 'money and fame' whatever the cost not only for Knausgaard but also for his intimates: 'The author's brother (Yngve) makes a profit on the covers, starts a publishing company and publishes books in the wake of this. The author's wife (Linda) suddenly takes the name Knausgaard and then publishes a book and becomes a columnist in a woman's magazine. Random? And the world can be fooled?'.[486] Desire for fame and desire for reward are according to Sapriro 'aggravating circumstances' because in that case 'the author has acted out of self-interest without thought for the consequences of his actions':

> The metaphor commonly used to designate this kind of act is 'prostitution', with the underlying analogy between selling one's body and selling one's pen, which refers to the personalization of the idea of the 'author', and the identification of the man and his work. The quest for fame can lead ambitious authors to break the law solely to get talked about, and by that means become famous.[487]

The feature articles do not only constitute an attack on the author's and publisher's intentions in publishing it, but also paint a negative portrait of Karl Ove Knausgaard and pass moral judgements on his behaviour. In the introduction

485 Sapiro, 'The Legal Responsibility of the Writer Between Objectivity and Subjectivity', 27.
486 Knausgaard, 'Hilsen fra onkel Gunnar'.
487 Sapiro, 'The Legal Responsibility of the Writer Between Objectivity and Subjectivity', 27.

to 'Character Assassination: Theoretical Framework', the editors propose seven methods by which attackers generally attack their targets: name-calling, making allegations, ridiculing, fearmongering, exposing, disgracing and erasing.[488] Among other things, Knausgaard's moral integrity is cast into doubt by his uncle, and he loses all sense of honour because he attempts to 'act as a victim'. Knausgaard's uncle portrays him as being placed outside 'good' society as an emblem of disgrace because he consistently humiliates the people he meets and does not care about the book's victims, which his uncle supports with a reference to his brother Yngve's statement: 'Karl Ove knows that there are many people in the family who will hate him for what he does, but he doesn't give a damn about this'.[489] One classic form of attack is 'erasing' or 'silencing', which refers to 'the practice of avoiding any reference to an individual and their work by the attacker'.[490] This 'silencing' is very prominent in the feature article written by Knausgaard's uncle, in which Knausgaard's name is consistently avoided in favour of the anonymous 'author' and his 'accomplice', which establishes a distance. At the same time, the name may be omitted in order to detach Karl Ove Knausgaard from the Knausgaard family, because along the way his uncle draws a picture of two groups and antagonists: 'his father's family' and 'his mother's family' [The Hatløys]. His uncle creates an image of a conspiracy, with *My Struggle* being a story of revenge prompted by Knausgaard's mother against the Knausgaard family: 'the truth about how *My Struggle* has been a collaborative project between publishers, the author's mother's family and himself is certainly unpleasant to present'.[491]

The character assassinations are also used as a defence against the novel's accusations (as a form of 'image repair'). Both feature articles indicate the victims' innocence and helplessness as 'manipulated' and 'involuntary extras', and they make it plain that there should have been a special obligation to protect the victims, as several of those affected have died and are unable to defend themselves. The attempt to increase the readers' antipathy towards Knausgaard is thus expanded by highlighting the loving, loyal and trusting grandparents, who fortunately did not themselves experience the negative effects of *My Struggle*, but

488 Martijn Icks, Sergei A. Samoilenko, Jennifer Keohane and Eric Shiraev, 'Character Assassination: Theoretical Framework', in *Routledge Handbook of Character Assassination and Reputation Management* (New York: Routledge, 2020), 11–24.

489 Knausgaard, 'Hilsen fra onkel Gunnar'.

490 Samoilenko, Shiraev, Keohane and Icks, 'Character Assassination', 443.

491 Knausgaard, 'Hilsen fra onkel Gunnar'.

who, according to Knausgaard's uncle, had their reputation, history and name dragged through the mud.

An effective attack must first imagine the target's response, and Knausgaard may have expected his uncle's counterattack against *My Struggle.* From volume six, we know that his uncle was furious when Knausgaard made his debut with the novel *Out of the World* (orig. *Ute av verden*, 1998), in which Knausgaard's father and his father's brothers also appeared but in an anonymous and fictitious form. *My Struggle* does not protect the people involved to the same extent, and in announcing *My Struggle,* Knausgaard stated that he had written the novels without taking his loved ones into account, which may have helped to provoke a counterattack. The family's feature articles had a great influence on the reception of *My Struggle* and on the debate concerning autobiographical novels in Norway. At the same time, the family's accusations helped to increase the media's attention on the novel, and their response created contexts that could be included in the last volume of *My Struggle* to tell a story about how ethics and morals are negotiated when someone oversteps social norms and boundaries that are not written down anywhere. In the following, I will show how Knausgaard's uncle's attack is exhibited in volume six and arouses new attacks and defences.

Exposing Knausgaard's uncle's attack

At the beginning of *My Struggle, book six*, the sun is shining, there isn't a cloud in sight, the world is wide open and the protagonist Karl Ove has an intense feeling of happiness. The publication of *My Struggle, book one* is approaching, but his joy is tinged with a sense of anxiety and 'unease'. Knausgaard's uncle has read the manuscript and has threatened to go to the papers and take the case to court. As readers, we already know that the media have got hold of the story and that the novel has had severe implications for the relatives, and it is this story we are about to learn. What were the consequences of writing these autobiographical novels? For him as a writer? For the family? How does it feel to overstep a social norm in this way? What happened when family and friends read the manuscript, and how did the media react? What kind of pressure did he meet, and how did it affect his writing?

In volume six, we go back in time and follow the publication process, during which Knausgaard sends the manuscript to the publishers and to everyone that plays a part in it. With a backwards composition, we learn about his uncle's reaction and 'abhorrent emails'[492] before Knausgaard sends him the manuscript

492 Knausgaard, *My Struggle. VI*, 45.

and waits for his answer in good faith: 'I argued against my unease, telling myself I hadn't written anything bad about the people now reading it'.[493] Knausgaard knows that his uncle will not be pleased with what he has written about his father and grandmother in volume one, but he doesn't think his picture of his uncle can give rise to displeasure because he comes out 'well' and is treated 'respectfully'.[494] But this polite picture of Knausgaard's uncle is about to change in book six, which contains a character assassination due to his counterattack on volume one, and this portrait may seem like some kind of vengeance.

In the novel, his first letter to his uncle is submitted; a letter that describes volume one and reveals Knausgaard's guilty conscience about the project, but at the same time provides his uncle with ammunition for his attack on the novels:

> I am laying bare the private life of our family, something neither you nor anyone else in the book has asked for. On the other hand, this is a book about me and my dad, that's what it deals with, my endeavour to understand him and what happened to him. [...] The fact that this story also involves other people, among them – and perhaps especially – you, torments me severely, but at the same time I've been unable to see any way around it. The rot and repugnance the book describes all comes down to Dad, no one else was to blame, but I can't describe any of it without reference to the context in which it took place. That's the way it is.[495]

Knausgaard says that he is prepared to change the names of his uncle and family and make their backgrounds anonymous, but he is aware that the problem lies elsewhere: 'that something you would prefer left alone, out of sight, is now going to be held up on display. Again, I'm sorry for that, but he was my father, the story I tell is my own, and unfortunately it looks like this'.[496] The problem arises because the author's life is inevitably intertwined with the history of other people (his family, friends and acquaintances), making it difficult to write autobiographically without including his relationship with other people. In Paul John Eakin's article 'The unseemly profession. Privacy, inviolate personality, and the ethics of life writing' (1999), private life is described as a kind of co-property, as our stories and lives are closely linked and inextricably intertwined.[497] When

493 Knausgaard, *My Struggle. VI*, 86.
494 Knausgaard, *My Struggle. VI*, 88.
495 Knausgaard, *My Struggle. VI*, 65.
496 Knausgaard, *My Struggle. VI*, 65.
497 Paul John Eakin, 'The Unseemly Profession. Privacy, Inviolate Personality, and the Ethics of Life Writing', in *How Our Lives Become Stories: Making Selves* (Ithaca and London: Cornell University Press, 1999), 169.

autobiographical material is used, it usually also becomes a biography of others. But it is not always the case that one's acquaintances want to give their consent to have their own story told, particularly if the story contains the more shadowy aspects of life. *My Struggle* raises the question of how to portray people who do not want to be included in fictional works written by others. Do you always have the right to tell your own story and thus involve others, or are our life stories also a form of private property? In 'Appropriating Other's Stories. Some Questions about the Ethics of Writing Fiction', Claudia Mills asks whether close relationships with friends and family involve some kind of agreed promise of confidentiality:

> Although friends or family members seldom ask us for explicit promises of confidentiality, this is only because confidentiality is so much taken for granted that no promise need to be given. We view our intimate relationships as enjoying certain protections: our homes, our families, our friendships provide protected zones in our lives where we can be who we want to be without fear of subsequent exposure or disclosure. Authors who expose family secrets, even those who simply publicize the quiet textures of everyday family life, may seem to transgress certain boundaries that appropriately protect intimacy.[498]

The writing of autobiographical fiction would be impossible, Mills says, without the author's licence to borrow from real life, including the real-life stories of those we know, love and hate. But the more the author's use of other people's stories is in a 'tension with ordinary moral requirements', the harder it is to justify, even acknowledging everything that we owe to literature:

> Authors have no special license to harm others, either by damaging their reputation or by causing them pain; authors have no special license to invade others' privacy or violate their confidentiality; authors, who are after all first and foremost human beings, need to respect their relationships with those about whom they write.[499]

Knausgaard's uncle's reaction is full of anger, as revealed by the newspaper feature articles. We are told that the subject line for his email to Knausgaard and the editor is 'verbal rape',[500] and that volume one is described as a 'despicable, immoral and self-centred shambles of a book' that is 'riddled with untruths, mean-spirited depictions'.[501] Knausgaard is attacked by calling his mental capacities

498 Claudia Mills, 'Appropriating Others' Stories: Some Questions about the Ethics of Writing Fiction', *Journal of Social Philosophy* 31/2 (2000), 202.
499 Mills, 'Appropriating Others' Stories', 205.
500 Knausgaard, *My Struggle. VI*, 95.
501 Knausgaard, *My Struggle. VI*, 96.

and moral integrity into question. He is lacking in empathy and has committed an act 'far worse than anything his father has ever done to him as he was growing up'.[502] His uncle wants to take legal action claiming damages, and he wants to stop the book from being published,[503] but at the beginning of the novel we hear how difficult it is to go to court if you have been offended by a novel without getting the attention you reacted to in the first place. As Knausgaard's friend Marie explains in a conversation about the uncle's possible court case: 'But if he doesn't want anyone to read what you've written, that wouldn't be the best way of going about it'.[504] In *The Treacherous Imagination* (2013), Robert McGill describes this problem of attention: 'when people feel aggrieved by fiction seeming to depict them, usually they are not eager to draw attention to the problem and risk further dissemination of the injurious representation'.[505] While Knausgaard is afraid that his uncle is going to take him to court, his friend Angell tells him to hope that this happens. A *succès de scandale* can get a commercial profit: 'Everyone'll be wanting your books if it comes to a court case! This is literary history in the making. And you'll be a millionaire. There's no better scenario'.[506]

One characteristic feature of autobiographies is the use of what James O' Rourke has called a 'legitimizing narrative', in which the narrator highlights his good intentions, and a 'shadow narrative', in which he talks about his discomfort in having to hurt others with his narrative.[507] Knausgaard performs an ethical attitude by criticizing his own project and acknowledging his uncle's right to be angry about the infringement of his private space: 'I've gone into detail in describing the place where it happened. That was his childhood home. I've written about my grandmother, right down to the smallest detail, and she was his mother. He grew up in those rooms. Of course it's an infringement, because it's a private space. His space'.[508] Knausgaard regards a court case as the worst possible scenario and imagines that he is sitting in the witness box having read the headlines in the newspapers: 'KNAUSGAARD THE LIAR; SHAMBLES; SHOULD NEVER HAVE BEEN PUBLISHED; ADMITS LYING; KNAUSGAARD RAPED

502 Knausgaard, *My Struggle. VI*, 96.

503 Knausgaard, *My Struggle. VI*, 103.

504 Knausgaard, *My Struggle. VI*, 17.

505 Robert McGill, *The Treacherous Imagination* (Columbus: The Ohio State University Press, 2013), 12.

506 Knausgaard, *My Struggle. VI*, 100.

507 James O' Rouke, *Sex, Lies and Autobiography: The Ethics of Confession* (Charlottesville: University of Virginia Press, 2006), 6.

508 Knausgaard, *My Struggle. VI*, 389.

ME'.[509] In the following quote, the imagined lawyer in this court expresses himself in a way that resembles Knausgaard's uncle's attack in the newspaper:

> You have offended these people, desecrated memories of two deceased members of your own family. You sold your father and grandmother for blood money. And all you can say is it's how you remembered it? Violating the privacy of your family is a serious enough matter on its own, a criminal offence, but to have lied about your uncle's mother and his brother exacerbates that offence tenfold. We're talking about defamation of character, carrying a sentence of up to three years' imprisonment.[510]

In his imagination, Knausgaard replies as follows: 'I've written about my father, it's my own story I'm telling. That can't be against the law, surely? Can it?'.[511] The question marks clearly invite the reader to consider these issues. Did he have the right to involve other people besides himself? What is so dangerous about the serial? He discusses his uncle's attack with Angell and alternately defends and accuses the project as if they were sitting in a courtroom, and again the scene invites reflections about how to defend the publication: 'The question is by what right. The right of literature? That means I'm saying literature is more important than the life of the individual. And not only that, I'm saying my literature is more important than his life'.[512] How should the invasion of privacy be weighed up against freedom of speech and artistic freedom? Geir has the role of defence lawyer for the novel: 'It's going to affect others. So what? Did you kill someone? Did you assault someone? Did you steal from someone? Did you write anything bad about them? No. You've written very kindly about Gunnar'.[513]

The portrait of Knausgaard's uncle becomes increasingly unsympathetic in the course of the story, and the rhetoric of both Knausgaard's uncle and *My Struggle* is intensified as the conflict escalates. His uncle is positioned as the attacker: 'If you go through with this, I'll take you to court. I'll make you bleed. I'll destroy you. You little shit of a nephew. That was what he was saying',[514] and Knausgaard and the novel are positioned as the target and the victim: 'I bowed my head in deep and heartfelt shame'.[515] But these descriptions of his uncle's reactions are also a new character assassination in which the attacker is Knausgaard and the

509 Knausgaard, *My Struggle. VI*, 184.
510 Knausgaard, *My Struggle. VI*, 187.
511 Knausgaard, *My Struggle. VI*, 187.
512 Knausgaard, *My Struggle. VI*, 117.
513 Knausgaard, *My Struggle. VI*, 270.
514 Knausgaard, *My Struggle. VI*, 123.
515 Knausgaard, *My Struggle. VI*, 124.

target is his uncle. We hear that his uncle makes absolute demands and wants himself and his wife removed completely from the book, as well as the description of his mother and the final phase of his brother's life. At the same time, he makes threats about going to the tabloid press and wants to sue for damages.[516] His uncle's emails are described as 'malicious',[517] and Knausgaard's brother Yngve receives an anonymous threatening letter that states the following: 'How bitter the thought that an abortion in 1964 could have given so many people a simpler life in 2010. We would have been spared the Hatløys. And your father would have been alive today'.[518] The readers' perceptions of the offensiveness of Knausgaard's uncle's act are increased by stressing the damage the action has caused for Knausgaard, who is going through 'hell' and feels an inner turmoil of distress and terror as if 'someone died'.[519] As we follow a condemnation of his uncle from Knausgaard's family and friends, we are invited to a similar response. The book asks if his uncle's rage can be justified.

In volume six, Knausgaard is under great pressure from the persons closest to him. His mother is worried about him and his family because he risks being made out to be some kind of criminal in the media. She asks him if it is worth it and warns him: 'I think the consequences for you are going to be quite far-reaching. If he goes to the papers or takes you to court. It'll be a huge strain. You're going to get a lot of negative publicity. The pressure will be enormous. People can crack in that situation'.[520] In the second part of volume six, this crack is described. Knausgaard can defend himself and the project from his uncle's accusations and claims; but the defence falls apart in relation to Linda, and the narrative develops from a character assassination against his uncle into a character assassination of himself because he can't legitimize *My Struggle's* consequences for Linda or assess the damage.

'Oh, Linda, Linda'

In the first part of the novel, we are waiting for Linda to read the manuscript for volume two, and the feeling of unease is now connected to Knausgaard's guilt towards her:

---

516 Knausgaard, *My Struggle. VI*, 139.
517 Knausgaard, *My Struggle. VI*, 860.
518 Knausgaard, *My Struggle. VI*, 407.
519 Knausgaard, *My Struggle. VI*, 320.
520 Knausgaard, *My Struggle. VI*, 156.

> There is nothing to be afraid of, she said. I can handle whatever, as long as it's true. But Linda was a romantic heart, she accepted the despondencies and conflicts of day-to-day life as long as the idea prevailed of there always being something else to fall back on, our love for each other, our lives together.[521]

At first, Knausgaard tries to defend the character assassination of Linda in volume two. He had been full of anger and frustrations when he wrote about the life in the family, 'the ordinary man's little hell',[522] and he wanted to break free from commitments and bonds and get 'into the open' as he writes with a reference to Hölderlin.[523] He had been afraid of 'the loudness of her voice, her sudden fits of anger, and had no idea how to handle it',[524] but at the same time, we learn that Linda's shifting moods and active and passive periods have a background in her struggle with mental illness.[525] In volume two, Knausgaard describes Linda as lazy, when she was actually depressed. As we learn more about Linda's anxiety and bipolarity, we start expecting a tragedy, and the author builds up to this with references to the myth about Faust.

In Goethe's *Faust*, the scholar Faust is dissatisfied with his life and embarks on a quest to find the true essence of life. He is frustrated with the limits of his knowledge and enjoyment of life, and this leads him to make a pact with the Devil and exchange his soul for unlimited knowledge and worldly pleasure. In *My Struggle*, Knausgaard's friend Geir Angell has the role of a demonic voice who tantalises him with freedom as in Thomas Mann's *Doctor Faustus*:[526]

> I allowed Geir to influence me to such an extent that his opinions became my opinions, that to a degree he was brainwashing me, and the distance that had opened up between Linda and me, which was due to my frustration, was a part of that. Geir was whispering in my ear about my life and her role in it, and before long it would make me leave her.[527]

For Knausgaard, life has become monotonous, he misses the intensity of life and he takes everything for granted, which is explained as 'poison', and his soul is described as 'cold'.[528] He wants to write no matter what and is willing to make any sacrifice in order to do so.[529] He defends the autonomy of the writer and is

521 Knausgaard, *My Struggle. VI*, 42–43
522 Knausgaard, *My Struggle. VI*, 43.
523 Knausgaard, *My Struggle. VI*, 365, 953.
524 Knausgaard, *My Struggle. VI*, 325.
525 Knausgaard, *My Struggle. VI*, 892.
526 Knausgaard, *My Struggle. VI*, 271, 969.
527 Knausgaard, *My Struggle. VI*, 331.
528 Knausgaard, *My Struggle. VI*, 937.
529 Knausgaard, *My Struggle. VI*, 62.

willing to sacrifice his love for Linda and lose his soul.[530] The aim of *My Struggle* is to tell the truth: 'Yes, my hands trembled at the very thought that I could actually describe everything as it was. That all I had to do was just go ahead and do it. What a treacherous thought!'.[531] He gains succes as an author, just as he desired, and people do fall for his 'tricks'.[532] But this is also presented as a story about hybris: 'Oh, it was going to be brilliant! Six books! Fuck, I was going to wipe the floor with them!'.[533] We hear that Knausgaard receives the Brage Prize for *My Struggle, book one*, and for this fame, there is a price to be paid. To understand this price, we get to know Linda better in volume six and learn more about their love for each other and the children. In the end, there is an accumulation of emotional significance, and the narrative is loading Linda with care that testifies to her goodness and loading Knausgaard with shame because he has sacrificed Linda's understanding of their love. Knausgaard remembers Linda's song for him at his birthday party. For the first time, Linda's own words are included, revealing something about her tenderness:

The days have turned to years
And my eyes are transfigured
Such a man, such a man is he
A touch of his hand made my life complete
He looked at me and smiled
I saw his lion heart and smiled
Karl Ove, my beloved
I love you so, I love you so.[534]

He loved her dearly at the beginning of their relationship but can't feel this until he is attacked by his uncle and he wants to 'be in the midst of my family, to live my life there, and so strong was my desire that it filled me with impatience, as if it would soon be too late'.[535] When his uncle attacks him, he feels defenceless against what is going on inside him.[536] The attack evokes his inner turmoil. But this is a feeling he has for a few days. We are about to see Linda defenceless on an entirely different level.

---

530 Knausgaard, *My Struggle. VI*, 881, 1017.
531 Knausgaard, *My Struggle. VI*, 912.
532 Knausgaard, *My Struggle. VI*, 971.
533 Knausgaard, *My Struggle. VI*, 71.
534 Knausgaard, *My Struggle. VI*, 889.
535 Knausgaard, *My Struggle. VI*, 266.
536 Knausgaard, *My Struggle. VI*, 314.

Knausgaard feels a rising sense of unease, and so does the reader as we sense that a tragedy is on its way. Knausgaard asks rhetorically: 'But there was nothing to be afraid of, was there?'.[537] We know that the fear is well-founded as we hear about *Oedipus Rex*, 'about a man who doesn't know and about what happens to him as he gradually enlightened and finally discovers the truth'.[538] As the narrative progresses, Knausgaard gains insight and feels guilty about his reactions to Linda. He now realizes that he wasn't there when her father died because he was writing about the death of his own father for *My Struggle*: 'my attempt to console her and be sympathetic was mechanical. When it came to the crunch, I failed her'.[539] As readers, we are touched by Linda's grief, and we hear about her cry for help in the airport on the way home from the funeral: 'Help!' she shouted in a loud voice. 'Help us!':

> At the time I had taken it literally, she wanted help carrying John, but when I reread the passage, it was impossible not to think of something else, something greater, a cry from her inner being, to me, I had to go to her rescue. I had to put everything aside, she was in distress, I had to help.
> I hadn't done that. I had lost my temper and was embarrassed. When she screamed in the night, I thought I should help her. I hope I can, I hope I am good enough. I hope I have learned.[540]

But we are going to see one more scene in which he doesn't understand her cry for help, and we are about to hear how she is affected when she reads *My Struggle*. When Knausgaard asks her to accept the manuscript for volume two, he knows that it is 'actually inhuman'.[541] Everyone now reads his version, his truth about them, and he ruins her ideas about romanticism and all the beautiful illusions about their relationship.[542] Everything has come into the open but the tragedy is on the way because Linda is hurt not only by his writings but also by the stories they have given rise to in the newspapers.[543] In the end, she collapses and breaks down, and once more he doesn't understand her cry for help, and it is almost unbearable to read. Karl Ove is going to Iceland to promote the novels, but Linda is afraid of being alone with the children because she is depressed. He tells her

537 Knausgaard, *My Struggle. VI*, 853.
538 Knausgaard, *My Struggle. VI*, 899.
539 Knausgaard, *My Struggle. VI*, 962–963
540 Knausgaard, *My Struggle. VI*, 969.
541 Knausgaard, *My Struggle. VI*, 987.
542 Knausgaard, *My Struggle. VI*, 987.
543 Knausgaard, *My Struggle. VI*, 994.

once more to pull herself together and shows us how coldly he reacts because the books are more important to him in this situation. Several times she begs him not to go, but he feels no empathy.[544] When he comes home, Linda is barely able to talk, and she has lost her grip and has fallen 'so far into her inner darkness that nothing around her had any meaning any longer'.[545]

> It was a terrible feeling, filled with gloom, because it was my fault she had ended up there, in the bedroom, in bed. I hadn't taken care of her. Had I done so, this wouldn't have happened. But I had done the opposite. I had made sure the pressure on her had been unbearable.[546]

> It hit her where she was most vulnerable, in the question of her identity, who she was. I held up a mirror, and not only did she see herself there, but so did everyone else.[547]

Knausgaard's portrayal of Linda is deeply moving, and, in the end, he attacks his own thoughtless and reckless behaviour. Now Linda is sick, she is the one who wants to be free, and this wish casts a shadow on his own wish for freedom.[548] She had struggled with her mental illness for all these years, and he had not recognized this. He has struggled with the feeling of living an unauthentic life, but this hadn't threatened him. Her struggle had been different from his and is described as a struggle between life and death.[549] In the end, Knausgaard writes about his love for Linda and the children. He is riddled with guilt because the consequences of the project were beyond his control: 'I am so happy about Linda, and I am so happy about our children. I will never forgive myself for what I've exposed them to, but I did it, and I will have to live with it'.[550] In relation to Linda, he understands the danger the novels have created by touching someone else's self-image and retelling someone else's story.

The novel as another place

In this chapter, I have shown how *My Struggle* elicited a response from Knausgaard's father's family in the newspapers and led to counterattacks. These assaults were an attempt to present a public reaction of anger, affect and moral judgement

544 Knausgaard, *My Struggle. VI*, 1061.
545 Knausgaard, *My Struggle. VI*, 1071.
546 Knausgaard, *My Struggle. VI*, 1092.
547 Knausgaard, *My Struggle. VI*, 1093.
548 Knausgaard, *My Struggle. VI*, 1141.
549 Knausgaard, *My Struggle. VI*, 1141.
550 Knausgaard, *My Struggle. VI*, 1152.

by increasing the audience's perceptions of the offensiveness of the novels. In volume six, Knausgaard includes this debate and creates a new, far worse character assassination of his uncle and his reaction to the novels, thereby exemplifying the danger of retaliating if you are attacked by a novel.

On the other hand, it is debatable whether Knausgaard commits a character assassination of his father in *My Struggle, book one*. On the surface, Knausgaard dissociates from his father and his downfall, which also led the family to write their feature articles to the newspapers. But in the course of the story, the relationship with Knausgaard's father, his responsibility for him and his love of him, become much more complex and ambiguous. A greater understanding of his father's anger and frustration in volume one is gained, as we see Knausgaard as a father in some of the same situations in volume two, and we hear about his mother's love for him.[551] Knausgaard is told that his father felt miserable about the distance to his sons and felt excluded and unwanted. This different view thus creates a greater ambiguity than the furious father the child fears in volume one. As readers, we are invited to understand that there is a rhetoric of fictionality in play. We can't just stay with the utterance's directly informative relevance but have to 'privilege the inferential of less immediate implicatures' and look for the narrative in which it participates.[552] We have go beyond the child's or the teenager's black and white image of his father and experience the complexity in this portrait when we notice the references between the novels of the six-volumes series and recognize Knausgaard's father's resemblance to Knausgaard as an adult. Particularly in volume six, Knausgaard has produced several scenes that establish these parallels between him and his father. We hear that they are both sensitive to noise: 'Dad really lived on his nerves, nothing was at peace inside him, one sudden noise and he exploded. Now it was my turn'.[553] Later, Knausgaard says how much he loves to drink, which indirectly explains his father's sad destiny and establishes a connection between them instead of the distance in volume one: 'I wanted to drink myself out of house and home, drink myself out of family and friends, drink myself out of everything I loved and held dear'.[554] Knausgaard recognizes his father's anger and has the same problems with venting his frustrations on his children. The differences between them as fathers are also described as differences between the two generations. His father hit him occasionally, just

551 Knausgaard, *My Struggle. II*, 573.
552 Walsh, 'Fictionality as Rhetoric', 411.
553 Knausgaard, *My Struggle. VI*, 906.
554 Knausgaard, *My Struggle. VI*, 930.

like his father before him. Today, it isn't acceptable to punish a child physically, but Knausgaard invites the reader to consider whether he might have reacted more like his father if they had belonged to the same generation with the same social and cultural conditions: '[We] think all our opinions and beliefs are personal and individual, reached by way of our mature considerations, completely ignoring the role played by time and the social mechanism'.[555]

The debate in the newspapers during the publication of the six volumes did not take into account how the novel's portraits are changed and nuanced during the serial, or how the reader is invited to be critical of the narrator and interpret the larger context of the narrative. There is a polyphonic complexity in relation to the sender position with differences between author and character-narrator, even though they share the same name, and the reader is invited to make comparisons across times, scenes, characters and pictorial motifs. In the newspapers, the novels were often read as news stories without taking their fictionality into account. In the public eye, the novels were read with an informative approach in a search for truth, which often aggravated the character assassinations or even created them. Knausgaard describes how the Norwegian newspapers ran front pages on the immorality of what he had done, and at the same time published his father's name, photographed his grandparents' house and called all the characters from the novels that they could track down.[556] The approach of one journalist from *Bergens Tidende* who is a former crime correspondent is shown as problematic,[557] and the portrait of his reading serves as a guideline for the dangers of a moral reading. This journalist's questions are accusations and an interrogation, and he speaks to Knausgaard as if he is a criminal.[558]

Knausgaard wanted to commit to reality in this project; but this becomes too hurtful as the narrative progresses and the outside world reacts to it. He changes the narratives after all the problems surrounding volume one and he can't fulfil his commitment to reality in volume four:

> I anonymised the village where I worked, calling it Håfjord instead of Fjordgård, as it was actually called, which the newspapers were not slow to pick up on. I gave different names to all the pupils and teachers, and I also furnished them with made-up characteristics or idiosyncrasies, all to escape the commitment to reality I could no longer fulfil.[559]

555 Knausgaard, *My Struggle. VI*, 235.
556 Knausgaard, *My Struggle. VI*, 972.
557 Knausgaard, *My Struggle. VI*, 863.
558 Knausgaard, *My Struggle. VI*, 866.
559 Knausgaard, *My Struggle. VI*, 976.

Volume six tells the story of how artistic freedom is negotiated in the debate in the media, with the fear of a court case and with the pressure from the reactions of the family. The reactions around his writings are meant to show 'the force of the social dimension' and how it regulates and controls the individual.[560] In a dialogue between Geir and Knausgaard, we are told how terrible it feels to overstep a social norm:

> 'Social boundaries, the things that regulate what we do and allow us to exist side by side with each other, aren't abstract. They're not thoughts. They're concrete, as you say. If you overstep the mark, it hurts. That's what you're sensing now.'
> 'Sensing? But it hurts like I killed someone. Oh! And not just anyone, but someone close to me. That kind of feeling. Like something irreparable has happened'.[561]

Knausgaard wanted *My Struggle* to expose the social norms and corrective mechanisms of our society and to gain an insight into how our social world observes certain rules and norms that are hidden. *My Struggle* shows the difficulties in life, the things we do not talk about, the things we conceal and suppress, the burdens we all bear on our own in the private sphere such as drinking problems and mental illnesses, and how we are affected by shame. But it is hurtful to mention the secret thoughts, to be as honest as possible and tell the truth: 'It hurts not to be considered and it hurts not to be considerate. This novel hurt everyone around me, it has hurt me, and in a few years, when they are old enough to read it, it will hurt my children. If I had made it more painful, it would have been truer'.[562]

In the last volume, he initially defends the project against the accusations of the media and his family, but in the end, he acknowledges that the consequences for Linda were beyond his control and that it is problematic to dramatize real people as characters in a story, representing them in the same way as fictional characters and thereby traducing them and their integrity.

The debate surrounding *My Struggle* shows that references to real people and events in a novel can be perceived as an attack on and a character assassination of the people involved because their private lives are exposed to the public without their consent. In family relationships and among friends, there is a kind of agreed confidentiality. You are in a private space where you can tell each other secrets and share difficult thoughts and experiences, so there is a special vulnerability attached to this space which Robert McGill also highlights in *The Treacherous*

560 Knausgaard, *My Struggle. VI*, 1007.
561 Knausgaard, *My Struggle. VI*, 348.
562 Knausgaard, *My Struggle. VI*, 1007.

Imagination: 'Those who experience intimacy together share an interrelational state involving a certain degree of exclusivity as well as affect, if not love, and thus are vulnerable to one another'.[563] This vulnerability also creates a great responsibility in passing on the life stories of others, and the research into character assassination raises the question of how much licence writers should have to base their narratives and characters on their loved ones without having received their prior consent and without anonymizing their stories and personal affiliations.

The danger of retelling the life stories of others has been exacerbated in our age by an interest in biographical accounts among both readers and the media, and the ease of confirming a novel's life stories via social media. Breaches of privacy are often aggravated in the epitext by the frequent appearances of authors and public interviews in connection with book launches, during which authors, listeners, critics and researchers all have a responsibility in relation to how life stories are discussed and framed. In the media's rendering of life stories in novels, character assassinations are often amplified, with the most shameful experiences or character traits being presented outside the more complex and nuanced context that the narrative establishes.

Character assassinations have previously been described and defined in a political context where the intention of the attack is clear, as the attacker tries to destroy someone else's reputation and influence and convince an audience. In fiction, it is not possible to approach character assassination in the same way due to the ambiguous nature of fiction: the words on the page are not supposed to be read as directly informative and literally as in a public debate. Novels are written with the quality of fictionality to arouse the reader's reflections in a special way, inviting the reader to interpret and compare separate scenes, different times, statements and motifs of different characters, and incorporate knowledge from various topics, figures and intertextual references.

Although character assassination works differently in fiction than it does in real life, it can still be devastating for the characters involved. People who comment on this fact in the media may well increase the problem by drawing even more attention to your story. This raises a number of ethical dilemmas, as it can be debated whether fiction should always be at the service of a higher cause that justifies breaching the agreed duty of confidentiality vis-à-vis friends and family. Literary theory has often been a little reluctant in relation to the ethical dilemmas in fiction, despite their place in the debates of today: 'Given the frequency with which autobiographical fiction is viewed as unethical, it might seem surprising

563 McGill, *The Treacherous Imagination*, 10.

that there has been virtually no serious study of the subject'.[564] Few literary theorists fancy an overly moral reading of literature and many writers argue that artistic freedom stands above norms and morality, as in William Faulkner's famous statement in an interview in *Paris Review* in 1956: 'The writer's only responsibility is to his art. He will be completely ruthless if he is a good one … If a writer has to rob his mother, he will not hesitate; the "Ode on a Grecian Urn" is worth any number of old ladies'.[565] This conquest of literary autonomy was a result of the struggle against the moral and political expectations from literature as described by Gisèle Sapiro: 'in response to the acusations some of them had to confront, writers invoked specific values which grounded their claim for autonomy, such as artistic license, disinterestedness, objectivity and truthfulness in the representation of reality'.[566] By studying the ethical issue at stake here, the interpretation may easily appear moralizing, conservative and idiosyncratic in advance, but the ethical dilemmas have become an essential element in the works themselves, and you risk overlooking important themes if you avoid the ethical dilemmas they express.

Among the theorists who have worked with the more moral issues related to the involvement of real people in fiction is the Norwegian literary theorist Marianne Egeland, who studies autobiographical literature in the article 'Freedom, equality and brotherhood in reality literature' (2015), in which 'the perspective […] lies on the inferior part of the asymmetrical relationship between the authors and their characters'.[567] She emphasizes that there is a lack of respect and recognition for people who are included in novels against their will 'when authors, publishers, reviewers and the public defend one's right to take on the other's life and identity'.[568]

In Norway, the debate about the ethical responsibility of involving real people's lives in literature has led the Norwegian Non-Fiction Writers and Translators Association (NFF) to draw up an ethical checklist to inspire writers and publishers in the hope that they may become more aware of their responsibilities. NFF writes:

---

564 McGill, *The Treacherous Imagination*, 12.

565 Joy Castro, 'Introduction: Mapping Hope', in Joy Castro, ed., *Family Trouble. Memoirists on the Hazards and Rewards of Revealing Family* (Lincoln and London: University of Nebraska Press, 2013), 1.

566 Sapiro, 'The Legal Responsibility of the Writer Between Objectivity and Subjectivity', 23.

567 Marianne Egeland, 'Frihet, Likhet og brorskap i virkelighetslitteraturen', *Edda. Scandinavian Journal of Literary Research* 115/3 (2015), 227.

568 Egeland, 'Frihet, Likhet og brorskap i virkelighetslitteraturen', 230–233.

> In ethical issues, different considerations must be weighed against each other. Here are a few final answers. Who is the weak party and needs protection, and what is to be understood as a critique of power, are questions that are open to debate. Authors themselves have the power owing to their language skills and access to the public. Defining power can be used to identify abuse and highlight forgotten stories. But it can also be used to inflict damage. Freedom of expression therefore entails responsibility for expression. (My translation).[569]

In light of this checklist, it is necessary to ask what the reasons are for publishing particularly sensitive information about other people. Is this information in the public interest, or is it too private? They emphasize that one must be particularly careful in relation to handing over stories about children and young people, mentally vulnerable or people who for some reason may find it particularly difficult to express themselves in the debate and express their own version. In the article 'The Ethics and Intentions of Writing Family' from 2017, Lesley Neale emphasizes that a deceased person is particularly vulnerable in certain respects because they cannot defend themselves. She is particularly interested in ways of writing responsibly about a deceased person without doing too much harm and with respect and understanding for the other person's struggles. She suggests that greater space for ethical reflection should be created in the work itself by using literary techniques that indicate that the full truth is not necessarily known. For instance, the perspectives of several different people can be included to show a relational ethics, and it is possible to emphasize that the version being presented is an individual choice and that it is therefore open to interpretation: 'Such questioning and authorial commentary on the writing process, within a narrative, may constitute uncertainty, yet position the reader to view the work as a writer's insight, not definite truths'.[570]

Research into character assassination paves the way for the study of how ethical dilemmas emerge in works of fiction themselves, and how ethics is discussed in the media and negotiated in relation to the people affected, thereby providing a glimpse of the conflictual and contrasting desires existing in the relationship between authors, publishers, readers and the individuals affected. Literature must be allowed to bear witness to traumatic and terrible events instead of portraying

---

569 The Norwegian Non-Fiction Writers and Translators Association, 'Etisk sjekkliste for sakprosa', <https://nffo.no/formidling/etisk-sjekkliste/innledning>, accessed 23 December 2021.

570 Neale Lesley, 'The Ethics and Intentions of Writing Family', *Vitae Scholasticae* 34/2 (2017), 117.

such events through rose-tinted spectacles in order to avoid any inconvenience or discomfort to others; but contemporary literature also shows us that excessive honesty in literature also comes at a cost and implies certain risks for the individuals involved.

Part IV: Broadening the Scope of Rhetorical Fictionality Theory

Samuli Björninen

9. On Being Lectured in and by Fiction: Rhetorical Directness and Indirectness of Fictional Instructiveness

Abstract: We intuitively know that fictions are often instructive, either in the moral or more broadly epistemological sense, but what are the implications of instructivity for the fictionality of fictions? The chapter looks into the uses of lectures in fiction. The lecture, a real-life instructive and non-fictional form, is contextualized within theories of fictional instructivity, and the embedment of lectures in fiction is theorized within the rhetorical accounts of fictionality and factuality. One of the key arguments in the rhetorical theory of fictionality is that fictional communication has no direct informative relevance. The case of the fictional lecture allows us a look behind the apparent simplicity of this claim and also to think about the question of instructivity in fictionality theory more broadly. The chapter also presents three distinct functions that lectures can have in novels. The different functions of lectures are illustrated in analyses of three contemporary novels: The Pale King by David Foster Wallace (2011), Oneiron by Laura Lindstedt (2018/2015), and The Underground Railroad by Colson Whitehead (2016). The analyses also show that there is more theoretical work needed on the diverse ways in which fictional and factual genres interact within the frame of fiction. A deeper understanding of these interactions will also help us articulate why fictions are capable of spreading misinformation and how they may contribute to the contemporary epistemological crises. Inversely, increased awareness of fictional and factual registers, genres and rhetoric will help us navigate the epistemologically precarious contemporary culture.

Keywords: lecture, the novel, fictionality, factuality, David Foster Wallace, Laura Lindstedt, Colson Whitehead

In real life, when we attend a lecture, we probably hope to gain insight and be instructed on its topic. When in fiction a lecture is addressed to fictional characters, at times this is what they are hoping, too. But what is the reader to do with such fictional lectures? When we read in a Harry Potter novel a chapter detailing a class of spellcasting, unlike the characters, we are not being primed to perform wizardry. In one sense or another, the reader's priming is more likely to be toward a more complete understanding of the work. In this case, perhaps toward a more thorough investment in the magical laws of the fictional world; or perhaps toward expecting plot twists – hairy situations which the young mages will conquer with the use of their new skills. In the former case, the lecture could be said to function as a type of exposition, and in the latter, as a type of foreshadowing or plot device.

To say that fictional lectures tend to perform functions other than actually instructing us about their topic is not to say that fictions never lecture us. When they do, however, it is often by other means – in authors' prefaces and other paratexts, in dialogue between characters, and in gnomic or authorial statements of the narrator. There are entire genres that are expected to treat us to a lesson or a moral, such as the *tendenzroman* (the tendential novel) and the exemplum; and a whole lot of works in other genres that come with a cause whether expected or not – and in doing so risk being perceived as tendentious, didactic, or mere commentaries of social issues.

Even if we agree that fictions are often didactic, when we think of fiction lecturing us about its themes or a cause we rarely envision reading about lectures. Lecture is, of course, a real-life *genre*, in the sense meant by Monica Fludernik: an empirical category that helps us understand actual texts. Lecture can be characterized or even defined by somewhat broader classificatory terms: it is typically *non-narrative*, *instructive* and *argumentative*. Such terms are called *macrogeneric* by Fludernik. For Fludernik, the distinction between *genres* and *magrogenres* emphasizes that empirical texts are not primarily classified (macrogenerically) into narratives, non-narratives, or argumentative texts but into genres like the novel, news report, or academic essay.[571] An author chooses to write a novel, not a narrative, and the readers tend to consciously assume they are reading a novel while only tacitly expecting the novel to be narrative. For my discussion, too, it is crucial that we understand the lecture as a real-life, empirical genre in which certain macrogeneric frames are operative (such as *instructiveness* and *non-narrativity*). This characterization of the lecture goes a long way towards explaining why lectures have gained little attention in narratology, which focuses on *narrative* genres, with an oft-acknowledged bias towards narrative fiction.

However, I also intend to give consideration to the narrative framing of the lecture, or, in other words, the embedding of the lecture within a narrative. It turns out that some the effects of this embedding point towards more general notions about the shortcomings or risks of narrative in communicating instructions or facts.[572] By the same token, it is clear that something happens to the

571 Monika Fludernik, 'Genres, Text Types, or Discourse Modes? Narrative Modalities and Generic Categorization', *Style* 34/2 (2000), 276, 280–281.

572 Maria Mäkelä et al., 'Dangers of Narrative: A Critical Approach to Narratives of Personal Experience in Contemporary Story Economy', Narrative 29:2 (2021), 155; cf. Liesbeth Korthals Altes, 'Factual or Fictional? The Interpretive and Evaluative Impact

instructiveness of the lecture genre when it is placed within fiction. In the following section will conceptualize the transformation of the lecture by the narrative and fictional framing in terms of narratology, the theories of text types, and the rhetoric of fictionality. After the theoretical contextualization, I will discuss particular functions of fictional lectures. The chapter at hand will not attempt a complete overview of functions the instructive (and factual) text type may take on in novels or fiction, but it will take a close look at three functions. The choice of these three functions is based on a structural similarity: each of them utilizes the possibility of having the lecture work as a clearly framed or embedded episode, a text within a text, as it were. For this reason, the three functions resemble those discovered by the scholars of the *mise en abyme*.[573] Further, in each case, the function of the embedded instructive text type of the lecture is more or less *metafictional*. The embedded text, therefore, while itself an instance of an instructive and non-narrative text type, acquires specific functions within the fictional context of use.

The discussion of lectures in narrative fiction paves way for more general arguments about how the current fictionality theory may be developed. A more encompassing approach based on this theoretical orientation could help us theorize how various text types and their rhetorical purposes interact and interfere with each other in different textual and generic contexts.

The three functions given to fictional lectures in this chapter are tentatively named and described as follows:

1. an aboutness function, which entails that the lecture foregrounds a central thematic concern of the novel, not because the lecture talks about it but because the lecture as a form allows it to be enacted;
2. a process function, which foregrounds an aspect of the writing process, because the lecture suggests something about the author's methods, and;
3. an emphasis function, which consists in the lecture being an exemplification or condensation of a discussion or debate that the novel contributes to on a larger scale. The third function is distinguished from the first mainly by its

of Framing Acts', in Monika Fludernik and Marie-Laure Ryan, eds., *Narrative Factuality: A Handbook* (Berlin: De Gruyter, 2020), 565–566.

573 E.g. Lucien Dällenbach, *The Mirror in the Text*, Jeremy Whiteley and Emma Hughes, trans. (Chicago: University of Chicago Press, 1989); Dorrit Cohn, 'Metalepsis and Mise en Abyme', Lewis S. Gleich, trans., *Narrative* 20/1 (2012); Brian McHale, 'Cognition *En Abyme*: Models, Manuals, Maps', *Partial Answers: Journal of Literature and the History of Ideas* 4/2 (2006), 175–189, <https://doi.org/10.1353/pan.0.0105>.

explicitness. While the aboutness of a text is often treated as an interpretive concern,[574] in this function, the lecture states its business rather unambiguously, and thus underlines some of the themes of the work for the reader.

The three functions will be illustrated via three novels, respectively: the aboutness function via *The Pale King* (2011) by David Foster Wallace; the process function via *Oneiron* (2018/2015) by Laura Lindstedt, and the emphasis function via *The Underground Railroad* (2016) by Colson Whitehead.[575] Apart from the embedded lectures, these works also resemble each other in other respects. They represent the contemporary Western novel that incorporates modernist and postmodernist innovations and complications of the narrative form: each of them leans towards the fragmentary or episodic form, complex emplotment, and the heteroglossia of viewpoints and styles.

The three analyses argue that using the instructive genre of the lecture can contribute to how literary works make statements about their themes and ethos, but also that the function of the lecture in each case is achieved only via an intertwining of the generic form of the lecture, its conventional association with factuality and instructiveness, and the fictional frame of the novel. The question arising from this constellation, as we will see shortly, concerns the *relevance* of the instruction given by the lectures. In short, and to return to the world Harry Potter, if a lecture on magic does not teach us how to do magic, can it still be instructive – does its information have instructive relevance in the rhetoric of the work? As a partial answer to this question, I will contextualize the lectures in my analyses within a framework of the *rhetoric of factuality*,[576] a development inspired by Richard Walsh's rhetorical theory of fictionality.[577] The need for this

574 Peter Lamarque, 'About', *JLT* 8/2 (2014), 257–269.

575 David Foster Wallace, *The Pale King: An Unfinished Novel* (New York and London: Back Bay Books, 2011); Laura Lindstedt, *Oneiron: A Fantasy about the Seconds after Death*, Owen Witesman, trans. (London: Oneworld, 2018); Colson Whitehead, *The Underground Railroad* (New York: Doubleday, 2016).

576 Samuli Björninen, 'The Rhetoric of Factuality in Narrative: Appeals to Authority in Claas Relotius's Feature Journalism', *Narrative Inquiry* 29/2 (2019), 352–370.

577 Richard Walsh, *The Rhetoric of Fictionality: Narrative Theory and the Idea of Fiction* (Columbus: The Ohio State University Press, 2007); Richard Walsh, 'Fictionality as Rhetoric: A Distinctive Research Paradigm', *Style* 53/4 (2019), 397–425. Walsh's theory has been debated and developed by: Henrik Skov Nielsen, James Phelan and Richard Walsh, 'Ten Theses about Fictionality', *Narrative* 23/1 (2015), 61–73; Paul Dawson, 'Ten Theses against Fictionality', *Narrative* 23/1 (2015), 74–100; the contributions to the *Style* 2019 special issue on the rhetoric of fictionality, among others.

move arises from the idea of relevance itself. The relevance theory framework is considered a key component of the theoretical reorientation undertaken by Walsh's theory, yet it arguably has ramifications that are hitherto underexplored.

My line of inquiry finds further motivation from the current trends and developments in (Western) literary cultures. As Markku Lehtimäki posits, in the twenty-first century novel, instruction as a literary mode is gaining both literary recognition and popularity among authors and readers. This, in turn, is due to the prevalence of real-world concerns that fiction engages with, such as environmental concerns and cultural issues of race and gender. According to Lehtimäki, while the use of fictionality in non-fictional contexts has been studied extensively, the role of informative, instructive, and factual discourses in fictional contexts – such as novels – merits more attention.[578] Arguably, in its current form, rhetorical fictionality theory runs the risk of failing to address the ways in which fictions aim to achieve particular rhetorical purposes and effects. The dictacticism of fictional works is more and more oriented towards the real world, but recent developments in the theories of fiction and fictionality have responded to this only partially. That is, they have fruitfully analysed the uses of fictionality outside fiction and in everyday rhetorical contexts. However, when it comes to fiction, fictionality theory has advanced an idea of fictionality as a question of global framing and shown relatively little interest in studying how and what, besides their own fictionality, fictions might be trying to communicate through those frames. Indeed, my approach to didactic and instructive aspects of fictions can be seen as a counterpoint to the studies of fictionality outside fiction that touch on contemporary cultural phenomena, often critically, and as an attempt to bring the rhetorical study of fictionality to bear on contemporary fiction.

Instructive fictions

As Lehtimäki points out, the instructive aspect of literary art tends to get overlooked in theories of fiction.[579] Fludernik's model offers one explanation for this: instructive text types or genres, such as the lecture, are considered both *non-narrative* and *nonfictional*, or *factual*, in Fludernik's terms.[580] Since our

578 Markku Lehtimäki, 'Fiction and Instruction', *Style* 53/4 (2019), 489–495.

579 Lehtimäki, 'Fiction and Instruction', 492–493.

580 Monika Fludernik, 'Non-Narrative Genres: Exposition, Lists, Lyric, etc.' in Paul Dawson and Maria Mäkelä, eds., Routledge Companion to Narrative Theory [italicize title] (New York: Routledge, 2022), 24–39.

question is, from the outset, how the novel, a fictional genre, incorporates an instructive and factual text type, the possible answers seem limited to two. Either a work of fiction can cease to be fictional and temporarily become factual, or the factual text type of lecture is somehow transformed by the global fictionality of the novel.

Fludernik's linguistically informed approach opts for the former alternative insofar as it posits that all texts may employ various *discourse modes*, regardless of their macrogeneric status: macrogenerically argumentative essays can contain narrative sections just like narrative novels can contain non-narrative exposition, lists, lyric etc.[581] Similarly, Fludernik argues that fictionality is found in genres not generally perceived as fictional, and, conversely, that factuality also occurs in fiction genres.[582]

In contrast, both answers are found in the currently much-discussed rhetorical theory of fictionality, a central concern of this book, among other recent publications. On the one hand, the lecture intervening in a fictional narrative can be treated as an instance of 'local nonfictionality', in which case the nonfictionality of the lecture would be 'subordinate to fictive purposes'.[583] On the other hand, by virtue of appearing in a novel, the factual and instructive text type of the lecture is embedded in the fictionality of the work, thus transmuting the nonfictional text into a part of the artistic whole that is 'globally' fictional. Walsh calls this the 'frame of fiction',[584] and with his co-authors Henrik Skov Nielsen and James Phelan, 'generic fiction'.[585] According to Walsh's theory, such a framing effects a shift in the *communicative relevance* of textual statements. In lay terms, when encountering a lecture in fiction, we would encounter it as a *fictional lecture*, and would be unconcerned with assessing the factuality of its content and the truthfulness of its arguments. Both answers manage the problem by cordoning off the instructive and factual aspects of the lecture from the province of fiction: in the first case of *local nonfictionality*, the lecture never properly becomes a part of the fiction but, rather, intervenes in it, and in the second case of *global fictionality*, the instructiveness and factuality of the lecture are always

581 Fludernik, 'Non-Narrative Genres'.

582 Fludernik, 'Non-Narrative Genres'; Monika Fludernik, 'Factual Narrative: A Missing Narratological Paradigm', *Germanisch-Romanische Monatsschrift* 63/1 (2013), 117–134.

583 Nielsen, Phelan and Walsh, 'Ten Theses about Fictionality', 67.

584 Walsh, *The Rhetoric of Fictionality*, 69–70.

585 Nielsen, Phelan and Walsh, 'Ten Theses about Fictionality', 62–63, passim.

already transformed by the context. This theoretical setup creates certain problems in practice, as we will see in the discussion of the cases.

The two answers, however, are the two sides of the same coin, as they both aim to explain the empirical fact that text types do not keep neatly apart. This notion of the mutability of text types within fiction resonates with well-known ideas in literary theory, such as the Bakhtinian idea of the novel as a meta-genre that can incorporate any discourse into its *heteroglossia*, and in doing so 'inserts into these other genres an indeterminacy, a certain semantic openendedness, a living contact with unfinished, still-evolving contemporary reality'.[586] Another view resonating here is the long tradition that treats literary art as indirect. According to Jacques Rancière, this view has bound together 'pure artists and social critics', whose seemingly divergent ways of understanding literature are unified in the view that literature expresses its meaning diffusely and that this 'expressivity' is the locus of its poetic power.[587]

This theoretical background partly suggests why instruction or didacticism is a somewhat neglected as a literary effect: the prevailing idea of literary indirectness suggests that even when literature uses rhetorical forms or text types of instruction, it renders their functions anew. My approach to the functions of fictional lectures aligns with this tradition, albeit critically, as I try to argue that while these functions may be particular to the literary or fictional context, it is well within their means to come across as factual and instructive. Further, their capability to be both altered by the fictional frame *and* retain the associations conventionally assigned to the discourse mode – of instructivity and factuality – is key to understanding why factual communication in narrative fiction is not without risks.

Fludernik comments on how the frame of fiction affects the instructive discourses embedded in narratives:

> [M]any narratives are instructive, persuasive or didactic and they, therefore, crucially involve the audience or reader in the narration. By contrast, in fictional tales, the narratee

586 Mikhail M. Bakhtin, 'Epic and Novel', in Michael Holquist, ed., *The Dialogic Imagination: Four Essays* (Austin: University of Texas Press, 1981), 7; see also 'Discourse in the Novel', in Holquist, *The dialogic imagination*.

587 Jacques Rancière, *Mute Speech: Literature, Critical Theory, and Politics*, James Swenson, trans. (New York: Columbia University Press, 2011), 67; see also Samuli Björninen, 'Poetics at the Interface: Patterns of Thought and Protocols of Reading in Studies of Thomas Pynchon's *V.*', Acta Universitatis Tamperensis 2360 (Tampere: Tampere University Press, 2018), 39–41.

> is usually less prominent (unless there is an intradiegetic narratee) and involvement is split between the extradiegetic narratee (or narrative audience; i.e., the narratee that the narrator addresses) on the one hand and, on the other, the 'real reader' (authorial audience in Rabinowitz's parlance), who usually is only in the position of decoder and who implicitly tries to establish the message of the text.[588]

This gives us another, distinctly narratological, view into the Harry Potter situation. Since the lecture is an intradiegetic instance of instruction, its instructees are also situated on the diegetic level (Fludernik's intradiegetic narratee). Hence it is the apprentice wizards who are instructed by the lecture and not us (whether we consider ourselves the real readers or members of the authorial audience). The question remains whether the lecture can have an instructive function to the reader or authorial audience even though, in the narratological sense, we cannot be its addressees.

Walsh himself has argued that the didacticism of novels is 'consonant with fictionality' insofar as it entails an indirect kind of informativity.[589] I will try to show in the following analyses that this argument about consonance merits further study; but I will also argue that this consonance does not mean that the rhetorical role of lectures or other embedded text types in fiction should be reduced to fictionality.

The Pale King: What does this lecture really inform us about?

David Foster Wallace's prose works have been read as a cornerstone of a twenty-first-century post-postmodernist aesthetic, labeled as *the new sincerity* by Adam Kelly (2010).[590] The apparent novelty of Wallace lies in that his fiction recalls postmodernist metafictional styles, while subverting their nihilistic playfulness by suggesting that overdoing self-reflection might be the best way to make it humanly meaningful. Thus, his fiction is populated by characters whose multilayered thought processes of self-perception and self-reflection Wallace painstakingly articulates.

This thematic pervades the lecture chapter in Wallace's *The Pale King*, but the chapter also serves as an example of the first function given above, the aboutness

---

588 Fludernik, 'Factual Narrative: A Missing Narratological Paradigm', 133.

589 Richard Walsh, 'Further Reflections on Fictionality', *Style* 53/4 (2019), 518.

590 Adam Kelly, 'David Foster Wallace and the New Sincerity in American Fiction', in David Hering, ed., *Consider David Foster Wallace: Critical Essays* (Los Angeles: Sideshow Media Group Press, 2010), 131–146.

function. In addition, it both illustrates and complicates the distinction between direct and indirect informative relevance in fictional communication. The chapter follows one of the characters through a lecture on tax regulations. The character David Cusk suffers from bouts of excessive sweating, which become incrementally more severe the more he worries about having them. The form of the lecture provides a sort of laboratory for exploring this nervous condition: the lecture affords an occasion for both paying close attention to something external to oneself and for feeling anxious about the visibility of one's own body and actions. Cusk has acknowledged these affordances as well as the psychology of his own condition in choosing a seat at the back of the room.

The actual tax lecture takes up a sizable portion of the chapter, and as Wallace scholars have pointed out, it discusses many factual particulars of Reagan-era tax reforms and their effects on the IRS.[591] Much of the lecture simply instructs the tax examiners on how to perform their tasks:

> The point for you is that 1040 exams are divided into rotes and Fats, and you're tasked to rotes, which are relatively simple 1040 and 1040As, hence Rote Exams. Fats are done in Immersive Exams, which are staffed by more senior, umm, staff, which under some regional organizations also handle 1065s and 1120s for certain classes of S corporation.[592]

Cusk's attention to the lecture is disturbed when a latecomer enters through the back of the hall and takes a seat behind him. Cusk now becomes more aware of the effort it takes to focus on the lecture instead of thinking about other things, among them, how he might appear to the newly arrived person, whom he starts to envision as female.

> He heard the distinctive sound of a seat being pulled down into position directly behind him and someone sitting and placing what sounded like two or more cases or personal items in the seat next to her and unzipping what sounded like a portfolio – for it was definitely a female, there was a smell of not only of floral perfume but of makeup, which has a distinct complex of scents in a warm room, as well as some type of floral shampoo, and Cusk could actually feel the twin disks of her eyes' pressure on the back of his head, since he could easily calculate that his head was at least partly within the girl's sight line of the podium. By watching the presentation, she would also be looking at least part of the rear of Cusk's head, and also his neck's rear, which his short haircut left bare, meaning any droplets that might emerge from the rear of his hair might be clearly visible.[593]

591 Ralph Clare, 'The Politics of Boredom and the Boredom of Politics in David Foster Wallace's *The Pale King*', *Studies in the Novel* 44/4 (2012), 428–446.

592 Wallace, *The Pale King*, 324.

593 Wallace, *The Pale King*, 329.

The pattern develops predictably toward an ever-greater tension between the close attention Cusk has to pay to the lecture to keep his sweating-inducing anxiety in check and between his inability to refrain from analyzing the near-subliminal signs of his environment and thinking how he might appear to the female onlooker.

Like most of the long chapters of *The Pale King*, the lecture chapter is a character study. More particularly, it is an exploration of male neuroticism and fragility. The lecture chapter delves into the innards of the male gaze in a rather inventive way, as it shows the male gaze as an internal mechanism of male psychology, automatized and independent of gazing understood literally. The seemingly ironic reversal – that Cusk imagines the pressure of the woman's gaze on the back of his head – is ultimately no reversal at all but merely another aspect of this mechanism. As part of the theme of self-reflection Wallace explores male gaze as a kind of nervous tick embedded in and enacted through quotidian social interactions. This, of course, comes as no news to the feminist theorists of the male gaze.[594]

The lecture chapter consolidates the theme of self-reflection as a double-edged sword, giving way on the one hand, to a serenity achieved via focused attention, and on the other, to a recursive form of neurotic self-consciousness. According to the scholars who have discussed the different roles of the *mise en abyme*, it is one of the most traditional roles of the device to facilitate interpretation by doubling or reiterating its theme – 'holding up to it a mirror in which its essential features could be contemplated'.[595] While the lecture does not represent *mise en abyme* in any of its exemplary forms, it shows a functional similarity. *Mise en abyme* is related to a larger-scale novelistic strategy of thematization, where the theme of the text is reflected in how the text organizes and presents itself as a text.[596] To put it very simply, this would mean that novels about human self-reflection are literarily self-reflexive (like *The Pale King*) or that novels about coping with boredom and annoyance deliberately bore and annoy their readers (again, like *The Pale King*). It is this literary strategy of doubling up on the theme that I am after in calling the function of the lecture 'aboutness function'.

---

594 E.g. Beth Newman, '"The Situation of the Looker-On": Gender, Narration, and Gaze in Wuthering Heights', *PMLA. Publications of the Modern Language Association of America* 105/5 (1990), 1029–1041.

595 McHale, 'Cognition *En Abyme*', 178.

596 See Björninen, 'Poetics at the Interface'.

The main question regarding the fictionality of the lecture is whether the character study and the lecture detailing tax laws, with many of the details factually accurate, are to be understood as equally fictional. To answer this question, we need make a brief digression into fictionality theory. Fictionality, in Walsh's well-known definition, is not a question of truthfulness but of relevance.[597] When we read fiction, the question of whether
the statements of the text are literally truthful need not arise.

This independence from literal truth is cast in two pairs of terms grounded in relevance theory: *direct* and *indirect informative relevance*, and *explicature* and *implicature*. The former pair of terms is coined by Walsh. The distinction explains why a sentence informing us about Clarissa Dalloway's presence in a room really does something else in the context of Woolf's *Mrs. Dalloway* – hence its indirect informative relevance.[598] The implication is that a formally and semantically equivalent utterance might have direct informative relevance outside fiction. This conceptual distinction is linked to the concepts of implicature and explicature from Dan Sperber and Deirdre Wilson's relevance theory. The authors describe the concepts thus:

> [W]e will call an explicitly communicated assumption an explicature. Any assumption communicated, but not explicitly so, is implicitly communicated: it is an implicature. By this definition, ostensive stimuli which do not encode logical forms will, of course, only have implicatures.[599]

Walsh acknowledges that indirectness of informative relevance does not provide a sufficient characterization of fictionality. Indeed, according to relevance theory, relevance overrides literal truth in communication *tout court*, and such communication that hinges only on direct informative relevance is not something we can set in contrast to fictional communication – it is perhaps nowhere to be found at all, as 'no explicature can stand alone, independent of implicatures'.[600]

In acknowledgement of the insufficiency of indirect informative relevance as the sufficient condition for fictionality, Walsh specifies in the latest large-scale elucidation of his theory that the distinguishing feature of fictionality 'is not merely its appeal to indirect informative relevance [...] but rather its manifest independence of direct informative relevance'.[601] To Walsh, this means that what

597 Walsh, *The Rhetoric of Fictionality*, 30.
598 See Walsh, 'Fictionality as Rhetoric', 412.
599 Dan Sperber and Deirdre Wilson, *Relevance: Communication and Cognition*, second edition (Oxford: Blackwell, 1995), 182.
600 Walsh, 'Further Reflections on Fictionality', 515.
601 Walsh, 'Further Reflections on Fictionality', 516.

the work implies could be wholly independent of what its utterances make explicitly manifest. In other words: 'The key to fictionality is that implicatures *can* stand alone, in the sense that they do not need to support or redeem the literal truth of an utterance when that expectation has been contextually suspended'.[602] However, relevance theory seems to give no reason to suspect that the ability of implicatures to stand alone is particular to fictionality. Although Sperber and Wilson's theory does not discuss fiction or fictionality at length, it does talk about communication based only on implicatures. I am pointing this out to interrogate the resulting, perhaps overly restrictive, view of fiction, rather than to contest Walsh's reading of relevance as such.

This brings us back to the topic of whether the fictional lecture can be fruitfully understood as instructive or factual. The treatment of the lecture under the aegis of the 'aboutness function' suggests that in the context of the work as a rhetorical and fictional performance the lecture is not about the United States' tax laws or about the rules, tasks and job positions of the IRS. Rather, it expounds on the thematics of the novel – boredom, self-consciousness, neuroticism, and the redemptive pleasure of attentiveness. This aligns with what the proponents of the rhetorical fictionality theory are suggesting: the frame of fiction changes our assessment of the relevance of the statements made in the text.

However, this might only pertain to the narrative of Cusk's sensations and anxieties, not the lecture as such. Many scholars, critics and readers have pointed out that much of the tax discourse in *The Pale King* is, indeed, based on actual US tax laws and IRS regulations.[603] The rhetorical choice to appeal to such factual authorities, might be described within the framework suggested in my earlier work: in terms of the rhetoric of factuality, making references to information from sources that are, in principle, fact-checkable, is a distinctive rhetorical choice.[604] The significance of this layer of factuality is underlined by something that might not be apparent if the reader is not already somewhat familiar with the facts presented: the actual tax laws and facts about the IRS are interwoven with made-up regulations, particularly the fictive or fictionalized Spackman Initiative that is geared toward turning the IRS into a revenue-driven business.

In contrast to this layer of fictionality, there is a narrative that details the thought processes and sensations of a fictional character. Is there a sense in which

602 Walsh, 'Further Reflections on Fictionality', 515–516.

603 E.g. Clare, 'Politics of Boredom'; Tom McCarthy, 'David Foster Wallace: The Last Audit', *The New York Times* (14 April 2011).

604 Björninen, 'The Rhetoric of Factuality in Narrative'.

both these informative strata are similarly indirect or similarly independent of direct informative relevance? If we subscribe to the idea of global fictionality, then, in terms of relevance, it should make little difference to us whether we know which parts of the information are accurate and which are fictitious. An alternate view opens up if we regard the lecture parts as instances of local nonfictionality, within which we find nested even more minuscule instances of (supra) local fictionality as the largely factual lecture is interspersed with parts detailing the made-up Spackman Initiative. However, neither approach accounts for the overall rhetorical strategy of bringing together a fictional narrative of a character's neurotic obsession with the overwhelmingly detailed and dull text of the lecture – that however requires the reader's close attention, or at least rewards it by revealing itself as a tapestry of facts and figments.

It should be added that the aboutness function of the lecture could be operational even if the statements made within the lecture were completely fictitious. As I mention above, something akin to the aboutness function is recognized in the literary theories of the fictional *mise en abyme*. However, the choice to embed a conventionally factual text type of the lecture within the frame of fiction, and then to have that lecture consist of factually accurate statements interspersed by invention, is a distinctive strategy particular to *The Pale King*. Interpreting its role in the novel requires seeing it in its rhetorical complexity, which is why lumping all of these fictional and factual layers within the frame of global fictionality seems reductive.

What is more, the resulting view of fictionality might hamper the ability of fictionality theory to make its fullest contribution to contemporary debates about the use of narrative and fiction to convey facts. The idea that narrative is conducive to causing confusion of fiction and facts can perhaps be explicated more thoroughly in this framework.[605] All narratives, not just fictional narratives, are about something. While they very often involve factual claims, the narrative may not be *about* those facts as such; they are not the theme or the point of the narrative. In such cases, verifying the facts presented in the narrative might seem like an auxiliary task. As the analysis of *The Pale King* shows, doing this may be rewarding from an interpretive standpoint, but even so, this work may be somewhat extraneous to simply grasping the point of the narrative. In a roundabout way, then, the aboutness function helps us see why embedding facts in a narrative makes them less amenable to fact-checking, even outside the frame of fiction but especially within it.

605 Cf. Maria Mäkelä et al., 'Dangers of Narrative', 155.

Oneiron: How to authorize factuality in fiction

Finnish author Laura Lindstedt won the prestigious Finlandia Prize for her 2015 novel *Oneiron*. Subtitled 'A Fantasy about the Seconds after Death', the novel is set in a bright void where seven newly deceased women of different ages and from different cultures meet for the first time. The protagonists try to understand their predicament – where they are, how and why they got there, and what they are to do next. In doing so they tell each other about their lives and what they know about their deaths. They present their theories of the afterlife and contemplate their fates and choices in life. As the characters come from different cultural, national, and religious backgrounds, the novel comes across as a tapestry of worldviews and notions about big themes like gender, family, work, love, sex, illness, and death. The novel takes perhaps a calculated risk with its multicultural ambitions, and, indeed, the way it handles these themes through the viewpoints of a diverse cast of characters has drawn both criticism and praise.

The fantastical *Oneiron* and the realist but metafictional *Pale King* are more alike than it might first seem. Like *The Pale King*, Lindstedt's novel is a veritable anthology of literary styles and techniques, as well as a long novel containing a glut of apparently factual information about all kinds of things, perhaps most prominently about the biological processes of death and theories of the afterlife. The Russian Polina lectures the other characters about the mystic Emanuel Swedenborg's visions of Heaven, while the American-Jewish Shlomith recalls an apocryphal description of Hell. These intertextual references are not overtly fictionalized but actually cite or paraphrase textual source materials.

However, the most striking factual text type featured in the novel is the lecture given by Shlomith. The story of Shlomith's life and death takes up a large portion of the novel's midsection: it details how she became a famous performance artist and died during her final performance, which involves her giving the lecture. Shlomith's performance is also an example of the second function of fictional lectures, the process function, as it foregrounds an aspect of *Oneiron's* creation. This example also allows us to look into the role of researched facts in fiction, as the lecture uses a footnote apparatus that makes visible that many of its points are backed up by institutionally approved research sources. I have discussed such references as part of *the rhetoric of factuality* that texts may choose to adopt.[606] The ways in which *Oneiron* employs these references reveals the concept of nonfictionality in fictionality theory as analytically insufficient. Further, the variable

606 Björninen, 'The Rhetoric of Factuality in Narrative'.

ways of appealing to institutionally authoritative sources in *Oneiron* will show that the tenet of independence from direct informative relevance can be called to question even within the global frame of fiction.

Shlomith's performance 'Judaism and Anorexia' takes the form of a lecture given in the Jewish Museum in New York and is produced in the novel as a (pseudo-)facsimile of the performance script. Therefore, the lecture becomes a clearly demarcated 'work' within the work, a potential *mise en abyme*. Another effect of this choice is that unlike other chapters telling Shlomith's story, the lecture seems to be given without the narrator's mediating voice. The choices made in the novel serve to authenticate the voice of the lecture as Shlomith's own.

The lecture contains factual references, for instance to rabbi Ignaz Maybaum's controversial 1965 study *The Face of God after Auschwitz*, a theological work explaining the mass extermination of the Jews in terms of biblical suffering. However, it juxtaposes its references to such sources with emphatically fictional statements. For example, there is a suggestion that Maybaum's book is hard to come by today because Shlomith bought all the copies she could find and burnt them in one of her performances.

What is more, Shlomith's lecture reads like a research paper, with references to actual studies in footnotes and a bibliography. After introducing her topic, Shlomith goes on:

> I begin with the undisputable fact that Jewish women suffer from anorexia and other eating disorders on average more than the general population. Although only two percent of the United States population is Jewish*, as many as thirteen percent of eating disorder clinic patients are Jews**.[607]

In the citation the two footnotes are located in the second sentence, one after each clause, linking the given percentages to the factual infrastructure of research-based data. Similar references accompany claims that secular Jews are more liable to develop eating disorders, because the Jewish faith 'emphasizes modesty and humility', and that 'nose jobs and hair straightening are very common in the Jewish community'.[608] Although nothing in the text clearly indicates this, the footnotes of the lecture all refer to actual published studies. The situation presented in *Oneiron* is, then: a character in a fictional narrative is giving a lecture that appeals to factual authorities of the actual world – and arguably the novel counts on us recognizing this rhetorical strategy.

---

607 Lindstedt, *Oneiron*, 240–241; asterisks added to indicate footnotes in the original.
608 Lindstedt, *Oneiron*, 244.

The footnotes seem to make a stronger-than-usual claim to *direct* informative relevance that the Walshian theory of fictionality all but excludes from fiction. This type of referencing takes the form of a communicative gesture that directly names a particular factual authority and connects the text to it. This fits relevance theory's notion of 'ostensive-inferential' communication far easier than the things we usually encounter in fiction.[609] Even such explicit communicative gestures are not without implicatures: for one, the reference implies, as a token of its own accountability, that it can be checked against the indicated source. In terms of the rhetoric of factuality, such a reference is an appeal to factual authority, even before we know whether the reference is veracious. More particularly, this gesture may be called an appeal to an *institutional* authority.[610] While such references in fiction can be made up or veracious, it would be hard to argue that the frame of fiction renders the assumption of veracity irrelevant. If relevance in communication consists in the hearer or reader choosing 'the first interpretation consistent with the principle of relevance', the obvious interpretation here is to assume that the reference names a source.[611]

Yet perhaps the role of factual references in fiction is not as straightforward as this. The notion of literary indirectness might intervene here, either as a narratological doctrine or in the guise of indirect relevance. Narratologically thinking, Shlomith is the intradiegetic writer of the lecture, and it is she who is using the footnotes. Thus, whatever the author might be communicating to us is still indirect because of this communicative layering. Curiously, though, the effect works here in a slightly counterintuitive way: the footnotes are legible to the authorial audience but go unseen by the diegetic audience who are *listening* to Shlomith's lecture. Because the use of the pseudo-facsimile form ensuring the real-world legibility of the footnotes is a strategy we must attribute to the (implied) author, the footnotes are clearly a rhetorical *resource* used to communicate something to the (authorial) audience.[612] However, the aura of indirectness persists even if somewhat conditioned by these observations.

In the context of rhetorical fictionality theory, fact-based discourses come to play in fiction as instances of 'local nonfictionality' that remain subordinated to 'fictive purposes'.[613] That is, the frame of fiction should preemptively guarantee

---

609 Walsh, 'Fictionality as Rhetoric', 411; Sperber and Wilson, *Relevance*, 54, 163.

610 Björninen, 'The Rhetoric of Factuality in Narrative', 360.

611 Sperber and Wilson, *Relevance*, 168–169, 257.

612 cf. James Phelan, *Somebody Telling Somebody Else: Toward a Rhetorical Poetics of Narrative* (Columbus: The Ohio State University Press, 2017).

613 Nielsen, Phelan and Walsh, 'Ten Theses about Fictionality', 67.

that whatever a factual genre or text type does in a novel, or in any other globally fictional text, is not quite what it does outside such a global frame. In Walsh's terminology, then, we could say that whatever the role of the references in *Oneiron*, their informative relevance remains indirect.

But my two examples thus far are showing that indirect informative relevance is a big tent – perhaps too big. Indirect informative relevance, insofar as it is largely coextensive with what relevance theory names implicature, would characterize communication so broadly that the regime of indirectness would end up including a gigantic variety of rhetorical strategies and purposes. The particular type of indirectness in the example from *Oneiron* could be approached by arguing that the function of the authoritative sources is not to show us that Shlomith represents the question of anorexia in Jewish cultures accurately. Rather, we might argue that the purpose of the footnotes is perhaps more broadly to convince us that the author's representation of 'Judaism and anorexia' is based on existing studies rather than her own ideas. Further, the use of the footnote apparatus can be seen as an indexical gesture suggesting a more general authorial ethos in question of representation: the novel's 'use' of characters is not fueled by ethnic stereotyping, or exotism, but is a *bona fide* attempt at a multicultural novel based on a careful study of cultural phenomena it represents – albeit one written by a white Finnish author. This is the particular function that the lecture acquires within the fictional frame, which I have labeled as the process function.

To grasp the specificity of the lecture chapter in *Oneiron*, we can compare it to other parts of the novel which also use the pseudo-facsimile form. The novel dedicates a newspaper clipping to each of its seven characters – stories about the events of their death, obituaries, even one job opportunity ad (to fill the deceased person's position). Unlike Shlomith's footnotes, these lookalike newspaper sources are not veracious. Actually, because they involve features conventional to the newspaper form – date, and the names of the paper and the journalist – it is possible to verify that these pages are not actual facsimiles of news stories. However, many of them are variations of stories that have appeared through various outlets roughly between 2010 and 2015, when the novel was published. For instance, in the novel the French Nina dies while pregnant with twins; after her dying scene we are presented with something that looks like a page from *Le Monde*, with a story of about a 'brain-dead' mother giving birth to twins.[614] Such a story was not actually run in *Le Monde* on 3 December 2011, but it is easy to

614 Lindstedt, *Oneiron*, 291–292.

find similar stories from the period of writing.[615] We could say that these are *fictionalized* versions of stories that have been available during the making of the novel, which the author may or may not have seen while writing it.

Relevance theory, as used by Walsh in his rhetoric of fictionality, would attest that not only does it not matter that such factual-looking things may or may not be actually true: because of the global assumption of fictionality, the question of their verifiability does not have to arise. Yet this view cannot account for the rhetorical difference between the veracious references in Shlomith's lecture and the fictional news stories that exploit the formal conventions of non-fiction genres. The former can be seen under the mark of indirect informative relevance, if perhaps not as fully independent of direct informative relevance. The latter, in contrast, represents fictionality in a sense quite successfully theorized within the rhetorical approach.[616] There is one sense in which the two are similar. Neither of them negates the frame of fiction in *Oneiron*: neither makes it any less a novel, a work of fiction. However, the difference is anything but inconsequential for the rhetoric of the novel, which suggests that the dynamic of direct and indirect relevance might have been oversimplified in the rhetorical theory of fictionality.

The process function also raises the question of whether a similar rhetorical strategy might be adopted for more nefarious purposes. If the genre of the novel allows factual text types to be framed in such a way that renders questions of factual accuracy less relevant while also being able to incorporate factual rhetoric outwardly quite similar to factual genres like academic papers or historical documents, this suggests that the novel could be quite efficient as a vehicle for misinformation. If fiction has no direct informative relevance, the question of misinformation need not arise. However, if we accept that the question of direct and indirect informativeness is more complicated than previously acknowledged, the rhetorical approaches to fictionality and factuality could make a substantial contribution to discussions about the epistemological affordances and risks of fiction.

---

615 E.g. 'Mom declared brain dead one month ago, gives birth to twins', *Fox News* (24 April 2012). Also, a Finnish case of 'the miracle-baby of Oulu' from 1984 was revisited in media during the year 2014, on the thirtieth birthday of a man born to a woman who was in life-support after aneurysm.

616 E.g. Stefan Iversen, '"Just Because It Isn't Happening Here, Doesn't Mean It Isn't Happening": Narrative, Fictionality and Reflexivity in Humanitarian Rhetoric', *European Journal of English Studies* 23/2 (2019), 190–205; Henrik Skov Nielsen, 'Factuality and Fictionality in "Fake News"', in Monika Fludernik and Henrik Skov Nielsen, eds., *Travelling Concepts: New Fictionality Studies* (Berlin: Peter Lang, 2020), 161–178.

The Underground Railroad: The consonance of didacticism and fictionality

Colson Whitehead's Pulitzer-winning *The Underground Railroad* is almost invariably classed as 'alternative history', a generic hybrid of historical and speculative fiction. The alternativeness of the novel's historical vision comes down to its highly intertextual style, and, most obviously, the titular subterranean railway network, which serves both as the main *novum* of the novel and its central literalized metaphor. Arguably, however, the novel is as striking for its historical realism or naturalism as it is for its speculative aspects. Nowhere is this more apparent than in its depictions of the brutal practices of slavery and the legal institutions enabling them. This has been contextualized by Stephanie Li as a kind of *speculative realism*, a term borrowed from Ramón Saldívar, that entails a critical stance to reality that posits 'the knowability of phenomena, even if we can't know the thing-in-itself'[617]. Li argues that it is precisely the inescapability of white supremacy that propels the speculative-cum-critical realism in the novel.[618]

After escaping a plantation in Georgia and narrowly evading capture in several states, the main character Cora ends up in a utopian all-black community in Indiana, and the part that I will discuss here is a town hall meeting held in that setting. The lecture is less clearly its own episode than in the previous two cases, and it is not demarcated as a text within a text with strong paratextual cues (such as constituting its own chapter, as in *The Pale King*) or material means (such as the pseudo-facsimile form in *Oneiron*). Further, it is actually a debate or perhaps a juxtaposition of two brief lectures. Yet by virtue of common features – being performed in front of a diegetic audience, establishing a clear division of duties between the narrator and the diegetic speakers – it is a represented or intradiegetic instance of instruction in the novel, and one that fulfils the third function suggested above, the *emphasis* function.

The two speakers are Lander, a light-skinned Bostonian of mixed ethnicity, and Mingo, an entrepreneurial former slave who has managed to buy freedom for himself and his entire family. Each of the speakers gives a prepared speech concerning the post-slavery possibilities of African Americans trying to find their place in the society. Mingo's speech invites the audience to consider themselves

---

617 Ramón Saldívar, 'The Second Elevation of the Novel: Race, Form, and the Postrace Aesthetic in Contemporary Narrative', *Narrative* 21/1 (2013), 1–18.

618 Stephanie Li, 'Genre Trouble and History's Miseries in Colson Whitehead's The Underground Railroad', *MELUS* 44/2 (2019), 1–23, <https://doi.org/10.1093/melus/mlz010>.

as an exemplary collective of individuals. After all, each of them has managed to escape slavery and join the privileged utopian community:

> 'We've accomplished the impossible,' Mingo said, 'but not everyone has the character we do. We're not all going to make it. Some of us are too far gone. Slavery has twisted their minds, an imp filling their minds with foul ideas. [...] You've seen these lost ones on plantations, on the streets of the towns and cities – those who will not, cannot respect themselves. You've seen them here, receiving the gift of this place but unable to fit in.'[619]

Mingo goes on to argue that the community can only persevere if it does not try to save everyone but only those with the potential to 'enter into American society as a productive member with full rights'.[620] Critics and scholars have pointed out that the exchange of views between Mingo and Lander echoes various debates in the African-American history; especially those between Booker T. Washington and W. E. B. DuBois.[621] Mingo's view aligns closely with Washington's, who advocated for African-American integration via economic independence and business ownership, but also embraced, perhaps strategically, the intellectual trends of Social Darwinism and Progressivism.[622] Lander, in contrast, is perhaps more utopian and radical than DuBois, but shares his conviction that former slaves did not have to earn or qualify for their freedom; rather, it was the duty of the privileged members of the African-American communities to vehemently advance the cause of equal rights for all.[623] Lander speaks thus:

> 'Brother Mingo made some good points,' Lander said. 'We can't save everyone. But that does not mean we can't try.[...]'
> [...]
> 'Color must suffice. It has brought us to this night, this discussion, and it will take us into the future. All I truly know is that we rise and fall as one, one colored family living next door to one white family.'[624]

---

619 Whitehead, *The Underground Railroad*, 283.

620 Whitehead, *The Underground Railroad*, 284.

621 Rich Smith, 'The Underground Railroad Is Bigger and Better Than You've Heard', *The Stranger* (8 September 2016), <https://www.thestranger.com/books/2016/09/08/24548834/the-underground-railroad-is-bigger-and-better-than-youve-heard>, accessed 7 January 2022.

622 See Wilson Jeremiah Moses, *Creative Conflict in African American Thought* (New York: Cambridge University Press, 2004), 148–150.

623 See W. E. B. DuBois, *The Souls of Black Folk* (New York: Oxford University Press, 2007), 43–44.

624 Whitehead, *The Underground Railroad*, 285–286.

The context of actual historical debates is significant here. However, *The Underground Railroad* does not make actual references to the speeches of Washington, DuBois, or other African American activists and thinkers, but merely evokes their arguments. The evocative quality is strengthened by the vaguely alternative historical setting that purposefully falls short of giving us a single historical moment as the context of the debate. Indeed, beyond the Washington-DuBois debate, Mingo and Lander reiterate points raised in by the Abolitionist movement, and later, those heard during the Civil Rights Movement of the 1960s.[625] A contemporary reading of Mingo's speech might highlight that the speaker has internalized white supremacist arguments about the successful 'good negro', who may be granted a degree of protection from structural racism because their success can be used as an argument against the prevalence of structural racism.[626] The fictional framing of the debate embeds various historically specific interpretations in the fictional representation, allowing them a place in the kind of *heteroglossia* that can flourish in fiction. Whitehead's strategy is one of fictionalization rather than of factuality, which helps establish the debate as an encapsulation of a recurring thematic that resurfaces in many guises both throughout the book and throughout the real historical struggle to secure human and civil rights for the racialized peoples of America.

The debate initiated by this exchange of views is cut short when a white mob descends on the Indiana farm and slaughters the participants of the meeting. Cora witnesses yet another monstrous act of racist violence before making yet another narrow escape. The point of the debate is trivialized as the mob destroys the community easily, with impunity, and, apparently, on a whim. All in all, it is not just the juxtaposition of views expressed in the two speeches that endows this chapter with a sense of didacticism. Rather, it is the stark contrast between, on the one hand, the community within which the very fact of public debate seems a utopian possibility and, on the other hand, the violent ideology intent on obliterating the forum enabling this possibility. Instead of Mingo and Lander's speeches the didactic message results from the design of the episode more holistically.

The lecture chapter in *The Underground Railroad* is both similar to and different from the other literary cases. All three novels use the communicative

625 E.g. Harvard Sitkoff, *The Struggle for Black Equality, 1945–1980* (New York: Hill and Wang, 1981).

626 Nikki Johnson Huston, 'The Myth of the "Good Negro"', *HuffPost* (6 November 2016), <https://www.huffpost.com/entry/the-myth-of-the-good-negr_b_8506570>, accessed 7 January 2022.

situation of the lecture within a fictional framing in ways that are comparable but dissimilar. Each of the works uses the framed situation to make a point or to expound on a theme, and in all three cases, it can be argued that the function of the lecture is somewhat independent of its explicature or content. The functions of the lectures can be described in rhetorical terms and also in terms that are familiar from literary theory. The functions of the lectures, which call to mind what scholars have said about *mise en abyme*, have a strong association with the kind of literariness that the frame of fiction can grant to its innards.

This means that in none of the cases can the role or purpose of the lecture be reduced to its message or content. While they are instructive in different ways and achieve their instructiveness via different rhetorical strategies, the informative relevance of the lectures themselves must ultimately be considered indirect in the sense proposed in the rhetorical fictionality theory. However, I have argued that both the argumentative structures and the specific references that appeal to knowledge-legitimizing authorities give rise to a rhetoric of factuality that often remains operational despite the global fictional frame of the novel. Appeals to authority can be detected both in the lecture addressed to the diegetic audience, as in *The Pale King*, and in the presentation of the fictional lecture as part of the work to its authorial audience, as in *Oneiron*.

In contrast, the kind of moral didacticism evident in *The Underground Railroad* might lie outside the purview of the rhetoric of factuality *per se*. Grasping the thematically emphatic role of the chapter staging the debate does not hinge on the factual authorities appealed to by the diegetic speakers. Rather, in this instance the emphasis function is achieved without any ostensibly factual rhetoric. Therefore, the didacticism of this example may be more closely linked to discussions about the kinds of *truthfulness* that fiction can achieve.[627] Unlike the other two examples, *The Underground Railroad* actually comes across as an instructive fiction in a specific sense discussed by Lehtimäki[628] and gestured towards by Walsh.[629] Indeed, the didacticism of its lecture chapter seem consonant with fictionality: Mingo and Lander's lectures, while opening up to a contextualization within particular historical social debates, juxtapose philosophies, ideas, or views expressed through fictional characters within the frame of fiction.

627 See Jukka Mikkonen, 'Truth in Literature: The Problem of Knowledge and Insight Gained from Fiction', in Monika Fludernik and Marie-Laure Ryan, eds., *Narrative Factuality: A Handbook* (Berlin: De Gruyter, 2019).

628 Lehtimäki, 'Fiction and Instruction', 492–493.

629 Walsh, 'Further Reflections on Fictionality', 518.

The least metafictional of the three lectures, the town hall meeting might also be functionally the most typical *mise en abyme* of the three: the lesson incorporated in the lecture serves to emphasize one of the main thematic concerns of the novel.[630] The lecture chapter is one episode in a series of quasi-historical racial parables in *The Underground Railroad*, each episode revealing a different facet of the same problematic: the insidiousness of white privilege and the ease with which it gives way to dehumanization and violence.

Conclusion: Why factuality and instructiveness make a difference to the relevance of fictions

The readings done here focus on two arguments from the rhetorical theory of fictionality: that fictionality is of indirect informative relevance, and, furthermore, that it is independent of direct informative relevance. In Walsh's fictionality theory, these arguments are assumed to describe the area of fictionality sufficiently and holistically, which might be questionable in the light of relevance theory. Even if the two arguments hold, they only demarcate the area of fictionality in very coarse terms. This, in fairness, may be all that the theory has set out to do; Walsh recapitulates time and time again that his theory is not an interpretive framework.[631]

I have tried to look into the multifarious rhetorical strategies at play *within* fictions. Rather than being reducible to fictionality and non-fictionality they point toward a host of more specific rhetorical purposes and strategies, including but not limited to those discussed under the rubric of factuality in this chapter. The novels analysed here build distinct rhetorical strategies by making factual appeals to authoritative sources and commonly held facts, employing (meta)fictional strategies of thematic emphasis, and exploiting the possibilities granted by the global frame of fiction. In each case, the sense of instructiveness is a result of a complex amalgamation of rhetorical choices. Walsh himself stresses that the question of relevance should not stop at fictionality, but, rather, the value of relevance theory lies in being a 'pragmatic and cognitive approach to communication in general'.[632]

I will end by briefly turning to certain contentious aspects highlighted in the reception of the novels discussed here. These literary controversies suggest that

630 See Dällenbach, *The Mirror in the Text*, 56; McHale, 'Cognition *En Abyme*', 178.
631 Walsh, 'Further Reflections on Fictionality', 525.
632 Walsh, 'Further Reflections on Fictionality', 513.

adopting a simplistic view of fiction's indirect relevance runs the risk of rendering the rhetorical approach to fiction and fictionality unable to contribute to contemporary literary debates that are inextricably linked to the way fictional and factual assumptions intermingle.

Each of the authors discussed here have been subject to public controversy for certain aspects of their literary works. The recent translation of Wallace's *Infinite Jest* (1996) into Finnish was accompanied by a kind of localization of the long-active debate about Wallace's misogyny.[633] For all the praise and honors coming its way, Lindstedt's *Oneiron* was also the subject of a significant debate about cultural appropriation, which mostly centered on the character of Shlomith and its depiction of eating disorders among the Jewish.[634] Criticisms of *The Underground Railroad* have accused Whitehead's novel of being a prime example of 'Southern Novel of Black Misery', a genre which the author himself once named and derided.[635]

These discussions about the ethics and politics of literature reveal a tension between different sets of assumptions about fiction that we can now describe in terms of rhetoric and relevance. We can discern a set of assumptions that allows fiction to have only indirect informational relevance, and another set, that may assume the possibility of fiction having both direct and indirect relevance. The long-standing view has been, of course, that sophisticated reading more or less requires a capability to recognize the indirectness of literary fiction – or, depending on one's theoretical frame, many varieties thereof. This view is often accompanied by the ultimatum that to argue otherwise is to fundamentally misunderstand what fiction is and does *as fiction*. In classical narratology, this would have been because the implied author might speak ironically, or because devices like free indirect discourse can make distinctions between speaking agents indeterminate and open to interpretation. The problematic morals and utterances can always be interpreted in a roundabout way, which sees, say, misogynistic speech as a way of studying the misogyny of the world and characters depicted

---

633 E.g., Deirdre Coyle, 'Men Recommend David Foster Wallace to Me', *Electric Literature* (17 April 2017), <https://electricliterature.com/men-recommend-david-foster-wallace-to-me/>, accessed 7 January 2022; Clare Hayes-Brady, 'Reading Your Problematic Fave: David Foster Wallace, Feminism and #metoo', *Honest Ulsterman* (June 2018), <https://humag.co/features/reading-your-problematic-fave>, accessed 7 January 2022.

634 Koko Hubara. 'Othe(i)ron', *Ruskeat tytöt* (8 February 2016), <https://www.lily.fi/blogit/ruskeat-tytot/otheiron/>, accessed 7 January 2022.

635 Li, 'Genre Trouble', 5.

in the novels, as the standard defense of Wallace would have it. The unspoken flipside of this argument is that taking direct offence from fiction betrays a naïve understanding of fiction.

The insight that fiction largely operates under the aegis of indirect informative relevance has its merits. However, my analyses have tried to demonstrate that the wide variety of rhetorical strategies found in fiction are not reducible to the fictionality theory's view of the fictional frame. Especially the strategies I have treated as instances of factual rhetoric foreground this variety: while it is possible and plausible to treat the informative relevance of these rhetorical means as indirect, it is difficult to argue that the rhetorical strategies of factuality are sufficiently explained by the binary notions of fictionality and nonfictionality, or direct and indirect informative relevance. As I have also tried to show, the strategies of embedding factual information in fictional narratives are available for many kinds of use. Studying these strategies might broaden our understanding of how narrative – including, perhaps controversially, fictional narrative – might become a vehicle for questionable factual rhetoric and even misinformation.

Also, regarding the literary controversies mentioned above, a more granular view of relevance might help the rhetorical theories become more conversant with debates about cultural issues raised in reference to fictions. After all, relevance theory is supposed to ask what kinds of assumptions are made manifest in communicative contexts.[636] To prescriptively limit the assumptions that fictional communication can make manifest by excluding the idea of direct informativeness from fictionality theory might hamper its applicability to the analysis of texts and diminish its potential to contribute to cultural discussions about the role of fiction and its relations with factual communication.

In focusing on ways in which works of fiction may seek to establish factuality, as well as on the rhetorical variety of fictional instructiveness, I have wanted to take tentative steps towards recognizing that a rich rhetorical field deserving of a closer analytical attention is routinely lumped aside as nonfictionality by the rhetoric of fictionality. By expanding the scope of rhetorical inquiry, we might gain a richer and more nuanced understanding of what works of fiction can be and do *as rhetoric*.

636 Sperber and Wilson, *Relevance: Communication and Cognition*, 118–119.

Henrik Zetterberg-Nielsen

10. Dangers of Fictionality, Human Sexuality and Sexual Fantasies

Abstract: The chapter applies the rhetorical turn in fictionality studies in the latest decades to the study of imaginary aspects of human sexuality. Rhetorical fictionality theory sees overtly invented stories as means for someone to achieve some purpose(s) of aesthetical, commercial, ethical kind or otherwise with someone else. The chapter continues the author's work on fictionality theory by exploring the relation between fictionality and human sexuality. Discussing three possible dangers in the context of sexual fantasy – 'assuming that what is rare in reality is also rare as fantasy; that fictionality does not have much real-world impact; and finally, that fantasies always amount to wish fulfilments', the chapter stresses the importance of distinguishing between fantasies of an overtly imagined nature and real wishes and acts, thus moving towards a de-pathologization of common sexual fantasies. Moreover, it is argued that sexuality is a common purpose of fictionality and demonstrated how a rhetorical approach to fictionality can shed new light on debated topics such as coercion fantasies, the importance of consensuality, and finally the point that some fictional narratives lend themselves to a didactics of sexuality in ways that can be healthy or unhealthy and sexist.

Keywords: fictionality, sexuality, sexual fantasies, imagination

Imagination, fictionality and human sexuality[637]

At a first glance, sex might appear as one of the most physical and carnal activities imaginable. The key word here, though, is imaginable, and reflection reveals that imagination and fictionality serve indispensable roles in what makes human sexuality human.[638] Fictionality is often put in the service of producing desired physical effects or working for the sole benefit of autonomous psychological pleasures. Fictional stories are on several levels central to sexuality, and sexual

637 I wish to thank Samuli Björninen and Maria Mäkelä for thorough comments that greatly helped improve the argument and clarity of expression, and also to thank the two anonymous reviewers who helped me tighten the connection between fictionality and danger in relation to the topic and to clarify my argument.

638 See Justin J. Lehmiller, *The Psychology of Human Sexuality* (Hoboken: Wiley Blackwell, 2014).

fantasies, in this context, are seen as something we make use of consciously and unconsciously, intentionally and unintentionally.

In this chapter, I examine fictionality in relation to sexuality with a specific view to the alleged and real dangers associated with sexual fantasies.[639] More on the status of fantasies as discourse and as narrative below.

Fiction, in and of itself, has been castigated recurrently throughout history. At a remove from reality; useless; dangerous; tempting; a gateway drug to real crime are just some of the (often mutually exclusive) accusations against fiction from Plato through early novel theories to discussions about computer games, movie violence and real-world assaults in recent decades.

No other instance of imagination and fictionality, however, has been under anywhere near the same degree of attack as the sexual fantasy, which has been condemned and denigrated by religion and psychology alike. Standing in an intimate (though not monogamous) relationship with masturbation and with other non-reproductive practices, the sexual fantasy has been considered dangerous in countless ways. Nowhere, thus, has the danger of fictionality seemed more obvious than at the crossroads with sexuality. In general, non-reproductive sexual practices have – even before any further contamination with fictionality and fantasy[640] – been considered among the most pathological manifestations across

---

639 See Donald S. Strassberg and Lisa K. Lockerd, 'Force in Women's Sexual Fantasies', *Archives of Sexual Behavior* 2/4 (1998), 408; Christian C. Joyal, Amélie Cossette and Vanessa Lapierre, 'What Exactly Is an Unusual Sexual Fantasy?', *The Journal of Sexual Medicine* 12/2 (2015), 334; Barbara Hariton and Jerome L. Singer, 'Women's Fantasies during Sexual Intercourse: Normative and Theoretical Implications', *Journal of Consulting and Clinical Psychology* 42/3 (1974), 313–322; Andrew Gilden, 'Punishing Sexual Fantasy', *William & Mary Law Review* 58/2 (2016), 419–492.

640 The alleged danger of masturbation very often brings along with it the alleged danger of sexual fantasies, and thus of fictionality. For most people, masturbation is difficult or impossible without any accompanying imagination or fantasy, and thus the masturbatory act and the sexual thought work in tandem to sever the necessary relation between reproductive copulation and sexuality. Masturbation, more paradigmatically than any other sexual practice, combines the non-reproductive or even anti-reproductive with the imaginary. In the immensely popular eighteenth-century treatise *ONANIA; OR THE DETESTABLE SIN OF Self-Pollution, AND ALL ITS Dreadful Consequenges (in both Sexes) CONSIDERED; WITH ADVICE TO THOSE THAT HAVE INJURED THEMSELVES BY THIS SHAMEFUL PRACTICE*, this is the very first accusation against masturbation: 'SELF-Pollution is that unnatural practice, by which persons of either sex may defile their own bodies without the assistance of others, while yielding to filthy imaginations' (Anonymous, *Onania: or, the heinous sin of self-pollution* (approx. 1712–23), 5). The necessary connection between the two

most psychological, psychoanalytical and psychiatric theories,[641] and have at the same time been, religiously speaking, considered among the worst sins. Onan, curiously, in the Bible, is never reported to have engaged in masturbation. Even as his name is so closely connected in many languages for synonyms for masturbation (Danish: 'Onani', German: 'Onanie', eighteenth century English: 'Onania') that was not his alleged crime. Onan's real crime has many names today: He left the church before the singing began; he got off at edge hill; he made a firefighter's special, had a nut gut; delivered a tummy cummy or something similar. In short, he used coitus interruptus as method of contraception (in the specific context of being ordered by his father to sleep with his diseased brother's wife).[642] Nothing suggests, either of the six times he is mentioned in the Bible, that he actually engaged in the activity still so closely associated with his name some 2500 years later, that of onanism in the form of masturbation.[644] Nevertheless, the result (spilled semen on the ground) was the same, and, as Monty Python has a catholic father explaining to his 63 children: 'If a sperm is wasted, God gets

---

is stated even stronger later: 'The supposition, that the action may be entirely free from mental impurity, is very dangerous: I cannot think it practicable' (Anonymous, *Onania: or, the heinous sin of self-pollution*, 28).

641 See Anonymous, *Onania: or, the heinous sin of self-pollution*; Kim M. Phillips and Barry Reay, *Sex before Sexuality: A Premodern History* (Cambridge, UK: Polity Press, 2011), 18; and even today American Psychiatric Association, *Diagnostic and Statistical Manual of Mental Disorders (DSM-5)* (Washington D.C.: American Psychiatric Publishing, 2013) to be discussed below.

642 'whenever he slept with his brother's wife, he spilled his semen on the ground' (Topverses, *The Bible,* New International Version, Genesis 38:9, <http://topverses.com/Bible/Genesis/38/9>, accessed 24 January 2022).

643 Onan is in a very specific and unusual situation: '"Sleep with your brother's wife and fulfill your duty to her as a brother-in-law to raise up offspring for your brother." [9] But Onan knew that the child would not be his'. In essence a rare situation of auto-cuckolding. Onan is asked to raise and provide for (what is legally and socially) another person's child – even to the point where he is asked, himself, to be the sperm-provider. At the very front page *ONANIA; OR THE DETESTABLE SIN OF Self-Pollution, AND ALL ITS Dreadful Consequenges (in both Sexes) CONSIDERED; WITH ADVICE TO THOSE THAT HAVE INJURED THEMSELVES BY THIS SHAMEFUL PRACTICE*, a translation is offered of Genesis 38, 9, which is different from the contemporary and which stresses this aspect: 'And Onan knew that the Seed would not he his', where the word 'Seed' serves to align sperm and child.

644 'Onanism', today, covers both meanings of masturbation and of coitus interruptus.

quite irate.'[645] So irate, in fact, with Onan, that God 'put him to death'.[646] The real crime, thus, was not masturbation per se. Rather, it was the refusal to engage in reproduction at all costs. There is a straight and uninterrupted (unlike Onan's intercourse with Er's wife) line from conceiving of this as a sin punishable by death, to later seeing rape and incest as relatively minor sins compared to sodomy and masturbation.[648] From there, the line continues to the widespread prohibitions against contraception in all forms across earlier and contemporary cultures to conceiving of non-genito-centric sexual preferences as intrinsically pathological even in the most recent editions of the most widely used psychiatric manuals.[649]

---

645 Terry Jones and Terry Gilliam, *Monty Python's The Meaning of Life* (United Kingdom: Celandine Films, The Monty Python Partnership, 1983).

646 Topverses, *The Bible*, New International Version, Genesis 38:9.

647 Seeing as God had already killed off Onan's brother, in a kind of pre-emptive contraception effectively preventing his wife from being impregnated by her husband's sperm, God is part of the pickle from the beginning, and not slow to execute death sentences for both brothers:

> [6] Judah got a wife for Er, his firstborn, and her name was Tamar. [7] But Er, Judah's firstborn, was wicked in the Lord's sight; so the Lord put him to death. [8] Then Judah said to Onan, "Sleep with your brother's wife and fulfill your duty to her as a brother-in-law to raise up offspring for your brother." [9] But Onan knew that the child would not be his; so whenever he slept with his brother's wife, he spilled his semen on the ground to keep from providing offspring for his brother. [10] What he did was wicked in the Lord's sight; so the Lord put him to death also. (Topverses, *The Bible*, New International Version, Genesis 38:9).

648 For a remarkably clear expression of this view, see again Anonymous, *Onania: or, the heinous sin of self-pollution*, 8: 'whether we commit abomination with our own sex, or with beasts, or that we defile our bodies with this shameful action, the consequences are the same to society and our species [...]. For fornication and even adultery itself we have frailty and nature to plead, though these are heinous sins: but Self-pollution is a sin not only against nature, but a sin that prevents and extinguishes nature'. See also Phillips and Reay, *Sex Before Sexuality*, 18, in the chapter on 'Sin':'The number and order of sexual sins varied from [premodern Christian] author to author, but most ranged from fornication (sex between an unmarried man and woman) as the least serious brand of lechery to the 'vice against nature' as the worst. A common ranking ran thus: fornication, adultery, incest, violation or debauchery, abduction-rape (raptus) and the 'vice against nature' (which generally encompassed all acts which could not result in procreation, including use of contraceptives, masturbation, anal or oral sex, same-sex practices and bestiality)'.

649 Much more on the fifth and latest edition of American Psychiatric Association, *Diagnostic and Statistical Manual of Mental Disorders (DSM-5)* below.

Throughout large parts of history, thus, the danger of non-reproductive sex has been considered larger than the danger of rape. Contemporary debates in America about whether rape or abortion (after rape) deserves the harshest punishment show just how present and prevalent that kind of thinking still is.

Against this backdrop of a multitude of accusations against fiction and sexuality – and more than anything against their overlap in the sexual fantasy so often aligned with non-reproductive sex – this chapter discusses three distinct possible dangers of fictionality in relation to sexuality and how they complicate each other. **First**, the danger to pathologize having and/or telling fictional fantasies about events or actions that would be dangerous, criminal or unethical in real life. **Second**, the reverse danger of thinking that fictive narratives do not have any bearing on reality does not influence real-world beliefs, and does not achieve real-world purposes. **Third**, the danger to think and to theorize that fictive sexual fantasies are always wish fulfillments. All three dangers directly connect the question of danger to the question of the relationship between fictionality and real-world beliefs and actions.

In sum, my purpose is ideological, theoretical and practical. I aim to demonstrate how the distinction between the overtly invented and imagined on the one hand, and the real and actualized on the other hand, allows us to de-pathologize the many widespread sexual fantasies. This, in turn, allows us to understand their roles in human sexuality, and to understand how it is possible that what would be disastrous in reality can be advantageous and pleasurable as fantasy.

It is quintessential to strike a balance between vehemently countering all aspects of abuse and any kind of rape myth acceptance, misogyny and sexism, and at the same time avoiding to pathologize or claim as rare or non-existing what is actually very usual fantasies or consensual practices on the other hand.[650] The latter kind of pathologizing only perpetuates the repressive line from religion, through nineteenth-century medicine to present-day diagnoses in manuals like *Diagnostic and Statistical Manual of mental disorders (DSM-5)* as I will detail below.

---

650 Joyal, Cossette and Lapierre, 'What Exactly Is an Unusual Sexual Fantasy?', 334. See also Hariton and Singer, 'Women's Fantasies during Sexual Intercourse: Normative and Theoretical Implications', 313–322. As for consensual practices see Juliet Richters, Richard Oliver de Visser, Chris E. Rissel, Andrew E. Grulich and Anthony M.A. Smith, 'Demographic and Psychosocial Features of Participants in Bondage and Discipline, "Sadomasochism" or Dominance and Submission (BDSM): Data from a National Survey', *The Journal of Sexual Medicine* 5/7 (2008), 1660–1668.

Recent fictionality theory and earlier approaches to similar questions

As far as fictionality is concerned, the theoretical horizon of this chapter and of the project of which it is a part, is that of rhetorical approaches to the issue in the wake of Walsh's 2007 publication *The Rhetoric of Fictionality*. Over the last decade, a large number of articles utilizing, expanding, criticizing and developing a rhetorical approach to fictionality have appeared by authors such as Mildorf, Hatavara, Mäkelä, Dawson, Zetterberg Gjerlevsen, Phelan, Iversen, Brix Jakobsen, Björninen and others.[651] In 2015 James Phelan, Richard Walsh and I suggested in 'Ten Theses about Fictionality', that the reorientation towards a rhetorical approach in the way of thinking about fictionality could be captured by three opening moves.[652] One, 'to distinguish between, on the one hand, fiction as a set of conventional genres (novel, short story, graphic novel, fiction film, television serial fiction, and so on) and, on the other hand, fictionality as a quality or fictive discourse as a mode'.[653] Two, to 'emphasize that the use of fictionality is not a turning away from the actual world but a specific communicative strategy within some context in that world'.[654] Three: 'to advance a general claim […]. The ability to invent, imagine, and communicate without claiming to refer to the actual is a fundamental cognitive skill'.[655] Together with Simona Zetterberg Gjerlevsen, I have defined fictionality as 'intentionally signaled invention in

651 In general, these and other scholars working in the area of rhetorical narrative theory have engaged with this new approach to fictionality and these theoretical moves; Henrik Skov Nielsen, James Phelan and Richard Walsh, 'Ten Theses about Fictionality', *Narrative* 23/1 (2015), 61–73; Simona Zetterberg Gjerlevsen, 'A Novel History of Fictionality', *Narrative* 24/2 (2016), 174–189; Simona Zetterberg Gjerlevsen, 'Fictionality', in Peter Hühn, ed., *The Living Handbook of Narratology* (Hamburg: Universität Hamburg, 2016); Paul Dawson, 'Ten Theses against Fictionality', *Narrative* 23/1 (2015), 74–100; Alexander Bareis, 'Randbereiche und Grenzüberschreitungen: Zu einer Theorie der Fiktion im Vergleich der Künste', in Anne Enderwitz and Irina Rajewsky, eds., *Fiktion im Vergleich der Künste und Medien* (Berlin: De Gruyter, 2016), 45–62; Mari Hatavara and Jarmila Mildorf, 'Hybrid Fictionality and Vicarious Narrative Experience', *Narrative* 25/1 (2017), 65–82.

652 The described reorientation had already resulted in The Aarhus Centre for Fictionality Studies where members are especially interested in issues of fictionality outside fiction.

653 Nielsen, Phelan and Walsh, 'Ten Theses about Fictionality', 62.

654 Nielsen, Phelan and Walsh, 'Ten Theses about Fictionality', 62.

655 Nielsen, Phelan and Walsh, 'Ten Theses about Fictionality', 63.

communication'.[656] The suggested definition has been widely used and discussed before and after publication.[657]

The way of approaching fictionality and sexuality suggested here thus continues the ways in which I have developed a rhetorical theory of fictionality and has this reconceptualization of fictionality as a premise.[658] To most people fictionality seems a device of extraordinary rather than ordinary language; perceived as belonging solely to the spheres of entertainment and aesthetics. In a decade-long devotion of my research to fictionality, I have aimed to consolidate the opposite assumption; that our everyday lives are permeated with fictionality. The ability to imagine is seen as one of the most fundamental human cognitive skills. When we communicate about non-actual state of affairs, we use our species-specific ability to fictionalize and to understand fictionality. We use fictionality to communicate about imagined state of affairs in political speeches, conversations, branding of companies, historical writings, job applications, witty remarks, court proceedings, diaries, fiction and in sexual fantasies if we tell them to partners, friends or researchers or publish them online.[659] If they remain in our own mind, they constitute imaginary narratives – the invented nature of

656 Simona Zetterberg Gjerlevsen and Henrik Skov Nielsen, 'Distinguishing Fictionality', in Cindie Aaen Maagaard, Daniel Schäbler and Marianne Wolff Lundholt, eds., *Exploring Fictionality. Conceptions, Test Cases, Discussions* (Odense: Syddansk Universitetsforlag, 2020), 19–40.

657 Walsh, Hatavara, Iversen, Bareis and many more.

658 See also Henrik Skov Nielsen, 'Fiktion og fortælling', *Kritik* 44/201 (2011), 113–123; Henrik Skov Nielsen, 'Fictional Voices? Strange Voices? Unnatural Voices?', in Per Krogh Hansen, Stefan Iversen, Henrik Skov Nielsen and Rolf Reitan, eds., *Narratologia* (Berlin: De Gruyter, 2011), 55–82; Simona Zetterberg Gjerlevsen, Jan Maintz and Henrik Skov Nielsen, *Fiktionalitet i litteratur, sprog og medier* (Frederiksberg: Dansklærerforeningens forlag, 2019); Gjerlevsen and Nielsen, 'Distinguishing fictionality'; Henrik Skov Nielsen, Louise Brix Jacobsen, Stefan Kjerkegaard, Rikke Andersen Kraglund, Camilla Møhring Reestorff and Carsten Stage, *Fiktionalitet* (Frederiksberg: Samfundslitteratur, 2013);, Nielsen, Phelan and Walsh, 'Ten Theses about Fictionality'; Richard Walsh, *The Rhetoric of Fictionality* (Columbus: Ohio State University Press, 2007); Catherine Gallagher, 'The Rise of Fictionality', in Franco Moretti, ed., *The Novel* (Princeton: Princeton University Press, 2006), 336–363; James Phelan, 'Authors, Resources, Audiences: Toward a Rhetorical Poetics of Narrative', *Style* 52/1–2 (2018), 1–34.

659 Hundreds of thousands of fantasies emphasizing fictionality are easily accessible online and thousands have been print-published following the theoretical work by Masters and Johnson and the empirical collections, especially by Nancy Friday.

which is intrinsically clear to the fantasizer and becomes signaled by signs of fictionality when communicated to others.[660]

The approach is in several respects different from earlier approaches combining the study of sexualities with discussions of fiction or literature. Story-oriented approaches to sexuality generally position themselves as specifically interested in literature and narratives as something different from, possibly even opposed to science and biology. Rohy's *Lost Causes*, which brilliantly discusses the history of the politics of pro-gay and anti-gay movements from the perspective of queer theory as well as narrative and literary theory, is exemplary in this regard:

> This study [...] does not address the scientific question of whether biological factors cause homosexuality, or the legal question of how best to secure equity. [...] Instead, this book examines the stories told about gay and lesbian etiology and the language in which they are told. Because the scholarly critique of biological determinism in the 1990s came largely from bioscientists and social scientists, there remains a need for readings of homosexual etiologies as narrative forms, hermeneutic strategies, and constellations of recurring tropes available to the methods of literary studies. Taking as its archive largely canonical fiction and nonfiction by British and American authors from Wilde to the present, this book turns from the present to the past, from the popular to the literary, from the polemical to the speculative, to show how fictional and nonfictional accounts of homosexual etiology afford new ways to frame the relations between causality and queerness.[661]

Rohy, thus, self-avowedly, disconnects the textual discussions and representations from scientific facts and biological factors even when speaking specifically about etiology.[662] Similarly, the editors in *Prose fiction and early modern sexualities* draw on Bruce Smith[663] to the point of overstatement in the introduction to drive home the point that literature about sexuality is a different and less reductive discourse than discourses within medicine and similar sciences.[664]

Here, I do not claim that literature or fiction provides for a special kind of language, or for otherwise completely unavailable insights but that invented

660 More on sexual fantasies as fictional or non-fictional and as narratives at the end of this section.

661 Valerie Rohy, *Lost Causes: Narrative, Etiology, and Queer Theory* (Oxford: Oxford Scholarship Online, 2014), 4.

662 Rohy, *Lost Causes: Narrative, Etiology, and Queer Theory*.

663 Bruce R. Smith, 'Premodern Sexualities', *PMLA* 115/3 (2000), 318–329.

664 Constance C. Relihan and Goran V. Stanivukovic, eds., *Prose Fiction and Early Modern Sexualities in England, 1570–1640* (New York: Palgrave Macmillan, 2004), 3.

narratives play important roles in human sexuality itself. Boyd, Gotschall and Carroll have all, individually and together, examined the role of narrative and storytelling for the evolution of human beings but not the direct interconnection between human sexuality and fictionality. In *Sapiens*, Harari insists on the importance of 'fiction'[666] and the emergence of 'fictive language'[667] for the ability of our species to organize and collaborate among other things, but again with no special view to sexuality.

Additionally, seeing fictionality as paradigmatic for human sexuality and vice versa means that even as I combine evolution theory and fictionality theory, my point and approach are completely different from that of literary Darwinists such as Saunders, who describes her approach in the following way:

> Literary Darwinists draw upon research and theory from evolutionary psychology to analyze fictional, dramatic, and poetic representations of human behavior. A product of imaginative and aesthetic energies, literature offers special insight into universals of human nature.[668]

My point is not a thematic one about the insights potentially offered by fiction, and not about human behavior in general. Rather, I contend that fiction is directly a product of as well as a driving force in human evolution in its close attachment to sexuality. In this sense, I am closer to Darwin's own description of imagination in *The Descent of Man*: 'The imagination is one of the highest prerogatives of man. By this faculty, he unites, independently of the will, former images and ideas, and thus creates brilliant and novel results'.[669]

Human beings have the ability to process, communicate about and signal the concern with non-actual states of affairs. Cognitively processing non-actual states of affairs can take the shape of just an idea or an image but often takes the shape of imaginary narratives, whereas intentionally signaling invention *in*

---

665 It is a common idea in queer approaches to literature that literature provides special or even unique insights about sexuality or queerness. This is different from my interest here in how narratives themselves *shape*, sustain and develop sexuality.

666 Yuval Noah Harari, *Sapiens: A Brief History of Humankind* (New York: Random House, 2014), 27.

667 Harari, *Sapiens: A Brief History of Humankind,* ix.

668 Judith P. Saunders, 'Darwinian Literary Analysis of Sexuality', in Todd K. Shackelford and Ranald D. Hansen, eds., *The Evolution of Sexuality* (Cham: Springer, 2015), 29.

669 Darwin [1871] quoted in Penelope Murray, 'Introduction', in John Cocking, *Imagination. A Study in the History of Ideas* (London: Routledge, 1991), 44 (with page 45 wrongly listed instead of 44).

communication constitutes fictionality in the rhetorical sense of the word. My view on fantasies as narratives has some affinity to Walsh's on dreams in 'Dreaming and Narrative Theory', except that many sexual fantasies are even more obviously narrative in nature than dreams. To Walsh, dreams as instances of fictionality dismiss existing explanations of fictionality:

> The fictionality of dreams in itself resists explanation in conventional narratological terms. Fictionality is treated, by both the pretense model of fictive discourse in speech act theory and the fictional worlds model of fictive reference, as fundamentally a problem of truthfulness. In the first case fiction is distinguished from seriously asserted narrative; in the second, it is distinguished from reference to the actual world. Yet it seems bizarre, on the one hand, to conceive of a dreamer pretending the dreamwork, or of dreaming as pretending to remember; and on the other hand the contingency of dream representations—their ad hoc fluidity in response to the demands of the moment, however those may be understood—exposes rather starkly the cumbersome redundancy of a fictional worlds account of fictive reference. Dreams suggest a view of fictive communication that is not subordinate to directly assertive communication at all, nor anchored by the assumption of a global referential ground, but rather accountable to generative principles of relevance or salience.[670]

Equally relevant is Walsh's utilization of dreams as fictions to shed light on the experience:

> Dreams are directly fictive and experienced directly [...]. Imagination, indeed, is precisely the relevant concept: it does not need to be redeemed by a dissociative framework providing for suspension of disbelief, willing or otherwise.[671]
> emotional valency, or affective value in general, is inherent in the process of (narrative) representation, rather than a secondary response to the products of representation. If this is so, the various ways in which narrative theorists and philosophers have sought to reconcile emotional involvement with fictionality are misconceived and redundant. Affective response does not depend upon suspension of disbelief or any equivalent framing of our engagement with fictions because it is inherent in, and continuous with, the semiotic process of representation[672]

Affective response, indeed, does not depend upon suspension of disbelief. In the sexual fantasy affective response, quite on the contrary, hinges on a perpetual awareness of the fictive nature of the fantasy. Using these insights in particular, and recent rhetorical fictionality theory in general to understand sexual fantasies,

670 Richard Walsh, 'Dreaming and Narrative Theory', in Frederick L. Aldama, ed., *Toward a Cognitive Theory of Narrative Acts* (Austin: University of Texas Press, 2010), 151.
671 Walsh, 'Dreaming and Narrative Theory', 154.
672 Walsh, 'Dreaming and Narrative Theory', 157.

we get a more precise understanding of how sexual fantasies often constitute manifestly fictive narratives as opposed to narratives confusable with representations of reality or narratives forming wish fulfillments. The sexual fantasy, which may very likely be the most common form of imaginary narrative, provides valuable insight into how human beings can use the invented as a very direct way of engaging with reality. Sexual fantasies – as the theoretical explanations above conclude, and as empirical research in form of questionnaires and surveys confirm[673] – are used and processed with a mental and/or verbal coding for imagination.[674] This means that sexual fantasies have real-world consequences, including producing affective and physiological responses in ways they would not if we were immersed in the specific sense of being temporarily unaware of the imagined nature and processing them as real. Fantasies of being forced and overpowered are at the very top of the most common fantasies, and they would not at all bring pleasure or work without a perpetual awareness of the fictive nature. Overtly invented narratives facilitate rather than preclude immersion in general and in sexual fantasies in particular. This also means that awareness of the imagined nature becomes a paramount factor in distinguishing rare pathological sexual desires about real coercion, abuse and non-consensual actions on the one hand from very common prevalent fantasies about imagined hierarchies, power play, and dominance and submission on the other hand.

From Walsh's perspective, in his article, dreams are mediated by the human cognitive apparatuses and produced in a process of semiosis, and in that sense communicated:

> The salient difference in kind between a memory and a dream is not that one is true and the other is false: there is such a thing as false memory, and dreams may represent actual experiences, without detracting from the integrity of either mental activity. The difference is that the generative principles of each are antithetical in a crucial respect: the dominant cognitive imperative of memory is its adequacy to prior experiential fact, however much that imperative may be coopted by subjective interests in the particular case;whereas the dominant cognitive imperative of dreaming, however much it takes account of adequacy to prior experience, is the satisfaction of present mental needs (some

673 See below for the findings of several large empirical studies.

674 See, for instance: Eileen L. Zurbriggen and Megan R. Yost, 'Power, Desire, and Pleasure in Sexual Fantasies', *Journal of Sex Research* 41/3 (2004), 291:

> We coded for frame when the words "I fantasize" or "I imagine" or "I dream" occurred in the fantasy. The category of frame indicated that the author qualified what was written, specifically stating that it was imagined and not real. An example of a frame is "I fantasize about sleeping with a co-worker."

> very obvious and general, such as the expression of desires or the management of anxieties, others rather more obscure or circumstantial). These cognitive drivers, I suggest, are of complementary rhetorical kinds: that is to say, the fundamental distinction between dreams and memories is not between falsehood and truth, still less between illusion and experience, but between fiction and nonfiction. Perception is a representation of the world: that is experience, but it is also the foundation of the cognitive narrative faculty, the products of which are available to (episodic) memory. The salient feature of dream percepts is that they are *fictive* representations, and that of dreams is that they are fictive *narratives*.[675]

The fantasy is typically more conscious than the dream and more intentional than even most lucid dreams. When communicated to others, it very clearly uses fictionality.[676] If not written down or spoken out, the fantasy works as an internal and imaginary narrative with experientiality, actions and events in verbal and/or visual semiotic forms used to produce desired effects hinging on a perpetual awareness of the invented nature of the narrative. For the current purposes, therefore, the rhetorical approach to fictionality applies to sexual fantasies when communicated; and the approach to imaginary narratives as overtly and intentionally invented rather than as pretendedly real and with a cognitive foregrounding of this invented nature instead of an alleged suspension of disbelief not only applies to but is strongly supported by internal fantasies.

Three dangers of fictionality in the context of human sexuality

The first danger of fictionality, in the current context of human sexuality and sexual fantasies, which I will attend to, is the danger of describing what is actually very prevalent, usual fantasies as rare and unusual, and then conceiving of them as pathological. Female fantasies about coercion or being forced are of a particularly peculiar and seemingly paradoxical nature. While sexual assault is a crime against humanity, in reality, being forced is among the most common sexual fantasies.[677] Interestingly, fantasies of committing violence are relatively

---

675 Walsh, 'Dreaming and Narrative Theory', 146.

676 The fantasy can partly or wholly draw on earlier, real experiences and regularly does. This does not make it non-fictional, since it is not just a recollection but a particular, deliberate, fictional use of memory: 'I imagine I am again with my ex-boyfriend'.

677 It is an obvious but important point that fantasizing entails agency while being subject to actual coercion or assault does not. Fantasizing about non-consensual sex does not entail real non-consensuality. Similar points are made in several articles on the subject. See, for instance, Jenny M. Bivona and Joseph W. Critelli, 'Women's Erotic Rape

rare for both sexes and rarer for men than for women, while fantasies about being the subject of violence and abuse are common in the form of fantasies of being overpowered for women (30–70%)[678] and about being pacified, whipped, humiliated, even castrated for men (25–36%).[679] Male fantasies about castration or forced chastity or about being 'cuckolded' are very common and are used by significant percentages for lust and arousal or by proxy seen represented in porn, as testified to by Pornhub's numbers for the views of the relevant categories.[680] Common to the mentioned male and female fantasies in contrast to other fantasies such as about sex in a deserted exotic place, is that few or no one would want them lived out in reality,[681] but that many use them in the form of imagination or communicated fantasy to achieve pleasure and desire.[682] The ethical and intellectual challenges of understanding such fantasies are attested to, among other things by the fact that I was recently, at a large conference, among the audience when a very prominent researcher stipulated to the audience that: 'No women have rape fantasies!'. Empirically, this is by a very large margin completely wrong, as large and small surveys show.[683] However, while on the one hand, it can be

---

Fantasies: An Evaluation of Theory and Research', *The Journal of Sex Research* 45/1 (2008), 58: 'Because individuals exert control over the contents of their own fantasies, many rape fantasies involve sexual activities that take place consistent with the will and desire of the fantasizer, even though these activities are against the will of her self-character in the fantasy.' Female fantasies of being forced are more common than both male fantasies about being forced and male fantasies about forcing and female fantasies about forcing. See, for instance, Joyal, Cossette and Lapierre, 'What Exactly Is an Unusual Sexual Fantasy?', 334.

678 Joyal, Cossette and Lapierre, 'What Exactly Is an Unusual Sexual Fantasy?', 334; Critelli and Bivona, 'Women's Erotic Rape Fantasies: An Evaluation of Theory and Research', 59–60.

679 Joyal, Cossette and Lapierre, 'What Exactly Is an Unusual Sexual Fantasy?', 334.

680 See also, for instance, Sai Gaddam and Ogi Ogas, *A Billion Wicked Thoughts: What the Internet Tells Us About Sexual Relationships* (New York: Plume Books, 2012), where it is stated that for heterosexual viewers, 'cuckold' is the second most common search term.

681 Although experiencing your partner with a third party is not particularly uncommon, it is still something that far more people fantasize about than wish to practice.

682 See Hariton and Singer, 'Women's Fantasies during Sexual Intercourse: Normative and Theoretical Implications', 313–322.

683 The exact numbers vary depending on the survey and depending on the phrasing of the question as 'being forced to have sex' (Hunt 1974 in Critelli and Bivona, 'Women's Erotic Rape Fantasies: An Evaluation of Theory and Research', 59), 'Forced Sexual Encounter' (Masters and Johnson 1979 in Critelli and Bivoni, 'Women's Erotic Rape Fantasies: An Evaluation of Theory and Research', 59), 'rape/force' (Wilson 1987 in

unfortunate to be judgmental about everyone's possible fantasies,[684] the desire and necessity to counter all aspects of abuse and any kind of rape myth acceptance on the other hand are both understandable and crucial. In what follows, I suggest that one contribution to achieve both; both a de-pathologization of the harmless and common and a steely resistance to any form of malignant rape myth belief, can be provided by the establishment of clear boundaries between communicating about invented fantasies and real actions; between fantasy and wish fulfillment, and between consensual practices and non-consensual crimes.[686]

Critelli and Bivoni, 'Women's Erotic Rape Fantasies: An Evaluation of Theory and Research', 60), 'Scene in which you have the impression of being raped' (Shulman and Horne 2006 in Critelli and Bivona, 'Women's Erotic Rape Fantasies: An Evaluation of Theory and Research', 60).

684 On this issue, I concur with Bivona and Critelli, "'The Nature of Women's Rape Fantasies: An Analysis of Prevalence, Frequency, and Contents', 58: 'an avoidance of this topic sends the false and disturbing message that there is something shameful about women's sexuality'. Doing so only perpetuates the repressive line from religion, through nineteenth-century medicine to present-day diagnoses like those of *DSM-5*.

685 See also Joseph W. Critelli and Jenny M. Bivona, 'The Nature of Women's Rape Fantasies: An Analysis of Prevalence, Frequency, and Contents', *The Journal of Sex Research* 46/1 (2009), 43:

> For the 14% of participants who reported having rape fantasies at least once a week, the mean proportion of sexual fantasies involving forced sex was 45%, with a median of 49%. Thus, for a sizable minority of women, rape fantasies comprise nearly one half of their sexual fantasies, suggesting that the rape theme has considerable appeal for millions of women in the United States. These results indicate that wording of rape fantasy items does make a difference. In this study, 52% of the sample reported having the fantasy, "being overpowered or forced by a man to surrender sexually against my will," whereas only 32% reported the fantasy, "being raped by a man."

686 See Nele De Neef, Violette Coppens, Wim Huys and Manuel Morrens, 'Bondage-Discipline, Dominance-Submission and Sadomasochism (BDSM) From an Integrative Biopsychosocial Perspective: A Systematic Review', *Sex Med* 7/2 (2019), 137:

> Additionally, Klement et al demonstrated significantly lower levels of sexism and rape myth acceptance in BDSM practitioners; contrasting insinuations that erotica involving sexually submissive women negatively impacts attitudes toward women and increases rape myth acceptance in men. [...] the fact that BDSM-related activities are classified as paraphilias implies that they are unusual or atypical; however, this stands in stark contrast with data showing that more than half of the general population has BDSM-themed fantasies. An internet survey conducted on 1,516 adults showed that only 9 of 55 sexual

Whereas narrative theory has limited scope in approaching clinical problems in general, fictionality theory provides fruitful insights into the two former, which also helps get a clearer with on the latter. These distinctions are virtually absent in the largest and most important psychiatric manual in the Western world, *The Diagnostic and Statistical Manual of Mental Disorders (DSM-5)*.[687] In the absence of such delimitations – the most important of which is probably the lack of a distinction of fictionality as signaling communicating about specifically invented and imagined states of affairs rather than real[688] – and without reference to disorder, dysfunction or disability, the chapter on 'Paraphilic Disorders' opens as follows:

> fantasies were deemed to be "unusual" (operationalized as being reported by <15.9%), including urine play, transgender dressing, or sexual abuse. Fantasies about sex with animals or children (age <12 years) were rare (as reported by <2.3%). Typical BDSM-related fantasies, such as being dominated, bondage, or spanking, were found to be more common (up to 34.5%), and could, thus, not be identified as unusual.

Ample literature shows that BDSM practitioners are typically highly educated. Sandnabba and colleagues found that more than one-third had a university degree, with an additional 21% having a college degree. Wismeijer & Van Assen similarly found that 70% had a higher education (i.e., bachelor's or master's degree), as compared with 34% in the general population. Martinez again showed that about half of their BDSM sample had a college degree, with another 33% having taken up to 1 year of college. In this line, they also had higher income levels than the general population.

687 Very far from being an inferior work, the importance of *DSM-5* can hardly be overrated. In their excellent review-article in *Journal of Sex Research*, 'Pathologizing Sexual Deviance: A History' from 2013, the philosophers De Block and Adriaens present the position of the changing editions of the DSM like this:

> The post–World War II history of psychiatry is characterized by the growing power of professional organizations. The American Psychiatric Association (APA) is perhaps the world's most powerful professional organization of psychiatrists. It is involved in health campaigns, the publication of psychiatric books and journals, and the organization of conferences. Its most visible work, however, is the preparation and publication of the *Diagnostic and Statistical Manual of Mental Disorders (DSM)*, a standardized psychiatric classification system. Today, it is the leading clinical diagnostic manual worldwide, and it is also used for research and administrative purposes all over the world. (Andreas de Block and Pieter R. Adriaens, 'Pathologizing Sexual Deviance: A History', *The Journal of Sex Research* 50/3–4 (2013), 284–285)

688 See Nielsen and Gjerlevsen, 'The Distinction of Fictionality'.

> Paraphilic disorders included in this manual are voyeuristic disorder (spying on others in private activities), exhibitionistic disorder (exposing the genitals), frotteuristic disorder (touching or rubbing against a nonconsenting individual), sexual masochism disorder (undergoing humiliation, bondage, or suffering), sexual sadism disorder (inflicting humiliation, bondage, or suffering), pedophilic disorder (sexual focus on children), fetishistic disorder (using nonliving objects or having a highly specific focus on nongenital body parts), and transvestic disorder (engaging in sexually arousing cross-dressing).[689]

Significantly, the introductory lines move seamlessly from the clearly or supposedly non-consensual (voyeurism and exhibitionism)[690] to the frotteurism explicitly specified to be non-consensual to masochism and sadism with no distinction made between widespread consensual practices and rare, criminal offenses. Subsequently, it moves on to pedophilia which can never be consensual, and then to fetishism which can only very rarely even *be* non-consensual in and of itself, to finally end with transvestitism, which cannot possibly be non-consensual.

The immediately following passage states:

> These disorders have traditionally been selected for specific listing and assignment of explicit diagnostic criteria in DSM for two main reasons: they are relatively common, in relation to other paraphilic disorders, and some of them entail actions for their satisfaction that, because of their noxiousness or potential harm to others, are classed as criminal offenses. The eight listed disorders do not exhaust the list of possible paraphilic disorders. Many dozens of distinct paraphilias have been identified and named, and almost any of them could, by virtue of its negative consequences for the individual or for others, rise to the level of a paraphilic disorder. The diagnoses of the other specified and unspecified paraphilic disorders are therefore indispensable and will be required in many cases.[691]

These are strange and illogical descriptions for several reasons, and they extend the confusion introduced in the opening passage. Relative commonness, of course, makes sense as criterion for inclusion, since a list of all paraphilias from the common to the uncommon is in principle endless.[692] *DSM*-5, however, then

---

689 American Psychiatric Association, *Diagnostic and Statistical Manual of Mental Disorders (DSM-5)*, 685.

690 From the context, it must be assumed that voyeurism and exhibitionism here means without consent or knowledge of other parties.

691 American Psychiatric Association, *Diagnostic and Statistical Manual of Mental Disorders (DSM-5)*, 685.

692 For instance lists with as many as 549 types have been made. See Anil Aggrawal, *Forensic and Medico-legal Aspects of Sexual Crimes and Unusual Sexual Practices* (Boca Raton: CRC Press, 2008), 369–382.

goes on to say that these have *all* been included because *some of them* can entail actions, which are classed as criminal offenses. First, this obscures the distinction between unethical and illegal acts on the one hand and mental disorders on the other hand, and second, it creates a continuum between allegedly unusual[693] sexual interests of no harm to anyone such as crossdressing at one end to abusive, illegal, coercive, non-consensual abuse in the form pedophilia or sadistic violence at the other end.

Towards the end, the passage directly states that almost any paraphilia can be a disorder because of its negative consequences for the individual or for others. This, more than anything begs the question of what counts at the basic constitutional characteristics of all members of the open-ended list of paraphilias. Dysfunction is not in the picture, and impairment is not at all consistently applied. Most paraphilias are not illegal or harmful to others,[694] and criminality normally does not amount to disorder anyway. It is shown in multiple studies, that just as persons with homosexual preferences are not lower functioning than persons with heterosexual ones; persons who engage in BDSM and fetish games or similar activities are not less educated, less happy or in other ways on average handicapped than persons who lack such interests.[695] It is recognized by *DSM-5* that this may be the case, and in fairness, the handbook does state that if the person feels no distress and does not act out (supposedly meaning in relation to non-consenting persons) then the paraphilia should be diagnosed as a sexual interest rather than a disorder. Then this leads to the question, why generally assume

---

693 In reality several of the listed paraphilias are not at all unusual – see below.

694 This also holds true for a large majority of the list in Appendix 1 in Aggrawal including, for example, the first nine among which are 'ablutophilia', 'acarophilia' and 'actirasty' designating having sexual preferences for baths, scratching and sun rays respectively.

695 Actually the reverse is true with clear statistical significance. See for instance Neef, Coppens, Huys and Morrens, 'Bondage-Discipline, Dominance-Submission and Sadomasochism (BDSM) From an Integrative Biopsychosocial Perspective: A Systematic Review', 137:

> Ample literature shows that BDSM practitioners are typically highly educated. Sandnabba and colleagues found that more than one-third had a university degree, with an additional 21% having a college degree. Wismeijer & Van Assen similarly found that 70% had a higher education (i.e., bachelor's or master's degree), as compared with 34% in the general population. Martinez again showed that about half of their BDSM sample had a college degree, with another 33% having taken up to 1 year of college. In this line, they also had higher income levels than the general population.

that the unspecified paraphilias almost all would have negative consequences and could constitute a disorder? Moreover, what do they have in common? The answer, it turns out, hides in the introductory conceptualization of the umbrella term rather than in any single instance of it, and in a way that is not and could not be manifested in diagnostic criteria:

> The term *paraphilia* denotes any intense and persistent sexual interest other than sexual interest in genital stimulation or preparatory fondling with phenotypically normal, physically mature, consenting human partners.[696]

This is the description of a necessary action and a necessary target for normophilic sexuality. For a sexual interest to not qualify as paraphilia, the target has to be phenotypically normal, physically mature and consenting, while the activity has to be stimulation of the genitals or preparing said stimulation of the genitals. With no further discussion, justification or even thematization, the description is an instance of emphatic genito-centric essentialism. The specification that fondling is allowed if (and only if) it serves preparatory purposes in relation to genital stimulation could draw a smile – were it not for the severely pathologizing effects this quasi-religious leftover has had and has.

In the lack of a common denominator in the dysfunctional, the harmful and the impairing, the result is that the non-normophilic or just unusual and in any case the non-genital becomes pathologized to the degree of being put on a par with assault, alcoholism and physical abuse.[697] This follows directly from the strong historical condemnation of masturbation and fantasies. What paraphilias really all have in common is that they present a perceived danger to reproductive sex, just as coitus interruptus and onanism do.

The single most important thing to notice, though, is recurrent through all the descriptions of all the paraphilias and consists of the very emphatic choice to **not** make a distinction between fantasy and reality and between internal feelings and

---

696 American Psychiatric Association, *Diagnostic and Statistical Manual of Mental Disorders (DSM-5)*, 685.

697 A telling example of the vagueness and broadness of the category is not only the great number of unspecified paraphilic disorders, but the section headlined 'Other Specified Paraphilic Disorders', which includes – as worth mentioning and specifying and giving a clinical term – dirty talk or in pathologizing greek: 'telephone scatologia' (American Psychiatric Association, *Diagnostic and Statistical Manual of Mental Disorders (DSM-5)*, 705). I recognize that uninvited obscene phone calls are verbal assault, but again the failure in *DSM-5* to distinguish between unwarranted and consensual behavior is detrimental.

external acts.[699] This is not by chance, as one phrase is repeatedly and deliberately stressed: 'fantasies, urges, or behaviors'. The phrase is formulaically repeated ad verbatim for seven of the eight paraphilias and stated with only a slight variation as 'fantasies, sexual urges, or behaviors' for the eighth 'Pedophilic Disorder'. This deliberate, paratactic assimilation is a main vehicle for the pathologizing rhetoric and effects of *DSM-5* where the fantasies and consensual practices of 50–90%[700] of the contemporary population in developed societies are described as rare, mental disorders. For a similar point from a different perspective, see de Neef et al. 2019:

> the fact that BDSM-related activities are classified as paraphilias implies that they are unusual or atypical; however, this stands in stark contrast with data showing that more than half of the general population has BDSM-themed fantasies. An internet survey conducted on 1,516 adults showed that only 9 of 55 sexual fantasies were deemed to be 'unusual' (operationalized as being reported by <15.9%), including urine play, transgender dressing, or sexual abuse. Fantasies about sex with animals or children (age <12 years) were rare (as reported by <2.3%). Typical BDSM-related fantasies, such as being dominated, bondage, or spanking, were found to be more common (up to 34.5%), and could, thus, not be identified as unusual.[701]

In 'What Exactly Is an Unusual Sexual Fantasy?', the authors find by reviewing almost 20 different surveys that fantasies about oral sex, anal sex, threesomes, being dominated, dominating, sex with an unknown, spanking, exhibitionism and many other fantasies are all common whereas the only two, rare fantasies even mentioned are sex with a child or with an animal.[702]

---

698 For a different, thorough discussion of this, see again Block and Adriaens, 'Pathologizing Sexual Deviance: A History', 276–298.

699 It is beyond the scope of this chapter about the dangers of fictionality to deal with fantasies about situations where consent of the other person is always impossible, such as murder or pedophilia. I would lean, though, on the side of thinking that if the imaginary nature of the fantasy is completely clear and opposed to any urge to actually act it out then there is little incentive to try to heal or change the thoughts. My interest here, though, is on the much, much more common fantasies of finding oneself – whether male or female – in the overpowered position.

700 See below on empirical studies on the percentages of diverse preferences.

701 Neef, Coppens, Huys and Morrens, 'Bondage-Discipline, Dominance-Submission and Sadomasochism (BDSM) From an Integrative Biopsychosocial Perspective: A Systematic Review', 136.

702 Joyal, Cossette and Lapierre, 'What Exactly Is an Unusual Sexual Fantasy?', *The Journal of Sexual Medicine* 12/2 (2015), 334.

In sum, the first danger to avoid is to stipulate on a purely speculative and non-empirical basis and without taking into account the distinction of fictionality that non-normative sexual fantasies are rare and/or pathological.

Whereas the first danger underestimates or entirely disregards the distinction of fictionality and thus the difference between imagining and acting out or actually wishing, the second danger goes in the opposite direction of underestimating the influence of fictionality.[703] Thus we now move from fantasies which are sometimes internal, imagined narratives or scenarios and sometimes told to other people, to fictional narratives always aimed at audiences.[704] In the discussion of the second danger, I examine the use of fictionality as a rhetorical act with social consequences and thus deliberately move to a completely different corpus of texts in the form of generic fictions such as literature and tv-series. Fiction is didactical and fictionality strongly influences beliefs and practices about the real world and about ethics, identities and actions.[705] Young people certainly learn more about norms, expectations, ethics and actions concerning sexuality and gender by watching partly or wholly fictionalized memes, TikTok videos,[706]

703 There is a strong, century-long tradition to take a special interest in the ways in which fiction is secluded and detached from real life. Versions of this reference Kant's concept of 'interesseloses Wohlgefallen', which distinguish the beautiful from the sublime as an argument to take interest in a purely and autonomous aesthetical space of fiction, whereas others argue for the importance of 'l'art pour l'art' to counter the risks of utilitarianism.

704 Naturally, fantasies, including purely internal ones, can also affect reality and real behavior; and they are also affected by the culturally available fictional representations. Internal fantasies can be almost entirely cognitive, nearly coextensive with the ability to imagine – and therefore, such versions couldn't possibly have rhetorical functions like didacticity.

705 Several studies provide empirical evidence for the ability of fiction to influence belief systems, though, in this context, I am drawing more on the tradition of rhetorical approaches to fictionality. See Nielsen, Phelan and Walsh, 'Ten Theses about Fictionality' for arguments supporting the view, including the use of fictionality as a persuasive strategy in politics. See also Nielsen and Gjerlevsen, "The Distinction of Fictionality" for a discussion of empirical cases supporting the assumption.

706 See for instance, Danah Boyd, *It's Complicated: The Social Lives of Networked Teens* (New Haven: Yale University Press, 2014); Anna Hickey-Moody, *Youth, Arts and Education: Reassembling Subjectivity through Affect* (Abingdon: Routledge, 2013); Susan Moore, Meredith Temple-Smith and Doreen Rosenthal, *Sexuality in Adolescence: The Digital Generation* (Hove: Routledge, 2016); Elaine O'Quinn, *Girls' Literacy Experiences In and Out of School Learning and Composing Gendered Identities* (Hoboken: Taylor and Francis, 2012).

and mass cultural products of fiction like *Euphoria*, *Elite*, *Atypical*, *Bonding*, and, well: *Sex Education* than by formal sex education.

Fictional literature, in the same vein, has always been didactical, and not least as far as sexuality is concerned. From early conduct books explicitly advertised as means to educate about romantic relationships, via romance novels[707] to modern-day series like the *Fifty Shades Trilogy* which has sold 100 million copies, and *The Twilight Saga* (120 million) fiction teaches readers how to behave (or abstain from behaving) sexually.

Consider, for example, the fairy tale by the Grimm Brothers, 'Der Froschkönig oder der eiserne Heinrich' ['The Frog Prince; or, Iron Henry'], the first fairy tale in all 17 editions of the tales. Versions of the story exist around the world and in more than 30 languages. The best-known element of the tale repeatedly referenced in pop culture, including in the 2009 Disney adaptation *The Princess and the Frog* is the transformation from frog to prince caused by the princess' kiss. The educational lesson of this version of the story seems straightforward: If as a woman, you are disgusted by the prospect of living the rest of your life with a

---

707 See Ellis and Symons on the gendered and evolutionarily based reading preferences between men and women. A main point in the article is an adaptionist explanation for the empirically confirmed expectation that men on average prefer 'Pornotopia' in the form of uncontextualized sex with more short-term partners, whereas women on average prefer 'Romance novels' where sex is predominantly a means to meet and remain with a lifelong partner. Both genres sell in the millions.
The most striking feature of male-oriented pornography is that sex is sheer lust and physical gratification, devoid of encumbering relationships, emotional elaboration, complicated plot lines, flirtation, courtship, and extended foreplay; in pornotopia, women, like men, are easily aroused and willing. Erotic romance novels, which are almost exclusively written by and for women, and which are so popular that a single title often sells millions of copies, differ profoundly from male-oriented pornography. Many modern romances portray sexual activity far more graphically than their historical predecessors did, and a modern romance heroine may have a career as interesting as that of the hero; but the basic fictional world of the romance—like the vastly different realm of pornotopia—has remained remarkably stable over the centuries (Mussell, 1984). [...] Romances are fundamentally about mate selection, and they vary widely in the degree to which sexual activity is graphically depicted (if it is depicted at all). "In all romances, the love story is the central action and the most significant motivating force.... [Romances] assert and reinforce a woman's desire to identify and marry the one right man who will remain hers for the rest of her life" (Mussell, 1984:11). (Bruce J. Ellis and Donald Symons, 'Sex Differences in Sexual Fantasy: an Evolutionary Psychological Approach', *The Journal of Sex Research* 27/4 (1990), 544).

revolting creature – **then** what you really want to do is comply with his every wish, give in to his sexual advances and obey his orders. If you succeed in this, you just might find that he will actually be a darling prince – or that you will begin to see him as one.

It is not clear to anyone exactly how and when the kiss entered the history of the transformations of the fairy tale.[708] In Grimm's published version, however, an entirely different response from the princess causes the transformation from beast to beauty. In Grimms's version, the princess loses her golden ball; the frog offers to get it for her from the pond, and in return, she offers everything she owns. The frog, however, does not want her things, but herself.[709] The repugnant nature of the frog's demand is underlined in the German use of the diminutive in its references to the princess' belongings; 'Bett**lein**' rather than just 'Bett' for example. The crucial point plays out very differently in Grimm:

> When she was in bed he crept to her and said, 'I am tired, I want to sleep as well as you, lift me up or I will tell your father.' At this she was terribly angry, and took him up and threw him with all her might against the wall. 'Now, will you be quiet, odious frog,' said she. But when he fell down he was no frog but a king's son with kind and beautiful eyes.[710]

The didactics seem to be exactly the reverse of the kiss-the-frog-versions. The transformation does not follow when and because she complies with him but, conversely, because and when she violently does not comply. The versions give

---

708 It is clear that already Edgar Taylor's 1823 English translation changed the original German version considerably. In his translation, the frog sleeps with the princess for three nights before the spell is broken and this is also one of the versions listed by the Grimm brothers themselves in their notes to versions of the tale.

709 See Brothers Grimm, 'Der Froschkönig oder der eiserne Heinrich', *Grimm Stories* (1812), https://www.grimmstories.com/language.php?grimm=001&l=de&r=en, accessed 24 January 2022: 'Was du haben willst, lieber Frosch', sagte sie, 'meine Kleider, meine Perlen und Edelsteine, auch noch die goldene Krone, die ich trage.' The frog can have all her things. Everything she owns. But the frog does not want her things, but herself: 'Der Frosch antwortete: "Deine Kleider, deine Perlen und Edelsteine, und deine goldene Krone, die mag ich nicht; aber wenn du mich liebhaben willst, und ich soll dein Geselle und Spielkamerad sein, an deinem Tischlein neben dir sitzen, von deinem goldenen Tellerlein essen, aus deinem Becherlein trinken, in deinem Bettlein schlafen: wenn du mir das versprichst, so will ich hinuntersteigen und dir die goldene Kugel wieder heraufholen'.

710 Brothers Grimm, 'The Frog King, or Iron Henry', *GENIUS* (1812), https://genius.com/Brothers-grimm-the-frog-king-or-iron-henry-annotated, accessed 24 January 2022.

very different lessons in the didactics of sexuality and are prescriptive about how to act when facing intrusive creatures. Today we see similar negotiations about similar subjects staged across our culture – not rarely with morals and value systems more in line with later, repurposed versions than with Grimm's published. For instance, products of mass culture such as the movie *365 days* and the tv-series *Game of Thrones* feature prominent 'heroines' 'trained' to eventually fall in love with their rapists in ways that are, for them on their level, entirely non-fictional. For better or worse, fictional representations teach receivers about sexual expectations and norms, and people, including young persons, accept, refuse and negotiate such expectations in the reading and viewing of fictional texts, which then inform their self-understanding as sexual/romantic and gendered persons.

The third danger of fictionality, and the final one that I will discuss in this context, is the widespread belief that the fictional, sexual fantasy amounts to a wish fulfillment. In terms of the topic of dangers of fictionality, this amounts to the danger of the non sequitur that the fictionality and narrativity on the one hand, and reality on the other hand, is such that one (only) dreams and fantasizes about that which one actually would want in reality.

Freud famously stated:

> … happy people never make phantasies, only unsatisfied ones. Unsatisfied wishes are the driving power behind phantasies; every separate phantasy contains the fulfilment [sic] of a wish, and improves on unsatisfactory reality.[711, 712,713]

Contemporary, empirical research shows that each of the contained statements are completely wrong – to the point that in each case almost the opposite is true. While unhappy people also fantasize, happy, content and confident people are

711 Sigmund Freud, 'The Relation of the Poet to Day-Dreaming', in Philip Rieff, ed., *Character and Culture* (New York: Collier Books, [1908] 1972), 37.

712 'Man darf sagen, der Glückliche phantasiert nie, nur der unbefriedigte. Unbefriedigte Wünsche sind die Triebkräfte der Phantasien, und jede einzelne Phantasie ist eine Wunscherfüllung, eine Korrektur der unbefriedigenden Wirklichkeit.' (Sigmund Freud, 'Der Dichter und das Phantasieren', in *Studienausgabe X* (Frankfurt am Main: Fisher Taschenbuch Verlag, 1982), 173–174). Compare to Sigmund Freud, 'Das Motiv der Kästchenwahl', in *Studienausgabe X* (Frankfurt am Main: Fisher Taschenbuch Verlag, 1982), 190–191: 'Wir wissen, dass der Mensch seine Phantasietätigkeit zur Befriedigung seiner von der Realität unbefriedigten Wünsche verwendet.'

713 This is all the more remarkable, since he also directly connects fantasizing to the work of the poets, whom he continuously pedestalizes.

more prone to engage in fantasies to achieve greater pleasure. Dissatisfaction is not a major driver behind fantasies. While some sexual fantasies take the form of a wish, which a high percentage of people would like to actually act out,[714] many fantasies do not.[715] While a few fantasies improve on a dissatisfactory reality,[716] most fantasies are sustained by confidence and sex-positive attitudes.[717] The pleasure in sexual fantasies, imagination and erotica, thus very often does not amount to wish fulfillment. The imaginary nature is manifest and many fantasies are about practices and experiences that one does decidedly not wish to really experience. While it remains highly problematic to depict scenarios of abuse and non-consent as run-of-the-mill, a matter of habit or even as finally beneficial to all parties, something completely different is at play in individual fantasies and stories about non-normative sex. Imagining same-sex relations, extra-couple copulations or being forced are three of the most common fantasies even for persons living in heterosexual, monogamous relationships.

Let us remember the fundamental role of imagination in human sexuality. It serves purposes that are not present in animals largely. Fantasies are a means to sexual arousal and pleasure whether solo or with others. In this particular respect, fantasies clearly serve real-world purposes. However, this is something entirely different from assuming that fantasies should reflect real-world wishes. The sexual fantasy can be (but does not always have to be) very different from non-sexual, wish-fulfillment fantasies, like, 'I imagine myself getting an A', or 'I imagine becoming a world-famous soccer player', or 'I dream that I become rich and can buy what I wish'. In all instances, of course, there is a difference between fantasy and reality but in most wish-fulfillment fantasies, one would actually like the fantasy to become real. The same does not at all necessarily hold true for the

714 Such as imagining having sex in a secluded setting like an island or cabin. A reported fantasy by 97% in one study (see Strassberg and Lockerd, 'Force in Women's Sexual Fantasies') compared to 75% (of the entire cohort) reporting being likely to act it out.

715 Such as engaging in extra-pair copulation (EPC) (A reported fantasy by 88% in one study (see Strassberg and Lockerd, 'Force in Women's Sexual Fantasies') compared to only 22% (of the entire cohort) reporting being likely to act it out; or the phantasy of being overpowered (a reported fantasy by 55% in one study (see Strassberg and Lockerd, 'Force in Women's Sexual Fantasies') compared to only 6% (of the entire cohort) reporting being likely to act it out.

716 See especially 'You Haven't Been on My Mind Lately'.

717 See Hariton and Singer, 'Women's Fantasies during Sexual Intercourse: Normative and Theoretical Implications', 313–322; Bivona and Critelli, 'The Nature of Women's Rape Fantasies: An Analysis of Prevalence, Frequency, and Contents', 45.

sexual fantasy. This is a point of crucial importance and one that when overlooked leads to blame, shame and guilt instead of pleasure. While some people will only have sexual fantasies about scenarios, they would like to experience in real life, many others will use distinctly unwanted scenarios to imaginatively trigger sexual arousal and pleasure. If someone imagines sex with a same-sex partner, or with their boss at work, or with several other persons at the same time this may or may not reflect events they would like to happen in real life, and very often it does not. Coercion fantasies and fantasies of abduction in women or castration in men and many other types of fantasies almost never reflect a real wish – but can sometimes work even stronger and give even more pleasure for that very reason.

In sexual fantasies, thus, there is not only the obvious difference between fantasy and reality, but also the additional difference between fantasy and *desired* reality. Sexual fantasies are not unconscious wish fulfillments.[718] The fantasy is a means; its content is not an end. The fantasy, rather, is a means to actual arousal,[719] often with a partner, and to pleasure. Sexual fantasies are very often, and very consciously used in this capacity and to that effect.

Sexuality as a purpose of fictionality

Above I have discussed three dangers of fictionality in the context of sexual fantasies in the form of assuming that what is rare in reality is also rare as fantasy; that fictionality does not have much real-world impact; and finally that fantasies always amount to wish fulfillments. I now move on to a short discussion of the relation between fictionality and sexuality in general, and then end by returning to some specific types of fantasies.

To approach the relation between sexuality and fictionality – at an intersection of which we find the communicated sexual fantasy – let us for a moment switch the perspective from the question about the importance of fictionality for understanding sexuality and the use of sexual fantasies to the inverse question about the importance of sexuality for the development and use of fictionality. One would probably imagine that of the enormous bulk of fictional texts (novels, short stories, tv-series, movies, short films etc.) a minor, marginal subpart is

---

718 See also Bivona and Critelli, 'Women's Erotic Rape Fantasies: An Evaluation of Theory and Research', 67.

719 Humans have the ability to use psychology and imagination rather than being dependent upon and determined by hormones.

concerned partly or wholly with explicitly sexual content. However, such an assumption is probably way off base. Consider the following numbers: One of the most famous books of the twentieth century, James Joyce's *Ulysses* has reached US sales figures of approximately 880,000 copies sold. At Pornhub.com[720] thousands of videos have more than a million views, numerous as many as 20–40 million. This includes mostly very quickly produced videos made in one take, such as 'College Girl Fucked In Her Dorm By 2 Guys – BLEACHED RAW – Ep II', with more than 30 million views, and many similar one-take, low-budget productions with 10–40 million views. It is immediately clear that porn is consumed in disproportionately large numbers compared to the fiction genres of interest to narratology. It is also produced much faster than non-porn reaching an audience. It is possible for hundreds of thousands of porn movies to easily reach viewer numbers which only a handful of bestselling books each decade can hope for, and which similarly only a very few cinema successes like *Titanic* and *Avatar* achieve. Very famous, widely discussed instances of so-called world literature can extremely rarely hope to reach a million copies sold.[721] Similarly, even bestselling authors such as Dick Francis, Tom Clancy and Patricia Cornwell do not reach an audience anywhere near any 'decent' pornhub producer such as for instance 'Wicked Fellow' with several videos with +4 million viewers, and more than 100,000 regular registered subscribers. Such numbers suggest that in terms of consumption, sexuality is not marginal but integral to storytelling.

It is remarkable, yet completely unnoticed in narrative studies and fictionality theory that sexuality still today may very well be the most common purpose of using fictionality, narrative and imagination. This applies to the enormous consumption of porn but not only to this.[722] Some porn is of a narrative nature and

720 While currently the largest porn provider online, Pornhub it itself one out of thousands of providers of porn on the internet.

721 See, for instance: Alex Hamilton, 'Fastsellers 2000: The Hot Paperbacks', *The Guardian* (6 January 2001).

722 Beyond porn consumption, our everyday imagination is not rarely sex oriented whether intentionally or unintentionally. When we daydream, sex is a common theme. There is ample empirical evidence for these claims. See for instance Ellis and Symons, 'Sex Differences in Sexual Fantasy: an Evolutionary Psychological Approach', 536:

> Questions 1 and 2 used a 0 to 7 rating scale with the alternative answers: Never, Once a week, Once a day or less, About once a day, 2 or 3 times a day, 4 to 6 times a day, 7 to 10 times a day, or More than 10 times a day. Question 1 asked, "Approximately how often do you have sexual fantasies?" and resulted in means

some is not; and some porn movies and videos are clearly fictional and some are not. These differences notwithstanding, all porn consumption is sex and sexuality by proxy. It would not work without some kind of 'empathy', emotional involvement and imagination.

To put it bluntly: When we experience sexuality, we tend to employ imagination and fictionality, and when we use our imagination, we tend to have sexuality on our minds.

Conclusion: Purposes of imagination, fictionality and sexual fantasies

The sexual fantasy, with its perpetual awareness of the imagined nature, allows human beings to awaken sexuality by use of thought, and to experience sexuality by proxy. This also means that the fantasy can be a means to decouple sexuality from reproduction and reality while attaching it to mental notions. Such notions and imaginations may, and often do include images and actions that may be dangerous or even lethal, if real, but which – as fantasies – stimulate sexuality. Prevalent sexual fantasies in both sexes are fantasies about something that would be unpleasant or in some instances even traumatic in reality. From an evolutionary perspective, actual occurrences of, say, coercion, castration or cuckolding would severely damage the possibility of passing on good genes. Therefore, a direct reference to reproductive success is not a helpful explanation, nor is the fantasy an expression of ancestral traits useful. Instead, insisting on the perpetual awareness of the imagined nature of the sexual fantasy, allows us to understand how human beings are able to awaken and use the fantasy as a means to draw on imagined scenarios such as establishing imaginary hierarchies. The fantasy in general as well as erotic fantasies of submission are – as fantasies and as opposed to reality – specifically a means to achieve pleasure. In 'Power, Desire, and Pleasure in Sexual Fantasies', Eileen L. Zurbriggen and Megan R. Yost[723] mention how under-studied this obvious aspect is:

> However, the desire for pleasurable physical sensation is clearly a centrally important sexual motive. This is especially true when one considers sexual fantasies, which are private mental events whose sole purpose would seem to be to induce pleasurable feelings

---

of 1.97 (*SD* = 1.16) for females and 3.22 (*SD* = 1.46) for males ($t = -8.33$, $df = 304$, $p < .001$).

723 Author of the attitude-towards-BDSM-scale-article.

> of sexual desire and arousal. It is surprising, then, that virtually no research on sexual fantasies has focused on desire and pleasure.[724]

The fantasy allows for the pleasurable imagination of mating with individuals higher or lower in the hierarchy. In fact, the establishment of hierarchical disparity in the form of teacher/student, master/slave, police/convict etc. is a commonplace in such plays and fantasies. Persons reporting to engage in fantasies or practices about overemphasized hierarchical disparity report higher sexual pleasure, more self-confidence and better relationships.[725] A direct link between hierarchical status and female arousal and even orgasm rate has been found in several species – with the perhaps most significant numbers in macaques.[726] Humans have a specific ability to use imagined scenarios (including scenarios that would be revolting as well as detrimental to their well-being and reproductive success) to sustain sexual arousal and reproductive success – not in the form of having intercourse often result in procreation, but in sustaining bi-parental investment in few children. In human sexuality – only apparently paradoxical thus – non-reproductive practices and preferences often work to optimize overall reproductive success.[727] The very common fantasy or play of establishing imaginary hierarchies attains part of its sexual energy from the substance of what is, for other animals, real and social hierarchies. Other sexual preferences such as fetishism and exhibitionism can be analysed along similar lines. Our

---

724 Zurbriggen and Yost, 'Power, Desire, and Pleasure in Sexual Fantasies', 289.

725 See Richters, de Visser, Rissel, Grulich and Smith, 'Demographic and Psychosocial Features of Participants in Bondage and Discipline, "Sadomasochism" or Dominance and submission (BDSM): Data from a National Survey', 1663; Neef, Coppens, Huys and Morrens, 'Bondage-Discipline, Dominance-Submission and Sadomasochism (BDSM) From an Integrative Biopsychosocial Perspective: A Systematic Review', 136–138; Eva Jozifkova, Ludek Bartos and Jaroslav Flegr, 'Evolutional background of dominance/submissivity in sex and bondage: the two strategies?', *Neuro Endocrinol Letters* 33/6 (2012), 637; Eva Jozifkova, Martin Konvicka and Jaroslav Flegr, 'Why Do Some Women Prefer Submissive Men? Hierarchically Disparate Couples Reach Higher Reproductive Success in European Urban Humans', *Neuro Endocrinol Letters* 35/7 (2014), 594; Bivona and Critelli, 'Women's Erotic Rape Fantasies: An Evaluation of Theory and Research', 63.

726 See Alfonso Troisi and Monica Carosi, 'Female Orgasm Rate Increases With Male Dominance in Japanese Macaques', *Animal Behaviour* 56/5 (1998), 1261–1266. I will return to this at the end of this chapter.

727 The same logic applies, it is speculated, to menopause: after a certain point in life, more offspring will detract from, rather than contribute to the overall reproductive success of a female. See Diamond, *Why is Sex Fun?*

species' special ability to imagine provides us, as species, with a means to achieve something similar to what other animals experience as physical and social reality but without the same risks and disadvantages.

Humans can play with and imaginatively construct scenarios, mating competitions and hierarchic disparities in ways animals cannot. Both the male and the female can take on roles that may or may not change and that may or may not reflect how they act in social and professional life. Non-normative fantasies provide evolutionary as well as individual advantages thus making it doubly significant and important that in many historical and cultural contexts, such fantasies have been castigated as religiously sinful, psychologically aberrant and pathological, and morally despicable.

If we move from religious superstition and psychological pseudoscientific prejudice to empirical studies, it soon becomes clear that most fantasies and so-called paraphilias are not uncommon, not unhealthy and not related to general sexual problems or dysfunctions. Avoiding the three dangers of fictionality examined in this chapter helps us understand why: **Fantasizing** about events or actions that would be rare, dangerous, criminal or unethical in real life is not in and of itself unusual or pathological. Instead, with a perpetual awareness of the imagined nature, they serve real-world purposes and influence real-world beliefs in ways completely different from acting out the fantasies. Finally, they very often do not constitute wish fulfillment. This gives us a theoretical understanding of the empirical fact that rather than being dysfunctions and impairments, such fantasies result in arousal, orgasm, self-reported relationship contentment and children.[728] This holds true for dominance-games or -fantasies, non-heterosexual and non-genito-centric practices and many other practices, preferences and orientations under the specific circumstances characterizing the living conditions of homo sapiens for the latest millennia. On an evolutionary level, they are part of the general disconnect between sexuality and reproduction and physiology that characterize our species as the most highly developed on the planet.

728 For the argument about the relation between non-reproductive sexuality and offspring, see above, and compare, for example, about higher reproductive success; Jozifkova, Konvicka and Flegr, 'Why Do Some Women Prefer Submissive Men? Hierarchically Disparate Couples Reach Higher Reproductive Success in European Urban Humans', 594, 598.

Bibliography

Abbott, H. Porter, 'Story, Plot, and Narration', in David Herman, ed., *The Cambridge Companion to Narrative* (Cambridge: Cambridge University Press, 2007), 39–51.

Abramson, Julia L., 'Translation as Metaphor in Hildesheimer's Marbot Eine Biographie', *Paroles gelées* 14/2 (1996), 103–114.

Aggrawal, Anil, *Forensic and Medico-legal Aspects of Sexual Crimes and Unusual Sexual Practices* (Boca Raton: CRC Press, 2008).

Akerman, Nick, 'Did Mueller Ever Stand a Chance Against Trump and Roger Stone?', *The New York Times* (13 July 2020).

Alba, Davey, 'False Claims That Biden "Lost" Pennsylvania Surge, and Tech Companies Struggle to Keep Up', *The New York Times* (11 November 2020).

———, and Ben Decker, 'Trump Spread Multiple Conspiracy Theories on Monday. Here Are Their Roots', *The New York Times* (1 September 2020).

Alter, Alexandra, 'She Pulled Her Debut Book When Critics Found It Racist. Now She Plans to Publish', *New York Times* (29 April 2019).

Althusser, Louis, 'Ideology and Ideological State Apparatuses (Notes towards an Investigation)', in Ben Brewster, trans., *Lenin and Philosophy and Other Essays* (New York: Monthly Review Press, [1969] 1971), 127–183.

Aly, Waleed, 'Trump, a Post-truth Man for a Post-truth World', *The Sydney Morning Herald* (5 November 2020).

American Psychiatric Association, *Diagnostic and Statistical Manual of Mental Disorders (DSM-5)* (Washington D.C.: American Psychiatric Publishing, 2013).

Anonymous, *Onania: or, the heinous sin of self-pollution* (approx. 1712–23).

Aristotle, *Poetics*, Malcolm Heath, trans. (London: Penguin Books, 1997).

Attridge, John, '"The Yellow-Dog Thing": Joseph Conrad, Verisimilitude, and Professionalism', *ELH* 77 (2010), 267–96.

Auster, Paul, *Report from the Interior* (New York: Henry Holt and Company, 2013).

———, *Winter Journal* (New York: Henry Holt and Company, 2012).

Baker, Djoymi, *To Boldly Go: Marketing the Myth of Star Trek* (London and New York: I.B. Tauris, 2018).

Baker, Peter, 'More Than Ever, Trump Casts Himself as the Defender of White America', *The New York Times* (6 September 2020).

———, and Lara Jakes, 'Fighting Election Results, Trump Employs a New Weapon: The Government', *The New York Times* (10 November 2020).

Bakhtin, Mikhail M., 'Discourse in the Novel', in Michael Holquist, ed., *The Dialogic Imagination: Four Essays* (Austin: University of Texas Press, 1981), 259–422.

———, 'Epic and Novel', in Michael Holquist, ed., *The Dialogic Imagination: Four Essays* (Austin: University of Texas Press, 1981), 3–40.

———, *Rabelais and His World*, Helene Iswolsky, trans. (Bloomington: Indiana University Press, [1965] 1984).

Bamberg, Michael, 'Positioning Between Structure and Performance', *Journal of Narrative and Life History* 7/1–4 (1997), 335–342.

———, 'Positioning with Davie Hogan: Stories, Tellings, and Identities', in Colette Daiute and Cynthia Lightfoot, eds., *Narrative Analysis. Studying the Development of Individuals in Society* (Thousand Oaks: Sage, 2004), 135–157.

Bareis, Alexander, 'Randbereiche und Grenzüberschreitungen: Zu einer Theorie der Fiktion im Vergleich der Künste', in Anne Enderwitz and Irina Rajewsky, eds., *Fiktion im Vergleich der Künste und Medien* (Berlin: De Gruyter, 2016), 45–62.

Barthes, Roland, 'There Is No Robbe-Grillet School', in Richard Howard, trans., *Critical Essays* (Evanston: Northwestern University Press, [1958] 1972), 91–95.

Beinart, Peter, 'The Real Reason Biden Is Winning? He's a Man', *The New York Times* (7 July 2020).

Bennett, Jessica, 'After #MeToo, the Ripple Effect', *The New York Times* (28 June 2018).

Bichlbaum Andy, Michael Bonanno, and Kurt Engfehr (dir.), *The Yes Men Fix the World* (2009).

Bivona, Jenny M., and Joseph W. Critelli, 'The Nature of Women's Rape Fantasies: An Analysis of Prevalence, Frequency, and Contents', *The Journal of Sex Research* 46/1 (2009), 33–45.

———, 'Women's Erotic Rape Fantasies: An Evaluation of Theory and Research', *The Journal of Sex Research* 45/1 (2008), 57–70.

Björninen, Samuli, 'Poetics at the Interface: Patterns of Thought and Protocols of Reading in Studies of Thomas Pynchon's *V.*', *Acta Universitatis Tamperensis* 2360 (Tampere: Tampere University Press, 2018).

———,'The Rhetoric of Factuality in Narrative: Appeals to Authority in Claas Relotius's Feature Journalism', *Narrative Inquiry* 29/2 (2019), 352–370.

———, Mari Hatavara, and Maria Mäkelä, 'Narrative as Social Action: A Narratological Approach to Story, Discourse and Positioning in Political Storytelling', *International Journal of Social Research Methodology* 23/4 (2020), 437–449.

———, and Merja Polvinen, 'Limits of Narrative: Introduction', *Partial Answers* (2022), 191–206.

Block, Andreas de, and Pieter R. Adriaens, 'Pathologizing Sexual Deviance: A History', *The Journal of Sex Research* 50/3–4 (2013), 276–298.

Bonheim, Helmut, 'Narration in the Second Person', *Recherches Anglaises et Américaines* 16 (1983), 69–80.

Boot, Max, 'The Three Reasons Conspiracy Theories Are More Dangerous Than Ever', *The Washington Post* (23 May 2020).

Booth, Wayne, *The Rhetoric of Fiction* (Chicago: University of Chicago Press, 1983).

Bouie, Jamelle, 'A Simple Theory of Why Trump Did Well', *The New York Times* (18 November 2020).

boyd, danah, *It's Complicated: The Social Lives of Networked Teens* (New Haven: Yale University Press, 2014).

———, 'Social Networking Sites as Networked Publics: Affordances, Dynamics, and Implications', in Zizi Papacharissi, ed., *Networked Self: Identity, Community, and Culture on Social Network Sites* (London: Routledge, 2011), 39–58.

Brown, Lee, '"Deepfake" Tom Cruise Goes Viral on TikTok with over 11 Million Views', *New York Post* (2 March 2021), <https://nypost.com/2021/03/02/deepfake-tom-cruise-goes-viral-on-tiktok-with-over-11m-views/>, accessed 20 June 2021.

Browse, Sam, Alison Gibbons and Mari Hatavara, 'Real Fictions: Fictionality, Factuality and Narrative Strategies in Contemporary Storytelling,' *Narrative Inquiry* 29/2 (2019), 245-267.

———, and Mari Hatavara, 'I Can Tell the Difference Between Fiction and Reality. Cross-fictionality and Mind-style in Political Rhetoric', *Narrative Inquiry* 29/2 (2019), 245–267.

Bruni, Frank, 'The Undertold, Undersold Story of Kamala Harris', *The New York Times* (14 August 2020).

Bucher, Taina, and Anne Helmond, 'The Affordances of Social Media Platforms', in Jean Burgess, Thomas Poell and Alice Marwick, eds., *The SAGE Handbook of Social Media* (London and New York: Sage Publications Ltd, 2018), online PDF-version, 2-19, <http://dx.doi.org/10.4135/9781473984066.n14>, accessed 5 October 2021.

Butor, Michel, *La Modification* (Paris: Minuit, 1957).

Calvino, Italo, *If on a Winter's Night a Traveler*, William Weaver, trans. (London: Picador, [1979] 1982).

———, *Se una notte d'inverno un viaggiatore* (Torino: Einaudi, 1979).

Cambridge Dictionary, 'deceit', <https://dictionary.cambridge.org/us/dictionary/english/deceit>, accessed 1 October 2021.

Castro, Joy, 'Introduction: Mapping Hope', in *Family Trouble. Memoirists on the Hazards and Rewards of Revealing Family* (Lincoln and London: University of Nebraska Press, 2013), 1–14.

Chatman, Seymour, *Story and Discourse. Narrative Structure in Fiction and Film* (Ithaca and London: Cornell University Press, 1980).

Cheney, Kyle, and Andrew Desiderio, 'How "Obamagate" and Hunter's "laptop from hell" fizzled', *Politico* (8 November 2020).

Christensen, Pernille Meyer, 'Hvorfor fortælle dig noget, du allerede ved? Om dufortællinger i dansk litteratur', *Passage* 35/3 (2020), 1–13.

Clare, Ralph, 'The Politics of Boredom and the Boredom of Politics in David Foster Wallace's *The Pale King*', *Studies in the Novel* 44/4 (2012), 428–446.

CNN.com, 'No, Tom Cruise Isn't on TikTok. It's a Deepfake', *CNN* (2021), <https://edition.cnn.com/videos/business/2021/03/02/tom-cruise-tiktok-deepfake-orig.cnn-business/video/playlists/business-originals-counterprogramming/>, accessed 20 June 2021.

Cohn, Dorrit, 'Metalepsis and mise en abyme', Lewis S. Gleich, trans., *Narrative* 20/1 (2012), 105–114.

———, 'Signposts of Fictionality: A Narratological Perspective', *Poetics Today* 11/4 (1990), 775–804.

———, *The Distinction of Fiction* (Baltimore: Johns Hopkins University Press, 1999).

———, *Transparent Minds. Narrative Modes for Presenting Consciousness in Fiction* (Princeton: Princeton University Press, 1978).

Conrad, Joseph, in J. H. Stape and Zdzislaw Najder, eds., *A Personal Record* (Cambridge: Cambridge University Press, 2008).

———, *Chance* (Oxford: Oxford University Press, 2002).

———, *Conrad's Prefaces to His Works* (London: J. M. Dent & Sons, 1937).

Costa, Elisabetta, 'Affordances-in-practices: An Ethnographic Critique of Social Media Logic and Context Collapse', *New Media & Society* 20/10 (2018), 3641–3656.

Davis, Jenny L., and James B. Chouinard, 'Theorizing Affordances: From Request to Refuse', *Bulletin of Science, Technology & Society* 36/4 (2017), 241–248.

Dawson, Paul, 'Ten Theses against Fictionality', *Narrative* 23/1 (2015), 74–100.

———, 'What is "The Narrative"? Conspiracy Theories and Journalistic Emplotment in the Age of Social Media,' in Paul Dawson and Maria Mäkelä, eds.,

The Routledge Companion to Narrative Theory (New York: Routledge, 2022), 71–85.

———, and Maria Mäkelä, 'The Story Logic of Social Media: Co-Construction and Emergent Narrative Authority', *Style* 54/1 (2020), 21–35.

Day, Amber, *Satire and Dissent: Intervention in Contemporary Political Debate* (Bloomington, IN, USA: Indiana University Press, 2011).

Dällenbach, Lucien, *The Mirror in the Text*, Jeremy Whiteley and Emma Hughes, trans. (Chicago: University of Chicago Press, 1989).

De Hard, Eric, 'Notes on Second-Person Narration. Tolstoj's First Sevastopol Story', *Amsterdam Journal for Cultural Narratology* (2006), <https://cf.hum.uva.nl/narratology/a06_haard.html>, accessed 27 April 2021.

Deirdre, Coyle, 'Men Recommend David Foster Wallace to Me', *Electric Literature* (17 April 2017), <https://electricliterature.com/men-recommend-david-foster-wallace-to-me/>, accessed 7 January 2022.

DelConte, Matt, 'Why *You* Can't Speak: Second-Person Narration, Voice, and a New Model for Understanding Narrative', *Style* 37/2 (2003), 204–219.

Depperman, Arnulf, 'Positioning', in Anna de Fina and Alexandra Georgakopoulou, eds., *The Handbook of Narrative Analysis* (Oxford: Wiley Blackwell, 2015), 369–387.

Dessem, Matthew, 'What's Fact and What's Fiction in *The Trial of the Chicago 7*', *Slate* (15 October 2020), <https://slate.com/culture/2020/10/trial-chicago-seven-aaron-sorkin-accuracy-netflix.html>, accessed 17 September 2021.

Dijck, José van, Thomas Poell, and Martijn de Waal, *The Platform Society: Public Values in a Connective World* (New York: Oxford University Press, 2018).

Dix, Hywel, ed., *Autofiction in English. Palgrave Studies in Life Writing* (Cham: Palgrave Macmillan, 2018).

Doležel, Lubomír, *Heterocosmica: Fiction and Possible Worlds* (Baltimore: Johns Hopkins University Press, 1998).

Douthat, Ross, '2020 will Not Be Decisive', *The New York Times* (3 November 2020).

Dowd, Maureen, 'Trump, Not so Statuesque', *The New York Times* (27 June 2020).

DuBois, W. E. B., *The Souls of Black Folk* (New York: Oxford University Press, 2007).

Durkheim, Emil, *Suicide: A Study in Sociology* (London: Routledge and K. Paul, 1952).

Eakin, Paul John, 'The Unseemly Profession. Privacy, Inviolate Personality, and the Ethics of Life Writing', in *How Our Lives Become Stories: Making Selves* (Ithaca and London: Cornell University Press, 1999), 142–186.

Egeland, Marianne, 'Frihet, Likhet og brorskap i virkelighetslitteraturen', *Edda. Scandinavian Journal of Literary Research* 115/3 (2015), 227–242.

Ellis, Bruce J., and Donald Symons, 'Sex Differences in Sexual Fantasy: An Evolutionary Psychological Approach', *The Journal of Sex Research* 27/4 (1990), 527–555.

Evans, Sandra K., Katy E. Pearce, Jessica Vitak and Jeffrey W. Treem, 'Explicating Affordances: A Conceptual Framework for Understanding Affordances in Communication Research', *Journal of Computer-Mediated Communication* 22/1 (2017), 35–52.

Fandos, Nicholas, and Catie Edmondson, 'As a Post-Impeachment Trump Pushes the Limits, Republicans Say Little', *The New York Times* (12 February 2020).

———, and Emily Cochrane, 'Republicans Back Trump's Refusal to Concede, Declining to Recognize Biden', *The New York Times* (9 November 2020).

Fernandes, Sujatha, *Curated Stories: The Uses and Misuses of Storytelling* (New York: Oxford University Press, 2017).

Fiske, John, and John Hartley, *Reading Television* (London: Routledge, 2004).

Fludernik, Monika, 'Factual Narrative: A Missing Narratological Paradigm', *Germanisch-Romanische Monatsschrift* 63/1 (2013), 117–134.

———, 'Genres, Text Types, or Discourse Modes? Narrative Modalities and Generic Categorization', *Style* 34/2 (2000), 274–292.

———, 'Introduction: Second-person Narrative and Related Issues', *Style* 28/3 (1994), 281–311.

———, 'Non-Narrative Genres: Exposition, Lists, Lyric, etc.' (forthcoming).

———, 'Second Person Fiction: Narrative *You* As Addressee And/Or Protagonist', *Arbeiten aus Anglistik und Amerikanistik* 18/2 (1993), 217–247.

———, *Towards a 'Natural' Narratology* (London and New York: Routledge, 2010).

Fowles, John, *The French Lieutenant's Woman* (Boston: Little, Brown, 1969).

Fredal, James, 'The Perennial Pleasures of the Hoax', *Philosophy & Rhetoric* 47/1 (2014), 73–97.

French, David (dir.), *How to Survive a Plague*, Public Square Films, 2012.

Frenkel, Sheera, 'How Misinformation "Superspreaders" Seed False Election Theories', *The New York Times* (23 November 2020).

Freud, Sigmund, 'Das Motiv der Kästchenwahl', in *Studienausgabe X* (Frankfurt am Main: Fisher Taschenbuch Verlag, 1982), 181–194.

———, 'Der Dichter und das Phantasieren', in *Studienausgabe X* (Frankfurt am Main: Fisher Taschenbuch Verlag, 1982), 169–180.

———, 'The Relation of the Poet to Day-Dreaming', in Philip Rieff, ed., *Character and Culture* (New York: Collier Books, [1908] 1972), 34–43.

Furst, Joshua, 'Aaron Sorkin's Moralizing Liberal Fantasy Betrays the Real Chicago 7', *Forward* (20 October 2020), <https://forward.com/culture/456814/aaron-sorkins-moralizing-liberal-fantasy-betrays-the-real-chicago-7/>, accessed 17 September 2021.

Gaddam, Sai, and Ogi Ogas, *A Billion Wicked Thoughts: What the Internet Tells Us About Sexual Relationships* (New York: Plume Books, 2012).

Gallagher, Catherine, 'The Rise of Fictionality', in Franco Moretti, ed., *The Novel* (Princeton: Princeton University Press, 2006), 336–363.

Gammelgaard, Lasse, Stefan Iversen, Louise Brix Jacobsen, Henrik Zetterberg-Nielsen, Simona Zetterberg-Nielsen, James Phelan and Richard Walsh, eds., *Fictionality in Literature: Core Concepts Revisited* (Columbus: Ohio State University Press, 2022).

Garnett, Edward, 'Introductory Essay', in *Conrad's Prefaces to His Works* (London: J. M. Dent & Sons, 1937), 1–34.

Gaver, William, 'Technology Affordances', *Proceedings of CHI'91* (1991), 79–84.

Genette, Gérard, *Narrative Discourse* (Oxford: Cornell University Press, [1972] 1980).

Georgakopoulou, Alexandra, 'Sharing the Moment as Small Stories: The Interplay Between Practices and Affordances in the Social Media-Curation of Lives', *Narrative Inquiry* 27/2 (2017), 311–333.

———, 'Small Stories Research and Social Media: The Role of Narrative Stance-Taking in Circulating A Greek News Story', *Sociolinguistica* 27 (2013), 19–36.

———, 'Storytelling on the Go: Breaking News as a Travelling Narrative Genre', in Mari Hatavara, Lars-Christer Hydén and Matti Hyvärinen, eds., *The Travelling Concepts of Narrative* (Amsterdam: John Benjamins, 2013), 201–224.

Gibson, James J., *The Ecological Approach to Visual Perception* (London: Routledge, 1979).

Gilden, Andrew, 'Punishing Sexual Fantasy', *William & Mary Law Review* 58/2 (2016), 419–492.

Gillespie, Tarleton, 'The Politics of "Platforms"', *New Media & Society* 12/3 (2010), 347–364.

Gitlin, Todd, 'Retrying the Chicago 7', *The American Prospect* (30 October 2020), <https://prospect.org/culture/retrying-the-chicago-seven/>, accessed 17 September 2021.

Gjerlevsen, Simona Zetterberg, 'A Novel History of Fictionality', *Narrative* 24/2 (2016), 174–189.

———, 'Fictionality', in Peter Hühn, ed., *The Living Handbook of Narratology* (Hamburg: Universität Hamburg, 2016).

———, and Henrik Skov Nielsen, 'Distinguishing Fictionality', in Cindie Aaen Maagaard, Daniel Schäbler and Marianne Wolff Lundholt, eds., *Exploring Fictionality: Conceptions, Test Cases, Discussions* (Odense: Syddansk Universitetsforlag, 2020), 19–40.

———, Jan Maintz, and Henrik Skov Nielsen, *Fiktionalitet i litteratur, sprog og medier* (Frederiksberg: Dansklærerforeningens forlag, 2019).

Goffman, Erving, *Forms of talk* (Philadelphia: University of Pennsylvania Press, 1981).

Goldberg, Richard, 'Trump Has an Iran Strategy. This Is It', *The New York Times* (24 January 2020).

Goodwin, Charles, 'Notes on Story Structure and the Organization of Participation', in J. Maxwell Atkinson and John Heritage, eds., *Structures of Social Action: Studies in Conversation Analysis* (London: Cambridge University Press, 1984), 225–246.

Grimm, Brothers, 'Der Froschkönig oder der eiserne Heinrich', *Grimm Stories* (1812), <https://www.grimmstories.com/language.php?grimm=001&l=de&r=en>, accessed 24 January 2022.

———, 'The Frog King, or Iron Henry', *GENIUS* (1812), <https://genius.com/Brothers-grimm-the-frog-king-or-iron-henry-annotated>, accessed 24 January 2022.

Grumsen, Stine Slot, and Louise Brix Jacobsen, 'Vitafictional Advertising, Fictionality and Celebrity Branding', in Cindie Aaen Maagaard, Daniel Schäbler and Marianne Wolff Lundholt, eds., *Exploring Fictionality: Conceptions, Test Cases, Discussions* (Odense: Southern Denmark University Press, 2020), 119–152.

Grüttemeier, Ralf, ed., *Literary Trials. Exceptio Artis and Theories of Literature in Court* (New York, London, Oxford, New Delhi, Sydney: Bloomsbury, 2016).

Hamilton, Alex, 'Fastsellers 2000: The Hot Paperbacks', *The Guardian* (6 January 2001).

———, 'Literary Trials as Mirrors. An Introduction', in *Literary Trials. Exceptio Artis and Theories of Literature in Court* (New York, London, Oxford, New Delhi, Sydney: Bloomsbury, 2016), 1–18.

Harari, Yuval Noah, *Sapiens: A Brief History of Humankind* (New York: Random House, 2014).

Hardaker, Claire, 'I Refuse to Respond to This Obvious troll. An overview of responses to (perceived) trollin', *Corpora* 10/2 (2015), 201–229.

———, '"Uh…not to be nitpicky, but…the past tense of drag is dragged, not drug.": An Overview of Trolling Strategies', *Journal of Language Aggression and Conflict* 1/1 (2013), 57–86.

Hardee, Gary M., and Ryan P. McMahan, 'FIJI: A Framework for the Immersion-Journalism Intersection', *Frontiers in ICT* 4:21 (2017), <https://doi.org/10.3389/fict.2017.00021>, accessed 7 January 2022.

Hariton, E. Barbara, and Jerome L. Singer, 'Women's Fantasies during Sexual Intercourse: Normative and Theoretical Implications', *Journal of Consulting and Clinical Psychology* 42/3 (1974), 313–322.

Hatavara, Mari, and Jarmila Mildorf, 'Hybrid Fictionality and Vicarious Narrative Experience', *Narrative* 25/1 (2017), 65–82.

———, 'Fictionality, Narrative Modes, and Vicarious Storytelling', *Style* 51/3 (2017a), 391–408.

Hayes-Brady, Clare, 'Reading Your Problematic Fave: David Foster Wallace, Feminism and #metoo', *Honest Ulsterman* (June 2018), <https://humag.co/features/reading-your-problematic-fave>, accessed 7 January 2022.

Herman, David, *Basic Elements of Narrative* (Hoboken: John Wiley and Sons Ltd, 2009).

———, 'Introduction', in David Herman, ed., *The Emergence of Mind. Representations of Consciousness in Narrative Discourse in English* (Lincoln: The University of Nebraska Press, 2011).

———, Manfred Jahn, and Marie-Laure Ryan, 'Second-Person Narration', in *Routledge Encyclopedia of Narrative Theory* (London: Routledge, 2010), <https://www.proquest.com/docview/2137959874?accountid=14468>, accessed 27 April 2021.

Hern, Alex, '"I Don't Want to Upset People": Tom Cruise Deepfake Creator Speaks Out', *The Guardian* (5 March 2021), <https://www.theguardian.com/technology/2021/mar/05/how-started-tom-cruise-deepfake-tiktok-videos>, accessed 20 June 2021.

Hickey-Moody, Anna, *Youth, Arts and Education: Reassembling Subjectivity through Affect* (Abingdon: Routledge, 2013).

Hight, Craig, and Jane Roscoe, *Faking It: Mock-Documentary and the Subversion of Factuality* (Manchester: Manchester University Press, 2011).

Holland, Norman, *Literature and the Brain* (Cambridge, MA: PsyArt Foundation, 2009).

Howard, Ron (dir.), *Apollo 13*, Universal Pictures, 1995.

Howell, Elizabeth, and Kimberley Hickok, 'Apollo 13: The Moon-Mission That Dodged Disaster', *Space.com* (31 March 2020), <https://www.space.com/17250-apollo-13-facts.html>, accessed 20 September 2021.

Hubara, Koko, 'Othe(i)ron', *Ruskeat tytöt* (8 February 2016), <https://www.lily.fi/blogit/ruskeat-tytot/otheiron/>, accessed 7 January 2022.

Huston, Nikki Johnson, 'The Myth of the "Good Negro"', *HuffPost* (6 November 2016), <https://www.huffpost.com/entry/the-myth-of-the-good-negr_b_8506570>, accessed 7 January 2022.

Hutchby, Ian, *Conversation and Technology: From the Telephone to the Internet* (Cambridge: Polity Press, 2001).

———, 'Technologies, Texts and Affordances', *Sociology* 35/2 (2001), 441–456.

———, and Simone Barnett, 'Aspects of the Sequential Organization of Mobile Phone Conversation', *Discourse Studies* 7/2 (2015), 147–171.

Hutcheon, Linda, *Irony's Edge. The Theory and Politics of Irony* (London and New York: Routledge, 1994).

Hyvärinen, Matti, 'Foreword: Life Meets Narrative', in Brian Schiff, A. Elizabeth McKim and Sylvie Patron, eds., *Life and Narrative: The Risks and Responsibilities of Storying Experience* (Oxford: Oxford University Press, 2017), ix–xxvi.

Hyvönen, Ari-Elmeri, 'Careless Speech: Conceptualizing Post-Truth Politics', *New Perspectives* 26/3 (2018), 1–25.

Ibarra, Herminia, and Kent Lineback, 'What's Your Story?', *Harvard Business Review* (January 2005), <https://hbr.org/2005/01/whats-your-story>, accessed 17 September 2013.

Icks, Martijn, Sergei A. Samoilenko, Jennifer Keohane and Eric Shiraev, 'Introduction', in *Routledge Handbook of Character Assassination and Reputation Management* (New York: Routledge, 2020), 1–8.

———, 'Character Assassination: Theoretical Framework', in *Routledge Handbook of Character Assassination and Reputation Management* (New York: Routledge, 2020), 11–24.

Iversen, Stefan, 'Disruptive Communication in Political Campaigning: On the Rhetoric of Metanoic Reflexivity', *Rhetoric Society Quarterly* 52/4 (2022).

———, '"Just because it isn't happening here, doesn't mean it isn't happening": Narrative, Fictionality and Reflexivity in Humanitarian Rhetoric', *European Journal of English Studies* 23/2 (2019), 190–205.

———, and Henrik Skov Nielsen, 'Invention as Invention in the Rhetoric of Barack Obama', *Storyworlds* 9/1–2 (2017), 121–142.

Jacobsen, Louise Brix, 'Fictional Characters in a Real World: Unruly Fictionalised Encounters in *Borat*, *The Ambassador*, and the Yes Men's media hoaxes', *European Journal of English Studies* 23/2 (2019), 206–223.

———, '"Måske ikke lige på Lorry". Om nyhedshoaxens kritiske transmedielle potentiale', in Louise Brix Jacobsen, Rikke Andersen Kraglund and Henrik Skov Nielsen, eds., *Satirisk Fake News* (Hellerup: Forlaget Spring, 2019), 104–122.

———, 'Paratext', in Lasse R. Gammelgaard, Stefan Iversen, Louise Brix Jacobsen, James Phelan, Richard Walsh, Henrik Zetterberg-Nielsen and Simona Zetterberg-Nielsen, eds., *Fictionality and Literature: Core Concepts Revisited* (Columbus: The Ohio State University Press, 2022), 141–160.

———,'Vitafiction as a Mode of Self-Fashioning: The Case of Michael J. Fox in Curb Your Enthusiasm', *Narrative* 23/3 (2015), 252–270.

———, Stefan Kjerkegaard, Rikke Andersen Kraglund, Henrik Skov Nielsen, Camilla Møhring Reestorff and Carsten Stage, *Fiktionalitet* (Frederikberg: Samfundslitteratur, 2013).

Jenkins, Henry, Sam Ford, and Joshua Green, *Spreadable Media: Creating Value and Meaning in a Networked Culture* (New York: New York University Press, 2013).

Jones, Terry, and Terry Gilliam, *Monty Python's The Meaning of Life* (United Kingdom: Celandine Films, The Monty Python Partnership, 1983).

Joyal, Christian C., Amélie Cossette and Vanessa Lapierre, 'What Exactly Is an Unusual Sexual Fantasy?', *The Journal of Sexual Medicine* 12/2 (2015), 328–340.

Jozifkova, Eva, Ludek Bartos and Jaroslav Flegr, 'Evolutional Background of Dominance/Submissivity in Sex and Bondage: The Two Strategies?', *Neuro Endocrinol Letters* 33/6 (2012), 636–642.

———, Martin Konvicka, and Jaroslav Flegr, 'Why Do Some Women Prefer Submissive Men? Hierarchically Disparate Couples Reach Higher Reproductive Success in European Urban Humans', *Neuro Endocrinol Letters* 35/7 (2014), 594–601.

Kaarsholm, Lotte Folke, 'I krig med de historiske løgne', *Information* (26 August 2004).

Kacandes, Irene, 'Are You in the Text? The "Literary Performative" in Postmodernist Fiction', *Text and Performance Quarterly* 13 (1993), 139–153.

———, 'Narrative Apostrophe: Reading, Rhetoric, Resistance in Michel Butor's *La Modification* and Julio Cortazar's "Graffiti"', *Style* 28/3 (1994), 329–349.

Karni, Annie, and Maggie Haberman, 'By Lowering the Debate Bar for Biden, Has Trump Set a Trap for Himself?', *The New York Times* (27 September 2020).

Katajala-Peltomaa, Sari, and Maria Mäkelä, 'Conversion As an Exemplary Experience in 14th Century and Today: Narrative-Comparative Approaches to the Exemplum', *Scandinavian Journal of History* 47/1 (2022), 16–38.

Kelly, Adam, 'David Foster Wallace and the New Sincerity in American Fiction', in David Hering, ed., *Consider David Foster Wallace: Critical Essays* (Los Angeles: Sideshow Media Group Press, 2010), 131–146.

Keyes, Ralph, *The Post-Truth Era: Dishonesty and Deception in Contemporary Life* (New York: St. Martin's Press, 2004).

Knausgaard (14 affected family members), 'Klassekampen, Schiøtz og Knausgaard', *Klassekampen* (3 October 2009).

Knausgaard, Bjørge, 'Hilsen fra onkel Gunnar', *Fædrelandsvennen* (16 November 2011).

Knausgaard, Karl Ove, *My Struggle. I-VI*, Don Bartlett, trans. (New York: Archipelago Books, [2009–11] 2012–18).

Knott, Matthew, 'Can You Trust the US Election Polls?', *The Sydney Morning Herald* (4 August 2020).

Kofod, Peter, 'Jeg fik noget af et chok, da jeg læste en skolebog og opdagede, hvor meget politisk slagside den havde', *Den korte avis* (4 June 2015).

Korthals Altes, Liesbeth, 'Factual or Fictional? The Interpretive and Evaluative Impact of Framing Acts', in Monika Fludernik and Marie-Laure Ryan, eds., *Narrative Factuality: A Handbook* (Berlin: De Gruyter, 2020), 565–575.

Kraglund, Rikke Andersen, 'Karaktermord, angreb og selvanklager omkring Karl Ove Knausgårds *Min kamp*', *Rhetorica Scandinavica* 25 (2021), 106–122.

———,'Karaktermord i 10'ernes danske skønlitteratur', *Passage* 36 (2021), 7–27.

Kristof, Nicholas, 'Help Me Find Trump's "Anarchists" in Portland: The President Has His Politically Driven Narrative. And Then There's Reality', *The New York Times* (29 July 2020).

Kruse, Michael, 'Trump's Crazy and Confoundingly Successful Conspiracy Theory', *The New York Times* (13 November 2020).

Kukkonen, Karin, 'Plot', in Peter Hühn, Jan Christoph Meister, John Pier and Wolf Schmid, eds., *The Living Handbook of Narratology* (Hamburg: Hamburg University, 2014).

Labov, William, and Joshua Waletzky, 'Narrative Analysis: Oral Versions of Personal Experience', *Journal of Narrative and Life History* 7/1 (1997), 3–38.

Lamarque, Peter, 'About', *JLT* 8/2 (2014), 257–269.

Lavocat, Francoise, 'Pseudofactual Narratives and Signposts of Factuality', in Monika Fludernik and Marie-Laure Ryan, eds., *Narrative Factuality: A Handbook* (Berlin and Boston: De Gruyter, 2020), 577–592.

Lee, Bri, 'Sharing Our Stories Is the Strength at the Heart of #MeToo. We Must Repeal Gag Laws', *The Guardian* (19 November 2018).

Legislationline, 'Criminal Code of the Kingdom of Norway (English version)', <https://www.legislationline.org/documents/id/8909>, accessed 23 December 2021.

Lehmiller, Justin J., *The Psychology of Human Sexuality* (Hoboken: Wiley Blackwell, 2014).

Lehtimäki, Markku, 'Fiction and Instruction', *Style* 53/4 (2019), 489–495, <https://doi.org/10.1353/sty.2019.0044>.

Leibovich, Mark, 'When the "Narrative" Becomes the Story', *The New Times Magazine* (8 December 2015).

Leitch, Vincent B., *The Norton Anthology of Theory and Criticism. Second Edition* (New York and London: W. W. Norton & Company, 2010).

Lesley, Neale, 'The Ethics and Intentions of Writing Family', *Vitae Scholasticae* 34/2 (2017), 110–126.

Levine, Caroline, *Forms: Whole, Rhythm, Hierarchy, Network* (Princeton, NJ: Princeton University Press, 2015).

Lexico, 'hoax', <https://www.lexico.com/definition/hoax?locale=en>, accessed 1 October 2021.

Li, Stephanie, 'Genre Trouble and History's Miseries in Colson Whitehead's The Underground Railroad', *MELUS* 44/2 (2019), 1–23, <https://doi.org/10.1093/melus/mlz010>.

Lindstedt, Laura, *Oneiron: A Fantasy About the Seconds After Death*, Owen Witesman, trans. (London: Oneworld, 2018).

'List of Awards and Nominations Received by The Trial of the Chicago 7', *Wikipedia* (7 May 2021), <https://en.wikipedia.org/wiki/List_of_awards_and_nominations_received_by_The_Trial_of_the_Chicago_7>, accessed 20 September 2021.

Lizza, Ryan, 'Trump's Blueprint for Victory', *Politico* (28 August 2020).

Lyotard, François, *La Condition postmoderne. Rapport sur le savoir* (Paris: Minuit, 1979).

Maçães, Bruno, 'How Trump Almost Broke the Bounds of Reality', *The New York Times* (12 November 2020).

Mäkelä, Maria, 'Disagreeing with Fictionality? A Response to Richard Walsh in the Age of Post-Truth Politics and Careless Speech', *Style* 53/4 (2019), 457–463.

———, 'Lessons from the Dangers of Narrative Project: Toward a Story-Critical Narratology', *Tekstualia* 1/4 (2018), 175–186.

———, 'Through the Cracks in the Safety Net: Narratives of Personal Experience Countering the Welfare System in Social Media and Human Interest Journalism', in Klarissa Lueg and Marianne Wolff Lundholt, eds., *Routledge Handbook of Counter-Narratives* (Abingdon: Routledge, 2020), 389–401.

———, 'Viral Storytelling as Contemporary Narrative Didacticism: Deriving Universal Truths from Arbitrary Narratives of Personal Experience', in Susanna Lindberg and Hanna-Riikka Roine, eds., *The Ethos of Digital Environments: Technology, Literary Theory and Philosophy* (London and New York: Routledge, 2021), 49–59.

———, and Hanna Meretoja, 'Critical Approaches to the Storytelling Boom', *Poetics Today* 43/2 (2022).

———, Samuli Björninen, Laura Karttunen, Matias Nurminen, Juha Raipola and Tytti Rantanen, 'Dangers of Narrative: A Critical Approach to Narratives of Personal Experience in Contemporary Story Economy', *Narrative* 29/2 (2021), 139–159.

———, and Samuli Björninen, 'My Story, Your Narrative: Scholarly Terms and Popular Usage', in Paul Dawson and Maria Mäkelä, eds., The *Routledge Companion to Narrative Theory* (Abingdon: Routledge, 2022), 11–23.

Manovich, Lev, *Software Takes Control: Extending the Language of New Media* (New York and London: Bloomsbury, 2013).

———, *The Language of New Media* (Cambridge, MA: The MIT Press, 2001).

Mar, Raymond A., and Keith Oatley, 'The Function of Fiction is the Abstraction and Simulation of Social Experience', *Perspectives on Psychological Science* 3 (2008), 173–192.

McCarthy, Tom, 'David Foster Wallace: The Last Audit', *The New York Times* (14 April 2011).

McGill, Robert, *The Treacherous Imagination* (Columbus: The Ohio State University Press, 2013).

McHale, Brian, '"A poet may not Exist": Mock-Hoaxes and the Construction of National Identity', in Robert J. Griffin, ed., *The Faces of Anonymity: Anonymous and Pseudonymous Publication from the Sixteenth to the Twentieth Century* (New York: Palgrave Macmillan, 2003), 233–252.

———, 'Cognition *En Abyme*: Models, Manuals, Maps', *Partial Answers: Journal of Literature and the History of Ideas* 4/2 (2006), 175–189, <https://doi.org/10.1353/pan.0.0105>.

———, *Postmodernist Fiction* (New York and London: Methuen, 1987).

McLean, Kate C., and Moin Syed, 'Personal, Master, and Alternative Narratives: An Integrative Framework for Understanding Identity Development in Context.' *Human Development* 58 (2015), 318–349.

Mencken, H. L., 'Joseph Conrad', in *A Book of Prefaces* (Garden City: Garden City Publishing Company, 1917), 11–64.

Meretoja, Hanna, *The Ethics of Storytelling: Narrative Hermeneutics, History, and the Possible* (Oxford: Oxford University Press, 2018).

———, 'Life and Narrative', in Paul Dawson and Maria Mäkelä, eds., The *Routledge Companion to Narrative Theory* (Abingdon: Routledge, 2022), 273–285.

———, *The Narrative Turn in Fiction and Theory: The Crisis and Return of Storytelling from Robbe-Grillet to Tournier* (London: Palgrave Macmillan, 2014).

Merriam-Webster, 'deceit', <https://www.merriam-webster.com/dictionary/deception>, accessed 1 October 2021.

———, 'mock', <https://www.merriam-webster.com/dictionary/mock>, accessed 1 October 2021.

Meyer, Pernille, 'Exploring the Boundaries of Second-Person Narrative: The Use of "You" in Maria Gerhardt's *Transfer Window*', *The Problems of Literary Genres* 65/4 (2023), 19–33.

Mikkonen, Jukka, 'Truth in Literature: The Problem of Knowledge and Insight Gained from Fiction', in Monika Fludernik and Marie-Laure Ryan, eds., *Narrative Factuality: A Handbook* (Berlin: De Gruyter, 2019).

Mikkonen, Kai, 'Can Fiction Become Fact? The Fiction-to-Fact Transition in Recent Theories of Fiction', *Style*, 40/4 (2006), 291–312.

Mildorf, Jarmila, 'Reconsidering Second-Person Narration and Involvement', *Language and Literature* 25/2 (2016), 145–158.

———, 'Studying Writing in Second Person: A Response to Joshua Parker', *Connotations* 23/1 (2013/2014), 63–78.

Miller, Alyson, 'Stylised Configurations of Trauma: Faking Identity in Holocaust Memoirs', *Arcadia* 49/2 (2014), 229–253.

Miller, Laura, 'The *New Yorker*'s "Cat Person" Story Is Great. Too Bad the Internet Turned It Into a Piping Hot Thinkpiece', *Slate* (11 December 2017), <https://slate.com/culture/2017/12/too-bad-twitter-turned-the-new-yorker-s-cat-person-story-into-a-piping-hot-thinkpiece.html>, accessed 29 April 2021.

Mills, Claudia, 'Appropriating Others' Stories: Some Questions about the Ethics of Writing Fiction', *Journal of Social Philosophy* 31/2 (2000), 195–206.

Moore, Lorrie, *Self-Help* (New York: NAL, 1985).

Moore, Susan, Meredith Temple-Smith and Doreen Rosenthal, *Sexuality in Adolescence: The Digital Generation* (Hove: Routledge, 2016).

Moser, Thomas C., 'Conrad, Ford, and the Sources of *Chance*', *Conradiana* 7/3 (1976), 207–224.

Moses, Wilson Jeremiah, *Creative Conflict in African American Thought* (New York: Cambridge University Press, 2004).

Murray, Janet, *Hamlet on the Holodeck: The Future of Narrative in Cyberspace* (New York: Free Press, 1997).

———, *Inventing the Medium: Principles of Interaction Design as a Cultural Practice* (Cambridge, MA: The MIT Press, 2011).

Murray, Penelope, 'Introduction', in John Cocking, *Imagination. A Study in the History of Ideas* (London: Routledge, 1991).

Nagy, Peter, and Gina Neff, 'Imagined Affordance: Reconstructing a Keyword for Communication Theory', *Social Media and Society* 1/2 (2015), 1–9.

Nahon, Karine, and Jeff Hemsley, *Going Viral* (Cambridge and Malden: Polity Press, 2013).

Neef, Nele de, Violette Coppens, Wim Huys and Manuel Morrens, 'Bondage-Discipline, Dominance-Submission and Sadomasochism (BDSM) From an Integrative Biopsychosocial Perspective: A Systematic Review', *Sexual Medicine* 7/2 (2019), 129–144.

Nelson, Lisa S., *Social Media and Morality. Losing Our Self Control* (New York: Cambridge University Press, 2018).

Newman, Beth, '"The Situation of the Looker-On": Gender, Narration, and Gaze in Wuthering Heights', *PMLA. Publications of the Modern Language Association of America* 105/5 (1990), 1029–1041.

Newman, Daniel, 'Your Body is Our Black Box: Narrating Nations in Second-person Fiction by Edna O'Brien and Jennifer Egan', *Frontiers of Narrative Studies* 4/1 (2018), 42–65.

Nguyen, Tina, 'The MAGA Movement Hits the Streets — And Trump Latches On', *Politico* (4 September 2020).

Nibbs, Kate, 'The Couch Jump That Rocked Hollywood', *The Ringer* (1 August 2018), <https://www.theringer.com/tv/2018/8/1/17631658/tom-cruise-oprah-couch-jump>, accessed 30 August 2021.

Nielsen, Henrik Skov, 'Factuality and Fictionality in "Fake News"', in Monika Fludernik and Henrik Skov Nielsen, eds., *Travelling Concepts: New Fictionality Studies* (Berlin: Peter Lang, 2020), 161–178.

———, 'Fictional Voices? Strange Voices? Unnatural Voices?', in Per Krogh Hansen, Stefan Iversen, Henrik Skov Nielsen and Rolf Reitan, eds., *Strange Voices in Narrative Fiction* (Berlin: De Gruyter, 2011), 55–81.

———, 'Fiktion og fortælling', *Kritik* 44/201 (2011), 113–123.

———, 'The Impersonal Voice in First-Person Narrative Fiction', *Narrative* 12/2 (2004), 133–150.

———, Louise Brix Jacobsen, Stefan Kjerkegaard, Rikke Andersen Kraglund, Camilla Møhring Reestorff and Carsten Stage, *Fiktionalitet* (Frederiksberg: Samfundslitteratur, 2013).

———, James Phelan and Richard Walsh, 'Ten Theses about Fictionality', *Narrative* 23/1 (2015), 61–73.

Niilo22, 'Ei oikeen kiinosta vielä mennä nukkuu' ['Don't Feel Like Going to Sleep'], *YouTube* (8 October 2018), <https://www.youtube.com/watch?v=YApgeoA9rIM>, accessed 27 April 2021.

———, 'Mikä Ilma Ja Kotiin Menossa' ['What Weather And Going Home'], *YouTube* (24 January 2018), <https://www.youtube.com/watch?v=H6qKb7eg47c>, accessed 27 April 2021.

Nilsson, Niels Christian, Rolf Nordahl and Stefania Serafin, 'Immersion Revisited: A Review of Existing Definitions of Immersion and Their Relation to Difference Theories of Presence', *Human Technology* 12/2 (2016), 108–134.

Nordic co-operation, 'Om det vore krig i Norden', *YouTube* (3 October 2012), <https://www.youtube.com/watch?v=LLJFSfKJxVw>, accessed 27 April 2021.

Norman, Donald, *The Psychology of Everyday Things* (New York: Basic Books, 1988).

Nussbaum, Martha, *Not for Profit. Why Democracy Needs the Humanities* (Princeton: Princeton University Press, 2010).

O' Rourke, James, *Sex, Lies and Autobiography: The Ethics of Confession* (Charlottesville: University of Virginia Press, 2006).

Oppenheim, Yael, and Aya Yadlin-Segal, 'Whose Dystopia Is It Anyway? Deepfakes and Social Media Regulation', *Convergence: The International Journal of Research into New Media Technologies* 27/1 (2021), 36–51.

O'Quinn, Elaine, *Girls' Literacy Experiences In and Out of School Learning and Composing Gendered Identities* (Hoboken: Taylor and Francis, 2012).

Page, Ruth, *Narratives Online. Shared Stories in Social Media* (New York: Cambridge University Press, 2018).

Palmer, Alan, 'Thought and Consciousness Representation (literature)', in David Herman, Manfred Jahn and Marie-Laure Ryan, eds., *Routledge Encyclopedia of Narrative Theory* (London and New York: Routledge, 2005), 602–606.

Papacharissi, Zizi, *Affective Publics: Sentiment, Technology, and Politics* (New York: Oxford University Press, 2015).

Pedersen, Jes Stein, and Hanne Budtz-Jørgensen, 'Hvis der var krig i Norden', *Bogfolk* (13 May 2016), <https://podtail.com/da/podcast/politiken-bogfolk/uge-19-hvis-der-var-krig-i-norden/>, accessed 27 April 2021.

Phelan, James, 'Authors, Resources, Audiences: Toward a Rhetorical Poetics of Narrative', *Style* 52/1–2 (2018), 1–34.

———, *Experiencing Fiction. Judgments, Progression and the Rhetorical Theory of Narrative* (Columbus: Ohio State University Press, 2007).

———, *Living to Tell about It: A Rhetoric and Ethics of Character Narration* (Ithaca: Cornell University Press, 2005).

———, 'Local Nonfictionality within Generic Fiction: Huntington's Disease in McEwan's *Saturday* and Genova's *Inside the O'Briens*', Zara Dinnen and Robyn Warhol, eds., in *The Edinburgh Companion to Contemporary Narrative Theories* (Edinburgh: Edinburgh University Press, 2018), 362–374.

———, 'Narrative Ethics', in Peter Huhn et al., eds., *Living Handbook of Narratology*, <https://www.lhn.uni-hamburg.de/node/108.html>, accessed 17 September 2021.

———, '"Self-Help" for Narratee and Narrative Audience: How "I" – and "You"? – Read "How"', *Style* 28/3 (1994), 350–365.

———, *Somebody Telling Somebody Else: Toward a Rhetorical Poetics of Narrative* (Columbus: The Ohio State University Press, 2017).

Phillips, Kim M., and Barry Reay, *Sex before Sexuality: A Premodern History* (Cambridge, UK: Polity Press, 2011).

Pillai, Jayesh S., and Manvi Verma, 'Grammar of VR Storytelling: Narrative Immersion and Experiential Fidelity in VR Cinema', *VRCAI '19: The 17th International Conference on Virtual-Reality Continuum and Its Applications in Industry*, Article 34 (2019), 1–6.

Polletta, Francesca, *It Was Like a Fever: Storytelling in Protest and Politics* (Chicago: University of Chicago Press, 2006).

———, and Nathan Redman, 'When Do Stories Change Our Minds? Narrative Persuasion About Social Problems', *Sociology Compass* 14/4 (2020), e12778.

Poovey, Mary, *A History of the Modern Fact: Problems of Knowledge in the Sciences of Wealth and Society* (Chicago: University of Chicago Press, 1998).

Prehn, Nikoline Linnemann, 'Vi glemmer, at flygtninge er individer, der lige så godt kunne være dig eller mig', *Jyllands-Posten* (24 February 2019).

Prince, Gerald, *A Dictionary of Narratology* (Lincoln: University of Nebraska Press, 1987).

Putterman, Samantha, 'What Aaron Sorkin's *The Trial of the Chicago 7* Gets Right and Wrong', *Poynter* (20 April 2021), <https://www.poynter.org/fact-checking/2021/what-aaron-sorkins-the-trial-of-the-chicago-7-gets-right-and-wrong/>, accessed 25 September 2021.

Qiu, Linda, and Michael D. Shear, 'Rallies Are the Core of Trump's Campaign, and a Font of Lies and Misinformation', *The New York Times* (26 October 2020).

Raahauge, Jens, 'Hvis der var krig i Norden', *Folkeskolen* (14 May 2016).

Rabinowitz, Peter J., *Before Reading: Narrative Conventions and the Politics of Interpretation* (Columbus: Ohio State University Press, [1987] 1998).

Ragsdale, Bruce A., *The Trial of the Chicago Seven: The True Story behind the Headlines* (e-artnow, 2021).

Raipola, Juha, 'Unnarratable Matter: Emergence, Narrative, and Material Ecocriticism', in Sanna Karkulehto, Aino-Kaisa Koistinen and Essi Varis, eds., *Reconfiguring Human, Nonhuman, and Posthuman in Literature and Culture* (London and New York: Routledge, 2019), 263–279.

Rancière, Jacques, *Mute Speech: Literature, Critical Theory, and Politics*, James Swenson, trans. (New York: Columbia University Press, 2011).

Rautajoki, Hanna, and Matti Hyvärinen, 'Aspects of Voice in the Use of Narrative Positioning in Polyphonic Storytelling: Ventriloquial Moves Within a Biographical Interview', *Journal of Interdisciplinary Voice Studies* 6/1 (2021), 55–73.

———, Jarkko Toikkanen and Pirkko Raudaskoski, 'Embodied ekphrasis of experience: Bodily rhetoric in mediating affect in interaction', *Semiotica* 235 (2020), 91–111.

Ray, Martin, 'Introduction', in Joseph Conrad, *Chance* (Oxford: Oxford University Press, 2002), x–xx.

Reilly, Ian, *Media Hoaxing. The Yes Men and Utopian Politics* (Lanham, Maryland: Lexington Books, 2018).

Reitan, Rolf, 'Theorizing Second-Person Narratives: A Backwater Project?', in Per Krogh Hansen, Stefan Iversen, Henrik Skov Nielsen and Rolf Reitan, eds., *Strange Voices in Narrative Fiction* (Berlin: De Gruyter, 2011), 147–174.

Relihan, Constance C., and Goran V. Stanivukovic, eds., *Prose Fiction and Early Modern Sexualities in England, 1570–1640* (New York: Palgrave Macmillan, 2004).

Richardson, Brian, 'At First You Feel a Bit Lost. The Varieties of Second Person Narration', in *Unnatural Voices: Extreme Narration in Modern and Contemporary Fiction* (Columbus: Ohio State University Press, 2006), 17–36.

Richters, Juliet, Richard Oliver de Visser, Chris E. Rissel, Andrew E. Grulich and Anthony M.A. Smith, 'Demographic and Psychosocial Features of Participants in Bondage and Discipline, "sadomasochism" or Dominance and Submission (BDSM): Data from a National Survey', *The Journal of Sexual Medicine* 5/7 (2008), 1660–1668.

Ricoeur, Paul, *A Ricoeur Reader: Reflection and Imagination*, Mario J. Valdés, ed. (New York and London: Harvester Wheatsheaf, 1991).

Rohy, Valerie, *Lost Causes: Narrative, Etiology, and Queer Theory* (Oxford: Oxford Scholarship Online, 2014).

Roine, Hanna-Riikka, 'Computational Media and the Core Concepts of Narrative Theory', *Narrative* 27/3 (2019), 313–331.

———, and Laura Piippo, 'Authorship vs. Assemblage in Computational Media', in Susanna Lindberg and Hanna-Riikka Roine, eds., *The Ethos of Digital Environments: Technology, Literary Theory and Philosophy* (London and New York: Routledge, 2021), 60–76.

Rosen, Charlotte, 'Aaron Sorkin's Inane, Liberal History Lesson', *The Nation* (3 November 2020), <https://www.thenation.com/article/culture/aaron-sorkins-inane-history-lesson/>, accessed 17 September 2021.

Roupenian, Kristen, 'Cat Person', *The New Yorker* (4 December 2017), <https://www.newyorker.com/magazine/2017/12/11/cat-person>, accessed 29 April 2021.

Rubin, Jerry, *Do It: Scenarios of the Revolution* (New York: Simon and Schuster, 1970).

Ruff, Orsolya, '"I Never Write to Provoke": Interview with Janne Teller', *Hungarian Literature Online* (6 May 2012), <https://hlo.hu/interview/inte rview_with_ janne_eller.html>, accessed 27 April 2021.

Rundle, Vivienne, 'Defining Frames: The Prefaces of Henry James and Joseph Conrad', *Henry James Review* 16/1 (1995), 66–92.

Ryan, Marie-Laure, *Narrative as Virtual Reality II: Revisiting Immersion and Interactivity* (Baltimore: Johns Hopkins University Press, 2015).

———, *Possible Worlds, Artificial Intelligence, and Narrative Theory* (Bloomington: Indiana University Press, 1991).

———, 'Postmodernism and the Doctrine of Panfictionality', *Narrative* 5/2 (1997), 165–187.

Sachs, Jonah, *Winning the Story Wars. How Those Who Tell – And Live – The Best Stories Will Rule the Future* (Boston, MA: Harvard Business Review Press, 2012).

Saldívar, Ramón, 'The Second Elevation of the Novel: Race, Form, and the Postrace Aesthetic in Contemporary Narrative', *Narrative* 21/1 (2013), 1–18.

Salmon, Christian, *Storytelling: Bewitching the Modern Mind*, David Macey, trans. (London and New York: Verso, 2010).

Samoilenko, Serhei A., Eric Shiraev, Jennifer Keohane and Martijn Icks, 'Character assassination', in Alena Ledeneva, ed., *The Global Encyclopaedia of Informality. Volume II* (London: UCL Press, 2018), 441–446.

Sapiro, Gisèle, 'The Legal Responsibility of the Writer Between Objectivity and Subjectivity: The French Case (Nineteenth to Twenty-First Century)', in Ralf Grüttemeier, ed., *Literary Trials. Exceptio Artis and Theories of Literature in Court* (New York, London, Oxford, New Delhi and Sydney: Bloomsbury, 2016), 21–47.

Saunders, Judith P., 'Darwinian Literary Analysis of Sexuality', in Todd K. Shackelford and Ranald D. Hansen, eds., *The Evolution of sexuality* (Cham: Springer, 2015).

Scanlon, Larry, *Narrative, Authority, and Power: The Medieval Exemplum and the Chaucerian Tradition* (Cambridge: Cambridge University Press, 1994).

Scarlett, Ashley, and Martin Zeilinger, 'Rethinking Affordance', *Media Theory* 3/1 (2019), 1–48.

Schaeffer, Jean-Marie. *Why Fiction?* (Lincoln: Nebraska University Press, [1999] 2010.)

Schultz, John, *The Conspiracy Trial of the Chicago Seven* (Chicago: University of Chicago Press, [1993] 2020).

Scott, Joanna, 'On Hoaxes, Humbugs, and Fictional Portraiture', *a/b: Auto/Biography Studies* 31/1 (2016), 27–32.

Shuman, Amy, *Other People's Stories: Entitlement Claims and the Critique of Empathy* (Urbana: University of Illinois Press, 2005).

Sidney, Sir Philip, *A Defence of Poesie and Poems*, David Price, ed. (London, Paris and Melbourne: Cassel and Company, [1595] 1891).

Sipher, John, 'The Intelligence Director Who Is Undermining Trust and Truth', *The New York Times* (20 October 2020).

Sitkoff, Harvard, *The Struggle for Black Equality, 1945–1980* (New York: Hill and Wang, 1981).

Smith, Bruce R., 'Premodern Sexualities', *PMLA* 115/3 (2000), 318–329.

Smith, Rich, 'The Underground Railroad Is Bigger and Better Than You've Heard', *The Stranger* (8 September 2016), <https://www.thestranger.com/books/2016/09/08/24548834/the-underground-railroad-is-bigger-and-better-than-youve-heard>, accessed 7 January 2022.

Sokal, Allan, 'Transgressing the Boundaries: Towards a Transformative Hermeneutics of Quantum Gravity', *Social Text* 46/47 (1996), 217–252.

Sorkin, Aaron (dir.), *Molly's Game*, STX Entertainment, 2017.

———, *The Trial of the Chicago 7*, Dreamworks, 2020.

———, *Trial of the Chicago 7: The Screenplay* (New York: Simon and Schuster, 2020).

Sperber, Dan, and Deirdre Wilson, *Relevance: Communication and Cognition*, second edition (Oxford: Blackwell, 1995).

Spielberg, Stephen (dir.), *Saving Private Ryan*, Paramount Pictures, 1998.

Starosta, Anita, 'Conrad's "Author's Notes": Between Text and Reader', *Yearbook of Conrad Studies* 3 (2007), 31–40.

Strassberg, Donald S., and Lisa K. Lockerd, 'Force in Women's Sexual Fantasies', *Archives of Sexual Behavior* 2/4 (1998), 403–414.

Taffel, Sy, *Digital Media Ecologies. Entanglements of Content, Code and Hardware* (New York and London: Bloomsbury Academic, 2019).

Tandoc, Edson C., Zheng Wei Lim and Richard Ling, 'Defining "Fake News"', *Digital Journalism* 6/2 (2018), 137–153.

Teller, Janne, *War: What If It Were Here?* (London: Simon and Schuster UK, 2016).

The Norwegian Non-Fiction Writers and Translators Association, 'Etisk sjekkliste for sakprosa', <https://nffo.no/formidling/etisk-sjekkliste/innledning>, accessed 23 December 2021.

'The Tom Cruise Scientology Video' (2008), posted on *Aleteuk*, <https://www.youtube.com/watch?v=UFBZ_uAbxS0>, accessed 30 August 2021.

theyesmen.org (The Yes Men's official site), <http://theyesmen.org/>, accessed 20 June 2021.

Thomas, Bronwen, *Literature and Social Media* (London: Routledge, 2020).

Thomas, Ebony Elizabeth, *The Dark Fantastic: Race and the Imagination from Harry Potter to Hunger Games* (New York: New York University Press, 2019).

'TikTok – Make Your Day, App Store', <https://apps.apple.com/us/app/id835599320>, accessed 20 June 2021.

Topverses, *The Bible,* New International Version, Genesis 38:9, <http://topverses.com/Bible/Genesis/38/9>, accessed 24 January 2021.

Treem, Jeffrey W., and Paul Leonardi, 'Social Media Use in Organizations: Exploring the Affordances of Visibility, Editability, Persistence, and Association', *Communication Yearbook* 36 (2012), 143–189.

Troisi, Alfonso, and Monica Carosi, 'Female Orgasm Rate Increases With Male Dominance in Japanese Macaques', *Animal Behaviour* 56/5 (1998), 1261–1266.

Turner, Susan, Huang Chih-Wei, Luke Burrows and Phil Turner, 'Make-Believing Virtual Realities', in Phil Turner and J. Tuomas Harviainen, eds., *Digital Make-Believe* (Cham: Springer, 2016).

Vaihinger, Hans, *A Philosophy of 'As if': A System of the Theoretical, Practical and Religious Fictions of Mankind* (London: Routledge and Kegan Paul, 1924).

van Dijck, Jose, *The Culture of Connectivity: A Critical History of Social Media* (Oxford: Oxford University Press, 2013).

Vasantola, Satu, 'Lukihäiriöinen nuori jäi ilman apua ja sitten ilman töitä – nyt Niilo22 on aikamies ja Youtube-tähti, joka lukee ylpeänä videoillaan, vaikka väärin menisi', *Helsingin Sanomat* (15 April 2017).

Vestergaard, Anne-Marie, 'Når litteratur bliver til debatindlæg', *Berlingske Tidende* (13 July 2017).

Vincent, James, 'Cruise Deepfake Creator Says Public Shouldn't Be Worried About "one-click fakes"', *The Verge* (5 March 2021), <https://www.theverge.com/2021/3/5/22314980/tom-cruise-deepfake-tiktok-videos-ai-impersonator-chris-ume-miles-fisher>, accessed 20 June 2021.

Wake, Paul, *Conrad's Marlow: Narrative and Death in Youth, Heart of Darkness, Lord Jim and Chance* (Manchester: Manchester University Press, 2007).

Wallace, David Foster, *The Pale King: An Unfinished Novel* (New York: Back Bay Books, 2011).

Walsh, Lynda, 'The Scientific Media Hoax: A Rhetoric for Reconciling Linguistics and Literary Criticism', in Patricia Bizzell, ed., *Rhetorical Agendas: Political, Ethical, Spiritual* (London: Routledge, 2005), 165–175.

———, *Sins against Science: The Scientific Media Hoaxes of Poe, Twain, and Others* (Albany, NY: State University of New York Press, 2006).

Walsh, Richard, 'Dreaming and Narrative Theory', in Frederick L. Aldama, ed., *Toward a Cognitive Theory of Narrative Acts* (Austin: University of Texas Press, 2010), 141–157.

———, 'Exploring Fictionality: Afterword', in Cindie Aaen Maagaard, Daniel Schäbler and Marianne Wolff Lundholt, eds., *Exploring Fictionality: Conceptions, Test Cases, Discussions* (Odense: University Press of Southern Denmark, 2020), 213–238.

———, 'Fictionality as Rhetoric: A Distinctive Research Paradigm', *Style* 53/4 (2019), 397–425.

———,'Further Reflections on Fictionality: Rejoinders to the Responses', *Style* 53/4 (2019), 508–530.

———, 'Person, Level, Voice: A Rhetorical Reconsideration', in Jan Alber and Monika Fludernik, eds., *Postclassical Narratology* (Columbus: Ohio State University Press, 2010), 35–57.

———, *The Rhetoric of Fictionality: Narrative Theory and the Idea of Fiction* (Columbus: Ohio State University Press, 2007).

Walton, Kendall, *Mimesis as Make-Believe: On the Foundations of the Representational Arts* (Cambridge, MA: Harvard University Press, 1990).

Wang, Yunwen, 'Humor and Camera View on Mobile Short-form Video apps Influence User Experience and Technology-Adoption Intent, an Example of *TikTok (DouYin)*', *Computers in Human Behavior* 110/9 (2020).

Wardle, Claire, 'Fake News. It's Complicated', *First Draft* 16 (2017), 1–11.

Wehner, Peter, 'Trump Lives in a Hall of Mirrors and He's Got Plenty of Company', *The New York Times* (2 November 2020).

Weimann, Gabriel, and Natalie Masri, 'Research Note: Spreading Hate on TikTok', *Studies in Conflict and Terrorism* (2020), 1–14.

Weiser, Benjamin, Michael S. Schmidt and William K. Rashbaum, 'Steve Bannon Loses Lawyer After Suggesting Beheading of Fauci', *The New York Times* (6 November 2020).

Westerlund, Mika, 'The Emergence of Deepfake Technology: A Review', *Technology Innovation Management Review* 9/11 (2019), 39–52.

White, Hayden, 'Historical Emplotment and the Problem of Truth', in Saul Friedlander, ed., *Probing the Limits of Representation: Nazism and the 'final Solution'* (Cambridge, MA: Harvard University Press, 1992), 37–53.

———, 'Historicism, History, and Figurative Imagination', *History and Theory* 14/4 (1975), 48–67.

Whitehead, Colson, *The Underground Railroad* (New York: Doubleday, 2016).

Wiener, Jon, ed., *Conspiracy in the Streets: The Extraordinary Trial of the Chicago Eight* (New York: The New Press, 2006).

Wierzbicka, Anna, '"Cultural Scripts": A Semantic Approach to Cultural Analysis and Cross-Cultural Communication,' *Pragmatics and Language Learning*, Monograph Series, 5 (1994), 1–24.

Willmore, Alison, 'Aaron Sorkin's Annoying Tics Are Actually Good in the Trial of the Chicago 7', *Vulture* (25 September 2020), <https://www.newsbreak.com/news/2069977337585/aaron-sorkins-annoying-tics-are-actually-good-in-the-trial-of-the-chicago-7>, accessed 17 September 2021.

Wood, Jennifer, 'The Unwavering Optimism of Aaron Sorkin', *GQ* (16 October 2020), <https://www.gq.com/story/the-unwavering-optimism-of-aaron-sorkin>, accessed 17 September 2021.

Yuan, Li, 'Coronavirus Weakens China's Powerful Propaganda Machine', *The New York Times* (26 February 2020).

Zuboff, Shoshana, *The Age of Surveillance Capitalism: The Fight for a Human Future at the New Frontier of Power* (London: Profile Books, 2019).

Zurbriggen, Eileen L., and Megan R. Yost, 'Power, Desire, and Pleasure in Sexual Fantasies', *Journal of Sex Research* 41/3 (2004), 288–300.

Literary and Cultural Studies, Theory and the (New) Media

Edited by Monika Fludernik and Sieglinde Lemke

Vol. 1 Zuzana Fonioková: Kazuo Ishiguro and Max Frisch: Bending Facts in Unreliable and Unnatural Narration. 2015.

Vol. 2 Michael Weber: Die Chronologie von Emily Brontës *Wuthering Heights*. 2017.

Vol. 3 Monika Fludernik / Henrik Nielsen: Travelling Concepts: New Fictionality Studies. 2020.

Vol. 4 Golnaz Shams: Social Minds in Drama. The Delineation of Mentalities and Collectives. 2020.

Vol. 5 Mara Cambiaghi: A.S. Byatt's Art of Memory. 2020.

Vol. 6 Michael Weber: Timelines in Emily Brontë's *Wuthering Heights*. 2020.

Vol. 7 Samuli Björninen / Pernille Meyer / Maria Mäkelä / Henrik Zetterberg-Nielsen (eds.): Dangers of Narrative and Fictionality. A Rhetorical Approach to Storytelling in Contemporary Western Culture. 2024.

www.peterlang.com

www.ingramcontent.com/pod-product-compliance
Ingram Content Group UK Ltd.
Pitfield, Milton Keynes, MK11 3LW, UK
UKHW041824031026
15587UKWH00002B/537

9 783631 851739